The Short Stories
of F. Scott Fitzgerald

The Short Stories
of F. Scott Fitzgerald
New Approaches in Criticism

Edited by Jackson R. Bryer

The University of Wisconsin Press

Published 1982

The University of Wisconsin Press
114 North Murray Street
Madison, Wisconsin 53715

The University of Wisconsin Press, Ltd.
1 Gower Street
London WC1E 6HA, England

First printing

Printed in the United States of America

For LC CIP information see the colophon

ISBN 0-299-09080-9 (cloth)
      0-299-09084-1 (paper)

Jacket illustration reprinted from *Grim Youth* by John Held, Jr.,
by permission of the publisher, Vanguard Press, Inc. Copyright © 1930
by Vanguard Press, Inc. Copyright renewed © 1958 by Mrs. Margaret Held.

For Hugh Holman

(1914–1981)

Something has spoken to me in the night, burning the tapers of the waning year; something has spoken in the night; and told me I shall die, I know not where. Losing the earth we know for greater knowing, losing the life we have for greater life, and leaving friends we loved for greater loving, men find a land more kind than home, more large than earth.

Whereon the pillars of this earth are founded, toward which the spirits of the nations draw, toward which the conscience of the world is tending—a wind is rising, and the rivers flow.

Thomas Wolfe — *"I Have a Thing to Tell You"*

CONTENTS

INDIVIDUAL STORIES

APPENDIX

The Short Stories of F. Scott Fitzgerald: A Checklist of Criticism

INTRODUCTION

F. Scott Fitzgerald wrote 178 short stories; 146 of them were published during his lifetime; 18 have been published since his death; 14 remain unpublished. Ernest Hemingway wrote 109 stories, 79 of which were published in his lifetime. Nine have been published posthumously and 21 remain unpublished. Both writers have been extremely popular with compilers of short story anthologies. Through 1979, 34 different Hemingway stories had been anthologized a total of 353 times, and 58 Fitzgerald stories had been anthologized 298 times. "Babylon Revisited" had been anthologized 63 times, by far the most of any Fitzgerald story, with "The Rich Boy" (34) and "Winter Dreams" (29) also frequently selected by editors. Thereafter, the list falls off sharply, with only "The Freshest Boy" (14), "The Baby Party" (11), and "The Jelly-Bean" (10) anthologized 10 or more times. The anthologizing of Hemingway's stories has been spread much more widely and evenly. Fourteen of his stories have been anthologized 10 or more times and 7 have been anthologized 20 or more times. But the fact remains that both writers' work in the short story is readily available to users of short story anthologies, as well as of course to those who purchase the highly popular Scribner's editions of their short fiction.

Given these statistics, the disparate critical attention which Hemingway's and Fitzgerald's short stories have received is astonishing. Again, figures do at least suggest this superficially. Through 1979, there were 287 articles or book chapters devoted to Hemingway's short stories; 46

Hemingway stories—nearly half he wrote—were the subjects of at least 1 full essay or chapter. For the same period, Fitzgerald's stories were the subjects of 75 articles or chapters; and only 22 stories—just about one-eighth of his total output—were dealt with in full essays or chapters. There were more essays on "The Short Happy Life of Francis Macomber" and "The Snows of Kilimanjaro" than on all of Fitzgerald's stories taken as a whole.

Behind these figures lie even more alarming specifics. If one glances at Section VII of the checklist appended to this volume, it will be noted that many of the "full" essays on individual Fitzgerald stories are either brief notes or bibliographical pieces with little or no critical content. The number of serious critical essays on the stories is probably no greater than 20. Many popular and frequently anthologized Fitzgerald stories have been ignored by critics. "The Rich Boy" is the subject of only 2 notes and a bibliographical article; "Winter Dreams" is the subject of 1 critical essay, 1 note, and 1 bibliographical article. "The Freshest Boy" and "The Baby Party" have not had any articles written about them. Only "Babylon Revisited," the subject of 20 essays, has received appreciable attention; and barely a half-dozen of these are serious critical pieces. *Babylon Revisited and Other Stories*, a Scribner Library paperback, is the most popular and accessible collection of Fitzgerald stories. It contains 9 stories, 7 of which are among his best. To date, these 9 stories are the subjects of only 45 essays and, as mentioned, 20 of these are on "Babylon Revisited."

Another way of illustrating the critical neglect of Fitzgerald's short fiction is to observe how many full-length studies of his work ignore it. Books like Milton Stern's *The Golden Moment* (1970), John F. Callahan's *The Illusions of a Nation* (1972), Aaron Latham's *Crazy Sundays: F. Scott Fitzgerald in Hollywood* (1971), and Thomas J. Stavola's *Scott Fitzgerald: Crisis in an American Identity* (1979) have virtually nothing to say about the stories; and the major collections of reprinted reviews and essays about Fitzgerald include no material on them. Each year, some 50 essays or chapters on Fitzgerald are published; rarely do more than 2 or 3 of these deal in more than a cursory way with the stories. Again by contrast, Hemingway's stories generate an annual figure of 15 or 20 essays. John A. Higgins's *F. Scott Fitzgerald: A Study of the Stories* (1971), while very useful as an introductory survey, tries to say something about every Fitzgerald story and, in the process, sacrifices depth for breadth of coverage.

Within the past two or three years, there have been signs that the neglect of Fitzgerald's stories may be approaching a long-overdue end.

Certainly a major source of encouragement for this awakening interest has been the publication of *Bits of Paradise* (1974) and *The Price Was High* (1979), collecting in book form for the first time 61 stories previously only available in magazines. *The Price Was High*, especially, insures that virtually all of Fitzgerald's short fiction is now readily accessible for serious critical and scholarly study. And this study seems to have begun. Worthwhile appraisals of "Crazy Sunday," "May Day," Absolution," and "Babylon Revisited" have appeared; and the most recent full-length critical study, Brian Way's *F. Scott Fitzgerald and the Art of Social Fiction* (1980), includes a very valuable 26-page chapter on the stories.

It is against this background of the recent availability in book form of almost all of Fitzgerald's stories and a remaining deplorable absence of worthwhile commentary that this collection is offered. Now that all but a handful of stories are conveniently available, it is surely time that critics and readers turn their attention from the critically well-perused pages of *The Great Gatsby* and *Tender Is the Night*—they annually account for close to 75 percent of the Fitzgerald criticism published—and assess his work in the short story, as well as the role short fiction played in his writing career.

To be sure, one of the reasons—other than their inaccessibility—that critics have neglected Fitzgerald's stories is the assumption that most of them were simply potboilers written solely and hastily for money to sustain their author during the financially fallow years between novels. And this assumption has been fueled by Fitzgerald's own remarks about his short fiction. He routinely referred to it as "trash" and generally deprecated it in his correspondence and autobiographical essays. Writing to John Peale Bishop in 1925, he lamented, "No news except now I get $2000 for a story and they grow worse and worse and my ambition is to get to where I need write no more but novels" (*Letters*, p. 355). The next year, in a letter to Maxwell Perkins, he expressed similar sentiments: "Isn't that a disgrace, when I get $2500, for a story as my regular price. But trash doesn't come as easily as it used to and I've grown to hate the poor old debauched form itself."[1] And, finally, there is his famous self-deprecating remark, in a 1929 letter to Hemingway when his price per story had reached its highest point: "Here's a last flicker of the old cheap pride: the *Post* now pays the old whore $4000 a screw. But now it's because she's mastered the 40 positions—in her youth one was enough" (*Letters*, p. 307). But even

1. *Dear Scott/Dear Max: The Fitzgerald-Perkins Correspondence*, ed. John Kuehl and Jackson R. Bryer (New York: Charles Scribner's, 1971), p. 134.

in the horrible sarcasm of this last reference there is at least a hint that Fitzgerald saw his stories as more than repetitive formulaic writing; and the careful reader of his letters and essays will find evidence of this as well. Writing in 1935 to his agent, Harold Ober, he explained, "all my stories are concieved like novels, require a special emotion, a special experience—so that my readers . . . know that each time it'll be something new, not in form but in substance."[2] And to Zelda in 1940, he wrote of his "high-priced writing for the magazines," calling it "a very definite trick," but adding, "The rather special things that I brought to it, the intelligence and the good writing and even the radicalism all appealed to old Lorimer [the editor of the *Saturday Evening Post*] who had been a writer himself and liked style" (*Letters*, pp. 17–18).

This collection of essays is predicated on the premise that the Fitzgerald of these last two remarks was more accurate than the one who downplayed his short stories. The essays which follow all seek, in one way or another, to redress two sorts of imbalances which have heretofore characterized Fitzgerald studies. The first, the lack of serious critical attention to the stories, has been alluded to and documented above; a second imbalance is the redundancy of most of the criticism which has appeared in the four decades since Fitzgerald's death. Despite the abundance of that commentary, much of it has tended to trace and retrace familiar patterns and approaches through the novels—Fitzgerald's ambivalence towards money and the wealthy, his "double vision," his attitudes towards women and man-woman relationships, romance versus realism in his fiction, the East and West contrast. Perhaps just because most of the critical attention has been focused on such a relatively small proportion of Fitzgerald's fictional canon, tunnel vision often has seemed to result. Another intention of this collection, then, is that by widening the scope of subject matter in Fitzgerald studies, new approaches will appear which it is hoped can then be reapplied into the other fiction, thus revitalizing that area of Fitzgerald criticism as well.

Lawrence Buell's piece on fantasy in Fitzgerald and Neil D. Isaacs's essay on the sports motif in "Winter Dreams" both use the short stories to introduce and explore in a preliminary yet suggestive manner aspects of Fitzgerald's art which have not received very much previous attention. Isaacs implies that an examination and study of Fitzgerald's inter-

2. *As Ever, Scott Fitz—: Letters Between F. Scott Fitzgerald and His Literary Agent Harold Ober 1919–1940*, ed. Matthew J. Bruccoli and Jennifer McCabe Atkinson (New York and Philadelphia: J. B. Lippincott, 1972), p. 221.

est in use of sports in his fiction is warranted. Joseph Mancini, Jr.'s highly speculative Jungian reading of the Basil stories will not convince all readers; it is included because it is provocative and because it hints at another plausible perspective through which Fitzgerald's fiction can be viewed. Kenneth E. Eble's essay on alcoholism and mental illness is the first to treat this obviously central issue in terms of the fiction rather than in terms of the glamorous details of the Fitzgeralds' lives. C. Hugh Holman brings to bear on Fitzgerald's three stories of Tarleton, Georgia, a lifetime of personal familiarity with and scholarly study of the South.

In his chapter on Fitzgerald's short stories, Brian Way observes, quite correctly, that the stories "are too often discussed as if they mattered only as aids to the understanding of his major novels."[3] Several of the essays in this collection seek to reverse that process by focusing on the stories and relating the novels to them. Richard Lehan's piece on the vectoring of self, place, and destiny uses the stories principally and the novels secondarily. Similarly, Scott Donaldson shows how Fitzgerald's changing attitudes towards money and marriage, subjects often discussed with respect to the novels, are revealed in the stories. Donaldson demonstrates how a totally ignored 1930 story, "A Snobbish Story," significantly reworks and alters material very similar to the Amory-Rosalind scenes in *This Side of Paradise*. Several of the essays deal with Fitzgerald and Hollywood, using the stories to expand greatly our understanding of that important relationship in Fitzgerald's life and work. Alan Margolies's essay suggests intriguingly how, in writing several of his stories, Fitzgerald clearly had "his eye on sales to Hollywood" and how this demonstrable fact affected the nature of the stories in question. Robert A. Martin studies two neglected stories, "Magnetism" and "Jacob's Ladder," showing how they, along with "Crazy Sunday" and the early Melarky-Kelly version of *Tender Is the Night*, "account for nearly all of the material, characters, and plot of *The Last Tycoon.*"

Another group of essays seeks to document Fitzgerald's artistic development through study of previously unnoticed short stories. It is not often remarked that Fitzgerald, unlike Hemingway and some other novelists of his generation, sought in each successive novel to experiment with and further refine his understanding and command of the novel form. Because Fitzgerald's themes and subject matter do not vary very much from one novel to another, relatively little attention has

3. Brian Way, *F. Scott Fitzgerald and the Art of Social Fiction* (New York: St. Martin's, 1980), p. 72.

been given to the fact that they are very different with respect to form and approach. Study of the short fiction which intervened between the novels can demonstrate this continual development and experimentation more convincingly. Ruth Prigozy's essay is particularly persuasive in this regard. She shows, through examination of stories written between 1929 and 1935, how Fitzgerald moved beyond "the romantic antics of young lovers" and began to deal with the serious and complex problems of marriage which he addressed in *Tender Is the Night*. Prigozy—and James L.W. West III in his article on Fitzgerald's *Esquire* stories—also offer convincing textual evidence that the sparer, terser short fiction of the late 1930s might well have lead in *The Last Tycoon* to a significantly "new" kind of Fitzgerald novel and a major artistic triumph. James J. Martine's study of "The Bridal Party" in connection with "May Day" and "Magnetism" also shows a development in Fitzgerald's attitudes towards wealth and success; examination of this little-known story alters in an important way our knowledge of his views on these central themes in his fiction.

The single greatest need in Fitzgerald studies has long been for close attention to the style and artistry of the texts themselves. The past five years have seen major and valuable close readings of sections of *The Great Gatsby* and *Tender Is the Night* as correctives to the sociological, historical, and biographical approaches which predominated in past decades. The short story form, of course, lends itself even more comfortably to this sort of essay; but very few of the critical articles in print on the stories have utilized it. The second half of this collection, essays on individual stories (arranged chronologically by each tale's first appearance), is designed to encourage this type of scrutiny. John Kuehl's is the first serious essay on "The Ice Palace," one of Fitzgerald's best and most popular stories. Kuehl draws profitably upon his extensive knowledge of Fitzgerald's life and work to present the story in terms of its North-South contrasts and the psychic tensions implied in that opposition. James W. Tuttleton's reading of "May Day" relates the themes and techniques of the story to major themes of Fitzgerald's fiction and to his reading in Norris and Mencken. Irving Malin presents an *explication de texte* of "Absolution," a story which most often previously has been studied either with regard to its relationship to *The Great Gatsby* or for what it tells us about its author's religious beliefs. Malin stays close to the text and emphasizes the structural and thematic oppositions in the story. Victor Doyno's piece on "Rags Martin-Jones and the Pr-nce of W-les," a story which has received virtually no critical attention, provides a model for how a Fitzgerald short story can profitably be approached from several different critical vantages—

stylistic, folkloristic, thematic, structural, genetic, and contextual. Doyno touches on a particularly promising area when he briefly examines the changes Fitzgerald made from manuscript to magazine to collection in a book. Christiane Johnson takes another entirely neglected story, "The Adjuster," and examines it closely, noting how it shows its author shifting his view of a young irresponsible woman to a depiction of a mature woman with a sense of control and responsibility. Melvin J. Friedman's reading of one of Fitzgerald's most unfairly ignored stories, "The Swimmers," deals with a number of stylistic and formal patterns against a background of the fascinating suggestion that with this story Fitzgerald participates in a Franco-American literary tradition which extends back to Poe and forward to Styron. Peter Wolfe and Sheldon Grebstein provide the first extended close readings of two of Fitzgerald's best and most famous stories, "The Rich Boy" and "Crazy Sunday." Carlos Baker's first sally into Fitzgerald criticism is a graceful study of the one Fitzgerald story which has received critical attention, "Babylon Revisited." But Baker provides a fresh approach by examining the motifs of freedom and imprisonment in the tale and relating them to events in Fitzgerald's life. And George Monteiro examines "Financing Finnegan" as Fitzgerald's answer to Hemingway's famous "poor Scott" remark in "The Snows of Kilimanjaro." Monteiro contends plausibly that Fitzgerald portrays Hemingway, through Finnegan, as the same sort of scapegoat that Hemingway made Fitzgerald in his story.

In selecting contributors for this volume, I called upon several persons whose credentials as Fitzgerald scholars need no explanation—Richard Lehan, Kenneth E. Eble, James L.W. West III, Ruth Prigozy, Alan Margolies, John Kuehl, Robert A. Martin. I also called upon several distinguished modernists whose previous work had often touched upon Fitzgerald but who had never previously worked specifically or entirely on his fiction—Carlos Baker, James W. Tuttleton, Irving Malin, Sheldon Grebstein, George Monteiro, Scott Donaldson, James J. Martine. I called as well on two young critics—Joseph Mancini, Jr., and Christiane Johnson. And, finally, I invited contributions from several scholars whose previous work had principally been outside modern American literature—Melvin J. Friedman, Peter Wolfe, Neil D. Isaacs, Lawrence Buell. The intention was to produce a volume of varied and suggestive approaches which would present a variety of critical perspectives through which the stories can be viewed. In a further attempt to achieve this variety, two types of essays were solicited—overview essays which dealt with several stories, and close readings of individual stories. Within the second category, I tried to include essays on the most popular and best stories—especially those in the Scribner Library paperback—as well as essays on stories which have been unfairly neglected. Obviously, this method has produced some repetition and redundancy; it is hoped such is minimal and even perhaps stimulating where it occurs.

If this collection causes critics and readers to look more carefully at Fitzgerald's stories, it will have achieved its major objective. These essays, explicitly and implicitly, suggest that to study and reread the stories is to broaden our appreciation and understanding of Fitzgerald as a literary artist.

For major assistance in the preparation of this volume, I would like to thank Ruth M. Alvarez, the General Research Board of the University of Maryland, and Peter Givler and Dennis Trudell of the University of Wisconsin Press.

ABBREVIATIONS

In order to simplify footnoting in the essays, wherever possible, references to individual Fitzgerald novels and stories, letters, and essays in collections are made internally, using the following abbreviations. In instances where consecutive quotes within a few lines are from the same page of the same work, a citation is inserted only after the last quote.

AA   *Afternoon of an Author.* New York: Charles Scribner's, 1957.

AF   *The Apprentice Fiction of F. Scott Fitzgerald: 1909–1917,* ed. John Kuehl. New Brunswick, N.J.: Rutgers University Press, 1965.

ASYM   *All the Sad Young Men.* New York: Charles Scribner's, 1926.

B&D   *The Beautiful and Damned.* Scribner Library Edition. New York: Charles Scribner's, 1950.

B&J   *The Basil and Josephine Stories,* ed. Jackson R. Bryer and John Kuehl. New York: Charles Scribner's, 1973.

Bits   *Bits of Paradise: 21 Uncollected Stories by F. Scott and Zelda Fitzgerald,* ed. Matthew J. Bruccoli and Scottie Fitzgerald Smith. New York: Charles Scribner's, 1973.

C-U   *The Crack-Up,* ed. Edmund Wilson. New York: New Directions, 1945.

1959 F&P   *Flappers and Philosophers.* New York: Charles Scribner's, 1959.

GG   *The Great Gatsby.* Scribner Library Edition. New York: Charles Scribner's, 1953.

LT   *The Last Tycoon.* Scribner Library Edition. New York: Charles Scribner's, 1970.

Ledger   *F. Scott Fitzgerald's Ledger.* Washington, D.C.: NCR/ Microcard Editions, 1972.

Letters   *The Letters of F. Scott Fitzgerald,* ed. Andrew Turnbull. New York: Charles Scribner's, 1963.

PH   *The Pat Hobby Stories.* New York: Charles Scribner's. 1962.

Price   *The Price Was High: The Last Uncollected Stories of F. Scott Fitzgerald,* ed. Matthew J. Bruccoli. New York: Harcourt Brace Jovanovich, 1979.

6TJA   *Six Tales of the Jazz Age and Other Stories.* New York: Charles Scribner's, 1960.

Stories   *The Stories of F. Scott Fitzgerald.* Selected by Malcolm Cowley. New York: Charles Scribner's, 1951.

TAR   *Taps at Reveille.* Scribner Library Edition. New York: Charles Scribner's, 1960.

TITN   *Tender Is the Night.* Scribner Library Edition. New York: Charles Scribner's, 1960.

TJA   *Tales of the Jazz Age.* New York: Charles Scribner's, 1922.

TSOP   *This Side of Paradise.* Scribner Library Edition. New York: Charles Scribner's, 1960.

OVERVIEWS

THE ROMANTIC SELF AND THE USES OF PLACE IN THE STORIES OF F. SCOTT FITZGERALD

RICHARD LEHAN

1.

Fitzgerald wrote many of his short stories for a popular audience, often because such stories were the source of quick and generous amounts of money. Despite these reasons, many of his stories are among the best writing of the 1920s and 1930s, and some of them helped him formulate the themes and the narrative situations of his major novels. The stories, in fact, can usefully be considered in the context of the novels that often followed them. To discuss Fitzgerald's stories hence involves a discussion of the major themes of the novels—the theme of youthful cynicism and disillusionment that characterized *This Side of Paradise* and *The Beautiful and Damned*, the theme of romantic limits that characterized *The Great Gatsby*, the theme of cultural and personal decline that characterized *Tender is the Night*, and the theme of romantic betrayal that characterized the unfinished *The Last Tycoon*. While these novels and stories treat new ranges of experience and meaning, all of them were firmly located in a specific place, which often shaped the meaning of character and narrative action; and Fitzgerald intensified that use of place in his very best writing.

The range of experience that Fitzgerald brought to his early short stories was severely limited. His subject involved youth and initial commitment. When set in a small city or town, these stories took place against a moonlit world of the country club dance and invoked the rituals of courtship and young love. But the country club could not contain the romantic imagination, and Fitzgerald invariably moved his early stories to New York, which was the ultimate landscape of rom-

3

ance, opportunity, and success. But one was only as good as one feared to be bad, and the other side of success was failure. In "My Lost City" (1932), Fitzgerald discussed how he projected each of these emotions onto New York and created two cities—the New York of his prep school and college days, which seemed limitless; and the more sobering post-war New York, when he worked in an advertising firm and seemed to be confined to "my drab room in the Bronx, my square foot of the subway" (C-U, p. 25). New York held its terrors as well as thrills, and he came to realize "that behind much of the entertainment that the city poured forth into the nation there were only a lot of rather lost and lonely people" (C-U, p. 28). After his success with *This Side of Paradise*, Fitzgerald came back to New York as a conquering hero; but he eventually used up the city and discovered that it "was not the endless succession of canyons . . . but *it had limits*—from the tallest structures he saw for the first time that it faded out into the country on all sides, into an expanse of green and blue that alone was limitless" (C-U, p. 32; Fitzgerald's italics). Where New York stopped, America began, and one could never escape the larger destiny that contained the city itself. The Puritan legacy—both as a business and a religious state of mind—would always be there. Beyond the heightened city was a regularized, provincial, soberly religious workaday world with family responsibilities—with "vulnerabilities," as he put it in another essay.[1]

Perhaps the earliest expression of these themes is in "The Spire and the Gargoyle," first published in the *Nassau Literary Magazine* (February, 1917). The title evokes the Gothic architecture of the Princeton campus; the spires suggest the buildings, while the gargoyle comes to stand for the preceptor who failed the young hero out of college. Five years have passed, and he is living in a Bronx flat, working in a New York office. As with Amory Blaine, Broadway with its "painted, pagan crowds" fills him with terror. His middle-class routine is at best dreary. Very early, Fitzgerald's imagination created two hells in which one could abandon the romantic self: one was a sexual realm, vaguely embodied by Broadway; the other was the mundane realm of the middle class. In contrast to both, Fifth Avenue takes on the same meaning in this story that it does in *This Side of Paradise*, supplying a sense of place commensurate with self. The story, however, does not end with Fifth Avenue possibilities. Instead the protagonist twice again meets the preceptor—first in a New York museum and then again on the Princeton campus, at which time he learns that the young instruc-

1. "What I Think and Feel at 25," in *F. Scott Fitzgerald in His Own Time: A Miscellany*, ed. Matthew J. Bruccoli and Jackson R. Bryer (Kent, Ohio: Kent State Univ. Press, 1971), pp. 214–22.

tor has left Princeton and is wearing himself out teaching in a Brooklyn high school in order to support his growing family. The gargoyle suddenly becomes a symbol to the young hero of what he has lost in leaving the university and of what he may become. As in *This Side of Paradise*, the story ends with a sense of all that impedes the self-creating imagination. Whatever its limitations, and they are many, "The Spire and the Gargoyle" reveals that very early in his career Fitzgerald had connected a sense of self with a sense of place, and both of these with a sense of destiny.

Almost all of the stories in Fitzgerald's first collection, *Flappers and Philosophers*, take on one or another aspect of this paradigm. In "The Offshore Pirate" (1920), a wealthy young man creates an imaginary self—that of an outlaw—to win Ardita. Significantly, he names himself Carlyle and at the end is praised for his romantic imagination. In "Head and Shoulders" (1920), two characters transform themselves and reverse their roles by an act of creative imagination. In "The Cut-Glass Bowl" (1920), the bowl embodies the hard and beautiful Evylyn to the extent that it follows her through life as both the agent and the symbol of her fate in a story where self and destiny are once again inseparable. In "Dalyrimple Goes Wrong" (1920), a young man disillusioned with the workaday world transforms himself, a la Nietzsche, into a criminal beyond good and evil, by becoming "a new psychological rebel . . . defying the sentimental a priori form of his own mind" (1959 F&P, p. 166), until he becomes indifferent to those he morally looks down upon—at which time he is given the opportunity to recreate himself once more, this time in the political arena.

These stories are admittedly slight, more interesting for what they reveal about Fitzgerald's early handling of character than for their literary substance. But one story in *Flappers and Philosophers* is among Fitzgerald's best, perhaps because he was able once again to move with total conviction between and among the ideas of self, place, and destiny. The story, "The Ice Palace" (1920), begins in the South, which Sally Carrol Happer feels has played itself out after the Civil War—that watershed of American history for Fitzgerald. He has Sally Carrol tell us, " 'I want to go places and see people. I want my mind to grow. I want to live where things happen on a big scale' " (1959 F&P, p. 50). She rejects the South because it is complacent and unable to invent itself anew. Its physical and moral equivalent is the cemetery, to which Sally Carrol is attracted because it is the embodiment of the glory that is now dead in the South. When Harry Bellamy comes South to propose, she accepts in the hope of finding both a new self and a new destiny in his Northern city (Fitzgerald's St. Paul). What she finds is a mirror image of the South: the North is energetic while the South is languorous, is committed to the practical and traditionless while the South seems content to glorify the past. Despite these differences, Sally Carrol comes to the conclusion that the North also has a tragic destiny—one that it is waiting to play out, and that death holds it in a firm grip. Fitzgerald would treat this theme repeatedly in his fiction: the aggressive, almost lawless, industrial North destroyed the aristocratic South and its old courtesies, creating a money-oriented world that engaged the new kind of man and would play itself out destructively. The embodiment of this inevitable death is the ice palace itself, within which Sally Carrol becomes lost and held as in a tomb. The ice palace is the physical equivalent of her Southern cemetery, only more terrifying as it creates in her a "deep terror far greater than any fear of being lost" (1959 F&P, p. 68). To create oneself anew in the face of this horror is too much for Sally Carrol, another of Fitzgerald's early characters who finds the task of creating the romantic self in a Northern city an overwhelming and frightening experience, one that tasks the romantic imagination and arrests a sense of destiny.

In a number of ways, Fitzgerald's second novel, *The Beautiful and Damned* (1922), picks up where *This Side of Paradise* leaves off. This is not to belie the essential differences in the characters of Amory Blaine and Anthony Patch. Amory is more self-conscious about what he is and is not, as one might expect, given the tradition of the *Bildungsroman* within which Fitzgerald was working. Amory is stumbling and fumbling; but he finally comes to the realization that the gods of the past are dead, that he has no desire to play out other men's lies, and that his romantic sense of self has been profaned by a selfish, materialistic, secular world.

In order to understand *The Beautiful and Damned*, we must see that Adam Patch, Anthony's grandfather, is the embodiment of Puritanism, that religious philosophy that controlled the land and its wealth in the name of God and work, then turned in upon itself and controlled the appetites and passions with the same severity. True to this pattern, Adam Patch turned his vast energies upon America after the Civil War, made a fortune, and then turned these same energies toward reform, in great part helping to bring about Prohibition, even naming his grandson after the reformer Anthony Comstock. Anthony's whole being is thus a matter of irony, and his life becomes an unconscious betrayal of his grandfather's ideals.

In *The Beautiful and Damned*, Fitzgerald once again deals with the creation of self, only Anthony does not know what to create. Around him other men are establishing themselves—Joseph Black (née Bloeckman) in the movies, Dick Caramel in publishing and film. At the same time that he is jealous of their success, Anthony feels above this kind of activity. He thinks that he can separate the money of his grandfather's legacy from where it came and for what it stands. Adrift in a world that he neither understands nor believes in, he drinks away his time and uses up his small inheritance.

The novel is told against the backdrop of New York, and we see Anthony and Gloria move from a comfortable brownstone apartment in the center of Manhattan to more dreary flats, finally to the Bronx, that middle-class hell for Fitzgerald, at which time Anthony tries unsuccessfully to take up as a salesman after a pep talk and a course that proves the sham of the old Puritan-Horatio Alger values. *The Beautiful and Damned* was Fitzgerald's most conscious attempt to show how impossible it was to create the romantic self in the face of our Puritan legacy, carrying as it did the seeds of its own destruction. It is no accident that Adam Patch was a product of the post-Civil War period, that time when the old aristocratic values of Jefferson, which would have encouraged the romantic self, gave way to the materialistic values of Hamilton; and a country was remade in an image that would no longer support that sense of privilege that Amory Blaine and Anthony Patch encourage, would no longer support an environment that they found hospitable to the dignity of a heightened imagination.

The stories that Fitzgerald wrote contemporaneous with *The Beautiful and Damned* rework these essential themes. "The Diamond as Big as the Ritz" (1922), for example, is a fantasy version of this material. The diamond is a mountain that Fitz-Norman Culpepper Washington discovered in Montana. Mr. Washington, a direct descendant of George Washington and Lord Baltimore, the founder of Maryland, is obviously carrying on the legacy of America. He finds the mountain just after the Civil War, giving up his Virginia estate to work the mine and turning these natural resources into a fortune on both the American and international money markets. His activity at this time parallels the events of American history: from 1870 to his death in 1900, his story "was a long epic in gold." He protects his interest, even to the extent of murdering, enslaving, and imprisoning in a period that for him are "years of progress and expansion" (*Stories*, p. 16). In order to get to the mountain, one must pass through the town of Fish, where sit twelve somber men, who have lost all religious zeal, all illusion and capacity for wonder, all sense of the heightened, inspired self. They are by-products of the Washington legacy, a dying vestige of an older, inspired religious order which has now lost its purpose and source of nourishment.

Mr. Braddock Washington has inherited the land from his father, and he and his family are now totally self-contained and self-sufficient: "A chaste and consistent selfishness ran like a pattern through their every idea" (*Stories*, p. 25). They bring in an occasional guest to amuse them, but the guest must be eventually destroyed in order to preserve their security—a metaphor that testifies to Fitzgerald's attitude toward this class. All who threaten the Washingtons are kept locked in the prison of the middle class, where they are given enough to survive but never enough to satisfy. The apocalyptic ending of this story reveals the destructive nature of Washington's legacy, defines once again the legacy that Adam Patch left Anthony, and anticipates the way Fitzgerald will portray the rich in *The Great Gatsby*, where the Valley of Ashes is the by-product of a land that has been ravaged and turned to waste, a grotesque inversion of the great wheat fields that once dominated the land.

"May Day" (1920) is also a postbellum story, only the war here is World War I. The story is held together by a use of place, New York, "the great city of the conquering people" (*Stories*, p. 83). New York embodies the social spectrum, and the story is a composite of several experiences in which we move from the Biltmore Hotel to the Yale Club, to Delmonico's, to a socialist newspaper office, to Child's Restaurant, to the Commodore Hotel—the locations, like the events revealed, spinning characters centrifugally away from any kind of moral center. The rich are portrayed as callow and hollow, the poor as ignorant and biased; political protest comes to naught; self-abandonment is the spirit of the times. Nothing pulls the separate fates of these characters together. Anything like a cultural unity has given way to discordant multiplicity. However, the illusion is still there, supplied by the city, especially Fifth Avenue, which held such symbolic significance for Fitzgerald with its "happy sun [which] glittered in transient gold through the thick windows of the smart shops, lighting upon mesh bags and purses and strings of pearls in gray velvet cases. . ." (*Stories*, p. 89). Even the sun gives token to money and gold, which is now what the city has come to embody.

In "The Popular Girl" (1922), Fitzgerald once again used the pattern of the young man (here woman) from the provinces tale. Yanci Bowman comes to New York to seek a heightened self, soon finds herself lonely and cut off from family and friends, realizes that the scale of the city is intimidating, and finds herself in a world where money opens doors and establishes relationships. As in many of Fitzgerald's stories, a tragic pattern is reversed by a sentimental ending, and Yanci finally succeeds in the money-dominated city, which seemingly had worn out the seeker. Despite the weakness of the ending, this little-known story convincingly portrays the way New York can be experienced and in what way both the height and depth of that experience involves the meaning of money.

Fitzgerald's is a romantic world which collapses when youth ends and marriage and domestic responsibility begin, especially when such responsibility takes place in the confines of the middle class. Even the lonely clerks have it better than this, and a number of stories make clear what dread Fitzgerald attached to marriage and domestic life. " 'O Russet Witch!' " (1921), for example, shows Alicia Dare (all is a dare) bringing magic to Merlin's life and changing him forever; the magic ends, however, when Merlin marries Olive and settles into a middle-class routine, where he lives for others and not himself. The story is told against the backdrop of New York, a constant reminder to Merlin of what he is missing as he grows old, until he realizes that it is too late—that life has passed him by. At this point Alicia appears again, and he tells her: " 'You were making an attempt at me. . . . But . . .it came too late . . .' " (6TJA, p. 117).

"The Lees of Happiness" (1920) is another story that works out the sad fate of life in the suburbs—that is, life where the city leaves off and domestic life begins. Still another story that describes marriage as an ordeal is "The Adjuster" (1925). And two other stories that establish a kind of marriage sequence are "Hot and Cold Blood" (1923) and "Gretchen's Forty Winks" (1925). Both deal with the need of young husbands to cope with problem wives. Although these stories are slight, even trivial, they clearly document that Fitzgerald could not warm to family life, that humdrum realm taking over where the city ends. Although often undercut by sentiment, these stories abound in sickness and mental illness, as does *The Beautiful and Damned*, all written long before Zelda's breakdown and Fitzgerald's own physical decline. One reads them a bit in awe, as if the writing is on the wall, the imagination anticipating a more personal fate.

2.

The Great Gatsby is Fitzgerald's singular achievement. In no other work was he so totally in control of his material, so effective in bringing the fictional elements into brilliant combination. Much of this material was rehearsed in the short stories, and it is useful to look briefly at the novel in the light of our present discussion of Fitzgerald's use of place.

Jay Gatsby was his own creation; he simply "sprang from his Platonic conception of himself" (GG, p. 99). Gatsby creates himself on two levels—the first is a level of "personality," the other a more substantial level involving what Fitzgerald earlier called "personage." "If personality is an unbroken series of successful gestures, then there was something gorgeous about him" (GG, p. 2), Nick Carraway tells us on the second page. The "gestures," of course, include the pink suits, the gold shirts, the silver ties, the gold car swollen with chrome, the clipped speech, the "old sports," the formal intensity of manner, the gracefulness on the ballroom floor, and the pretensions to Oxford gentility. Personage involves moving beyond personality to an essential self. Beyond the accidents of person, we have Gatsby modeling himself on Dan Cody (William "Buffalo Bill" Cody?) and of course having Daisy Fay for his wife. Dan Cody is the last of the frontier speculators, the last of a pioneer tradition: "a product of the Nevada silver fields, of the Yukon, of every rush for metal since seventy-five." A millionaire many times over, he literally comes sailing into Little Girl Bay "as James Gatz's destiny" (GG, p. 100). Given this background, Gatsby's fate is bound to be strange—as strange as the violent contradictions that exist between Gatsby as personality and personage, as well as those between Gatsby the western "roughneck" and Gatsby the Oxfordian.

Nick of course spots the contradictions and is more amused than offended by the pink suits and silver ties, by the ignorance that locates San Francisco in the Midwest, and by Gatsby's tales of hunting big game in Paris, Venice, and Rome. Only Gatsby's intensity of purpose holds together the contradictions that undermine his creation of self.

But difficulties do not stop with the creation of self. Gatsby compounds his problem by bringing a Dan Cody mentality to New York, the money center of the world. The most serious lapse in Gatsby's education is that he cannot really see the difference between East Egg and West Egg and believes that Daisy can be won with Meyer Wolfsheim's kind of money. To put this differently, Gatsby never comes to understand the city—that city which rises "up across the river in white heaps and sugar lumps all built with a wish out of non-olfactory money" (GG, p. 69). He never comes to understand that some money smells and some does not. He lacks Amory Blaine's instinctual fear of Broadway and attaches himself to Meyer Wolfsheim—a "denizen of Broadway" whom he first meets in a 43rd Street poolroom—as readily as he attached himself to Dan Cody. Gatsby never realizes that he is moving between worlds that cannot be bridged by any one conception of self. As a result, he will never understand why Daisy will both be attracted and repulsed by his personality, why she will abandon him when she learns the source of his money, and why she is offended from the beginning by his parties, "appalled by West Egg, this unprecedented 'place' that Broadway had begotten upon a Long Island fishing village" (GG, p. 108).

Gatsby tries to play out a Western paradigm in the East. To the urban maze he brings a pioneer disposition and a Benjamin Franklin trust in himself and his purpose; and he plays out these aspects of self on the West Egg-Broadway-underworld axis, thinking that there he can find the credentials to enter the world of East Egg. In *The Great Gatsby*, Fitzgerald brilliantly shows how a conception of self is inextricably connected with the meaning of place, both of which are played out as destiny. As Nick tells us, Gatsby "told me the strange story of his youth with Dan Cody—told it to me because 'Jay Gatsby' had broken up like glass against Tom's hard malice, and the long secret extravaganza was played out" (GG, p. 148).

And personal destiny parallels a national destiny; as Gatsby left an ideal in the past, so did America itself. The "green breast of the new world" that the Dutch sailors saw when they came to the new continent has become the Valley of Ashes, where gigantic mounds of ashes instead of wheat are brought forth in grotesque display, as if some horrible process has short-circuited the connection between man and nature. Something has been lost in the past; something has preyed upon an ideal that was left behind us "somewhere back in that vast obscurity beyond the city, where the dark fields of the republic rolled on under the night" (GG, p. 182)—somewhere back, that is, in the realm of Jefferson, before the Civil War and before the rise of the city rich, personified by the Buchanans.

In "The Diamond as Big as the Ritz" and in *The Beautiful and Damned*, Fitzgerald had treated this theme before, had shown in what way the past had been altered and the legacy tainted; however, never had he developed such meaning with the poetic intensity that he brought to *The Great Gatsby*, never with such brilliant detail. The horror that he associated with the Bronx is overwhelmingly conveyed in the terrible party that Myrtle Wilson and Tom Buchanan host up on 158th Street, the tenuousness of married life by the marriages of both Tom and Daisy and Myrtle and George Wilson, the irony of Gatsby's almost religious intensity by his standing vigil over Daisy's house while she is in the kitchen "conspiring" with Tom over cold fried chicken and ale, the self-protectiveness of the established rich by Tom Buchanan's callous ability to direct George Wilson murderously toward Gatsby when he knows that Daisy was driving the car that killed Myrtle, and the insubstantiality of Gatsby's world by the contrast between a "world's-fair" effect of his parties and his lonely burial. Gatsby goes to his grave watched over only by servants; by the owl-eyed man (a kind of Tiresias figure), who gives us Gatsby's epitaph; by Gatsby's father, who never understands what has happened; and by Nick, who understands all too well. But what is remarkable about Gatsby is that he dared—dared to create something unique of himself, as contradictory as it turned out to be; dared to challenge the city, ignorant of its secrets and of its ways; to recreate the idealized moment of love, even though it was lost forever; to take on the established rich with fraudulent credentials; to challenge time itself; dared to play out the vision of self that linked his fate with America.

The stories that are satellites to *The Great Gatsby* are "Absolution," "Winter Dreams," " 'The Sensible Thing,' " "The Last of the Belles," and "The Rich Boy." "Absolution" (1924) is directly related to the novel because it was originally written as a description of Gatsby's childhood before Fitzgerald decided to make that part of Gatsby's background less detailed. The connections with the novel are obvious. Rudolph Miller does not believe that he is the son of his parents; his father and mother seem too pathetic for his rampant imagination. Rudolph puts himself ahead of God, brings down God from the heavens, and endows himself with the religious intensity that goes beyond his father's fumbling admiration for James J. Hill—the St. Paul mineral and railroad king to whom Gatsby's father refers at the end of the novel. Terrorized at the thought that he has committed a sacrilege by going to communion after having lied in the confessional, Rudolph distances this act by creating a superior self, which he names Blatchford Sarnemington, whose "suave nobility" allows him to escape prosaic reality and enter the privileged world of the imagination. Because he is able to rise to this level, he can escape the "terror" and confirm his "own inner convictions" that life offered "something ineffably gorgeous somewhere that had nothing to do with God" (*Stories*, p. 171). Father Schwartz, on the verge of a nervous breakdown, confirms these convictions, telling him that life can be turned into "an amusement park," a world's fair, so long as we "don't get up close" (*Stories*, p. 171). The story ends on a note of fertile life going on, the hot sun of afternoon reality giving way to the cool moon of evening imagination within which "blonde Northern girls and tall young men from the farms [would lie] out beside the wheat" (*Stories*, p. 172). In *The Great Gatsby*, Fitzgerald would move this landscape to the city, turn the wheat fields into a Valley of Ashes, turn out the lights at Gatsby's self-created world's fair, smash the imagination with the machinations of the city rich, and show how the religious intensity that Gatsby brought to his sense of self ends in a world totally secularized, materialistic, and brutalized.

Dexter Green of "Winter Dreams" (1922) brings the same intensity of purpose to winning Judy Jones, his summer love. Once again, we have a character who must move beyond his parents, especially his "Bohemian [mother] of the peasant class [who] . . . talked broken English to the end of her days" (*Stories*, p. 135). What he creates in place of his past is an image of self which he thinks is worthy of Judy and her wealth. *The Great Gatsby* was a summer novel, moving from the first weeks of June, 1922, to the first weeks of September. Dexter's was a summer love. In both instances death follows the summer—and it is the death of self, the product of winter dreams.

" 'The Sensible Thing' " (1924) is another version of the Gatsby experience and of Fitzgerald's own experience in winning Zelda. George O'Kelly had fallen in love with Jonquil Cary when he was working in the oil fields of Tennessee. When the story opens, he is living in the Bronx, working as a forty-dollar-a-week insurance clerk, "his dream slipping fast behind him" (*Stories*, p. 147). He returns to Tennessee, is unsuccessful in getting Jonquil to marry him, and then ships out for Peru, where he eventually makes his fortune. When he returns once again to Jonquil, it appears that he will eventually overcome her hesitancy and that they will be married. The romantic egoist is a fated man—unhappy as he desires, unhappier as he possesses. That is why all of these characters are sad young men, why all these stories end on a note of loss, and why the cemetery is the logical ending for the Gatsby figure—the lonely death metaphorically perfect for that singular dream that can never be shared and never won.

In its use of detail, "The Last of the Belles" (1929) is even closer than "Winter Dreams" to *The Great Gatsby*. Fitzgerald once again pursues the idea of personality, self as gesture. Like Gatsby, Earl Schoen is Nobody from Nowhere, the equivalent of being a streetcar conductor from the milltown of New Bedford, Massachusetts. What he lacks in intelligence, education, and social graces is made up for by his good looks and his impressive officer's uniform. Ailie Calhoun, already a proven *femme fatale*, falls in love, encourages him, and awaits his return after the war. When he arrives without his uniform, the deficiencies of self—the "gestures" that reveal personality—are quickly exposed. Earl Schoen cannot go beyond "gesture," cannot create the self that will hide the differences of class, cannot prolong Ailie's interest by bringing Gatsby's vitalized imagination and intensity of purpose to such a task—and his fate is inseparable from himself. The emotion of this loss is intensified in this story, as it is in *The Great Gatsby*, by being personalized by a narrator, who tells the story with the same feeling of loss that we sense in Nick Carraway.

The last of the stories that can be linked to *The Great Gatsby* is "The Rich Boy" (1926), where we find the Tom Buchanan figure treated in some depth. Fitzgerald tells us "the rich are different from you and me. They possess and enjoy early, and it does something to them" (*Stories*, p. 177). What it does is embodied in the character oi Anson Hunter, who has such a sense of superiority that he can never reconcile himself to having been turned down by the beautiful Paula Legendre. Anson gets his revenge of sorts by winning and then dismissing Dolly Karger and by driving Cary Sloane to suicide for having an affair with his uncle's wife. Like Tom Buchanan, he knows how to possess, how to protect what he has, and how to destroy what threatens him. "This was his city," he tells us as he walks up Fifth Avenue (*Stories*, p. 198), and he plans to keep it that way through "resourcefulness and a powerful will—for his threats in weaker hands would have been less than nothing" (*Stories*, p. 199). This sense of superiority that he brings to everything has been damaged by the loss of Paula, the full meaning of which he bitterly realizes when he sees her happily married to Peter Hagerty, quite content in the life that she has made for herself. His damaged sense of self is arrested only when he learns that Paula has died in childbirth, at which point he resumes his old superiority, regains his old self. "I was glad he was himself again [the narrator tells us] or at least the self that I knew, and with which I felt at home. I don't think he was ever happy unless some one was in love with him, responding to him like filings to a magnet, helping him to explain himself, . . . [nursing and protecting] that superiority he cherished in his heart" (*Stories*, pp. 207–8). The only Fitzgerald story in which the self is finally left intact—the only story that does not end with a sense of romantic loss—involves the rich. Anson Hunter does not have to worry about fraudulent gestures and contradictions in personality, does not have to play out a sense of the created self in a tenuous world, and does not have to find himself in the city. He knows who he is, lives his sense of superiority, is at one with himself and the city in a way that "no change could alter" (*Stories*, p. 199), and has every reason to believe that his destiny is of a different magnitude.

3.

After *The Great Gatsby*, Fitzgerald's sense of place changes. We move across a different landscape, away from the American provinces, which encourage a heightened conception of self, away even from New York, which is the inevitable stage upon which this drama of self was played, away finally from America. The changes here cannot be separated from his own personal experiences—his trip to Europe, his initial experience in Hollywood, and his response to the Depression, to Zelda's breakdown, and to his own bouts with illness, depression, and alcohol. The emphasis shifts from the romantic solitary to the family man— who was always vulnerable, even in Fitzgerald's earlier stories—and from America to Europe, the landscape of the western world containing the seeds of an American destiny as well as its own.

In *Tender Is the Night*, Fitzgerald equates two historical events, the American Civil War and World War I. Both bring an end to the old aristocracy. The Battle of the Somme is a "love battle" because the aristocracies destroy each other. The Civil War is "mass butchery" because one social order is destroyed by another. Out of the ravage comes the Warren family (war end?), for whom trains crisscross the country and a working class toils. Beneath this new, industrialized feudalism is something rotten, something sick, symbolized by Devereux Warren's incestuous relationship with his daughter. Nicole's illness, Abe (Abraham Lincoln) North's decline, the inverted sexual roles of the deracinated Europeans—all reveal this malaise. To this sickness Dick brings his vitality, only to have it exhausted. The betrayal of self comes from within and from without, violates the moral spirit of the aristocratic father, who dies at the point when Dick loses self-control and whose death is followed by Dick's seducing Rosemary Hoyt. Since he had previously protected Rosemary like a father, her seduction is thus an act which symbolically parallels the incest of Devereux Warren. In his earlier work, Fitzgerald had shown the romantic self playing itself out in the aftermath of American Puritanism. In *Tender Is the Night*, he reveals the man of genius playing himself out at the end of western civilization. Indeed, the man of vitality contains the sickness within him, and here destiny involves the doubled self, which like the moon has both a shiny and a dark side.

The story that most directly contains the seed of *Tender Is the Night* is "One Trip Abroad" (1930). The Kellys, Nicole and Nelson, have come to Europe, where among others they meet the Mileses, who have been "worn away inside" by fifteen years of the international scene (AA, p. 143). After four years of life in Europe, the Kellys are as jaded as the Mileses, their marriage at the edge of ruin, and their health sapped. The story ends in a sanatorium in Geneva (this detail is significant) at the lake which "is the center of Europe," by placid "waters that are a little sinister beneath the surface with all the misery that has

dragged itself here from every corner of Europe. Weariness to recuper-
ate and death to die" (AA, pp. 161–62). Here the Kellys try to take
stock of themselves, try to understand their "unlucky destiny" (AA, p.
162), try to discover why they lost " 'peace and love and health, one
after the other' " (AA, p. 164). As in T. S. Eliot's *The Waste Land*, a
work that deeply influenced Fitzgerald, their thoughts are interrupted
by a peal of thunder, at which time they see again the couple who have
shadowed them through Europe, now " 'harder-looking and . . . dissi-
pated' " (AA, p. 155); and the Kellys realize that their own fate is part
of the general cultural malaise.

Writing these stories in the Depression, Fitzgerald seemed to feel that
he had every right to be pessimistic about the world condition, justified
in his Spenglerian belief that western culture was destructively playing
itself out, and confirmed in his belief that one's personal destiny was
part of a larger process. The imaginative consent he had given to the
golden years between seventeen and twenty-nine now had a curious
parallel in history with the Jazz Age beginning after the war and
ending with the Depression of 1929. Their European experience had
ended with Zelda's mental breakdown, and his vitality was on the
wane. This sense of emotional depletion Fitzgerald anticipated in "The
Rough Crossing" (1929), in which the Adrian Smiths realize that they
are destroying each other. When Adrian no longer feels secure that he
can generate vitality on his own, he is attracted to the beautiful Betsy
D'Amido, whose "youth seemed to flow into him, bearing him up into
a delicate romantic ecstacy that transcended passion. He couldn't relin-
quish it; he had discovered something that was lost with his own youth
forever" (*Stories*, pp. 263–64). A story that obviously anticipates the
Dick Diver-Rosemary Hoyt sequence of *Tender Is the Night*, and perhaps looks back to Fitzgerald's own feelings toward Lois Moran, the
movie star he met in Hollywood in 1927, "The Rough Crossing" also
reveals a changing attitude toward character. For the first time a Fitzgerald character is no longer self-contained, looks to another for the
energy and vitality that he had once supplied himself, and willingly
links his destiny to that of another.

"Two Wrongs" (1930) reveals the consequence of such action. Bill
McChesney, a successful stage producer, takes sympathy on a young
dancer, Emmy Pinkard, whose career rises as his falls, until "he had
come to lean, in a way, on Emmy's fine health and vitality" (*Stories*,
p. 300). Like Dick Diver, McChesney loses self-control and begins to
rely on others rather than himself, until he is alone and in a state of
ruined health; illness is the constant in these stories.

The loss of this vitalized self is part of something larger, as we clearly see in "Babylon Revisited" (1931), where the dissipation of Charlie Wales cannot be separated from the spirit of the times. Throughout Fitzgerald's fiction the past has a way of consuming the present; here it follows Charlie like a ghost in the persons of Duncan Schaeffer and Lorraine Quarrles, with whom he had once lived riotously, and once again we have a story that ends on a note of loss which seems part of a larger destiny.

"The Swimmers" (1929), surprisingly untreated by Fitzgerald's critics, brings the material of this period into relief and reveals the way Fitzgerald related a sense of personal and historical destiny. The story opens in Paris, where Henry Clay Marston, a Southerner close now to being an expatriate, works in a bank. The details are significant because we see at the outset how he has betrayed his past aristocratic tradition, given himself to a foreign culture, and is at one with the fume-choked, money-oriented city. He refuses Judge Waterbury's request to return to a well-paying job in America and goes home to Choupette, his French-born wife, only to surprise her in the arms of a lover. Overwhelmed, he suffers a nervous collapse. His recovery brings with it " 'the Continental attitude,' " which accommodates adultery. This physical and moral sickness is broken by a vacation on the Riviera, where Henry, who cannot swim, goes to the help of a young girl who has suffered a cramp. In gratitude, the girl offers to give him swimming lessons, telling him that she swims " 'to get clean.' " He feels a vitality in this girl that seems gone from his own life, and in the water he begins to understand the source of it; not only does he experience a new physical well-being, but he begins to feel morally intact. When Henry finally accepts Judge Waterbury's offer and brings his family back to America, he discovers that Choupette is having an affair with Charles Wiese, one of the new money-men who now dominate the South. " 'Money is power, Marston,' " Wiese tells him and then delivers a speech on how we are all in the grip of money: " 'Money made this country, built its great and glorious cities, created its industries, covered it with an iron network of railroads. It's money that harnesses the forces of Nature, creates the machine and makes it go when money says go, and stop when money says stop' " (*Bits*, p. 205). This speech is delivered in a motorboat where Wiese, Choupette, and Marston have gone to discuss terms of the divorce. Marston insists that he must be given custody of his children, whom he feels will be lost under the protection of Wiese and Choupette. When Wiese reaches the end of his speech on the triumph of money over nature and the machine, the engine of the boat stops, and Wiese cannot get it started again. Letting the other two believe that they will drift to their deaths at sea, Marston gets the promise of custody before he swims to a lighthouse for help. His strength comes from what is simple and fundamental in nature and allows a triumph over the modernized European woman and the city man and his machines. This scene illuminates the end of *Tender Is the Night*, where Dick Diver is no longer able to perform upon the aquaplane board. Unlike Henry, Dick has become too much a part of a sick culture, has cut himself away from the strength that abides in nature, from which the vitality of self must not be separated. Henry Marston comes to believe that what was true of his own regained vitality could be true for America as well—that beneath "the ugly débris of industry the rich land still pushed up"; if this force could be tapped, perhaps it could bring new life to the sickness of western culture in general because "the best of America was the best of the world" (*Bits*, p. 209). This remarkable story is surely a transition piece between the Fitzgerald of *The Great Gatsby* and the Fitzgerald of *Tender Is the Night*— between a belief in a cultural vitality that stems from those dark fields somewhere beyond the city and that lost self that finds a pathetic equivalent on the battlefields of a worn-out Europe. "The Swimmers" ends precisely on this note. All that separates these two destinies is the matter of self—that is, "a willingness of the heart" (*Bits*, p. 210).

"The Swimmers" offers us a means to speculate on why Fitzgerald turned during this period to a new subject and the sequence we know as the Basil and Josephine stories, which are set for the most part in the Midwest and chart the growth of himself and Ginevra King, the imaginative source of the Jay Gatsby-Daisy Fay experience. These stories supplied a source of quick money from the *Saturday Evening Post*. But need seldom explains Fitzgerald's fiction, since he could not write a story unless he could bring to it a genuine emotion. It is possible that these stories of adolescence, which deal with the turmoil of the emerging self, may have helped him regain through the imagination the sense of vitality that he was losing in person. Booth Tarkington had, after all, written the Penrod stories after a bout with alcoholism. But if Tarkington's motives initiated these stories, the results differ finally from the Tarkington model. Tarkington's young man encapsulates a social process that brings him from a Huck Finn-like antipathy toward society into conformity with his genteel world. Fitzgerald's young man creates something more privileged, more unique, more strangely and singularly destined—and he wrote these stories that anticipate a romantic destiny when he was brooding over characters like Dick Diver, who are on the verge of a tragic destiny. A telescope has two ends, and Fitzgerald seemed to need both views at this time. Despite the sense of a world in decline, he held on to the belief that things could get better—and inseparable from this hope was his belief in the power of the youthful imagination to create an image of self in a world that was still vital.

4.

Unquestionably, Fitzgerald brought both a sense of hope and of doom to his work on *The Last Tycoon.* The novel opens with Monroe Stahr moving like a star across the heavens, in an airplane moving east to west, fated to play out his brilliance in what Fitzgerald called "a lavish, romantic past that perhaps will not come again into our time" (LT, p. 141). From a childhood in the Bronx, Stahr "had flown up very high to see, on strong wings, when he was young" (LT, p. 20) and had become a new kind of prince, in a world that cannot sustain him. Stahr's end is anticipated at the beginning of the novel by the suicide of Manny Schwartz on the doorstep of Andrew Jackson's Hermitage. Once the head of a large combine, now down-and-out, Schwartz "had come a long way from some ghetto to present himself at that raw shrine" (LT, p. 13). Manny Schwartz and Andrew Jackson—dissimilar names, dissimilar men, whose lives are inextricably connected because they both were acted out as part of an American destiny, a destiny that will also drop Stahr from the sky. Beneath the reality of death, however, something vital lives on. Cecilia Brady intuits it on the backroads of Tennessee when she contrasts in her mind a Negro and "real cows, with warm, fresh, silky flanks" with a flock of sheep, the first she had ever seen, "hundreds of them" (LT, p. 9), that are part of the setting for a movie. We have moved away from something vital in the land to the grotesque world of Hollywood. Monroe Stahr brings to all that is lavish the vitality of his own imagination, but it is an imagination severed from everything but its own vision. Alone, detached, aloof, his dream is exhaustible because it feeds on itself and is cut off from a more elemental vitality.

Any discussion of the uncompleted *The Last Tycoon* must be tentative. But even as a fragment, the novel documents the way Fitzgerald's imagination creatively worked; and despite Fitzgerald's disclaimer about writing another novel of deterioration, a magnanimous Monroe Stahr does undergo a process of decline. The last scene that Fitzgerald wrote before his death, the confrontation between a drunken Stahr and the radical Brimmer, involves an abrupt change in Stahr's character—moves him a bit too quickly from competent prince to incompetent fool. Since all the energy came from within him, Stahr was bound to wear out; too many people were tapping that energy, and the sources of renewal were gone.

Fitzgerald had anticipated such a character fate as early as 1928 in the story "Magnetism." George Hannaford, a handsome actor, feels himself becoming exhausted by the contradictory demands being made on him by Helen Avery, a beautiful young actress who wants him to return her love; by Kay Tompkins, his wife who feels that their marriage is being tested; by Margaret Donovan, a studio employee who is willing to blackmail him to win his attention; even by the Mexican maid, whose strategies are also aimed at "a possible admission to the thousand delights and wonders that only he knew and could command" (*Stories*, p. 239).

Another story that anticipates *The Last Tycoon* is "Crazy Sunday" (1932). The principal character, a Hollywood screenwriter named Joel Coles, makes a fool of himself at a Sunday afternoon cocktail party hosted by the successful director Miles Calman and his actress wife Stella. Hurt pride does not prevent him from showing a romantic interest in Stella. As Joel gets closer to the Calmans, he discovers two Miles Calmans—the brilliant director and the more bumbling husband: "The fine instinct that moved swiftly and confidently on the set, muddled so weakly and helplessly through his personal life" (*Stories*, p. 412). Like Stahr, Miles dies in a plane crash, a death that seemed inevitable to Joel, who suddenly realizes that a man of Miles's temperament was doomed in Hollywood, that he had used himself up and been used, did not live in a world that could sustain him. Along with *The Last Tycoon*, "Crazy Sunday" reveals the last of the princes, the last of the aristocrats, the last of the artists trying to function in a world that is no longer worthy of him—a world that cannot nourish and hence can only destroy. Once again, Fitzgerald played out a romantic conception of self as tragic destiny and revealed how romantic tragedy could not be separated from the modern landscape which gave it its being.

Sometime in the middle of 1939, Fitzgerald must have realized that romantic destiny could be lived out comically as well as tragically— that a fraudulent system would more easily generate the fraud than the man of integrity and that such a character would live on a less heroic scale. Such, I believe, explains the creation of Pat Hobby, about whom Fitzgerald wrote seventeen short stories, all submitted to *Esquire* between September, 1939, and the end of 1940. Once a successful Hollywood writer, now forty-nine years old and down-at-the-heels, Pat scavenges a living as a hanger-on at the studio. Although he has never forgotten what it means to be at the top, remembers the day the top executives invited him to lunch with the president of the United States ("A Patriotic Short"), can even be moved to violence when the hierarchy of the system is threatened (" 'Boil Some Water—Lots of It' "), Pat is now "too far gone" to work within the system—and he even has trouble getting through the studio gates ("Pat Hobby and Orson Welles"). Held to the system by memories, Pat has no illusions about its integrity, comes to accept his fate as a scavenger and turns it into a way of life. When it is suggested that writers are hard-working, he replies, " 'Listen, if you tried all the doors in the Writers' Building you'd find a lot of them locked and don't you forget it' " (PH, p. 132). The system exploits and justifies exploitation in return, an idea that could be played out bitterly, except that Pat is so inept that his behavior is far more comic than sinister, far more pathetic than evil. In at least five of the stories, he tries to steal credit for a script or a script idea ("A Man in the Way," "Teamed with Genius," "Pat Hobby's Secret," "Pat Hobby's Preview," and "No Harm Trying"); in another he is guilty of attempted blackmail ("Pat Hobby's Christmas Wish"); and in another of passing himself off as a friend of the stars ("The Homes of the Stars"). Pat hates pretensions (see "Two Old-Timers"), refuses to take himself seriously, and is not taken seriously in return. He lives off the fat of the system, off its waste, its debris. The idea here is more significant than the artistic achievement, and in an inchoate way Fitzgerald was showing that survival had its merits. But Pat's survival is at the expense of a heightened conception of self, and Fitzgerald had come a long way from the genteel and romantic hero, from the *homme épuisé* and the Faustian prince. He could not give up easily his belief that such heroes were necessary despite the shoddy world that destroyed them. Even Pat Hobby can warm to a romantic occasion. In his last years Fitzgerald seemed to toy with two very different conceptions of self—and two different calls to fate. Survival was not enough. If the modern air would not sustain heroic flight, the attempt to fly was still worth the effort.

If at the end Fitzgerald was amused by Pat Hobby, he was committed to Monroe Stahr—that last great romantic projection of his imagination, whose destiny could not be separated from Hollywood and the dream of self-fulfillment. Such a dream had its origins in the Enlightenment, when birthrights gave way to natural rights and moved west across an ocean with the early settlers and then across a whole continent, until it hit the sea and, like Monroe Stahr, had nowhere else to go when it tragically turned back upon itself.

THE SIGNIFICANCE OF FANTASY IN FITZGERALD'S SHORT FICTION

LAWRENCE BUELL

Fitzgerald's use of fantasy is a rather neglected subject worth closer scrutiny not just for its own sake but for what it can tell us about his literary methods in general and his place in the history of modern American fiction. We can best appreciate this through a survey of the fantastic in his short stories, especially "The Diamond as Big as the Ritz." As with Henry James, Ernest Hemingway, and a number of other novelists, Fitzgerald is often more experimental in his shorter fiction. The relative lack of critical attention paid to it has surely contributed to a general underestimation of the extent to which he was, by design, an artist of the fabulous.[1]

Fitzgerald's readers have often noticed in passing what might loosely be called a "surreal" quality to his imagery. Perhaps the most familiar

---

1. The present essay is the first systematic study of Fitzgerald's use of fantasy, but important commentary on certain aspects of the topic can be found in Richard D. Lehan, *F. Scott Fitzgerald and the Craft of Fiction* (Carbondale: Southern Illinois Univ. Press, 1966), Chapters I–II; Robert Sklar, *F. Scott Fitzgerald: The Last Laocoön* (New York: Oxford Univ. Press, 1967), Chapter VI; Robert A. Ferguson, "The Grotesque in the Novels of F. Scott Fitzgerald," *South Atlantic Quarterly*, 73 (Autumn 1979), 460–77; and Dawn Trouard, "Fitzgerald's Missed Moments: Surrealistic Style in His Major Novels," *Fitzgerald/Hemingway Annual*, 11 (1979), 189–205. Tristram P. Coffin, "Gatsby's Fairy Lover," *Midwest Folklore*, 10 (Summer 1960), 79–85; Scott Donaldson, " 'No, I am Not Prince Charming': Fairy Tales in *Tender Is the Night*," *Fitzgerald/Hemingway Annual*, 5 (1973), 105–12; and Peter L. Hays, "Gatsby: Myth, Fairy Tale, and Legend," *Southern Folklore Quarterly*, 41 (1977), 213–23, try with varying success to relate Fitzgerald to folktale and fairy tale conventions. I have also been much aided by the thoughtful comments of Leonard Podis and the inspirations of W. Patrick Day.

example is the description, in Chapter II of *The Great Gatsby*, of the wasteland dominated by the pseudodivine gaze of Dr. T. J. Eckleburg. The descriptions of Gatsby's radiant smile repeat this device in a major key. In each case normative reality seems to dissolve as one feature of an otherwise faceless face is disproportionately emphasized and converted into a symbolic motif that becomes almost obsessive with repetition. These motifs are reinforced at every turn by images of the grotesque and the unexpected, like Wolfsheim's cufflinks made of human molars and Nick's sudden fancy that a flock of sheep may be about to come around the city street corner. Such touches, which recur throughout Fitzgerald's works, have rightly been seen as causing his fiction to hover somewhere between the domain of manners and that of myth.

Nor is Fitzgerald always content to limit himself merely to the presentation of a heightened or distorted reality. At certain times, his instinct for hyperbole carries him into outright supernaturalism. In the novels, one thinks of Amory Blaine's vision of the devil with the face of Dick Humbird in *This Side of Paradise* or the motif of Gloria Gilbert as the incarnation of Beauty in *The Beautiful and Damned*. The seemingly magical fulfillment of Jerry Frost's dream of becoming president in *The Vegetable* is a related device. But most of Fitzgerald's experiments with anti-realism occur in a dozen or more short stories from as early as 1911 ("The Room with the Green Blinds") to as late as 1936 ("Thank You for the Light"),[2] the most distinguished example being "The Diamond as Big as the Ritz" (1922). The following essay will reverse the usual procedure of Fitzgerald criticism by taking these works as its central vantage point for an analysis of "surrealism" in his writing as a whole, rather than viewing them as a somewhat aberrant, inferior byproduct of his imagination.

The latter has been the prevailing view. Fitzgerald's critics have tended, with some justice, to be impatient with his handling of the fantastic. Fitzgerald "was always in danger when he was writing fantasy," Arthur Mizener notes, "for he was inclined to use material which was more extravagant than its point justified and to make so much

2. This story is described in Jennifer McCabe Atkinson, "Lost and Unpublished Stories by F. Scott Fitzgerald," *Fitzgerald/Hemingway Annual*, 3 (1971), 52–53: a "tired corset saleswoman, dying for a cigarette," enters a cathedral, falls asleep, and is visited by the Virgin, who "comes down and lights her cigarette." The date given here indicates probable time of composition; elsewhere dates indicate first publication (and, where appropriate, publication of revised versions).

fantastic that nothing seemed remarkable."[3] This is precisely what's wrong with *The Vegetable*: the wish-fulfilling dream gimmick becomes banal. Equally prevalent but less justifiable have been objections to the intrusion of fantasy into predominantly realistic works. Milton Stern, for instance, argues in the case of the Humbird-as-devil passage that Fitzgerald "made a critical error in not presenting a dramatization that would at once be symbolic and also in keeping with the realistic mode of the rest of the book."[4] In a somewhat similar vein, Sergio Perosa and John A. Higgins criticize Fitzgerald for unconvincing psychology in the characterization of the leading couple in "One Trip Abroad" (1930).[5] This story, anticipating *Tender Is the Night*, sketches the rather mysterious moral deterioration of Nelson and Nicole Kelly, ending in their sudden recognition that an elusive second couple, whose path they have crossed several times and whose decline they have already observed, is none other than themselves. At this point the doubles vanish. Of each above work one could ask, however, might it not have been in Fitzgerald's interest to create a sense of disjunction between the fictive world and "reality" so as to prevent either a symbolic or a realistic reading? A closer look at Fitzgerald's fantasies should reinforce this suspicion and in the process suggest another approach to the perennial question of what was Fitzgerald's primary literary mode.

This question is usually put as follows: Was Fitzgerald essentially a romanticist or a realist? Was he "perhaps the last notable writer to affirm the Romantic fantasy . . . of a personal ambition and heroism, of life committed to, or thrown away for, some idea of self"?[6] Or was he "the Social Historian of the Jazz Age," the writer whom John O'Hara credited with Belasco-like ability to create real people, real talk, real clothes, real cars?[7] Or was he a bit of both, a split personality? None of these alternatives, I think, quite does justice to the element of aesthetic

3. Arthur Mizener, *The Far Side of Paradise: A Biography of F. Scott Fitzgerald* (Boston: Houghton Mifflin, 1965), p. 170; cf. Henry Dan Piper, *F. Scott Fitzgerald: A Critical Portrait* (New York: Holt, Rinehart and Winston, 1965), p. 77.

4. Milton Stern, *The Golden Moment: The Novels of F. Scott Fitzgerald* (Urbana: Univ. of Illinois Press, 1970), p. 62n; cf. Trouard, pp. 195–96.

5. Sergio Perosa, *The Art of F. Scott Fitzgerald*, trans. Charles Metz and Sergio Perosa (Ann Arbor: Univ. of Michigan Press, 1965), p. 101; John A. Higgins, *F. Scott Fitzgerald: A Study of the Stories* (Jamaica, N.Y.: St. John's Univ. Press, 1971), p. 120.

6. Lionel Trilling, *The Liberal Imagination* (1950; rpt. Garden City, N.Y.: Doubleday, 1954), p. 240.

7. James W. Tuttleton, *The Novel of Manners in America* (Chapel Hill: Univ. of North Carolina Press, 1972), p. 164; John O'Hara, "*An Artist Is His Own Fault*": *John O'Hara on Writers and Writing*, ed. Matthew J. Bruccoli (Carbondale: Southern Illinois Univ. Press, 1977), p. 136.

distance or romantic irony in his style—to the continual reminders, especially in the fantasies, that the work before us is an artifact, that the fictive world is something more or less than a representation of social reality or the expression of somebody's commitment or dream. When Nick breaks his narrative-in-progress to document Gatsby's past, when *This Side of Paradise* and *The Beautiful and Damned* lapse *Moby-Dick*-like into drama, when Prince Agge suddenly sees "Lincoln" in *The Last Tycoon*, we are instantly reminded that we have been experiencing an artifice. This is because two contrasting modes of presentation have been laid side by side. We are made uncertain about the locus of reality, and we are made more conscious of the artist as manipulator of his characters and of ourselves. Much the same is true of the interjection of the supernatural previously noted in *This Side of Paradise* and "One Trip Abroad." We should resist the temptation to ascribe these effects to incompetence or a misguided lingering undergraduate cleverness. Though they may sometimes be no more than that, in general they reflect a serious aesthetic strategy, which should become more evident as we review the main techniques and themes involved in Fitzgerald's use of the fantastic.

Fantasy in Fitzgerald's work seems to occur in five main forms. First, as in the two early novels and in "One Trip Abroad," it may be used to complicate an essentially realistic presentation. Another such case is "The Adjuster" (1925), where a disintegrating marriage is held together by the mysterious Doctor Moon, whose ability to anticipate the self-indulgent wife's plans to desert her ailing husband seems clairvoyant and eventually intimidates her into becoming a loyal spouse. " 'Tell me who you are!' " she finally cries, and she gets the strange reply: " 'I am five years' "—the period of the adjustment (6TJA, p. 159). A second type of fantasy is the whimsical reinvention of history. We find this in Fitzgerald's apprentice fiction. "The Room with the Green Blinds" (1911) pictures John Wilkes Booth alive and hiding out in Georgia after the Civil War; "The Conquest of America" (1915) humorously imagines a German invasion repelled at Princeton; "Tarquin of Cheapside" (1917, 1921) is built around the idea that Shakespeare must have raped some real-live Lucrece in order to gain the experience to write his poem. All three tales unfold in a circumstantial, pseudodocumentary manner that contrasts with the impossibility of the situation. In the first, an illusion of factuality may be intended; the latter two are plainly comic *tours de force*.

A third group of tales dispenses with the illusion of a historical anecdote and builds upon situations that are inherently fabulous. In "The Curious Case of Benjamin Button" (1922), the title character is born as a seventy-year-old man and grows younger until he dies of extreme infancy. In "A Short Trip Home" (1927) ("my first ghost story"),[8] a Yale sophomore confronts and exorcizes a ghoul who has kept himself alive by preying upon young women he meets on railroad trains. In "The Diamond as Big as the Ritz," John T. Unger from Hades, Mississippi, spends a summer vacation in Montana with his prep school friend Percy Washington, whose family lives in unparalleled luxury atop a mountain that contains the largest diamond in the world, waited upon by a phalanx of slaves who don't know that the North won the Civil War.

Two other types of Fitzgerald fiction treat rationally explicable events in ways that merely seem fantastic. In the one, a wish-fulfilling dream apparently comes true by magic but is later revealed as illusion. *The Vegetable* follows this pattern. Likewise, in " 'O Russet Witch!' " (1921), Merlin Grainger, an ironically-named bookstore clerk, devotes his life to musing about a beautiful, impulsive woman whom he comes to believe is an enchantress with a special revelation for him, only to find in old age that her motives were prosaic and disreputable and her interest in him was nil. Related to this type of story are comparatively more realistic works that portray temporary delusions or fantasies that we immediately recognize as such: e.g., Rudolph Miller's dream of himself as Blatchford Sarnemington in "Absolution" (1924) and the father-daughter game of make-believe in "Outside the Cabinet-Maker's" (1928). These make integral use of fantasy, though they are not written in the fantastic mode.

Finally, on the periphery of the fantastic are stories about mundane events where the structure or texture is so exaggerated that we are forced to read the work as deliberate stylization rather than as mimesis. An early example is "Jemina, the Mountain Girl" (1916, 1921). A ridiculous hillbilly tale of two lovers killed in a Hatfield-McCoy feud, it burlesques frontier narrative and sentimental love conventions ("He was wonderful. When he talked his lips moved" [TJA, p. 314]). In "Head and Shoulders" (1920), a boy genius, socially inept, marries an actress; then the two change places: he becomes a trapeze artist, she becomes a writer. Beyond a point, admittedly, one has trouble distinguishing between conscious and unintended fantasy in stories of this

8. *As Ever, Scott Fitz—: Letters Between F. Scott Fitzgerald and His Literary Agent Harold Ober 1919–1940*, ed. Matthew J. Bruccoli and Jennifer McCabe Atkinson (New York and Philadelphia: J. B. Lippincott, 1972), p. 102.

kind.[9] Perhaps the best summary statement would be that the distinction can seem as strong as Fitzgerald's own general awareness of the gap between dream and fact, or as shadowy as his periodic confusion of the two in life.

The main reason it is hard to tell where fantasy starts or breaks off in Fitzgerald is not biographical, however, but aesthetic. Almost all the works just described, even those of the second and third types, are grounded at some point in a recognizable social reality (e.g., nineteenth-century Baltimore in "Benjamin Button" and the exclusive Northeastern prep school in "Diamond"). The fantasy takes shape, gradually or abruptly, by moving away from this environment or by transforming it into something bizarre. To put this another way, fantasy in Fitzgerald usually involves an interplay or tension between the sense of a "real world" and the sense of an anti-world of the implausible or the outlandish. The characteristic themes of Fitzgerald's fantasies all arise from this interplay.

One of these is of course an awareness of the way people want and need to impose their private visions upon reality. Through fantasy this need is both dramatized and shown to be comic or pathetic or dangerous. A related theme is the compulsion to arrest or rearrange time. The historical fantasies do this in an obvious manner, but a number of the other stories also play upon the idea of altered time. "Benjamin Button," following a hint from Mark Twain that the worst part of life shouldn't have to come last, reverses the life cycle.[10] Some broader, undeveloped comment on Southern cultural nostalgia may also be implicit in the fact that the aged Benjamin is born in Baltimore on the eve of the Civil War (1860): does time make the bankrupt old South an increasingly vital illusion, until its regressiveness becomes patent? In "The Adjuster," Dr. Moon, whose name suggests time, personifies, as we have seen, the effect of elapsed time on the heroine. If he seems to belong to a different world from hers, that is because he represents the underlying law that unifies her time-bound state of flux and development. Likewise the ghoul in "A Short Trip Home" seems to be a variant of the older man in Fitzgerald's "Daddy's Girl" narratives, where the

9. For instance, in " 'The Sensible Thing' " (1924), the youthful hero, initially rebuffed by his sweetheart on the ground of poverty, unexpectedly makes a fortune in Peru. Since the latter episode is not handled in a tone that would suggest authorial awareness of an incongruity in the shift from the level of manners to the level of extreme romance, I would classify the ending as unconscious rather than conscious fantasy; but it is risky to insist on such precision in Fitzgerald's case.

10. F. Scott Fitzgerald, *Tales of the Jazz Age* (New York: Charles Scribner's, 1922), p. ix.

protagonist tries to stave off middle age through affairs with young women.

As some of these examples show, fantasy can also be a way of dramatizing absolutes, as with Dr. Moon. The doubles in "One Trip Abroad" represent another psychological law, a law of decay. Again, the supernaturalism of *The Beautiful and Damned* shows, on one level, Gloria as the essence of beauty. The fantasy, at least for a moment, provides a kind of moral center for the narrative, a center of authority, although its appearances are sufficiently evanescent as to make that authority seem problematic.

Perceiving this, we arrive at still another use of fantasy in Fitzgerald. Sometimes it seems to have an almost purely ludic function, to be engaged in as a sport, for the sake of virtuosity or exhibitionism. This seems especially true of the undergraduate pieces. ("Admiral Von Nose-itch was swimming across with the fleet. Pandemonium reigned in the great city, women and tenors were running frantically up and down their rooms, the men having all left. . . .")[11] Fortunately, this kind of rhetoric gets toned down in the later fiction, yet in a tempered way it continues to infuse a leavening of unreality into such passages as Gatsby's guest list and the imagistic catalogues of a sketch like " 'Show Mr. and Mrs. F. to Number—' " (1934):

> We are married. The Sibylline parrots are protesting the sway of the first bobbed heads in the Biltmore panelled luxe. The hotel is trying to look older. (C-U, p. 41)

Here we have the fifth type of fantasy: one may think of it as mimetic, but the mimesis is so stylized that the perceptions are almost solipsistic, reflecting the private world of the young marrieds. They retaliate against imagined disapproval by locating it in the chatter of the Biltmore's parrots and express the phoniness of the place (and their own insecurity, too) by personifying the hotel as youth trying to act mature. The sketch as a whole is not *just* a playful exercise; it also can be read as a rather somber study of how thirteen years of aimless wandering turns honeymooning into a wearisome routine. But this undertone is created by the persistence of the device of having the speakers react to the external world as a mere toy on which to vent their ennui.

11. F. Scott Fitzgerald, "The Conquest of America," in *F. Scott Fitzgerald in His Own Time: A Miscellany*, ed. Matthew J. Bruccoli and Jackson R. Bryer (Kent, Ohio: Kent State Univ. Press, 1971), p. 77.

The combination of fantasy and irony in this sketch is characteristic of Fitzgerald. Whether or not the intent of his fantasies happens to be deeply satirical, they usually have the effect of calling attention to the illusory, pasteboard quality of what is being depicted, even though their airiness and hyperbole may also induce a temporary euphoria. One conjectures that the fantasy starts as a kind of romantic exuberance, then turns into parody or satire through its own excess, so that the extravaganza finally seems sick or grotesque. Needless to say, this dual effect is very much in keeping with Fitzgerald's known ambivalence toward himself, his age, and the manners and values of the characters he usually portrays. Ultimately the most distinctive feature of Fitzgerald's fantasies is this peculiar tone, which mocks the pretended solidity of his realistic portrayals and the high seriousness of his straightforwardly romantic passages.

We can see this very clearly in his most successful fantasy, "The Diamond as Big as the Ritz,"[12] which incorporates all the themes just mentioned. This story is also his most succinct critique of the American dream. Regarding its composition, Fitzgerald tells us, "I was in that familiar mood characterized by a perfect craving for luxury, and the story began as an attempt to feed that craving on imaginary foods."[13] Here as elsewhere Fitzgerald's fictional practice illuminates Freud's idea of the link between poetry and daydreaming: "Diamond" is both an indulgence in and, in the process, an exorcism of the notion of "material possibilities run wild."[14] Through the use of a naive center of consciousness, the schoolboy John Unger, Fitzgerald can revel in the splendors of the Washingtons' Montana estate yet also convey the foolishness and hazards of such wide-eyed enthusiasm.

Actually three sorts of illusion are developed: John's, the Washington family's, and the narrator's own game of pseudo-mimesis.

John has imbibed what Fitzgerald implies is the standard American middle-class fascination with wealth: "The simple piety prevalent in Hades has the earnest worship of and respect for riches as the first article of its creed" (*Stories*, p. 9). Later, Hades is implicitly equated with the "hell" of the underground prison where Braddock Washington keeps a melting-pot full of trespassers; both suggest "The hell of middle-

---

12. All general studies of Fitzgerald's writing mention "Diamond" at least in passing, but the two most important critical readings are Sklar, pp. 140–47, and Marius Bewley, *The Eccentric Design: Form in the Classic American Novel* (New York and London: Columbia Univ. Press, 1959), pp. 259–70. I have profited from both.

13. *Tales of the Jazz Age*, p. viii.

14. Bewley, p. 267.

class life."[15] Hence it is that young John is sent by his ambitious parents to St. Midas School; hence he is conditioned to believe, " 'The richer a fella is, the better I like him' " (*Stories*, p. 7). The Washingtons' materialistic paradise is the realization of this dream, later shown as nightmare; the fantasy, on this level, is an appropriate mirror of John's immature mind.

Second, the Washingtons themselves are dreamers in that they too are committed to maintaining the impossible and have previously acted out the transformation that John briefly experiences. They are associated with all the stock emblems of American success and *noblesse*. They are antebellum planter aristocrats, pioneers who struck it rich, capitalist plutocrats who rule a miniature technological state. The clan's leader, Braddock Washington, as his name implies, epitomizes the way the American republic might revert—perhaps had reverted—to the imperialism it was founded to overthrow.[16] As the story unfolds, Braddock and John, the two characters most fully developed, begin to be cast in a guru-novice relation faintly analogous to Gatsby and Nick or, better, Uncle Ben and Willy Loman in *Death of a Salesman*.

Third, the story is narrated in such a way as continually to flaunt its own illusoriness. As previous commentators have noted, it resembles the fairy tale and the tall tale, both forms that deliberately heighten and exaggerate.[17] But the narration's most significant feature is the way it combines overtones of these forms with the appearance of documentary realism, so that the pretense of mimesis is set up only to be undercut immediately. "John T. Unger came from a family that had been well known in Hades—a small town on the Mississippi River—for several generations." Everything is prosaic here except for the place name, which turns the whole sentence into a (facile) *double entendre*. "John's father," the narrator blandly continues, "had held the amateur golf championship through many a heated contest" (*Stories*, p. 5). Again the pretense of exposition dissolves into a deliberate cliché ("heated contest") which puns on the Hades idea. Later, our natural tendency to read John's tearful departure for St. Midas seriously is defeated by the narrator's playful handling of his affection for "the old-fashioned Victorian motto" over the city gates, even though it's "a little depressing." The sign, which Mr. Unger wants to replace with one that

15. Lehan, p. 104.

16. Edward Braddock (1697–1755), British general during the French and Indian War, conducted a raid against Fort Duquesne that proved disastrous when, according to American legend (inaccurate), he ignored George Washington's advice to prepare for Indian ambush.

17. Bewley, p. 259, and Sklar, p. 143 and *passim*.

has "a little more push and verve," presumably reads something like "Give up all hope, ye who enter." Throughout the story Fitzgerald continues to play with the illusion of mimesis in similar fashion, so that the reader is made very aware of the extent to which the narrative, like the two main characters, fails to reinvent reality. Perhaps the most striking instance is the cold-bloodedness of Braddock Washington's policy of preserving his empire through slave labor, life imprisonment of interlopers, and execution of guests. Washington's urbane manner of explaining himself in his conversation with his prisoners creates an atmosphere of matter-of-factness that is simultaneously undercut by the monstrousness of the situation.

The unreality of the Washington lifestyle is dramatized partly as a quixotic defiance of time. Braddock's empire was founded on the refusal to accept the consequences of the Civil War and maintained against increasingly greater odds as technology improved (geologic surveys, invention of aircraft). It is finally defeated by the rise of modern warfare. Just before his demise, Braddock, first seen as "about forty" and "robust," suddenly and fittingly ages into "a broken, white-haired man." This process starts during the scene where he tries to bribe God to turn back the clock, "calling to witness forgotten sacrifices, forgotten rituals, prayers obsolete before the birth of Christ." Through this ritual the symbolic implications of Braddock's character are momentarily given full extension, and he appears for an instant as an archetypal being who transcends all temporal limits. As "king and priest of the age of gold," he is not just the richest American entrepreneur, but a primal figure—"Prometheus Enriched," as the narrator somewhat enigmatically calls him (*Stories*, p. 34).[18] Even before he finishes praying, however, his dimensions begin to shrink, and the failure of his prayer implies either the obsolescence of his faith or the traditional idea that the gold-worshipper is bound to the wheel of fortune, which is a time-bound condition. When Braddock destroys himself, we seem to have returned to a world of comparatively normal time and probability. The chateau has virtually disappeared; John, Kismine, and Jasmine discover that they have no diamonds, only rhinestones; John tells us that his hometown isn't, after all, the prototypical Hades but just an ordinary place. All this is a bit like Alice waking up from her dream of wonderland.

Or from the dream of youth. The stars, Kismine says,

18. Fitzgerald probably meant to suggest that Braddock Washington, like Prometheus, was a usurper and God-defier but for the sake of self-aggrandizement rather than for public benefit.

". . . make me feel that it was all a dream, all my youth."

"It *was* a dream," said John quietly. "Everybody's youth is a dream, a form of chemical madness." (*Stories*, p. 38)

Like Braddock, John too has misunderstood or refused to accept the consequences of human time. Almost willfully failing to draw any connection between himself and the prisoners, John doesn't see how his summer must end. His absorption in his love affair with Kismine shows the same naive attempt to orient life around himself that the Washingtons have displayed in the creation of their estate. He admires—and imitates—the "chaste and consistent selfishness" of Kismine, Percy, and their father. Significantly, John's reintroduction to "real life" is almost as abrupt as Braddock's downfall. Realization of his plight, his escape, and the chateau's destruction all happen in less than a day. Almost the entire story consists of these events, plus events leading up to and including John's first day at the estate. There is no correspondence between chronological time and the proportions of the story. July passes in a hazy instant.

Although Braddock and John accept the frustration of their dreams, the story itself continues with the same interplay between fantasy and mimesis until the end. Here the analogy to *Alice* breaks down. The final conversation between John and the Washington sisters, which has struck many readers as mawkish, is instead probably a piece of calculated mock-sentimentalism.[19] Fitzgerald continues to show John as a compound of cliché (" 'let us love for awhile' ") and precocious remarks he half-understands (" 'His was a great sin who first invented consciousness' " [*Stories*, p. 38]). The speed with which he then falls asleep is disconcerting—and maybe also pathetic: perhaps he would like to return to his dream. Above all, the tone of the whole conversation is oddly out of place. As party chatter, it is conceivable; as the immediate aftermath of holocaust, it is bizarre. The characters are too unshaken, too unscarred. They are puppets, like Candide or Cabell's Jurgen and his women; the narrative remains fabulous even as it reenters reality. Perhaps this effect is meant to imply that the characters have only begun to develop into genuine persons. More likely, though, the ending implies that both the rich and the middle class must remain trapped in what we recognize as a fantasy world of their own making. John's claim that the original Hades is abolished seems, then, a bit premature.

Altogether, "Diamond" admirably realizes what for Fitzgerald was perhaps the most significant potential of the fantastic mode: its ability

19. Bewley, p. 269, also makes this point.

to convey at the same time that dreams of a metamorphosed reality are emotional and social necessities which we cannot help but indulge, and that they are in another sense insubstantial, ludicrous, pathetic. In this respect fantasy was well suited to mirror Fitzgerald's complex attitude toward his times ("It was an age of miracles, it was an age of art, it was an age of excess, and it was an age of satire" [C-U, p. 14]) and to measure up to his famous "test of a first-rate intelligence"— namely "the ability to hold two opposed ideas in the mind at the same time, and still retain the ability to function" (C-U, p. 69).

Even the critics who take "Diamond" most seriously treat it as a prelude to *Gatsby*. That is understandable. The two works share a number of motifs in common: the time-forestalling dream, the intoxication with luxurious decor, the amazing house and car, the mysterious central figure or family viewed by the relatively conventional middle-class outsider, the narrative pattern of romantic exuberance abruptly cut short.[20] Here as elsewhere Fitzgerald can retrospectively be seen as using his short fiction to test out devices later used in the novels. This very legitimate approach to "Diamond" should not, however, keep us from appreciating the extent to which it and Fitzgerald's other fantasies constitute a distinct and significant achievement in their own right. We may perceive this more clearly through a brief survey of how Fitzgerald's work fits into the history of modern anti-realistic fiction.

Though literary influences are notoriously hard to specify, it seems fair to assert that Fitzgerald, like most serious writers, learned to write fantasy partly on his own and partly from inspiration supplied by a variety of models. In particular, we know that he was stimulated during his formative years by a number of late nineteenth-century and early twentieth-century writers who use anti-realistic devices in ways that anticipate his own practices: Samuel Butler, George Bernard Shaw, Oscar Wilde (*The Picture of Dorian Gray*), Mark Twain (*The Mysterious Stranger*), James Branch Cabell (*Jurgen*), and Anatole France (*Thaïs, The Revolt of the Angels*) being probably the most important precursors. Perhaps H. L. Mencken should also be included due to his brand of rhapsodic invective, which verges on fantasy. To all of these writers Fitzgerald paid homage at one time or other. Though this hardly amounts to positive proof that he recognized a tradition of literary fantasy or consciously aligned himself with it, the point is worth stressing as a complement to the standard picture of Fitzgerald's artistic development as a process of evolution from the "novel of saturation"

20. Some of these motifs, of course, reappear in *Tender Is the Night* and *The Last Tycoon*—e.g., the sumptuous house (symbolic of overreaching) and the use of the naive witness (Rosemary, Cecilia).

(Wells, Mackenzie, later Norris) to the "novel of selection" (James, Conrad), both of which are essentially realistic modes.[21] In particular, this scheme of Fitzgerald's development minimizes or overlooks the relevance for his art of the vogue of mock-romantic or satirical fantasy represented by most of the writers just listed. They are seldom taken very seriously as analogues or models for Fitzgerald's mature style.[22]

One measure of their importance to Fitzgerald is the fact that at one crucial point in his career he saw himself as developing into a nonrealistic writer. This was during the years 1921–23, which saw the publication of "Diamond," "Benjamin Button," " 'O Russet Witch!' " and *The Vegetable*, plus the republication of "Tarquin." Fitzgerald was almost invariably excited about these works. "Diamond" was "the best thing I've ever done" (*Letters*, p. 471); "Benjamin Button" was one of his two favorite stories; the play was "the best American comedy to date & undoubtedly the best thing I have ever written"; later on, "The Adjuster" was "a peach."[23] Fitzgerald's second collection of stories, *Tales of the Jazz Age* (1922), contained a subsection called "fantasies," including "Diamond," "Benjamin Button," "Tarquin," and " 'O Russet Witch!' " These, Fitzgerald coyly explained, "are written in what, were I of imposing stature, I should call my 'second manner.' "[24] Seven months earlier, he had called Maxwell Perkins' attention to "my 'new' manner" when he first announced his plan for the collection.[25] This was in February, 1922, shortly after finishing "Benjamin Button" and while the revision of "Diamond" (November/December, 1921) was still fresh in his mind.

At this point, Fitzgerald was most enthusiastic about both the aesthetic and commercial possibilities of the fantasy form. His next

21. See especially James E. Miller, Jr., *F. Scott Fitzgerald: His Art and His Technique* (New York: New York Univ. Press, 1964), Chapters I–III.

22. The most notable exception is Sklar's thoughtful analysis of the Twain-Fitzgerald relation, pp. 138–47. For Mencken-Fitzgerald, see William Goldhurst, *F. Scott Fitzgerald and His Contemporaries* (Cleveland and New York: World, 1963), Chapter III. A brief but very helpful account of Fitzgerald's literary enthusiasms is John Kuehl, "Scott Fitzgerald's Reading," *Princeton University Library Chronicle*, 22 (Winter 1961), 58–89, which refers to all the authors mentioned above. For testimony (unsympathetic) as how mock-romantic fantasy would have been seen in the 1920s as a more vital, important tradition than we are now inclined to associate with the period, see, for instance, Peter Munro Jack, "The James Branch Cabell Period," *New Republic*, 89 (January 13, 1937), 323–26. Fitzgerald's penchant for fantasy would also have been reinforced by the somewhat patronizing and erratic counsel of Edmund Wilson; see Piper, pp. 77, 95.

23. *Dear Scott/Dear Max: The Fitzgerald-Perkins Correspondence*, ed. John Kuehl and Jackson R. Bryer (New York: Charles Scribner's, 1971), p. 62; *As Ever*, p. 70.

24. *Tales of the Jazz Age*, p. viii.

25. *Dear Scott/Dear Max*, p. 54.

novel, he thought, "will not be a realistic one." He predicted that his
new collection would outsell *Flappers and Philosophers* "because all
the fantasies are something new & the critics will fall for them."[26]
Unfortunately his literary agent, Harold Ober, was finding "Diamond"
hard to market; it finally went to the highbrow but unremunerative
Smart Set, and Fitzgerald did his best to console himself with the
prestige. "Benjamin Button," he fancied, would do better "because it
does not 'blaspheme,' " and he turned out to be right—but only, it
seems, after considerable salesmanship on Ober's part. By September,
1922, Fitzgerald was quite aware that "the magazines want only flapper stories from me—the trouble you had in disposing of *Benjamin
Button + The Diamond as Big as the Ritz* showed that." In the meantime, he experimented (unsuccessfully) with the writing of movie scen-
arios, intending to do more of the same "if this works out," since "it
seems unlikely that the satyrical short stories I feel moved to write at
present (*Ben Button* + the *Diamond in the Sky*, for instance) will *ever*
bring me any movie money."[27] Again Fitzgerald's instinct was right. His
next major attempt at fantasy, *The Vegetable*, on which he spent a
year of off-and-on work, turned out to be a "catastrophic experiment"
both aesthetically and financially, as Henry Dan Piper has said.[28] Its
failure may well have had a good deal to do with the fact that Fitzgerald thereafter largely ceased practicing in his "second manner." He
would have been reinforced by the fact that his two later pieces that
came closest to pure fantasy did not fare well commercially. "A Short
Trip Home" was accepted grudgingly by the *Saturday Evening Post*;
"Thank You for the Light" proved unmarketable.[29]

Fitzgerald's second manner continued to lead a thriving sublimated
existence, however, in his penchant for injecting destabilizing devices
into his later fiction. The evaporation of the ghostly doubles in "One
Trip Abroad" is an obvious case. Almost equally disconcerting is the
way Dr. Pirie, in "The Long Way Out" (1937), ends his story of the
insane patient who waits every day for her dead husband: " 'There's
always the chance . . . that some day he will be there' " (*Stories*, p.
446). The reader cannot be sure that this is *merely* the doctor's awkward attempt to end what has become for the whole party a most
depressing tale. Again, consider the point from which we began: Fitzgerald's fondness for proliferating bizarre and/or discontinuous im-

26. Ibid., pp. 57, 55.
27. *As Ever*, pp. 35, 48, 42. "The Diamond in the Sky" was the working title of
"Diamond."
28. Piper, p. 77.
29. *As Ever*, p. 103; Atkinson, pp. 52–53.

agery, as in the thirteen-year marriage sketch, or Rosemary Hoy·'s introduction to the movie set-like salon in the Rue Monsieur, where she meets "the three cobra women" who speak ill of the Divers (TITN, p. 73).

An especially striking example is Nick Carraway's first glimpse of the Buchanan house, an exercise in disorientation. The grass "seemed to grow a little way into the house"; the rug ripples like the sea:

> The only completely stationary object in the room was an enormous couch on which two young women were bouyed up as though upon an anchored balloon. They were both in white, and their dresses were rippling and fluttering as if they had just been blown back in after a short flight around the house. I must have stood for a few moments listening to the whip and snap of the curtains and the groan of a picture on the wall. Then there was a boom as Tom Buchanan shut the rear windows and the caught wind died about the room, and the curtains and the rugs and the two young women ballooned slowly to the floor. (GG, p. 8)

Thematically, the passage is an obvious piece of foreshadowing: brutish Tom will deflate Daisy's fairy balloon. The rhetoric of the passage, however, does not bring us to earth; rather it establishes the sense of a fictive world in which houses become organic in strange ways and ladies levitate. This is not exactly an idyllic fairyland; the impression is rather one of delicate but vaguely repellent strangeness, and of light irony rather than of intense concern. So the rhetoric does in the long run exercise in a sophisticated way an influence parallel to what Tom does crudely. The magic has an alienating as well as enticing effect. This eventually sets us up for the voice of the sober, earnest, dutiful, organizing commentator, who is rarely long absent in Fitzgerald's mature fiction. But the reader only accepts his post-Victorian moralizing (e.g., the orgiastic green light passage) as a result of having sensed the disconcerting otherness of the magical world witnessed here and elsewhere.

This underlying perception of "reality" as fabulous and of "romanticism" as pathological, and the dramatizing of such perceptions through the use of the discontinuous, the grotesque, the bizarre, and (ocasionally) the supernatural, makes Fizgerald a forerunner of the succession of anti-realistic, ironic experimentalist writers from Nathanael West to Donald Barthelme who have established what may very well come to be recognized as *the* main current in late twentieth-century American fiction. Fitzgerald, Jay Martin notes, was "a kind of literary father to

West," whose work he admired and helped to promote.[30] West is justly recognized as the first thoroughgoing practitioner of black humor in America. Yet West's dystopian fantasy, *A Cool Million*, a mock-Alger story in which the naive hero loses most of his bodily organs, recalls a work like "Diamond" in its deadpan treatment of cruelty, its sense of the protagonist as a throwaway character, its use of hyperbole to achieve a pose of ironic nonchalance.

That is not to equate the two works, or the two authors, but merely to emphasize that Fitzgerald leads somewhere other than just to John O'Hara and to the realistic and sentimental sides of J. D. Salinger. To the extent that Fitzgerald can legitimately be grouped with a writer like West, the explanation lies in that second manner of his. Seeing this, we may finally want to identify Fitzgerald, in William Goldhurst's phrase, not only as the moralist or the recorder but also as the "fabulist" of his age.[31]

30. Jay Martin, *Nathanael West: The Art of His Life* (New York: Farrar, Straus, 1970), p. 387.
31. Goldhurst, p. 228.

TOUCHES OF DISASTER:
ALCOHOLISM AND MENTAL ILLNESS
IN FITZGERALD'S SHORT STORIES

KENNETH E. EBLE

"The test of a first-rate intelligence," F. Scott Fitzgerald wrote in the first of "The Crack-Up" essays, "is the ability to hold two opposed ideas in the mind at the same time and still retain the ability to function" (C-U, p. 69). This concern with the ability to function amidst conflicts marks Fitzgerald's career as a writer and is an underlying theme of all his fiction. For very few periods of his life, drunk or sober, suffering from his own real and imagined ills or confronting Zelda's incipient and confirmed schizophrenia, did Fitzgerald stop functioning as a writer, exerting the power of mind over language which so much defines rationality.

Though Fitzgerald is commonly, and not erroneously, regarded as a romantic, a side of him posed a keen, dispassionate rationality as the ideal. The male protagonists with whom Fitzgerald most sympathized—Nick Carraway, Gatsby, Dick Diver before his decline—are above all rational men, sober amidst much insobriety, able to function amidst disorder around them, and capable of establishing moral and emotional stability for a time even though it will eventually yield to chaos. His harshest judgment fell upon careless people, like Tom and Daisy, "who retreated back into their money or their vast carelessness . . . and let other people clean up the mess they had made . . ." (GG, pp. 180–81).

That admiration for mind, however, coexisted with an admiration for physical vigor; his greatest personal defeats (aside from losing Ginevra King) were his not becoming a football star and not getting into the war overseas. His idealism was both classical—a sound mind in a sound body—and contemporary American—he came to maturity in the Teddy Roosevelt era, during the first flush of the mating of academic life with intercollegiate football. At the peak of his powers he could show most contempt for Tom Buchanan, the hulking brute who displays what little mind he possesses in a sentimentality which burlesques rational thought. Only with "The Crack-Up" essays did he abandon the idea of being an "entire man in the Goethe-Byron-Shaw tradition, with an opulent American touch" (C-U, p. 84). In the end, he would be partial to mind, "the fine quiet of the scholar," he wrote in *Tender Is the Night*, "which is nearest of all things to heavenly peace" (TITN, p. 116).

In attacking physical control and mental functioning, alcoholism and mental illness must have posed for Fitzgerald the worst of fates. From his mid-twenties on, they were ever-present in his life, and they seem to be almost as conspicuous facts of modern life. Malcolm Cowley, in writing about Fitzgerald, observes: "We have been living through an age of emotional breakdown."[1] They are not simply modern; the concepts of the Apollonian and Dionysian are classical, and Fitzgerald's struggle between the two may account in part for the note of tragedy in his life and work. If we do not accord him tragic stature, it may be both our fault and his. Drinking and mental illness in American society are not suitable to tragic feelings either in the writer or the audience. For the former, the long history of struggle with Demon Rum, the conventions which have long sentimentalized even as they condemned, and those which made Prohibition the national joke make it difficult to treat drinking seriously in fiction. As to the latter, it has become commonplace, chic, the province of lay and professional psychologizing in ways that make even the worst of mental ills something other than tragic.

Yet both conditions have something in common with the view that lay behind classical tragedy—"Whom the Gods would destroy they first make mad." Both represent a clouding of the rational mind, a loss of clear sight, an invitation to err which is part of what causes or accompanies the fall of a powerful figure. Both seem to belong to those afflictions by which some people are accursed and yet for which the individual appears to have some responsibility. I am not claiming that the Fitzgeralds—the one an alcoholic writer, the other diagnosed as schizophrenic—are tragic because of those facts, though I do claim

---

1. Malcolm Cowley. Introd., *The Stories of F. Scott Fitzgerald* (New York: Charles Scribner's, 1951), p. xxi.

that the public has long sensed something tragic in their lives and that much of the fiction conveys the sense of tragedy. My primary aim here, however, is to discuss how Fitzgerald treated alcoholism and mental illness in his fiction, perhaps thereby to cast some light on larger questions.

Looking back on his early career, Fitzgerald wrote in 1937: "All the stories that came into my head had a touch of disaster in them—the lovely young creatures in my novels went to ruin, the diamond mountains of my short stories blew up, my millionaires were as beautiful and damned as Thomas Hardy's peasants" (C-U, p. 87). The number of stories like "Bernice Bobs Her Hair" (1920) and their surface appeal made it easy to pass over his darker views. Moreover, what has been said about American attitudes toward drinking and mental illness applies specifically to Fitzgerald's early works. In both *This Side of Paradise* and *The Beautiful and Damned*, the depiction of drinking and its consequences is so often in terms of melodramatic conventions that it is hard to take it seriously. As to a serious regard for mental illness, one can say that "being crazy," like being drunk, was the thing to be in the world readers attributed to the Fitzgeralds.

Drinking is a conventional undergraduate diversion in *This Side of Paradise*, but it is also conventionally sinister. Drinking is the cause of Dick Humbird's fatal accident, and his ghostly face appears before Amory Blaine much as other ghosts are aroused by sexual sins. *The Beautiful and Damned* drew heavily upon the kind of drinking and partying life the Fitzgeralds were living. Adam Patch disinherits Anthony almost on the spot when he comes upon Anthony and Gloria in the midst of a typical drinking party. From that point on, Anthony's drinking accompanies his steady decline. Fitzgerald's language contributes to the staginess of scenes which were intended to be crucial. *"Bedlam creeps screaming out of the bottles"* (B&D, p. 273), he writes, and at *"the high tide of his life's depravity"* (B&D, p. 275), one of the characters crawls forward to make a boozy remark to the outraged Adam Patch. As if that were not sufficient, Fitzgerald adds that just that morning Adam had contributed $50,000 to the cause of national prohibition. Drunk each day, hating to be sober, Anthony suffers one of the conventional fates of drunks—two brutal beatings, one by a cab driver with whom he quarrels—and it is finally in a drunken rage that he departs from sanity altogether.

In Fitzgerald's career, it is often hard to know whether art mimics life or life mimics art. We do not know whether the beating scene in *The Beautiful and Damned* came out of an actual incident (Fitzgerald was far enough advanced in his becoming a belligerent drunk that it could have), but we do know that an actual fight, beating, and jailing provided the basis for a very similar scene in *Tender Is the Night*. Dick Diver's collapse is signaled by his turning to drink, and the low point of that downward path is reached in the beating scene. Just as Fitzgerald began drinking early and working it into his fiction, so did he begin to exact actual and fictional penance for doing so. Nevertheless, in the early fiction of Fitzgerald and in particular in the short stories appearing in popular magazines, drinking was often seen in good American terms, the source of hi-jinks, the mark of a good time, the ritual acts of college undergraduates, and as a generalized social problem rather than as a serious individual affliction. Most of the stories that brought Fitzgerald popular acclaim were like "The Camel's Back" (1920), in which Percy Parkhurst is an amiable and successful drunk and which Fitzgerald wrote by breaking off from a drinking party to complete the story within twenty-four hours. Though he did not have much affection for the story, it was included in the *O. Henry Memorial Award Prize Stories for 1920*. Even in such a serious story as "May Day" (1920), the interpolated tale of Mr. In and Mr. Out barely escapes being an account of Ivy Leaguers out on an amusing drinking spree. Instead, Fitzgerald uses it as a heavy-handed ironic contrast to Carrol Key's earlier death and Gordon Sterrett's later suicide, both related to excessive drinking.

This more serious regard for the excessive drinker appears very early in Fitzgerald's short fiction and in a number of stories in the 1920s. As early as 1915, in "Shadow Laurels," the central character is trying to find traces of his father who is revealed to have been a drunk, "bright and clever—when he worked, he worked feverishly hard, but he was always drunk" (AF, p. 74). "The Pierian Springs and the Last Straw" (1917), his last story written while he was at Princeton, is largely a character sketch of "Uncle George," who "used to be such a pathetic, innocent little boy" (AF, p. 171) but who has become a chronic drinker. In "The Cut-Glass Bowl" (1919), the central male character's drunkenness provides the pivotal melodramatic action of the story. "One of My Oldest Friends" (1924) foreshadows "Babylon Revisited" (1931). The earlier protagonist, also named Charlie, gets drunk and seeks a loan to replace funds he has misappropriated. "Not in the Guidebook" (1925) follows the course of a marriage in which the husband is a no-good drunk, "a morbid and broken man" (*Price*, p. 171). In "One Trip Abroad" (1930), important to the development of *Tender Is the Night*, Nelson Kelly is described as "not a drunk, he did nothing conspicuous or sodden, but he was no longer willing to go out socially without the stimulus of liquor" (AA, p. 157).

As Fitzgerald grew more aware of the consequences of drinking upon his work, his depiction of drinking in his stories became more convincing. A decade later, in "Babylon Revisited," Fitzgerald goes beyond the obvious social moralizing of "May Day" to focus upon the situation and character of Charlie Wales, a reformed drinker. Shades of melodrama still fall over the story—"that terrible February night . . . a slow quarrel that had gone on for hours . . . turned the key in the lock in wild anger. . . . How could he know she would arrive an hour later alone, that there would be a snowstorm in which she wandered about in slippers. . . . Then the aftermath, her escaping pneumonia by a miracle" (*Stories*, p. 396). But the contrast between the generosity and meanness of spirit in Charlie Wales and Marion Peters, the affection between father and daughter, and the refusal of Fitzgerald to pose either a calamitous or happy resolution make the story ring true. Fitzgerald's larger apprehensions about creating meaning in a world moving always to disarray are indicated in these reflections, quietly offered by Charlie Wales as he revisits the Montmartre: "All the catering to vice and waste was on an utterly childish scale, and he suddenly realized the meaning of the word 'dissipate'—to dissipate into thin air; to make nothing out of something" (*Stories*, p. 389).

By the time "Babylon Revisited" was written, Fitzgerald was aware that he was not just an ingratiating (sometimes) and obnoxious (often) drinker, but an alcoholic. Like most alcoholics, he did not easily or fully accept the fact, but the fiction of the 1930s includes an increasing number of stories and sketches which deal with the actualities of his condition. "Family in the Wind" was written in early 1932, after Zelda's second breakdown and following their return to the United States the previous fall. The central character is a Dr. Forrest Janney, a once brilliant surgeon until "he had committed professional suicide by taking to cynicism and drink" (*Stories*, p. 422). The plot defies easy delineation, but the central action requires that Dr. Janney get sober enough to remove a bullet from the brain of a Southern redneck, a relative he has every right to wish dead. Tornadoes occur in the area, and Dr. Janney resumes his professional role both in treating those injured by the storm and in performing (though to no avail) the brain surgery. "The story is spoiled," as Piper says, "by two rather melodramatic hurricanes and certain sentimentalities. But at the end Dr. Janney decides to adopt a small orphaned girl, and make himself into a responsible person once more."[2]

2. Henry Dan Piper, *F. Scott Fitzgerald: A Critical Portrait* (New York: Holt, Rinehart and Winston, 1965), p. 168.

The story, I think, matches the sentimental mood of the 1930s, and Fitzgerald thought enough of it to include it in *Taps at Reveille*. Though it is, as Arthur Mizener says, "a result of his attempt to adjust to the wreckage of his own career and his present condition,"[3] it is an unsuccessful attempt both to regain his writing powers and to alter his alcoholic condition. As a piece of fiction, it is marred by the author's excessive sympathy for the alcoholic central character and by elaborations of plot which evade a simpler, more painful, examination of that character. Something of the same can be said of other short fiction in which drinking figures prominently.

In "Two Wrongs" (1930), Fitzgerald draws upon his own worsening condition and Zelda's dancing obsession. The central character is Bill McChesney, "a fresh-faced Irishman exuding aggressiveness and self-confidence" (*Stories*, p. 287) at the beginning of the story and a tired and unconfident tubercular departing for an unlikely cure at the end. Drinking is not really central to McChesney's malaise, nor does it figure prominently in the story except as part of the contrived incident which precipitates his decline. McChesney's insecurities and aggressiveness are made ugly by drinking, and Fitzgerald can again do penance through that display. Like Charlie Wales's locking his wife outside in the snow and thus causing her near-fatal pneumonia, Bill McChesney fails to be on hand; his wife is forced to go to the hospital alone, falls getting out of the taxi, and delivers their child stillborn. Such a contrivance has to be acknowledged as Fitzgerald's doing, but the story nevertheless has power in its attempt to understand just why McChesney has lost both the will and vitality which characterized his success. The diagnosed tuberculosis is not used to excuse McChesney's behavior nor even to explain his loss of vitality. It chiefly serves to emphasize his uneasy dependence on Emmy (she has enjoyed great success as a ballet dancer) and as a device of plot enabling him to leave Europe and Emmy and accomplish his decline alone in the West. The reader is forced, probably unwillingly, to sympathize with McChesney at the end—"he had brought all this on himself" (*Stories*, p. 304)—and with his wan hope that Emmy will somehow show up to be with him when he expires.

Fitzgerald's best-known Hollywood story, "Crazy Sunday" (1932), reveals both the actuality of Fitzgerald's drinking and his masquerading of it in his fiction. The incident behind the story was a party given by Irving Thalberg—later the model for Monroe Stahr in *The Last*

3. Arthur Mizener, *The Far Side of Paradise: A Biography of F. Scott Fitzgerald* (Boston: Houghton Mifflin, 1965), p. 284.

Tycoon—and Norma Shearer. According to Dwight Taylor,[4] a fellow writer at MGM who accompanied him to the party, Fitzgerald got drunk, insulted Robert Montgomery, and insisted on singing a banal song about a dog. The song embarrassed everyone, though Norma Shearer sent Fitzgerald a telegram the next day: "I THOUGHT YOU WERE ONE OF THE MOST AGREEABLE PERSONS AT OUR TEA,"[5] which Fitzgerald used almost word for word in the story (*Stories*, p. 408). At the end of the week he was fired. In his fictionalizing of the story, Fitzgerald described Joel Coles, the drunken writer, in such a way as to be identified with Taylor and gave himself the role of the writer who tried to save him. No perceptive reader of Fitzgerald's stories is likely to be fooled, for the central character clearly betrays the conscience, guilt, moralizing, and defiance with which Fitzgerald viewed his drinking.

"A New Leaf" (1931) and "An Alcoholic Case" (1937) directly confront alcoholism by name and an alcoholic's unsuccessful attempt to reform or be cured. In "A New Leaf," Dick Ragland is an excessively handsome man of twenty-eight whose alcoholic behavior—"drink, women, jails, scandals, killed somebody with an automobile, lazy, worthless"—has caused him to be socially ostracized. " 'Like so many alcoholics,' " a male foil character explains to Julia, the girl who has become interested in him, " 'he has a certain charm. . . . Just when somebody's taken him up and is making a big fuss over him, he pours the soup down his hostess' back, kisses the serving maid and passes out in the dog kennel. But he's done it too often. He's run through about everybody until there's no one left' " (*Bits*, p. 299).

Ragland is an obvious projection of Fitzgerald, and the paragraph in which Ragland answers the girl's question of why he drinks so much is worth quoting at length:

> "About the time I came into some money I found that with a few drinks I got expansive and somehow had the ability to please people, and the idea turned my head. Then I began to take a whole lot of drinks to keep going and have everybody think I was wonderful. Well, I got plastered a lot and quarreled with most of my friends, and then I met a wild bunch and for a while I was expansive with them. But I was inclined to get superior and suddenly think 'What am I doing with this bunch?' They didn't like that much. And when a taxi that I was in killed a man, I was sued. It was just a graft, but it got in the papers, and after I was

4. Dwight Taylor, *Joy Ride* (New York: G.P. Putnam's, 1959), pp. 234–50.

5. Aaron Latham, *Crazy Sundays: F. Scott Fitzgerald in Hollywood* (New York: Viking, 1971), p. 74.

released the impression remained that I'd killed him. So all I've got to show for the last five years is a reputation that makes mothers rush their daughters away if I'm at the same hotel." (*Bits*, pp. 302–3)

As applied to Fitzgerald's own case, the above makes the story both worse and better than it was. Ragland didn't begin drinking until after he had left Princeton; and Fitzgerald's drinking never resulted, even indirectly, in anyone's death. The mixture of minimizing and exaggerating the consequences of drinking are made more interesting by a subsequent scene when the drunken Dick Ragland appears before Julia for the first time:

His face was dead white and erratically shaven, his soft hat was crushed bunlike on his head, his shirt collar was dirty, and all except the band of his tie was out of sight. . . . His whole face was one prolonged sneer—the lids held with difficulty from covering the fixed eyes, the drooping mouth drawn up over the upper teeth, the chin wobbling like a made-over chin in which the paraffin had run—it was a face that both expressed and inspired disgust. (*Bits*, pp. 303–4)

Though Ragland is the dominant figure in the story, the focus is much upon the girl Julia, "who never drank," and her falling in love with this immensely attractive but doomed man. For a time he is able to break from drinking and she convinces herself, against the advice of friends, that she can risk marrying him. During a brief separation, Dick has a meaningless affair which he confesses to Julia. They break off and he sails to London with the faint hope he will return a changed man. The foil character breaks the news to Julia that Dick has committed suicide by jumping overboard. When she asks whether Dick was drinking, the honest second-choice (they subsequently marry) tells her what she wants to hear, though he knows that Dick had resumed his old habits.

Julia's comments are probably Fitzgerald's: " 'Oh, isn't life cruel sometimes—so cruel, never to let anybody off. . . . He broke rather than bent; he was a ruined man, but not a bad man' " (*Bits*, p. 314). What I find even more revealing is the mothering Dick Ragland (as well as other male protagonists of these stories) so much craves. As I will mention later, it seemed to be Fitzgerald's need as well. "After a week," Fitzgerald wrote, "Dick's depression lifted. When he was sad,

Julia made him her baby, holding his handsome head against her breast" (*Bits*, p. 310).

The Ragland story precedes Fitzgerald's periods of hospitalization, in which being nursed was a reality and which furnished details for a number of stories. In "An Alcoholic Case" (1937), the focus is not on the male alcoholic but on the nurse who moves in the course of the story from wanting to be taken off the case to deciding to go back and finally to, " 'It's just that you can't really help them and it's so discouraging—it's all for nothing' " (*Stories*, p. 442). Similarly, the nurse in "Her Last Case" (1934) has to take care of Ben Dragonet, a prematurely-old Virginian who drinks, walks incessantly, and relives the past. She, too, must decide whether she will stay or leave an essentially hopeless case. The story is a contrived one but is full of hints about Fitzgerald's feelings toward his past and present condition. The hospital ward turns up in other stories, as it did in the New York *Post* interview by Michel Mok captioned "Scott Fitzgerald, 40, Engulfed in Despair." Further amplification about how Fitzgerald viewed himself during these years is to be found in the autobiographical sketches, most notably in "Afternoon of an Author" (1936), in which he says to the face in the mirror, "The perfect neurotic, by-product of an idea, slag of a dream" (AA, p. 425).

It is fair to say that in this last quote and in most of the later sketches, Fitzgerald is able to view himself with some irony and detachment. The same tone in his fiction gets into the Pat Hobby stories and "Financing Finnegan" (1938). Nothing much had changed in his life; he was still getting ruinously drunk and Zelda was to be a mental patient to the end of her days. But the writer in him, as he affirmed it in "The Crack-Up" essays, made the most of the has-been Pat Hobby, admittedly a rummy and a dreamer but still living by his wits, albeit in a much reduced state. In 1929, Fitzgerald wrote "A Short Autobiography" for the *New Yorker*, a kind of smart-aleck piece that detailed his life in the liquor drunk in various places. In 1939, he wrote "The Lost Decade," a chilling fictional sketch that echoed the entry in his notebooks, "Then I was drunk for many years, and then I died" (C-U, p. 191). Here a young editor takes a visitor on a vaguely reminiscent walk through Manhattan. The visitor notices a building he designed in 1928, ten years previously, for the first time. He had been drunk all the while between.

If these stories and others I have not mentioned are limited in their understanding of alcoholism, so to this day is our general understanding of it. Since Fitzgerald's death, it has come to be regarded more as a disease than as a moral failing, but its origins are by no means clearly understood. Dr. Donald Goodwin, who investigated Fitzgerald's alcoholism under U.S. Public Health grants in 1970, concluded: "The origin of his alcoholism is as inscrutable as the mystery of his writing talent."[6] Dr. Goodwin reviews the various possibilities lodged in Fitzgerald's heredity, family relationships, success and failure, personal problems, and the like. He began drinking early, drank heavily at Princeton, was an alcoholic in a clinical sense by the mid-1920s. From that time on, it was a dominating fact of his life.

Goodwin, like other observers, notes the connection between alcoholism and writing and offers some points at which writing and alcohol may intersect:

> Writing is a form of exhibitionism; alcohol lowers inhibitions and brings out exhibitionism in many people. Writing requires an interest in people; alcohol increases sociability and makes people more interesting. Writing involves fantasy; alcohol promotes fantasy. Writing requires self-confidence; alcohol bolsters confidence. Writing is lonely work; alcohol assuages loneliness. Writing requires intense concentration; alcohol relaxes.[7]

But he adds, "This, of course, may explain why writers (and many other people) drink, but does not explain alcoholism."

The hint I find most provocative in Dr. Goodwin's presumably (from the medical point of view) authoritative article is his mention of a possible meeting point of writing talent and alcoholism in manic-depressive disease. "Fitzgerald's enthusiasms," he writes, "at times bordered on hypomania but were never, it appears, frankly manic." As to clinically diagnosed depression, Goodwin finds that in Fitzgerald's description of his three episodes of depression (one at Princeton, the other after the war, and the third at the time of his crack-up) in "The Crack-Up" essays, "the symptoms were classical, their description incomparable."[8] He goes on to say that alcoholism and other disorders are almost always linked.

If we seek another major cause, it may reside in Fitzgerald's relations with his parents, particularly with his mother. What are we to make of his long entanglement with a novel that began as "The Boy Who Killed His Mother," became for a time "The Drunkard's Holiday," and

6. Donald Goodwin, "The Alcoholism of F. Scott Fitzgerald," *Journal of the American Medical Association*, 212 (April 6, 1970), 90.

7. Ibid.

8. Ibid., p. 89.

ended as an examination of Zelda's schizophrenia and his own malaise? Moreover, the extraneous mother and her more explainable daughter—the Hoyts in *Tender Is the Night*—were never removed despite his long struggle to give the novel focus and direction. What are we to make of the "mothering" mentioned previously in this essay and so often present in his fiction? And finally, to pick out only one of the many remarks Fitzgerald made about both parents, what of this outburst to Maxwell Perkins in 1926: "Why shouldn't I go crazy? My father is a moron and my mother is a neurotic, half insane with pathological nervous worry" (*Letters*, p. 199).

Dr. Goodwin's essay includes a letter Fitzgerald wrote to a psychiatrist in 1931. It is an account of a dream in which Fitzgerald is living with his mother, "old, white-haired, clumsy and in mourning." On another floor are handsome and rich young men and a dance going on to which Fitzgerald is not invited. Mother and son quarrel, he goes into the ballroom, realizes he is not invited, leaves the house, calling back to his mother "some terse and furious reproach." More friction and misunderstandings between mother and son occur, this time involving a book, and "the dream becomes an ominous nightmare."[9]

The possible link between alcoholism and mental illness calls obvious attention to the facts of Scott's and Zelda's lives together. But Fitzgerald first saw in his father the mysterious loss of vitality which is so prominently attached to male characters in his fiction and which he was to describe of himself in "The Crack-Up." Appearing less often in his short fiction than drinking, mental illness is used in early and late stories to explain a character's inability to function. In "The Lees of Happiness" (1920), a blood clot in his brain reduces the central male character to a vegetable existence sacrificed over by his wife. In both "The Adjuster" (1925) and "Your Way and Mine" (1927), male protagonists have nervous breakdowns and recover. Jennifer McCabe Atkinson, in looking at the unpublished stories, observes that despite Fitzgerald's attempts to use his experiences with clinics and psychiatrists in his short fiction of the 1930s, "he never drew upon it in the right way—or at least in a commercially successful way."[10] One of his attempts, "Nightmare" (1932), is a "zany, humorous story" in which four rich brothers are all committed to a psychiatric clinic.

Fitzgerald's mother, for all she doted on him, was a source of embarrassment through much of his early maturity. What may have threatened Fitzgerald most in his relation with his parents was also the threat

9. Ibid., p. 90.
10. Jennifer McCabe Atkinson, "Lost and Unpublished Stories by F. Scott Fitzgerald," *Fitzgerald/Hemingway Annual*, 3 (1971), 32–63.

which hung over his whole life: the loss of vitality, in part physical but more related to exercise of will and mental competence. It was depressing indeed that his parentage raised doubts about his own ability to function and that his alcoholism and Zelda's mental illness would attack that same spot of vulnerability.

Of Fitzgerald's writing directly concerned with mental illness, *Tender Is the Night* and "The Crack-Up" are the most consequential. The novel has been both praised and blamed for Fitzgerald's understanding of psychiatry. A psychiatrist reviewing the novel in the *Journal of Nervous and Mental Diseases* (1935) praised it for the author's psychological acuteness.[11] Piper excuses minor inaccuracies, but he finds serious fault with Fitzgerald's handling of the psychiatrist-patient relationship.[12] My interest here in that novel is limited; however, I perceive it as adding to the number of central male characters who experience a vaguely explained loss of vitality in which drinking is both symptom and cause. It was Fitzgerald's most ambitious attempt to explore mental illness, though concentrated on Zelda's specific condition. ("The Long Way Out" [1937] is the one piece of short fiction that confronts mental illness as Zelda was experiencing it.) And as I have mentioned, the various themes taken up in Fitzgerald's wrestling with the novel and the difficulties in bringing this material to a satisfactory order shed light upon his deepest psychic tensions. In its best parts, the novel is often symbolic of irrationality threatening the rational, of disorder defying the semblance of order. In shorter form, the story "One Trip Abroad" (1930) covers some of the same ground. The inexplicable decline of a wealthy, handsome couple takes place against backgrounds conveying an air of vague, meaningless terror also present in *Tender Is the Night*.

The last of Fitzgerald's writings I will discuss are the three essays that appeared as "The Crack-Up" in 1935 and are reasonably accurate analyses of his breakdown that year. I say "reasonably" accurate because for all that the essays purport to lay bare the past for clues to his present condition, no mention is made of his father or mother or Zelda, and only one short passage (and that a disavowal) mentions that alcoholism might have played any part in the crack-up. Nevertheless, the essays convey as few other short works have the truth of that most commonplace of mental afflictions, anxiety in its acute and chronic forms.

11. Jackson Bryer, "A Psychiatrist Reviews *Tender Is the Night*," *Literature and Psychology*, 16 (Nos. 3–4, 1966), 108–9.
12. Piper, p. 223.

The metaphors Fitzgerald uses to describe his condition are consistent with the nameless dread, the "vastation" by which others have described the experience. He writes of feeling that he is standing at twilight on a deserted firing range with an empty rifle and all the targets down, of "silence with only the sound of my own breathing" (C-U, p. 78). What is missing in this emptiness is both the will to do anything and the vitality to perform even were there the will. It is a frightening condition for Fitzgerald as for anyone who suffers it, for it defies rationality and continuity and purpose in indefinable ways. It all at once and without argument or exposition struck down Fitzgerald's "passionate belief in order" and faced him with the task of reconstructing altogether.

Importantly involved in that reconstruction is the exercise of his own powers of thought. He had done very little thinking, he confesses, and the effort to do so was like the "moving about of great secret trunks." The analysis which followed in the essays displeased some of his friends, and as I have pointed out, it hides as well as reveals. On close examination, the essays emphasize again that Fitzgerald's power is more in the aptness of individual phrases than in the exercise of analytic thought. Too much attention, for example, is given to airing old conflicts between the writer and his public. The tone is splenetic when he picks out "the slime of Mr. Tiffany Thayer"; cynical but brilliantly so when he hangs the sign *Cave Canem* over his door at the end of the last essay.

Two main resolves come out of Fitzgerald's analysis: to become a writer only, and to accept "that the natural state of the sentient adult is a qualified unhappiness" (C-U, p. 84). Neither is a very new avowal for Fitzgerald. Indirectly, "The Crack-Up" would have you believe that all Fitzgerald's work was invested with the full powers of his mind and heart. But clearly throughout his career, he went back and forth between pursuing his highest ambitions and functioning pretty much as what he calls "a writer only." As to his espousing a pessimistic view of life, the touch of disaster was present in his earliest fiction.

What so interests me in these essays is his grappling, once again, with the inexplicable loss of will and vitality. "Of all natural forces," he writes, "vitality is the uncommunicable one. . . . You have it or you haven't, like health or brown eyes or honor or a baritone voice" (C-U, p. 74). Vitality occupies an important place in Fitzgerald's fiction, as does physical violence, as if they flowed unformed beneath the surface of existence, coming forth in the robustness of Myrtle Wilson and the brutality of Tom Buchanan, running thin in Mr. Wilson, abundant but uncontrolled in Zelda, at hand but capricious in his own drives and enthusiasms, running out in Anthony Patch, Dick Diver, and other fictional characters. Both alcoholism and mental illness rob their victims of purposeful vitality, let loose the chaotic violence that flows beneath, and nullify the rational processes by which the sober and sane maintain control.

The tensions Fitzgerald felt between his once vital self and the cracked plate he had become in "The Crack-Up" are present in other opposites within his persistently dualistic perspective. His preoccupations with success and failure, with materialism in conflict with idealism, have been much discussed. Other opposites, having a closer relationship with the subject at hand, are as apparent: sobriety vying with inebriation, sanity with insanity, youth and beauty with age and decay, order with chaos. The moral perspective is dualistic, too. As Fitzgerald contrasted them in his fiction, one is often good, the other bad: the sober man of affairs as contrasted with the drunk making a fool of himself, the clear-headed psychiatrist as contrasted with the befuddled patient, the young idealist believing that "the rock of the world was founded securely on a fairy's wing" (GG, p. 100) and the slightly older man realizing that one cannot both have and spend.

Underneath his recognition of these dualities is a kind of sentimental and vague wishing it were not so, that one could always be young, the world always beautiful and good. The vitality cf youth enables one to deny the dualities or to merge them or to act in defiance of their truth. Fitzgerald's reaction to what has happened to him in "The Crack-Up" is only in part a stoic, possibly tragic, acceptance of life as equally comprised of birth and death, ripeness and decay. To some degree his response is the same as he expressed in his ledger of 1928: "Thirty two, Years Old (And sore as hell about it)" (*Ledger*, p. 183).

Whether Fitzgerald would have developed in wisdom and power as a writer if he had lived longer is an idle conjecture. We only have enough work of his last three or four years to suggest no overwhelming change, no sudden flooding in of understanding and insight. We do know of his life that he continued to function and took some pride in the fact. That part of him which so prized the ability to function, together with the fiction in which loss of function is the looming threat, reach us amidst our own faintnesses and palpitatings. They give us strength in our own tenuous hold on equilibrium or sanity, our own losses of will and vigor, both sharing our morbid states and reminding us of vital health that may have been—and may still exist in sufficient store to give us a place to stand, to provide "a momentary stay against confusion."

FITZGERALD'S CHANGES
ON THE SOUTHERN BELLE:
THE TARLETON TRILOGY

C. HUGH HOLMAN

That the South should play a significant role in the work of F. Scott
Fitzgerald was inevitable.[1] Though he was born in St. Paul, Minnesota, and spent much of his life there before he went to Princeton, he
saw himself as torn between the vigorous, successful, and aggrandizing
North and an ancestral dignity, grace, and good manners associated
with the South. His father, an ardent pro-Confederate advocate, was
of Maryland ancestry stretching back to colonial times; among his
ancestors Scott Fitzgerald was proudest of Francis Scott Key, author of
the national anthem. John Kuehl has pointed out that "his financially
inept but 'Old American stock' father came to symbolize pre-Civil War
southern aristocracy while his mother's financially successful but 'black
Irish' relatives came to represent post-Civil War northern *nouveaux
riches*."[2] In a letter to John O'Hara, Fitzgerald said, "I am half black
Irish and half old American stock with the usual exaggerated ancestral
pretensions. The black Irish half of the family had the money and
looked down upon the Maryland side of the family who had, and really
had, that certain series of reticences and obligations that go under the

1. Fitzgerald's connections with the South have been explored in detail by Scott
Donaldson in "Scott Fitzgerald's Romance with the South," *Southern Literary Journal*, 5
(Spring 1973), 3–17. For biographical data I am indebted to Donaldson, to Arthur
Mizener, *The Far Side of Paradise: A Biography of F. Scott Fitzgerald* (Boston: Hough-
ton Mifflin, 1965), and to Andrew Turnbull, *Scott Fitzgerald* (New York: Charles Scrib-
ner's, 1962).
2. John Kuehl, ed., *The Apprentice Fiction of F. Scott Fitzgerald: 1909–1917* (New
Brunswick, N.J.: Rutgers Univ. Press, 1965), p. 35.

poor old shattered word 'breeding.' . . . I spent my youth in alternately crawling in front of the kitchen maids and insulting the great" (*Letters*, p. 503). This sense of two selves clearly at war with each other and of one of them associated with what may be called the Shintoism of the South had made Fitzgerald's military service at Camp Sheridan near Montgomery, Alabama, an experience that one aspect of himself was ready to welcome as, in a sense, a return to an appropriate ancestral home.

In Montgomery he had been a part of the social life of that small city for a brief time, and there on the rebound he fell in love with Zelda Sayre, the reigning queen of the society of young, reasonably well-born girls who entertained the officers at Sheridan. Her friend and fellow entertainer of the time, Sara Mayfield, may be exaggerating when she calls Zelda "the reigning prom queen in the Deep South," but Zelda did certainly attend the dances at the University of Alabama, the University of Georgia, and Sewanee; and at Auburn her admirers formed a fraternity called Zeta Sigma, in which the qualifications for membership were a pledge of devotion to Zelda and proof that the candidate had had at least one date with her in Montgomery.[3] With a difficulty that is charted in his own stories and particularly in Zelda's novel *Save Me the Waltz*, Fitzgerald at last won the hand of the belle of Montgomery, and their wedding in 1920 in New York City began one of the most famous marriages in American literature. Zelda shows up repeatedly as a character in Scott's work, by no means always assigned residence in the South. He said on one occasion, "I married the heroine of my stories."[4]

The South also appears repeatedly in Fitzgerald's work. It is the setting of the Dorothy episode in *The Beautiful and Damned* and of Gatsby's courtship of Daisy Fay in *The Great Gatsby*. It is the locale for a simple and rather poor murder story, "The Dance" (1926). It is the setting for "Two for a Cent" (1922), a story about two Southern men who take contrasting attitudes toward the North. It is the home of the protagonist in "Dice, Brass Knuckles & Guitar" (1923) and of the heroine of "Two Wrongs" (1930). The South is the setting for most of the action in " 'The Sensible Thing' " (1924) and is present, as it frequently is, in a casual reference to the wife in "Gretchen's Forty Winks" (1924): "She was a Southern girl, and any question that had to do with getting ahead in the world always tended to give her a headache" (6TJA, p. 176). It is also the primary setting of the Tarleton trilogy of

3. Sara Mayfield, *Exiles from Paradise: Zelda and Scott Fitzgerald* (New York: Delacorte, 1971), p. 45.

4. Nancy Milford, *Zelda: A Biography* (New York: Harper and Row, 1970), p. 77.

stories, "The Ice Palace" (1920), "The Jelly-Bean" (1920), and "The Last of the Belles" (1929). In this trilogy Fitzgerald said the most about the South and the contrast of North and South that he was to say, and there the Southern belle and her role are most clearly delineated.

John A. Higgins says that the Tarleton trilogy, "which began with youthful affirmation of the romantic attitude in 'The Ice Palace' and moved to disenchantment in 'The Jelly-Bean,' terminates with mature acceptance of reality in 'The Last of the Belles.' The cycle in these three stories is a microcosm of Fitzgerald's thematic evolution."[5] This acceptance of reality is reiterated in " 'The Sensible Thing,' " and the whole North-South theme is summarized, though badly, in the story "Dice, Brass Knuckles & Guitar." When these stories are examined, and the Tarleton trilogy is seen as a unit, what Fitzgerald was doing with the contrast of North and South becomes very clear.

Fitzgerald, like Thomas Wolfe, saw the North as masculine and the South as feminine. For Wolfe the North was an enfabled rock; the South was a "ruined Helen burning in his blood." For both, the North was an arena for action, for adventure, for accomplishment, for energy and vigor. The South was a warm, pleasant, and lazy place, a home of good manners and elegant traditions, a garden which, for Fitzgerald, grew Southern belles and jelly-beans. "Jelly-Bean" was, Fitzgerald said, "the name throughout the undissolved Confederacy for one who spends his life conjugating the verb to idle in the first person singular" (6TJA, p. 17).[6] Fitzgerald's South and its people were described directly in Wolfe's picture of South Carolinians:

> They drawl beautifully. There is the most wonderful warmth, affection, heartiness in their approach and greeting. . . . Sometimes their women have the honey skins, they are like gold and longing. They are filled with the most luscious and seductive sweetness, tenderness, and gentle mercy. But the men are stricken. They get fat about the bellies, or they have a starved, stricken leanness in the loins. . . . They drawl softly in front of the drug store, they palaver softly to the girls when the girls drive up, they go up and down the streets of blistered, sun-wide, clay-dust little

5. John A. Higgins, *F. Scott Fitzgerald: A Study of the Stories* (Jamaica, N.Y.: St. John's Univ. Press, 1971), p. 105. Although many critics mention the common setting of these three stories, only Higgins sees them as related by more than autobiography and locale. He calls them the "Tarleton trilogy," but does little beyond the suggestion in the quotation given above toward examining that trilogy.

6. Today a "jelly-bean" is called "a good ole boy."

towns in their shirt-sleeves, and they are full of hearty, red-faced greetings.[7]

These men must go North to accomplish anything, and those with imagination or ambition have gone to college in the North or have migrated there to make their fortunes.[8] But the North is not only the home of accomplishment, effort, and hard work, the bedrock of reality; it is also a killer, or at the very least a duller, of the romantic dreams of youth which the South represents. Hence for Fitzgerald the South is a land of beauty and romance, of a lost order, of tradition and dignity, and of a glorious past. It is to be dreamed of and to be loved in youth, but it must be abandoned in maturity. It sums up, with its families, its homes, its discipline and order, and its Confederate graveyards, the "precious, the incommunicable past."[9] Fitzgerald found particularly in Confederate cemeteries a symbol of a departed glory. According to Sheilah Graham, when a friend remarked that the pickets in a fence at a house Fitzgerald lived in near Los Angeles looked like "gravestones in a Confederate graveyard," the place was made "livable" for him.[10]

Allen Tate, also a celebrator of Confederate cemeteries, said: "With the war of 1914–1918, the South reentered the world—but gave a backward glance as it stepped over the border: that backward glance gave us the Southern renascence, a literature conscious of the past in the present."[11] Fitzgerald in the Tarleton stories cast a similar backward glance at what seemed to him a lost world of tradition, graciousness, and beauty. Out of the resulting nostalgia and the sense of loss, he develops the strongest emotion these stories evoke, for they are all tales built around the backward glance.

Although the Tarleton trilogy is by no means local color and the town of Tarleton exists in the three stories as an ambience, an atmos-

7. Thomas Wolfe, *The Web and the Rock* (New York: Grosset & Dunlap, 1939), p. 14.

8. Wolfe describes the Southerner in the city repeatedly in *Of Time and the River* and particularly in *The Web and the Rock*: "The city is the place where men are constantly seeking to find their door" (*The Web and the Rock*, p. 229). See all of Chapters 13 and 14 of *The Web and the Rock*, pp. 219–49.

9. The concluding phrase of Willa Cather, *My Ántonia* (Boston: Houghton Mifflin, 1918). For Fitzgerald's debt to Cather, see James E. Miller, Jr., *F. Scott Fitzgerald: His Art and Technique* (New York: New York Univ. Press, 1964), pp. 87–92. Henry Dan Piper, *F. Scott Fitzgerald: A Critical Portrait* (New York: Holt, Rinehart and Winston, 1965), also discusses this debt and perhaps exaggerates it.

10. Sheilah Graham, *Beloved Infidel* (New York: Holt, 1958), pp. 266–67.

11. Allen Tate, "The New Provincialism," *Essays of Four Decades* (Chicago: Swallow, 1968), p. 545.

phere, and a feeling rather than a very specific place with streets, houses, and landmarks that can be compared, there seems little reason to question that Fitzgerald drew accurately from a precise memory the details of the town in which, in July, 1918, he had met Zelda Sayre. For the Tarleton of these stories is a very thinly disguised Montgomery, Alabama, even to the size of its population—in "The Jelly-Bean" Fitzgerald calls it "a little city of forty thousand" (6TJA, p. 17), the size of Montgomery at the time when Fitzgerald was stationed at Camp Sheridan. It has, as Montgomery had during World War I, an airfield and an army camp. Tarleton is a lingering outpost of the "undissolved Confederacy"; Montgomery had been the capital of the Confederacy. It was, Sara Mayfield remembered, a city with "a classical dignity, a respect for law and order, for authority and degree. Its sleepy oak-vaulted streets held no threat of violence by day or terror by night."[12]

The stories share not only a common setting but a common group of characters who play roles of varying degrees of importance in the different stories. Sally Carrol Happer, the protagonist of "The Ice Palace," also appears in the other two stories; Nancy Lamar, the leading girl in "The Jelly-Bean," is also in "The Last of the Belles." Clark Darrow, the Southern swain of Sally Carrol in "The Ice Palace," is an important minor character in "The Jelly-Bean." Marylyn Wade and Joe Ewing are recurrent characters in the group of officers and Tarleton belles in the series. In each of the stories, an outsider's affair with the girl threatens to remove her from Tarleton. In "The Ice Palace," Harry Bellamy of Minnesota is Sally Carrol's fiancé; in "The Jelly-Bean," Ogden Merritt of Savannah, whose family makes the Merritt Safety Razors, is Nancy Lamar's suitor; in "The Last of the Belles," Bill Knowles from Harvard and Earl Schoen from Connecticut pursue Ailie Calhoun. These outsiders are threats to Tarleton because, as Clark Darrow says in "The Jelly-Bean," "Seems like all the best girls around here marry fellas and go off somewhere" (6TJA, p. 23). Ailie Calhoun speaks for the lot of them, apparently, when she says that "she didn't think she'd marry a Southern man" (*Stories*, p. 242).

In "The Ice Palace," Sally Carrol's deep affection for the South is defined by the scene in which she goes with her Minnesota fiancé to a Confederate cemetery and tries to tell him why she feels as she does when she reaches the rows of graves whose crosses bear just the date and the word "Unknown":

> "These were just men, unimportant evidently or they wouldn't
> have been 'Unknown'; but they died for the most beautiful thing

12. Mayfield, p. 16.

in the world—the dead South. You see . . . people have these dreams they fasten onto things, and I've always grown up with that dream. It was so easy because it was all dead and there weren't any disillusions comin' to me. I've tried in a way to live up to those past standards of noblesse oblige—there's just the last remnants of it, you know, like the roses of an old garden dying all around us—streaks of strange courtliness and chivalry in some of these boys an' stories I used to hear from a Confederate soldier who lived next door, and a few old darkies." (*Stories*, p. 66)

But Sally Carrol goes to Minnesota to visit her fiancé's people and to see the country to which her marriage will commit her, and she finds the people cold, selfish, and vigorous, and finds that her fiancé believes of modern Southerners that

"They're sort of—sort of degenerates—not at all like the old South-erners. They've lived so long down there with all the colored people that they've gotten lazy and shiftless. . . .

"They're all right when they come North to college, but of all the hangdog, ill-dressed, slovenly lot I ever saw, a bunch of small-town Southerners are the worst!" (*Stories*, p. 75)

At last when she becomes lost and almost freezes to death in an ice palace at a winter carnival, Sally Carrol realizes that the cold North and its people are not for her, and she rushes back home to Clark Darrow, her languid Southern swain.

In "The Jelly-Bean," Jim Powell, the last of a family who once owned large blocks of land and a house with four tall columns, has become a town ne'er-do-well, a casual worker on automobiles, a driver of taxis at odd times, but predominantly a gambler with dice. He is reintro-duced by his friend Clark Darrow to "the old crowd, the crowd to which, by right of the white house, sold long since, and the portrait of the officer in gray over the mantle, Jim should have belonged" (6TJA, p. 19). He meets and falls in love with Nancy Lamar, a wild and lovely Tarleton girl who drinks excessively and gambles. He rescues her by cheating at dice in order to reclaim two checks, at least one of them worthless, which she has lost in a game at the country club after the dance at which he has fallen in love with her. She leaves with Ogden Merritt, the outsider, after having drunk too much bootleg whiskey. The next day Jim resolves to try to reclaim his position in this society by going off to work with his uncle on a family farm, so that he can become a proper suitor for Nancy, only to discover that the night before while drunk, she had married Merritt. Jim now turns back to being what he had been before she entered his life, a jelly-bean.[13]

"The Last of the Belles" is the reminiscence of Andy, a Harvard man who had been stationed some fifteen years before near Tarleton in an Army training camp. He is introduced to a Southern beauty, Ailie Calhoun, who is pleased with her conquests, regards herself rather proudly as having driven a suitor to commit suicide in a plane crash, and is fascinated by Lieutenant Earl Schoen from New Bedford, Connecticut, a good officer but from the lower levels of society. Ailie and Schoen become engaged; the lieutenant is transferred, and then the war ends. He comes back in civilian clothes obviously unsuited in every way to the gracious life which Ailie Calhoun represents, and they part. Six years later the narrator, Andy, returns to Tarleton. The reason for his returning South is having seen a girl at twilight at a railway station in Indiana greeting a man who got off a train and then hurrying him to a waiting car:

> It seemed to me that she was bearing him off into the lost midsummer world of my early twenties, where time had stood still and charming girls, dimly seen like the past itself, still loitered along the dusky streets. I suppose that poetry is the Northern man's dream of the South. (*Stories*, p. 251)

Back in Tarleton, Andy finds Ailie still unmarried, a slowly aging but remarkably beautiful party girl, and he realizes that he has returned to something that has been dear and lovely to him. He tells Ailie that he is in love with her, but she says that she cannot consider him a suitor, for she is not in love with him. At his insistence, the two of them order a taxi and go out to the site of the camp where they had shared a farewell party. The camp has now been torn down, and the narrator wanders about seeking in vain the place where a splendid part of his youth had been spent:

> . . . I stumbled here and there in the knee-deep underbrush, looking for my youth in a clapboard or a strip of roofing or a rusty tomato can. . . .

13. Jim Powell is the protagonist in Fitzgerald's 1923 short story "Dice, Brass Knuckles & Guitar." In this story he goes North to make an improved living by running a school to teach rich youths social grace and self-defense. When he learns that the rich regard him as "just a servant," he heads bitterly back to the South and to being a jelly-bean.

> All I could be sure of was this place that had once been so full of
> life and effort was gone, as if it had never existed, and that in
> another month Ailie would be gone, and the South would be empty
> for me forever. (*Stories*, p. 253)

In " 'The Sensible Thing,' " a story which Malcolm Cowley has called
"autobiographical in the strict sense; it is the story of his broken and
renewed engagement to Zelda Sayre,"[14] Fitzgerald returned to this
theme of the fading of youthful romantic dreams for the Northern man
in love with a Southern girl. In this story, which is set in Tennessee, the
protagonist George O'Kelly is very much in love with Jonquil Cary.
Because she is unwilling to marry him until he is financially better off,
they break the engagement; he leaves, makes a fortune in Peru in a
little over a year, returns, and their engagement is resumed.

> Yet he knew that that boy of fifteen months before had had some-
> thing, a trust, a warmth that was gone forever. The sensible
> thing—they had done the sensible thing. He had traded his first
> youth for strength and carved success out of despair. But with his
> youth, life had carried away the freshness of his love. (*Stories*, p.
> 156)

The plot lines in each of the Tarleton stories rest upon a contrast
between North and South, and the central figure in that contrast is to
a certain extent the Northern outsider who finds in the South an
attractive beauty and order. Each of the outsiders finds in the South
something very much like what Andy in "The Last of the Belles" remembers:

> We parked under the broken shadow of a mill where there was the
> sound of running water and restive squawky birds and over every-
> thing a brightness that tried to filter in anywhere—into the lost
> nigger cabins, the automobile, the fastnesses of the heart. The
> South sang to us—I wonder if they remember. I remember—the
> cool pale faces, the somnolent amorous eyes and the voices. (*Sto-
> ries*, p. 248)

Yet when these people leave the South, it is sadly but finally, like the
farewell dinner in the mess shack in "The Last of the Belles":

14. Malcolm Cowley, *The Stories of F. Scott Fitzgerald* (New York: Charles Scribner's, 1951), p. 4.

> We toasted ourselves and the South. Then we left our napkins and
> empty glasses and a little of the past on the table, and hand in
> hand went out into the moonlight itself. Taps had been played.
> (*Stories*, p. 248)

Something precious but irrecoverable has been lost. The demands that
the North, a type of reality, will make of them, will render the South
the stuff that dreams are made on, the dreams of vanished youth.

But the central image in these stories, the pivot upon which their
meaning hinges, is not this Northern outsider and his experience, however intensely autobiographical and meaningful it was for Fitzgerald,
nor is it the indolent Southern male trapped in a sleepy and sun-smitten
inertia like Jim Powell. The central image of these stories is the Southern belle, and it is in the group of Tarleton belles that Fitzgerald finds
his most effective way of defining the special emotion these stories
evoke. The controlling metaphors for the South, Fitzgerald and the
Northern outsiders remember in sweet sorrow, are Sally Carrol Happer,
Nancy Lamar, Ailie Calhoun, and Marylyn Wade, a bevy of beauties
in their late teens raised in an intensely ordered social world, beautifully decorative in their physical presence, giddy, laughing, happy to
be the Southern hostesses to the officers of the adjoining Army camp.
They are the embodiments of a tradition that stretched back before the
Confederacy and that enchanted and hypnotized men for a century,
permanent embodiments of the dream of beauty and youth and the
romantic aspiration of the aggressive male.

Nancy Milford describes this essentially dreamlike quality of the
Southern belle effectively by recalling the toast offered by a University
of Alabama club during its dances: "To woman, lovely woman of the
Southland, as pure and chaste as the sparkling water, as cold as this
gleaming ice, we lift this cup, and we pledge our hearts and our lives
to the protection of her virtue and chastity."[15] In this tradition of
adulation and submissive protection, the Southern belle had certain
prerogatives which, in the changing times of World War I, she was
beginning to exercise with vigor and some indiscretion, prerogatives
she had won by her beauty, her social graces, and above all her ability,
as Nancy Milford suggests, "to manage men without seeming to do so."
She and her beauty and her social characteristics had had a long history
in the South. As early as 1854, George Fitzhugh had said, "So long as
she is nervous, fickle, capricious, delicate, diffident and dependent,
men will worship and adore her. Her weakness is her strength, and her

15. Milford, p. 21.

true art is to cultivate and improve that weakness."[16] In 1920, the introduction to a biographical account of the United Daughters of the Confederacy declared of the Southern belle:

> "It took the civilization of an Old South to produce her—a civilization whose exquisite but fallen fabric now belongs to the Dust of dreams. . . . The old queen passes, but the young queen lives; and radiant, like the morning, on her brow, is Dixie's diadem,"[17]

a statement that, however grandiose in phraseology, expresses fairly well the feelings of each of the Northern protagonists in the Tarleton trilogy.

But this Southern belle was a creature torn between two worlds. Zelda Fitzgerald wrote, ". . . it's very difficult to be two simple people at once, one who wants to have a law to itself and the other who wants to keep all the nice old things and be loved and safe and protected."[18] Frances Newman described her heroine in *The Hardboiled Virgin* as being

> a girl who began by believing everything her family and teachers said to her, and ended by disbelieving most of those things, but by finding that she couldn't keep herself from behaving as if she still believed them . . . a girl who was born and bred to be a southern lady, and whose mind could never triumph over the ideas she was presumably born with.[19]

Frances Gray Patton, attempting to define the Southern belle, once said, "Her role is essentially passive—to excite admiration without appearing to demand it, to create an illusion of fragility without looking sick, to sustain an atmosphere of gentle gaiety without seeming bat-

16. George Fitzhugh, *Sociology for the South* (Richmond, Va.: A. Morris, 1854), p. 214.

17. Lucian Lamar Knight, Introduction to Mrs. Bryan Wells Collier, *Biographies of Representative Women in the South* (n.p., n.d.); quoted in Anne Firor Scott, *The Southern Lady from Pedestal to Politics 1830–1930* (Chicago: Univ. of Chicago Press, 1970), pp. 221–22.

18. Zelda Fitzgerald, *Save Me the Waltz* (Carbondale: Southern Illinois Univ. Press, 1967), p. 56. This double role of the Southern lady or the Southern belle is a major theme of Anne Firor Scott's important study cited above.

19. *Frances Newman's Letters*, ed. Hansell Baugh (New York: H. Liveright, 1929), p. 30.

brained."[20] Her role in life, for all its seeming vigor and even occasional betrayal of convention, is essentially man-oriented. Zelda Fitzgerald once said that women's "excuse and explanation is the necessity for a disturbing element among men."[21] The Tarleton belles playing this traditional role symbolize in these stories the nature of a South so firmly fixed in the romantic dreams of youth and the haunting beauty of a lost past. In them Fitzgerald finds his clearest method of expression, and he was quite explicit in assigning the three belles of the Tarleton stories most of the characteristics of such women. Sally Carrol has, he says, "several rather clearly defined sides" (*Stories*, p. 65). She grieves over the grave of Margery Lee, who died in 1873 at the age of twenty-nine, and pictures for herself what this departed Southern belle was like:

> ". . . she always wore her hair with a ribbon in it, and gorgeous hoop-skirts of alice blue and old rose. . . . And she was the sort of girl born to stand on a wide, pillared porch and welcome folks in. I think perhaps a lot of men went away to war meanin' to come back to her; but none of 'em ever did." (*Stories*, p. 65)

Sally Carrol, in common with the other Southern girls, is not playing a role; they are indeed what they appear to be, and when Sally Carrol reaches Minnesota, "she had the feeling for almost the first time in her life that she was acting a part" (*Stories*, p. 70).

Nancy Lamar "had a mouth like a remembered kiss and shadowy eyes and blue-black hair" (6TJA, p. 20). Ailie Calhoun

> had the adroitness sugar-coated with sweet, voluble simplicity, the suggested background of devoted fathers, brothers, and admirers stretching back into the South's heroic age, the unfailing coolness acquired in the endless struggle with the heat. There were notes in her voice that ordered slaves around, that withered up Yankee captains, and then soft, wheedling notes that mingled in unfamiliar loveliness with the night. (*Stories*, p. 241)

These girls, products of a long tradition, are for Fitzgerald moving and effective symbols, and they should be viewed in the roles they play in

20. Frances Gray Patton, "Anatomy of the Southern Belle," in *Chapel Hill Carousel*, ed. Jessie Rehder (Chapel Hill: Univ. of North Carolina Press, 1967). Originally published in *Holiday*, 26 (November 1959), 76, 120, 123–26.

21. Milford, p. 44. In *This Side of Paradise*, Fitzgerald assigns this observation of Zelda's to his character Rosalind.

Tarleton and in the Northern outsiders' feelings about Tarleton. Scott Donaldson is obviously right in saying, "The romantic appeal of the South was obviously mingled in Fitzgerald's mind with the golden girl."[22] Fitzgerald himself referred to Zelda as "the golden beauty of the South" and himself as "the brilliant success of the North."[23] But I believe Donaldson errs when he sees Ailie Calhoun as "Fitzgerald's ultimate rejection of the Southern belle."[24]

For the Tarleton belles do not themselves shatter the illusions of the protagonists nor, I believe, of the author. They simply body forth a stage in the growth of an individual, a stage which inevitably is left behind. The problem in " 'The Sensible Thing' " is not that Jonquil Cary has forced a change in George O'Kelly's view of her but that they must inevitably do "the sensible thing"—and that in the process of doing it, something of youth and romance and beauty is left behind. The problem at the end of "The Last· of the Belles" is not that the protagonist goes back to Tarleton and loses one whom he realizes he has loved; it is rather that in going back, he knows that she and all she represents has already been lost through the passage of time itself. It was not Ailie who tore down the camp and rusted the tomato cans; it was time, and the Southern belle has her greatest value as a symbol of that time arrested in the emotions. For Scott Fitzgerald she had a potent aura, one which he made his readers feel. The Southern belle, at least in Tarleton, was wistful nostalgia made flesh.

22. Donaldson, p. 6.
23. Milford, p. 306.
24. Donaldson, p. 7.

"KISSING, SHOOTING, AND SACRIFICING": F. SCOTT FITZGERALD AND THE HOLLYWOOD MARKET

ALAN MARGOLIES

It is well known that because of F. Scott Fitzgerald's unusual financial needs, many of his short stories were composed quickly and with the requirements of the popular magazines in mind. As a result, their quality suffered, a fact he was fully aware of. Of "The Camel's Back" (1920), for example, Fitzgerald boasted in *Tales of the Jazz Age* that he had written this story in one day "with the express purpose of buying a platinum and diamond wrist watch which cost six hundred dollars."[1] To Harold Ober he admitted that "The Popular Girl" (1922) was "a cheap story . . . written in one week while the baby was being born. . . ."[2] And even if he did feel that many of the stories written for the *Saturday Evening Post* were "at least not any spot" on him and "honest," he wrote Ober that "if . . . *their* form is stereotyped people know what to *expect when* they pick up the Post."[3] But in addition, a few of the short stories suffered further because they were written with an eye on sales to Hollywood as well. In this case, the evidence can be found not only in Fitzgerald's correspondence but in the stories themselves.

Ironically, early in his career Fitzgerald expressed a dislike for the types of movies that Hollywood was then making. In 1921, for example, he told an interviewer that the average movie consisted of "creaky

1. F. Scott Fitzgerald, *Tales of the Jazz Age* (New York: Charles Scribner's, 1922), p. vii.

2. *As Ever, Scott Fitz—: Letters Between F. Scott Fitzgerald and His Literary Agent Harold Ober 1919–1940*, ed. Matthew J. Bruccoli and Jennifer McCabe Atkinson (New York and Philadelphia: J.B. Lippincott, 1972), p. 36.

3. *As Ever*, p. 168.

mid-Victorian sugar."[4] In his essay " 'Wait Till You Have Children of Your Own!',", published three years later, he criticized motion picture producers who "rummaged among the ash heaps for shoddy ideas,"[5] endangering the minds of young children. These feelings continued into the early 1930s. In 1931, in the essay "Echoes of the Jazz Age," he attacked the film producers of the early 1920s for having been "timid, behind the times and banal . . ." (C-U, p. 17). Similar negative opinions can be found in his short stories; one of the most blatant is in "On Schedule" (1933), in which a scientist educates his daughter and his nineteen-year-old sweetheart because he believes that " 'they must not be educated by the money changers of Hollywood' " (*Price*, p. 443).

Despite this contempt, however, the young Fitzgerald felt no pangs of guilt in attempting to take advantage of the large sums that Hollywood was paying for stories. To his aunt and uncle in late 1920 he wrote about an outline he had submitted to D. W. Griffith: "I am not averse to taking all the shekels I can garner from the movies. I'll roll them joy pills (the literary habit) till doomsday because you can always say, 'Oh, but they put on the movie in a different spirit from the way it was written!' " (*Letters*, p. 466).

As early as 1919, before the publication of *This Side of Paradise*, Fitzgerald had written a number of film scripts, but like most of his works during this period, they were rejected. After the acceptance of his first novel, he wrote editor Robert Bridges of *Scribner's Magazine* of his inability to work on a second novel and of his need for money. " 'The Diary of a Literary Failure' was a literary failure," he lamented. "In the middle of its revision I gave out + consigned it to the drawer of unfinished manuscripts. As for short stories I've only done one since I left New York and its pitifully pathetic. So expect to see huge billboards announcing CHARLEY CHAPLIN in Scott Fitzgeralds new comedy 'Slapstick Sam.' As soon as I turn out anything respectable I'll send it on to you."[6] Shortly after, he wrote Maxwell Perkins that he had "just sent $1000 worth of movies to the *metro* people,"[7] but this material was rejected, too.

Soon after this, however, Fitzgerald sold the movie rights to three short stories, "Head and Shoulders" (released in 1920 by Metro Pictures

4. Frederick James Smith, "Fitzgerald, Flappers and Fame," *Shadowland*, 3 (January 1921), 75.

5. *F. Scott Fitzgerald in His Own Time: A Miscellany*, ed. Matthew J. Bruccoli and Jackson R. Bryer (Kent, Ohio: Kent State Univ. Press, 1971), p. 196.

6. *Correspondence of F. Scott Fitzgerald*, ed. Matthew J. Bruccoli and Margaret M. Duggan (New York: Random House, 1980), pp. 49–50.

7. *Dear Scott/Dear Max: The Fitzgerald-Perkins Correspondence*, ed. John Kuehl and Jackson R. Bryer (New York: Charles Scribner's, 1971), p. 25.

as *The Chorus Girl's Romance*), "Myra Meets His Family" (released that same year by Fox Film as *The Husband Hunter*), and "The Offshore Pirate" (released under the same name in 1921 by Metro). In addition, during this period he wrote "The Camel's Back," which was sold to Hollywood in 1923.

None of the first three films received exceptional reviews; *The Chorus Girl's Romance*, the earliest released, clearly earned the best. One contemporary newspaper referred to it as "comedy perfection" and "an extremely clever story," and another headlined "Type of Plot Good in Films," stating that this was "an example of the kind of story that works over into a good photoplay." Other reviews, however, were not as favorable, one for example finding it "dragging in spots."[8] But more important, the film exhibitors' trade publication *Wid's Daily*, later known as the *Film Daily*, found it a "splendid comedy full of originality" and suggested that the exhibitors feature Fitzgerald's name in the advertising, advising that they "dwell on the fact that he is a new author with new ideas."[9]

Wid's Daily greeted *The Husband Hunter* as well as *The Offshore Pirate* film much less enthusiastically. The reviewer of *The Husband Hunter* criticized both director and editor, who he said had devised "its moments of very rough comedy that will hardly appeal to a high class audience." While the reviewer did praise the "moments of good comedy" that he thought were "probably retained from F. Scott Fitzgerald's original story," in his summary he wrote: "AS A WHOLE—Some bright spots in this comedy; unreasonable story . . . STORY—Hardly any. . . ."[10] Of *The Offshore Pirate*, *Wid's* praised actress Viola Dana's performance and labeled the film amusing, but once again criticized the story, this time finding it slim for the length of the film and suggesting that the film should have been released in five reels rather than six. The reviewer stated, "There isn't enough in the plot to keep it going over five thousand feet."[11] This is ironic, considering that the filmmakers had tacked onto the beginning the tale of a Russian fortune hunter who arranges a holdup and rescues wealthy Ardita Farnam— all part of a plan to marry her for her money—before Toby Moreland as well as the remainder of Fitzgerald's original plot was introduced.

All of the short stories on which these films were based had contained visual effects important to the movies. The informal neighbor-

8. The reviews are in Fitzgerald's scrapbooks in the F. Scott Fitzgerald Papers, Princeton Univ. Library, Princeton, N.J.

9. *Wid's Daily*, August 22, 1920, p. 3.

10. Ibid., September 5, 1920, p. 25.

11. Ibid., February 13, 1921, p. 17.

hood vaudeville show in "Myra Meets His Family" (1920), ending with Myra Harper's song with its Al Jolson-like conclusion, as well as Marcia Meadows's stage performances and Horace Tarbox's trapeze act in "Head and Shoulders" (1920), could be easily converted to the silent screen. The short story version of *The Offshore Pirate* (1920) contained tableaux and lighting effects that also would have appealed to a movie cameraman. At one point in Fitzgerald's story, for example, Ardita Farnam and Toby Moreland are silhouetted in front of a blazing sun, reminiscent of the backlighting effects found in many of the films of the time. "Suddenly against the golden furnace low in the east," Fitzgerald wrote, "their two graceful figures melted into one, and he was kissing her spoiled young mouth" (1959 F&P, p. 44). (The fourth story, "The Camel's Back" [1920], also contained several visual sections, including a wedding and several parties, but when it was finally released by Warner Brothers Pictures in 1924 as *Conductor 1492*, all that remained of Fitzgerald's original plot were the two men going to the masquerade in the camel's costume, the remainder of the film in no way resembling Fitzgerald's story.)

Furthermore, Fitzgerald had specifically alluded to filmmaking in two of these short stories. In "The Offshore Pirate," when Ardita Farnam's uncle cautions her about a disreputable male friend, she replies that the description of the friend's escapades sounds like a movie plot: " 'Thrilling scandals by an anxious uncle,' yawned Ardita. 'Have it filmed. Wicked clubman making eyes at virtuous flapper. Virtuous flapper conclusively vamped by his lurid past. Plans to meet him at Palm Beach. Foiled by anxious uncle' " (1959 F&P, p. 20). Later, when Toby Moreland disguised as Curtis Carlyle boards Ardita's yacht, Ardita becomes curious about Moreland's past. " 'Why,' " queries Moreland. "Going to write a movie about me?' " (1951 F&P, p. 27). And in "The Camel's Back," Fitzgerald had introduced Perry Parkhurst's girlfriend with another film allusion. "I want you to meet his Love," he wrote. "Her name is Betty Medill, and she would take well in the movies" (6TJA, p. 35).

It seems possible that these were more than just metaphors. For by this time Fitzgerald was writing a few stories with film sales in mind. How autobiographical, one wonders, was at least a certain aspect of Richard Caramel, the successful author of *The Demon Lover* and friend of Anthony Patch in *The Beautiful and Damned*? Very early in his conversations with Bloeckman, the movie magnate, Caramel learns how to fashion his writing for eventual movie sale. " 'The main thing in a moving picture,' " he discovers, " 'is a strong story,' " ironically just what *Wid's Daily* had found wanting in both *The Husband Hunter* and *The Offshore Pirate* film. Bloeckman further states, " 'So many novels are full of talk and psychology. Of course those aren't as valuable to us. It's impossible to make much of that interesting on the screen.' " And Caramel replies, " 'You want plots first' " (B&D, p. 96). Thus within a two-year period, this novelist earns more than $25,000 by selling to popular magazines short stories that can be easily converted into film scripts:

> He received seven hundred dollars for every story, at that time a large emolument for such a young man—he was not quite thirty—and for every one that contained enough "action" (kissing, shooting, and sacrificing) for the movies, he obtained an additional thousand. His stories varied; there was a measure of vitality and a sort of instinctive technic in all of them, but none attained the personality of "The Demon Lover," and there were several that Anthony considered downright cheap. (B&D, p. 222)

Late in 1922 (the year of publication of *The Beautiful and Damned*), Fitzgerald deprecated a short story—most probably from the date and other evidence, "Dice, Brass Knuckles & Guitar"—that he was trying to sell to the magazines. To Harold Ober he wrote in December: "Im sure its best not to try the Metropolitan on this story. Its pretty bad stuff on second thots, but I still think it will make a magnificant movie." Just before publication, this time specifically naming the story, Fitzgerald asked if there had been any "movie nibbles."[12] When it appeared, "Dice, Brass Knuckles & Guitar" (1923) blatantly reflected the hoped-for Hollywood sale. After introducing his heroine, Amanthis Powell—a blonde-haired beauty sleeping in a hammock—Fitzgerald gave tongue-in-cheek instructions for filming:

> Now if this were a moving picture (as, of course, I hope it will some day be) I would take as many thousand feet of her as I was allowed—then I would move the camera up close and show the yellow down on the back of her neck where her hair stopped and the warm color of her cheeks and arms, because I like to think of her sleeping there, as you yourself might have slept, back in your young days. Then I would hire a man named Israel Glucose to write some idiotic line of transition, and switch thereby to another scene that was taking place at no particular spot far down the road. (*Price*, p. 48)

12. *As Ever*, pp. 50, 54.

Fitzgerald then immediately introduced his hero, Jim Powell, in a situation similar to those found in slapstick movies of the silent screen. Jim and his servant are encumbered by an ancient automobile with loose upper and lower sections. At times they must "dismount, shove the body on the chassis, corner to corner, and then continue onward, vibrating slightly in involuntary unison with the motor" (*Price*, p. 48). As the car passes the sleeping Amanthis, the body of the car falls off, dust rises and drifts slowly away, and the two riders stare at the separate halves.

All of this is merely introductory to a tedious, episodic story in which Jim Powell opens a school in Southampton for instruction in dice-throwing and guitar-playing as well as defense with brass knuckles, but fails socially as well as financially. The conclusion of the story also resembles the ending of many film comedies of the period. After Jim and his servant drive off in a "preposterous cloud of dust," the jalopy stops at the first bend and the two occupants dismount and realign the two halves of the chassis, return to their seats, restart the car, and soon are out of sight, "leaving only a faint brown mist to show that they had passed" (*Price*, p. 68).

Three years later Fitzgerald considered this story for inclusion in *All the Sad Young Men*, calling it "Exuberant Jazz in my early manner,"[13] but then, after having devoted much time to deleting a thousand words and making a great many other changes in the tearsheets of the story, he substituted "The Adjuster" (1925), confessing that the latter was a "better one."[14]

During this period Fitzgerald finally achieved financial if not artistic success for work in the film industry. In 1923 he received $10,000 for writing a treatment of *This Side of Paradise*, but the film was never made. He also wrote the titles for the 1923 Paramount film *The Glimpses of the Moon* based on Edith Wharton's novel and directed by Allen Dwan, at the time a friend of the Fitzgeralds. Finally, that same year he wrote the story for the Film Guild production of *Grit* starring Glen Hunter and Clara Bow. This film, according to a *Film Daily* reviewer, was a "Crook melodrama in which a weakling hero, born as his father is killed by a gang he had quit, is kept a coward through his fear of a gun. . . ." Finally, however, he "overcomes his fear, is the means of exposing a desperate gang and is eventually happy with Orchid, a girl of the underworld." The reviewer said that the film was "far from being good even with F. Scott Fitzgerald's name attached to

13. *Dear Scott/Dear Max*, p. 112.
14. Ibid., p. 119.

it; an amateurish looking picture both in production and acting." Furthermore, the reviewer specifically criticized Fitzgerald's contribution, calling it "a rather weak and poorly developed crook theme. . . ."[15] Apparently, Richard Caramel's theory of "kissing, shooting, and sacrificing" was not enough to produce a successful script. A year later Fitzgerald added his own critique of *Grit* when he wrote to John Peale Bishop: "Christ! You should have seen [the Film Guild's] last two pictures—one from my story" (*Letters*, p. 356).

But this criticism did not deter him from attempting to earn more money from the film industry. "The Adjuster," the story that had been substituted for "Dice, Brass Knuckles & Guitar" in *All the Sad Young Men*, was one of three stories—a fourth was discarded—that Fitzgerald wrote between September, 1924, and January, 1925, soon after he told Harold Ober that he was now making a conscious effort to write stories that would satisfy both the *Saturday Evening Post* and Hollywood. "Considering the fact that of the eleven stories I've written this year 4 of the 7 that have been published were run 1st in their issues," he wrote, "I think I've had hard luck with the movies. I must try some love stories with more action this time. I'm going to try to write three that'll do for Famous-Players as well as for the Post."[16]

However, none of the three stories completed during this period, "The Adjuster," "Love in the Night" (1925), or "Not in the Guidebook" (1925), was ever sold for filming. "The Adjuster" is a talky psychological study of Luella Hemple, a restless and selfish young woman who is helped to brave the death of her baby and her husband's nervous breakdown by a mysterious Dr. Smith (the name was changed to Moon when collected in *All the Sad Young Men*). Although Luella eventually matures and becomes relatively happy, this gloomy tale—easily the best of the three—was certainly not the kind of story that a Bloeckman-type producer would have purchased. Furthermore, since the plot was so different from the usual Fitzgerald story, it is difficult to believe that Fitzgerald's name would have increased ticket sales had "The Adjuster" been made into a film. On the other hand, "Love in the Night," the second story, though more representative of Fitzgerald's work, had a generally uneventful plot. This tale of a young Russian-American who returns impoverished to the Riviera after eight years of the Russian Revolution to find waiting for him the woman of his past, now a wealthy widow, contained a few pictorial scenes at or near the water, but it would have needed additional material to serve as the basis for a full-length movie.

15. *Film Daily*, January 6, 1924, p. 7.
16. *As Ever*, p. 66.

Of course, one cannot be absolutely certain that "The Adjuster" or "Love in the Night" were two of the tales combining love with action referred to in Fitzgerald's letter. "Not in the Guidebook" (1925) seems an even more likely possibility. Fitzgerald's tale of young Milly Cooley, married to a shiftless war veteran who falsely claims to be a war hero and soon leaves her in France, is set against several pictorial backgrounds that would have attracted a prospective producer. A ship scene, a train scene, and several tours of Europe make this the most visual of the three stories. Conveniently (for a filmmaker), Milly meets a tourist guide, Bill Driscoll, who takes her and the reader through Paris. Once again Fitzgerald pointedly referred to a scene that would interest a film director: "If someone had tipped off a multi-millionaire or a moving-picture director—at that time American directors were swarming over Europe looking for new locations—about Bill Driscoll, he would fortify himself with two cups of coffee, adorn his person with his new dinner-coat and show them the most dangerous dives of Montmartre in the very safest way" (*Price*, p. 167). Fitzgerald's wordy conclusion, both sentimental and pictorial, might also have appealed to silent filmmakers. Milly and Bill, now married, begin their honeymoon riding in a huge car with some two dozen vacant seats, and as they proceed, they pick up riders "along the white poplar-lined roads . . ." (*Price*, p. 176). The story ends with a description of the tour progressing through a number of French cities and towns.

Fitzgerald's correspondence with Harold Ober during this period and later mentions other stories—"The Jelly-Bean" (1920), "The Diamond as Big as the Ritz" (1922), "The Popular Girl" (1922), "The Third Casket" (1924), "John Jackson's Arcady" (1924), and "Majesty" (1929)—that the novelist hoped Hollywood would purchase.[17] But in none of these do we find similar ineffectual humorous comments referring to Hollywood filmmaking, unnecessarily drawn-out pictorial scenes, or any other purposeful attempts to attract the movie moguls. And with the exception of "Majesty," which he commended for its dramatic form and dramatic scenes,[18] in none of this correspondence does Fitzgerald suggest any technical reasons why Hollywood should express interest in these stories.

Fitzgerald's attempts to write short stories that would also interest Hollywood seem to have ended in 1925. His failure was at least partially due to his inability to accept the fact that until then he had only been dabbling in filmmaking. In late 1927, while working in Holly-

17. Ibid., pp. 28, 34, 62, 65, 109, 169.
18. Ibid., p. 169.

wood on the script of the never-to-be-made college film *Lipstick*, he spoke of this lack of knowledge to a movie reporter who had asked him about screen flappers. "I know nothing of their evolution," he apologized. "You see, we've been living on the Riviera for three years. In that time the only movies we've seen have been a few of the very old pictures, or the Westerns they show over there."[19] And in 1937, while traveling to Hollywood to work for Metro-Goldwyn-Mayer, he confessed how ignorant of scriptwriting he had been. "I honestly believed," he wrote of the *Lipstick* venture, "that with *no effort on my part* I was a sort of magician with words—an odd delusion on my part when I had worked so desperately hard to develop a hard, colorful prose style" (*Letters*, p. 16). Finally he realized that he still had much to learn about the movies.

19. Margaret Reid, "Has the Flapper Changed?," *Motion Picture Magazine*, 33 (July 1927), 104.

MONEY AND MARRIAGE
IN FITZGERALD'S STORIES

SCOTT DONALDSON

I write about Love and Money; what else is there to write about?

—Jane Austen

1.

Most authors constantly repeat themselves, Scott Fitzgerald observed in 1933. "We have two or three great and moving experiences in our lives," he continued, and on the basis of these experiences "we tell our two or three stories—each time in a new disguise—maybe ten times, maybe a hundred, as long as people will listen" (AA, p. 132). One of the two or three stories Fitzgerald told was about the struggle of the poor young man to win the hand of the rich girl. That had "always" been his situation, he remarked. He grew up " 'a poor boy in a rich town; a poor boy in a rich boy's school; a poor boy in a rich man's club at Princeton' "—above all, a poor boy in love with a rich girl. " 'The whole idea of Gatsby,' " he said, " 'is the unfairness of a poor young man not being able to marry a girl with money. The theme comes up again and again because I lived it.' "[1]

He exaggerated his poverty. The Fitzgeralds were not badly off, except in relation to the fabulously wealthy. But they did have less money than most families whose sons and daughters went to dancing school or college with Scott, and so he thought of himself—and this is the crucial point—as "a poor young man" whose financial condition put him at a disadvantage in courting rich girls. Love and money became almost inextricably entangled in his mind—and in his fiction. Almost everyone who has written about Fitzgerald has commented on his obsession with this topic, but usually they have concentrated on the

---

1. Andrew Turnbull, *Scott Fitzgerald* (New York: Charles Scribner's, 1962), p. 150.

novels. Until now there has been no wide-ranging attempt to trace how his *stories* reveal his changing attitudes toward money and marriage. Moreover, some of the stories discussed below have only recently become available in book form and so have received little or no critical attention.

Rudolph Miller in "Absolution" (1924) suffers a "furious" attack of shame when he has no money for the church collection box, since Jeanne Brady, in the pew behind him, might notice (*Stories*, p. 168). In "Rags Martin-Jones and the Pr-nce of W-les" (1924), an imaginary merchant offers to sell the rich and beautiful Rags "some perfectly be-*oo*-tiful love." If he runs out, he'll gladly send for a fresh supply since there's "so much money to spend" (ASYM, pp. 140–41). But if you don't have anything for the collection box, the girl will notice. And if you don't have enough to spend, the merchant will not bother. No money, no love. "If you haven't got money," Philip Dean instructs the hapless Gordon Sterrett in "May Day" (1920), "you've got to work and stay away from women" (*Stories*, p. 87).

Sterrett is a weakling who commits suicide when he wakes from a sodden drunk to find himself rejected by the society girl who used to love him and married to a Jewel of the lower classes. Though he is the only protagonist driven to this extremity, in many other stories the poor young man engages in unequal combat with a wealthy competitor. "Remember," a precociously cynical Fitzgerald wrote at nineteen, "in all society nine girls out of ten marry for money and nine men out of ten are fools" (AF, p. 126). He often felt discriminated against in such an environment. Occasionally he treated his predicament humorously:

> Those wealthy goats
> In raccoon coats
> can wolf you away from me

he complained in "Oh, Sister, Can You Spare Your Heart," a jingle in his notebooks.[2] But such levity was rare, for he had been badly hurt. "It was one of those tragic loves doomed for lack of money. . . . In the years since then I have never been able to stop wondering where my friends' money came from, not to stop thinking that at one time a sort of *droit de seigneur* might have been exercised to give one of them my girl" (C-U, p. 77). In his literary notebooks he typed out a suggestion

2. "Oh, Sister, Can You Spare Your Heart," in *The Notebooks of F. Scott Fitzgerald*, ed. Matthew J. Bruccoli (New York and London: Harcourt Brace Jovanovich, 1978), p. 135.

for dramatic treatment of this concept: "Play about wife and Prince Droit de Seigneur."[3]

The play went unwritten, but Fitzgerald rang variations on the theme in his two best novels and in dozens of short stories. These were based—sometimes loosely, sometimes with almost photographic fidelity to the facts—on his love for two girls, Ginevra King and Zelda Sayre. Fitzgerald wooed Ginevra King of Chicago throughout 1915 and 1916, but she remained unwilling to commit herself to him. In August, 1916, he went to visit her at her summer home in Lake Forest. "Once I thought that Lake Forest was the most glamorous place in the world," he wrote two decades later. "Maybe it was" (*Letters*, p. 84). As Ginevra's visiting beau, he escorted her to parties, dinners, and dances. But he also spent a "bad day at the McCormicks," endured a " 'Disappointment,' " and heard someone—probably Charles King, Ginevra's father—declare, "Poor boys shouldn't think of marrying rich girls" (*Ledger*, p. 170).[4] A few months later he and Ginevra broke up conclusively, but Fitzgerald did not soon lose his feeling for her.

He fell in love with Zelda Sayre of Montgomery, Alabama—so his ledger records—in September, 1918, the month of Ginevra's wedding to William Mitchell ("beautiful Billy Mitchell," Fitzgerald had noted in his entry for August, 1916). Zelda was widely known in Montgomery for her daring; Fitzgerald thought that "by temperament she was the most reckless" of all the women he ever knew. Nonetheless, Zelda "was cagey about throwing in her lot" with him before he had proved himself as a moneymaker. So at war's end Fitzgerald went off to New York, "the land of ambition and success," to make his fortune. When the fortune failed to develop, Zelda's devotion flagged; and after a desperate trip back to Montgomery, Fitzgerald boarded a Pullman car for her benefit and then sneaked back into the daycoach when the train got underway. In the summer of 1919 he gave up his job in New York, went west to St. Paul, where he rewrote *This Side of Paradise*, and in September learned that Scribner's would bring out his novel in the spring. "Would it be utterly impossible for you to publish the book Xmas—or say by February?" Fitzgerald wrote Maxwell Perkins. "I have so many things dependent on its success—including of course a girl. . . ." Meanwhile, he cranked out short stories and wired to the South such materialistic messages of love as "I HAVE SOLD THE MOVIE

3. Ibid., p. 110.
4. Mrs. Marjorie King Belden, Ginevra's sister, recalls that her father often gave young Fitzgerald "a piece of his mind": Richard D. Lehan, *F. Scott Fitzgerald and the Craft of Fiction* (Carbondale: Southern Illinois Univ. Press, 1966), p. 54.

RIGHTS OF HEAD AND SHOULDERS TO THE METRO COMPANY FOR TWENTY-FIVE HUNDRED DOLLARS I LOVE YOU DEAREST GIRL."[5]

Each of these situations—the poor boy spurned by the rich girl, the poor boy put off by the not-so-rich girl until he can demonstrate his financial capacities—occurs in several Fitzgerald stories. Almost all the stories he began selling to the *Saturday Evening Post* in 1919 and 1920 dealt with young love (". . . essentially I got my public with stories of young love" [*Letters*, p. 128]) in high society. As early as New Year's Eve of 1920, in fact, he was complaining to Perkins that he'd "go mad if I have to do another debutante, which is what they want" (*Letters*, p. 145). Readers started a Fitzgerald story not always sure of a happy ending, but with confidence that he would provide a glimpse of a glamorous social world few of them had ever inhabited. So stereotyped was this social setting that his illustrators usually presented the characters as handsome wraithlike creatures in full evening dress. The men wore tuxedos or tails, the women gowns, though there might be no reason whatever, on the basis of the story itself, for them to be so attired. In "The Bowl" (1928), for example, the male protagonist is described as customarily wearing tan or soft gray suits with black ties. Yet in the illustrations he appears in formal evening dress.[6]

Fitzgerald's novels of love and money usually attack the wealthy. The Buchanans treat Jay Gatsby brutally, then retreat into their carelessness while his dream and life blood ebb away. The Warrens retain Doctor Diver until they've used up his vitality, then casually dismiss him. The stories are far less consistent in their attitude toward the wealthy. Yet most of them can be classified as falling within one of two strains. One group of stories depicts the success, or seeming success, of the poor young man in wooing the rich girl. In the other, more effective group, the young man is rejected in his quest or subsequently disappointed.

2.

The usual trouble with stories of the first kind is that they are not persuasive. At least subconsciously, Fitzgerald must have realized this, for he often tricked out such tales with fantasy or with outrageous challenges to reader disbelief. "The Offshore Pirate" (1920) provides a

5. Arthur Mizener, *The Far Side of Paradise: A Biography of F. Scott Fitzgerald* (Boston: Houghton Mifflin, 1965), pp. 79–104.

6. F. Scott Fitzgerald, "The Bowl," *Saturday Evening Post*, 200 (January 21, 1928), 6–7, 93–94, 97, 100; collected in *Price*, pp. 256–77.

case in point. It is—as the first sentence declares—the "unlikely story" of the winning of Ardita Farnam, a yellow-haired embodiment of the golden girl. Ardita is bored by the predictable round of her social life, and eager—so she says—to cast her lot with anyone who will show some imagination. That someone turns out to be Toby Moreland, a rich boy playing at poverty. He attracts her interest by pretending to be a musician who has risen to wealth first by way of his talent, then by stealing the jewels of society matrons. He commandeers Ardita's yacht but though fascinated, she withholds her hand.

> "We can get married in Callao."
> "What sort of life can you offer me? I don't mean that unkindly, but seriously, what would become of me if the people who want that twenty-thousand-dollar reward ever catch up with you?" (1959 F&P, p. 40)

It would be different if she were "a little poor girl dreaming over a fence in a warm cow country" and he, newly rich with ill-gotten gains, had come along to astonish her with his munificence. Then she'd stare into the windows of the jewelry store and want the " 'big oblong watch that's platinum and has diamonds all round the edge' " but would decide " 'it was too expensive and choose one of white gold for a hundred dollars.' " And he'd say, " 'Expensive? I should say not!' " and " 'pretty soon the platinum one would be gleaming' " on her wrist (1959 F&P, p. 40). She wishes it were that way, but it isn't, so Ardita turns her suitor down—until his identity is revealed at the end, and she finds to her relief that he is both imaginative *and* respectable. Imagination alone is not enough. A rich boy may charm his girl by pretending to have been poor, like Toby Moreland and like George Van Tyne in "The Unspeakable Egg" (1924), who wins his Fifi by playing the role of a bearded, disheveled roustabout (*Price*, pp. 126–42). But it does not, of course, work the other way around.

A good many Fitzgerald stories hinge upon an actual rather than imaginary reversal of fortune. In these tales, he posits an America where the ambitious hard-working lad is bound to rise and then to receive the romantic reward due him. Generally, stories that conform to this "boy makes money, gets girl" pattern are among the worst Fitzgerald ever wrote. They tend to be overplotted to the point where manipulation of character and circumstance becomes blatantly obvious. They lack verisimilitude and conviction and achieve only sentimentality.

Commenting on two such stories—"Presumption" and "The Adolescent Marriage"—written in the fall and winter of 1925–26, Robert Sklar observes that the author of *The Great Gatsby* had "put his matured art and intellectual perception into the requirements of slick magazine stories . . . as if he were an adolescent boy forced to wear short pants."[7] In "Presumption," the more interesting of these two, Juan Chandler pursues a rich debutante, Noel Garneau. Juan comes from middle-class circumstances in Akron, and swims beyond his depth in the social waters of Culpepper Bay. " 'You're not in any position to think anything serious about Noel Garneau' " (*Price*, p. 187), his cousin Cora reminds him. And Noel does in fact reject him at first, though only partly because of his poverty; Juan really loses his chance when he foolishly tries to make her jealous. Still, he can think of but one way to remedy the situation: by making a proper fortune. " 'I haven't any money and I'm in love with a girl who has' " (*Price*, p. 189), he confesses to a golfing partner who turns out, by that sort of coincidence that makes these stories embarrassing, to be Noel's father. Mr. Garneau advises Juan to stick it out:

> "Does the girl care about you?" he inquired.
> "Yes."
> "Well, go after her, young man. All the money in the world hasn't been made by a long shot." (*Price*, p. 189)

Driven by these words of encouragement, Juan drops out of college to get wealthy and eighteen months later represents himself to Noel as a rich young man. Though she is now engaged, he follows her from Boston to New York, where he presents his case to her aunt, the *soignee* Mrs. Poindexter:

> "I've been called presumptuous in this matter, and perhaps to some extent I am. Perhaps all poor boys who are in love with wealthy girls are presumptuous. But it happens that I am no longer a poor boy, and I have good reason to believe that Noel cares for me." (*Price*, p. 200)

Here, as Sklar points out, is a reworking of the *Gatsby* plot, and when Juan reads the note Noel has left directing her aunt to dismiss the

7. Robert Sklar, *F. Scott Fitzgerald: The Last Laocoön* (New York: Oxford Univ. Press, 1967), pp. 215–16.

" 'intolerable bore' " who is pursuing her with his " 'presumptuous whining' " (*Price*, p. 201), it seems as if story and novel will have the same sorry end. At this point Juan realized, Fitzgerald writes, "that fundamentally they were all akin—Cousin Cora, Noel, her father, this cold, lovely woman here—affirming the prerogative of the rich to marry always within their caste, to erect artificial barriers and standards against those who could presume upon a summer's philandering" (*Price*, p. 201). The words could hardly ring truer. But wait! It's a case of mistaken identity, and the bore Noel speaks of is Mr. *Templeton*, the man she'd been engaged to, and of course she'll be delighted to see and fall in love with and marry Mr. Chandler.

"Presumption" ran as the lead story in the January 9, 1926, *Saturday Evening Post*. Like everything Fitzgerald ever wrote, it has its moments. But, along with such other *Post* publications as "The Adolescent Marriage" (1926), "The Rubber Check" (1932), "More Than Just a House" (1933), and "The Family Bus" (1933), it fails for lack of feeling. John O'Hara wrote Fitzgerald admiring his portrait of Lew Lowrie, the "climber" in "More Than Just a House." He always did the "climber" well, O'Hara told him, and rightly so, for Fitzgerald the author felt a natural kinship for the poor young man on the make. But as he grew older, he could no longer care very much whether his young man won the golden girl. The magazines wanted him to continue turning out commercial love stories, but by the mid-1930s he had lost interest in such "inessential and specious matters" and could no longer write them convincingly.[8]

Occasionally Fitzgerald shifts the sexes as a variation on his basic theme. Thus in such early stories as "Myra Meets His Family" (1920) and "The Popular Girl" (1922), a poor girl sets her cap for a rich boy. Fitzgerald's obvious sympathy lies with the girl in this situation; he cannot or will not identify with the rich young man. At twenty-one Myra Harper "can still get any man" she wants, and she wants Knowleton Whitney: " 'You know what a wiz he is on looks, and his father's worth a fortune, they say. . . . He's smart as a whip, and shy—rather sweetly shy—and they say his family has the best-looking place in Westchester County' " (*Price*, pp. 13–14). Warned about Myra's reputation as a gold-digger, Whitney invites her out to the mansion where he tests her devotion by introducing her to awful people (actors hired for the occasion) masquerading as his parents. Then he confesses his plot, but Myra still exacts her revenge by staging a phony wedding, then leaving him cold on a train for Chicago immediately afterwards.

8. Turnbull, p. 300.

The rich boy is bested, albeit rather cruelly. In "The Popular Girl," Yanci Bowman pretends to a wealth and social position that will, she thinks, impress her rich beau. But he loves her, not her background, and once she has spent her last dime they blissfully ride into Manhattan—and the future—together.

3.

Fitzgerald's tales of rejection and disappointment are far more effective than those where true love unpersuasively conquers all. They are more deeply felt, more to the life. The stories of rejection also serve to demonstrate the author's growing maturity of outlook, his disturbing sense that pursuit and capture of the golden girl was not really worth all the trouble and heartache. He felt anything but philosophical about the matter when he wrote *This Side of Paradise*, however. The section of that novel called "The Debutante"—really a short story in the form of a playlet, with dialogue and stage directions—painfully relives Fitzgerald's rejection by Ginevra King.

When Amory Blaine first meets Rosalind Connage, she describes herself as a commodity—" 'Rosalind, Unlimited.' Fifty-one shares, name, good-will, and everything goes at $25,000 a year" (TSOP, p. 174). They fall in love, and though Amory is making a paltry $35 a week, she agrees to marry him:

> "Amory," she whispered, "when you're ready for me I'll marry you."
> "We won't have much at first."
> "Don't!" she cried. "It hurts when you reproach yourself for what you can't give me. I've got your precious self—and that's enough for me." (TSOP, p. 188)

Mrs. Connage puts a stop to the match through the weapon of sarcasm. " 'You've already wasted over two months on a theoretical genius who hasn't a penny to his name,' " she tells Rosalind, " 'but go ahead, waste your life on him. *I* won't interfere' " (TSOP, p. 190). Both mother and daughter know that Rosalind is extravagant, that Amory's income wouldn't even buy her clothes, and so the rich girl breaks her promise. " 'I can't, Amory. I can't be shut away from the trees and flowers, cooped up in a little flat, waiting for you' " (TSOP, p. 195). And again, " 'I don't want to think about pots and kitchens and brooms. I want to worry whether my legs will get slick and brown when I swim in the summer' " (TSOP, p. 196). She will marry the rich Dawson Ryder, instead. Her selfishness is appalling, but Fitzgerald is not yet ready to condemn her. In the concluding stage direction, in fact, he assigns her a romantic capacity for feeling akin to his own: "(*And deep under the aching sadness that will pass in time, Rosalind feels that she has lost something, she knows not what, she knows not why)*" (TSOP, p. 197).

A decade later, in "A Snobbish Story" (1930), Fitzgerald reworked the same material with much less sympathy for the rich girl involved. In this story, as in four others of 1930–31, she is Josephine Perry, Lake Forest debutante. She is attracted to John Bailey, a Chicago *Tribune* reporter and aspiring playwright, but Bailey comes from Bohemia, not the upper-class suburbs, and even has a wife who lives apart from him. Bailey casts Josephine as the lead in his play (called *Race Riot!*) and comes to the Perrys' home one summer Saturday to interest her father in investing in the production. While he's there, however, a policeman comes with the news that Bailey's wife has tried to take her life. Bailey disappears forever, while Mr. and Mrs. Perry chastise their daughter:

> "What I can't understand is why you should have to know people like that. Is it necessary to go into the back streets of Chicago?"
> "That young man had no business here," her father thundered grimly, "and he knew it." (B&J, p. 267)

Josephine accepts their criticism, and determines that she will no longer interest herself in potential geniuses. She decides that "any value she might have was in the immediate, shimmering present—and thus thinking, she threw in her lot with the rich and powerful of this world forever" (B&J, p. 269).

While Rosalind Connage had supposedly been tender-hearted, though hardheaded on the question of marriage, Josephine Perry is equally tough of heart and head. The difference clearly lay not in the girl who sat for both portraits but in Fitzgerald's perception of that girl and the nature of the struggle to win her hand. In his better stories of the 1920s, he gradually de-romanticized the girl and de-emphasized the glory of the quest. The poor young man who commits himself to that pursuit must begin with abundant supplies both of ambition and energy. Like Dexter Green in "Winter Dreams" (1922), he must be driven to possess not merely Judy Jones but all she represented: "He wanted not association with glittering things and glittering people—he wanted the glittering things themselves. Often he reached out for the best without knowing why he wanted it—and sometimes he ran up against the mysterious denials and prohibitions in which life indulges" (*Stories*, p. 130). The young man must also have the talent and energy to go out and make a success of himself, if only to get the girl's attention. Dexter's ability to earn money dramatically transforms his relationship with the wealthy Judy Jones. On their first dinner date, she confesses that she's had "a terrible afternoon. There was a man I cared about, and this afternoon he told me out of a clear sky that he was poor as a church-mouse" (*Stories*, p. 135). Her interest in him, she admits, had not been strong enough to stand the shock. Then this dialogue ensues:

> "Let's start right," she interrupted herself suddenly. "Who are you, anyhow?"
> For a moment Dexter hesitated. Then:
> "I'm nobody," he announced. "My career is largely a matter of futures."
> "Are you poor?"
> "No," he said frankly, "I'm probably making more money than any man my age in the Northwest. I know that's an obnoxious remark, but you advised me to start right."
> There was a pause. Then she smiled and the corners of her mouth drooped and an almost imperceptible sway brought her closer to him, looking up into his eyes. (*Stories*, p. 136)

And they kiss, her kisses "like charity, creating want by holding back nothing at all." But Dexter does not win the girl after all, and at the end of the story, he is disillusioned to hear Judy spoken of as " 'faded' " and " 'a little too old' " for her husband in Detroit (*Stories*, pp. 144–45).

The loss of romantic illusions provides a central motif in stories of this type. Jonquil Cary, in " 'The Sensible Thing' " (1924), fends off the proposal of George O'Kelly until he is "ready" for her. By this code word—also used by Rosalind Connage to Amory Blaine and Zelda Sayre to Scott Fitzgerald—Jonquil meant that her suitor must first establish himself financially. Until he did so, she would remain "nervous" (another code word uttered both by Zelda and Jonquil) about the prospect of marriage. The ambitious O'Kelly strikes out for South America, makes his pile, and returns to claim the girl. But some of the magic has gone: "as he kissed her he knew that though he search through eternity he could never recapture those lost April hours. . . . There are all kinds of love in the world, but never the same love twice" (*Stories*, p. 158).

A still bitterer disillusionment awaited some of those who—like George O'Kelly—eventually win the girl. Then they are liable to find, as in "Gretchen's Forty Winks" (1924) and "The Adjuster" (1925), that they have married creatures of exquisite irresponsibility and selfishness. What's more, Fitzgerald implies that the possession of money—and the idle hours it can supply—encourages adultery. Luella Hemple in "The Adjuster" is bored. She "honestly wanted something to do. If she had had a little more money and a little less love, she could have gone in for horses or for vagarious amour. Or if they had had a little less money, her surplus energy would have been absorbed by hope and even by effort" (6TJA, p. 142). But she falls in between, and concentrates instead on making her husband's life miserable.

Money also confers a license for misbehavior on Anson Hunter of "The Rich Boy" (1926). He feels no more compunction about breaking hearts than about getting drunk. Like Henry Ford II, when caught in a compromising situation he will not apologize afterwards: "Never Complain, Never Explain."[9] But Anson pays dearly for his privileges, since he is unable to commit himself to any one woman, even the woman he thought he loved. His financial capacity is balanced by an emotional incapacity. He cannot give, only receive:

> I don't think he was ever happy unless some one was in love with him, responding to him like filings to a magnet, helping him to explain himself, promising him something. What it was I do not know. Perhaps they promised that there would always be women in the world who would spend their brightest, freshest, rarest hours to nurse and protect that superiority he cherished in his heart. (*Stories*, pp. 207–8)

Fitzgerald's mature view of the relationship between love and money is that too much money militates against true love. Such wealth is destructive because "those who have it lose the capacity to feel for others."[10] This is true of the Buchanans and Warrens of his novels, and of the Anson Hunters and Josephine Perrys of his stories. In this re-

9. Ford made the "Never Complain, Never Explain" comment when discovered in the company of a model who appeared in Ford Motor Company commercials.

10. William F. Kennedy, "Are Our Novelists Hostile to the American Economic System?," *Dalhousie Review*, 35 (Spring 1955), 33.

spect, the young man on the rise actually holds an emotional advantage over both his rich competitor and the golden girl he seeks to wed.

The story which best illustrates Fitzgerald's altered perception of this relationship is "The Bridal Party," published in the *Saturday Evening Post* for August 9, 1930. On the surface this appears to be yet another tale about the poor boy who loses his girl to a much better-off young man. Michael Curly is in Paris when he runs across his old girl, Caroline Dandy, and her fiancé, Hamilton Rutherford. As Michael himself reflects,

> He had met Caroline Dandy when she was seventeen, possessed her young heart all through her first season in New York, and then lost her, slowly, tragically, uselessly, because he had no money and could make no money; because, with all the energy and good will in the world, he could not find himself; because, loving him still, Caroline had lost faith and begun to see him as something pathetic, futile and shabby, outside the great, shining stream of life toward which she was inevitably drawn. (*Stories*, p. 271)

Her "entire clan," Michael believes, had been against him: "What a little counter he was in this game of families and money!" (*Stories*, p. 272)

Now, on the brink of Caroline's marriage, Michael comes into an inheritance and determines to take up his courtship once again. This effort fails, though not for lack of resources. Caroline preferred Rutherford for his solidity and decisiveness, she tells Michael. "It was that more than the question of . . . money" (*Stories*, p. 276). And she proves the point by sticking with Rutherford when he discovers, on the night of his stag party, that he has lost every cent he's made and must start over. Michael goes to the wedding expecting to feel only sorrow. But his financial windfall combines with champagne and the "ceremonial function" itself to obliterate the wound: "All the bitterness melted out of him suddenly and the world reconstituted itself out of the youth and happiness that was all around him, profligate as the spring sunshine." This is not a conventional happy ending, however, for though Michael is "cured" of his sorrow, he may also be "cured," the last sentence suggests, of ever feeling so deeply again. "He was trying to remember which one of the bridesmaids he had made a date to dine with tonight as he walked forward to bid Hamilton and Caroline Rutherford goodby" (*Stories*, p. 286).

Through its ironic view of the narrator-protagonist, "The Bridal Party" repudiates the belief, often implied and sometimes articulated in Fitzgerald's early fiction, that money could purchase almost anything or anybody one wanted to buy. To young Dalyrimple, returning from World War I, it seemed that "happiness was what he wanted—a slowly rising scale of gratifications of the normal appetites—and he had a strong conviction that the materials, if not the inspiration of happiness, could be bought with money" (1959 F&P, p. 166). Fitzgerald wrote "Dalyrimple Goes Wrong" in 1920. Ten years later, in such stories as "The Bridal Party," "The Swimmers" (1929), and "Babylon Revisited" (1931), he demonstrated the relative impotence of money. In "The Swimmers," Henry Marston is deceived by his French wife, Choupette, and faces the problem of divorcing her while keeping custody of their children. His wife's lover, an aggressive American businessman named Wiese, tells Marston that he has no chance, that Wiese's money will insure that the children remain with Choupette. " 'Money is power,' " Wiese insists. " 'Money made this country, built its great and glorious cities, created its industries, covered it with an iron network of railroads. It's money that harnesses the forces of Nature, creates the machine and makes it go when money says go, and stop when money says stop' " (*Bits*, p. 205). As if to illustrate how wrong he is, the motorboat in which Wiese delivers this speech sputters to a halt, and they are drifting out to sea—apparently at the mercy of the Atlantic—when Marston, the only swimmer of the three, agrees to swim for help in return for custody of the children. Skill and knowledge carry the day. For Marston as for Fitzgerald, it was not money but "a willingness of the heart" that made America.

"Babylon Revisited" also focuses on the issue of child custody. During the boom of the 1920s, Charlie Wales got rich, then wasted his time on drinking and lost his wife to illness. Charlie was so badly off when his wife died that her sister and brother-in-law, Marion and Lincoln Peters, assumed care of Honoria, the Wales's daughter. Now that the boom has turned to bust, a reformed Charlie comes to Paris to try to get Honoria back. At the end he finds he cannot have custody of her yet and reflects with bitter irony on the days and nights of the boom when it seemed, for a while, that one could purchase even forgetfulness—when a man could lock his wife out in the snow (as he had done) "because the snow of twenty-nine wasn't real snow. If you didn't want it to be snow, you just paid some money" (*Stories*, p. 402). Charlie's money seems to him to have been as much a handicap as a blessing. Marion still resents the lavish way Charlie had spent his money after making a killing in the stock market of the 1920s. Now that he has lost that fortune and started to build another anew, he alienates her once again by announcing how well he's doing. Nor can he, yet, entirely shake loose of the drunken companions his money had enabled him to dissipate away his life with a few years before. So he must wait still longer for Honoria, the only girl left for him. In the meantime he could at least "send her a lot of things," though, he thinks in anger, that "was just money—he had given so many people money . . ." (*Stories*, p. 402).

In the mid-1920s, Jacob Booth—the hero of "Jacob's Ladder" (1927)—made $800,000 in real estate. Then "he had tried—tried hard—for a year and a half to marry one of the richest women in America" (*Bits*, p. 162). If he had loved her, he could have had her. But Jacob did not love her; he had pursued her because of the glitter of wealth that surrounded her. A similar halo hovered in the vicinity of many of the rich girls Fitzgerald's young men were forever pursuing in his stories of the 1920s. But during his last years as a writer, he rarely sent poor boys out in quest of the golden girl. He had learned by then that the halo was slightly tarnished and the glitter not always gold. He had also discovered that there were other things as powerful as money and come to realize that the power wealth did exert rarely worked to the benefit of those who possessed it. Besides, by then he had told his story of money and marriage—sometimes poorly, sometimes superlatively well—often enough.

TO BE BOTH LIGHT AND DARK: THE JUNGIAN PROCESS OF INDIVIDUATION IN FITZGERALD'S BASIL DUKE LEE STORIES

JOSEPH MANCINI, JR.

In the early spring of 1928, F. Scott Fitzgerald temporarily suspended work on his difficult fourth novel and began to turn out magazine pieces chronicling the early adolescent exploits of the precocious and presumptuous Basil Duke Lee, a remarkable likeness of Fitzgerald as a young man. The author's assessment of this year-long project was ambivalent: on the one hand, he depreciated the nine stories by labeling them "watered goods" and planning them as "a nice *light* novel, almost" and "in the direct line of my so-called 'work' "[1]; it is this appraisal that seems to confirm a critical perspective characterizing the work as an escape into the past from an onerous present, and as a potboiler crammed with nostalgic reminiscences in lieu of any substantial material. On the other hand, Fitzgerald wrote to an admirer that he "was glad you like them—I thought they were rather better than the response they had" (*Letters*, p. 495). In another remark to this friend, Fitzgerald seems to resolve his contradictory estimations by noting that the mistake lay in the execution rather than in the conception of the stories: "it was too much good material being shoved into a lousy form" (*Letters*, p. 495).

If in fact the Basil stories do comprise "good material," it clearly concerns the maturation of a youth from ages eleven through seventeen. What makes this otherwise banal material "good" is Fitzgerald's ability not only to transmute many personal memories into a universal

---

1. Jackson R. Bryer and John Kuehl, eds., *The Basil and Josephine Stories* (New York: Charles Scribner's, 1973), pp. ix, viii.

context but also to weave from seemingly insignificant elements a rich tapestry displaying the process of growing up. Because this process is essentially psychological, analysis of its pattern may well benefit from the contribution of a discipline devoted to understanding human motivation. As Norman Friedman has noted, "A psychological scheme may indeed *come* from someplace outside of literary studies but its *use* can remain strictly within [that] framework. . . ."[2] Thus, psychology offers literary criticism a way of conceptualizing and thereby illuminating how human characters, however different, will respond in essentially similar ways to internal and external stimuli. A writer need not consciously write according to any psychological formula for his work to be open to such investigation. The fact that readers can respond at all to the work suggests the presentation, whether conceptualized or not, of an essentially universal sense of how humans behave.

The intricacies of this presentation can be defined with the help of psychological systems, most of which, though they differ, do overlap, as Friedman points out. These systems agree, for instance, that hidden causes influence behavior, that repression of undesirable feelings issues in their projection onto other people or in eruptions of irrational behavior, that neurotic psyches tend to be compartmentalized, and that psychic disturbances can be traced, in part, to childhood traumata.[3] Still, since the orientations do differ, the critic must make a choice. Friedman suggests a criterion: "Where we have insufficient bases for choosing one scheme over another in terms of its truth value, we should choose heuristically that model . . . which seems to us the most illuminating in terms of its explanatory value. . . ."[4]

Fitzgerald's respect for the theories of Carl Jung is evident in a 1932 letter to Mrs. Turnbull, where he declared that "if one is interested in the world into which willy-nilly one's children will grow up, the most accurate data can be found in the European leaders, such as Lawrence, Jung, and Spengler . . . (*Letters*, p. 433). When in 1931 Zelda was being treated at a clinic located in Zurich, Jung's research center, Fitzgerald "often discussed psychiatry" with the Jungian Margaret Eglov and asked her to analyze his dream about his burdensome, suffocating mother[5] (who resembles in some respects Basil's parent). Though it can only be conjectured when he "probably read" Jung's

2. Norman Friedman, "Psychology and Literary Form: Toward a Unified Approach," *Psychocultural Review*, 2 (Spring 1978), 79.

3. Ibid., p. 80.

4. Ibid., p. 81.

5. Andrew Turnbull, *Scott Fitzgerald* (New York: Charles Scribner's, 1962), pp. 206–8.

Psychological Types[6] (first American edition by Harcourt Brace, 1923), Fitzgerald might well have known something of the psychotherapist's work before 1930 when he began the Josephine stories, companion pieces to the Basil sequence; in the initial story, "First Blood," he mentions Jung by name along with one of his theories about the male dimension in a female (B&J, p. 190). However, none of this information is intended to suggest that Fitzgerald was a Jungian or wrote in accordance with the psychologist's theories; these facts are provided only to demonstrate that Fitzgerald was at least not adverse to Jung's conception of human behavior. The value of the ensuing Jungian interpretation of the Basil stories must rest on its making substantial sense out of Basil's seemingly unrelated activities and feelings.

1.

In *Psychological Types*, Jung describes the process of individuation; a brief overview of this pattern of psychic growth may help prepare the reader for the more elaborate analysis and application to follow. According to Jung, the goal of individuation is "the development of the psychological *individual* as a being distinct from the general, collective psychology."[7] The individual learns to distinguish himself from two modes of collective life, the unconscious realm or ground of all being, and the conscious world of society. The former world, which Jung calls the Self, is the transpersonal, incorruptible, eternal center of every life, "the central source of life energy, the fountain of our being which is most simply described as God."[8] This Self or God belongs to no one in particular and everyone in general.

In the state of earliest infancy, the ego or consciousness has not yet emerged from complete identification with this inner God or unconscious ground common to all men. Though the infant's ego is only part of this paradisal original wholeness, it has at this point no consciousness to make the distinction and thus is *unconsciously inflated* with the attributes of deity; the infant's world is one with God. As the ego issues into consciousness from its collective source, it becomes the center of

6. John Kuehl, "Scott Fitzgerald's Reading," in *Profile of F. Scott Fitzgerald*, ed. Matthew J. Bruccoli (Columbus, Ohio: Charles E. Merrill, 1971), pp. 71, 72.

7. C. G. Jung, *Psychological Types*, in *The Collected Works of C. G. Jung*, ed. Sir Herbert Read et al., trans. H. G. Baynes, rev. R. F. C. Hull (Princeton, N.J.: Princeton Univ. Press, 1976), 6, p. 448; hereafter cited in the text as PT.

8. Edward F. Edinger, *Ego and Archetype: Individuation and the Religious Function of the Psyche* (Baltimore: Penguin Books, 1973), p. 178; hereafter cited in the text as ED.

the individual's unique, subjective identity. In order truly to break away from the inner deity, the ego ultimately must *consciously* inflate itself beyond its actual limitations and assume God-like powers just as Adam and Eve defied God, ate the apple to become like Him, and emerged out of the womb of Eden into consciousness and self-responsibility. Such an action is experienced as a sin, but also as a prerequisite for self-awareness. Each child, in rebelling against its mother or any authority that reflects the nutritive, protective, but possibly suffocating aspects of the Self, reenacts the *felix culpa* of Adam. We will see how Basil also follows this universal pattern of human life in defying his mother's control.

Too often, however, this necessary sin of inflation serves to assert more than individual identity; the inflated ego then becomes the center of the world, viewing all things and God as merely aspects of itself, rather than the other way around. Such a puffed-up individual may, like Basil, earn the epithet "Bossy" or a much more pejorative one. But Jung notes that individuation properly understood does not lead to such solipsism but to "more intense and broader collective relationships" (PT, p. 448). For to exist as an individual without a social context against which to define onself is an impossibility. In short, "we are both unique indivisible units of being and also part of the continuum [the Self] which is the universal wave of life" (ED, p. 178). Thus individuation involves both the differentiation and reconciliation of opposites: the ego must distinguish itself from the Self to exist at all, but it must also finally reunite with this inner divinity, the ground of its being. When this reunion occurs, it is not a fusion with the Self as in the state of original wholeness and unconsciousness but rather a conscious, individual relationship to God, now experienced as the Other.

To prepare for this ultimate confrontation with the Self which can be realized fully only in the latter half of life, the ego must learn to relate to but not fuse itself with a reflection of the collective inner Self embodied in the transpersonal standards of the outer world of society. Adapting to society involves developing what Jung calls the social mask or *persona*, the side of the ego turned outward toward conformance with societal norms. We will see that Basil spends much of his adolescence trying on various personae to "fit in" with one or another of his social environments. While the collective mask is a practical necessity for easing social interaction, the persona, if the ego identifies completely with it, will hide or destroy the ego's other, individual side. For the persona is formed by the ego's repressing into the dark unconscious certain of its once-known traits that are not directly acceptable to society. These individualizing attributes then form what Jung identifies as the *shadow*, which constantly and sometimes ruthlessly seeks the light of consciousness and reconciliation with the persona. In being assimilated by the collective mask, the shadow qualifies the persona and thus prevents the individual from becoming the anonymous mass-man Basil is during his fervent acting in the role of the perfect, ultra-virtuous man.

Being the inner side of the ego, the shadow also points the ego towards the even darker and less accessible realm of the Self. But if the individual is to make contact with the Self, which is always alienated to some degree when consciousness appears, this God within must provide the opportunity by trying to make the ego aware of one or another of its dimensions which Jung has labeled the archetypes. As functions of the Self, the archetypes provide the ego with the universal patterns of growth, spontaneously emerging whenever the person's conscious orientation needs to be "corrected" or compensated, not by some repressed individual trait (the shadow) and not by the societal image of the Self but rather by the Self *per se*. One of these archetypes, the *anima* or eternal feminine, arises in a male from his transpersonal center whenever he is obsessed with professing the masculine traits of logical planning, impersonality, and engagement with the public realm. She offers him the use of her universal "feminine" attributes of emotionality, irrationality, creativity, and relatedness. Whenever Basil opens to the mysterious beauty of life and the magic of girls, he is being influenced by his inner anima.

In the latter half of a male's life, his anima, because of her quality of relatedness, can also lead him to the Self from which she issued. Basil's adolescent chronology, therefore, reflects primarily the first phase of individuation, which involves the inflationary act of separating his ego from the Self, developing personae to adapt to society, recognizing his shadow, and becoming dimly aware of his contrasexual nature or anima. But Basil by no means follows this multi-faceted course of growth with ease and uninterrupted progress. His continual backslidings and failures to understand what is happening to him make the way of individuation for him (as for everyone else) a long and arduous road whose end is rarely seen.

2.

Basil's first task is to dissociate from unconscious identification with the Self. Because the Self must be experienced to be distinguished from the ego but cannot be truly confronted as the Other except by a fully developed consciousness, the God within a dimly conscious child is sensed indirectly by its being unconsciously projected onto somebody in the external world who seems to embody or mirror the Self as the source of wholeness, generative energy, direction, and nurturing. As Jung points out, "Projections change the world into the replica of one's unknown face."[9] The central and first embodiment or symbol of the Self is the mother: "in the primary relationship the mother as the directing, protecting, and nourishing source represents the unconscious and, in the first phase, also the Self and . . . the dependent child represents the childish ego and consciousness."[10] As the child rebels against the mother, he simultaneously but unconsciously weakens his fusion with the Self. Although Basil has passed beyond the infantile state at the beginning of his recorded history, he nevertheless never quite escapes being influenced by his mother, whose subtle presence in every story but the last is hovering in the background via either her actual person or a figuration of her motherliness. This influence is all the more encompassing because, with the loss of his father after the first story, Basil has no model to follow in counterpointing what can be maternal suffocation of his ego.

As the embodiment of the directive and protective functions of the Self, Basil's mother warns him about the danger of kissing girls too early, about worrying excessively over the need for long pants, and about coming to bed to get sufficient rest for his activities. Her "deputies" who promote these functions include the mothers who descend upon the infamous kissing party and call their children home from the Whartons' backyard: Mrs. Van Schellinger, who looks for the "proper" companions for her Gladys; and Mrs. Bissel, who oversees youthful escapades from her window.

Reflecting the nurturing dimension of the Self, Mrs. Lee constantly feeds Basil—most of their discussions take place over one or another of the daily meals. According to his mother, unless Basil eats the special dinner she has prepared for his debut as a playwright, he "won't be able to act" (B&J, p. 114), both in the theatrical and existential senses. Feeding her son breakfast is also her way of calming Basil's anxiety over the expected arrival of his long pants. Though Basil resists these ministrations, he also consistently comes home to eat chocolate cake or

---

9. C. G. Jung, *Aion: Researches into the Phenomenology of the Self*, trans. R. F. C. Hull, in Bolligen Series 20 (Princeton, N.J.: Princeton Univ. Press, 1968), p. 9; hereafter cited in the text as AI.

10. Erich Neumann, "The Significance of the Genetic Aspect for Analytical Psychology," *Journal of Analytical Psychology*, 9 (July 1959), 133.

strawberries and drink large quantities of milk. In returning to his mother's influence, especially after abortive attempts to fashion his ego in the world inhabited by Imogene and other girls who like long pants on boys, Basil is unconsciously rejuvenating himself by contact with the Self via his mother; yet he is also endangering the relative autonomy and growth of his ego by passively accepting what is often unreservedly and too easily given to him. Only much later does he discover that "An indulgent mother had given him no habits of work and this was almost beyond the power of anything but life itself to remedy" (B&J, p. 75). At St. Regis, he learns to qualify his passive acceptance of motherly nurturing by *stealing* food from the pantry, a symbol of the mother, and then later *paying* for his meals in New York, albeit with money his mother has sent to him.

Basil is constantly tormented by that period in life "when youth fluctuates hourly between one world and another—pushed ceaselessly forward into unprecedented experiences and vainly trying to struggle back to the days when nothing had to be paid for" (B&J, p. 79). Though he presses his mother for long pants, he wonders once she pays for them whether he will ever be able to jump hydrants again. He also too easily avoids the difficulties of emulating Elwood's prowess with girls, reminding himself of his promise to his mother to be home early, and later watching Elwood and company from a distance, safely situated in a box with the mother-dominated Gladys and her parents. Yet Basil is also capable of contravening his mother's excessive influence by pitting her nurturing against her protecting function; as a child, he asks for more gravy to distract her from his planning an orgy of kissing, and as an adolescent, requests a larger allowance, ostensibly for shoe laces but really for a probably "scandalous" New York show. He also tries to separate from his mother by defying her less threatening substitutes: Irma the maid; Albert Moore, "son of his mother's best friend and thus a likely enemy" (B&J, p. 4); and Carpenter Moore, Albert's crippled brother and avenger as well as the voice of those parents who disapproved of such "disgusting stuff" as kissing.

Mrs. Lee likewise fluctuates between one world in which she inhibits Basil's separation from her and another in which she counsels his departure: "Whenever a new responsibility devolved upon Basil, he was 'a boy almost sixteen,' but when a privilege was in question, he was 'a fifteen-year-old boy'" (B&J, p. 99). If she discourages kissing, she nevertheless first offers to get his party started and then leave; if she thinks it silly that he is frantic about acquiring long pants, she also sends him down to the clothiers after breakfast; if she ignores his need to stay awake to write his play and suggests he come to bed, she nonetheless yields to his desire that she not smile at him when he comes on stage but rather, " 'Just act as if I was anybody else' " (B&J, p. 114). And if she sends a letter to St. Regis inquiring about her son's low grades, she also wants him "to do just as you like" (B&J, p. 69) about leaving that school for one in Europe. Only when Basil is close to going to college does she truly foster his individuality by allowing him to try paying his own way to Yale when the family nears bankruptcy. When an unsaleable property is finally sold, Basil is unfortunately preserved from an important growth experience, yet his mother refuses to bail him out of another predicament with Mrs. Reilly, to whom she asserts, " 'I don't see that it's my affair' " (B&J, p. 163).

What Basil might have become if he had remained identified with his mother and thereby with the Self is revealed in a comparison between him and the homesick, extremely dependent Lewis Crum, whose mother "canonized all his timidities as common sense." When they go away to school, Basil's sense of self is preserved because he "had lived with such intensity on so many stories of boarding-school life that, far from being homesick, he had a glad feeling of recognition and familiarity" (B&J, p. 56). While this life is familiar and therefore not threatening and still protective, Basil moves a step closer toward being on his own.

In contrast, Lewis "had grown entirely dependent on the stimulus of a hearty vital mother, and as he felt her slipping farther and farther away from him, he plunged deeper into misery and homesickness" (B&J, pp. 55–56). Still virtually identified with the Self projected onto his smothering mother, Lewis passively and with dim consciousness experiences his undeveloped ego as being "canonized," as being the center and circumference of the world, as being inflated with the attributes of deity. When faced with deflation and alienation from the Self, Crum flees Basil's challenge of his inhibiting authority. Crum then yearns for his mother to inter his embryonic ego in the paradisal state of original wholeness; in that state there is no conflict with the Self which has no consciousness set against it. To split apart this wholeness would be a crime for Crum, who reacts with disbelief at Basil's intended transgressions against the masters, the surrogates of the mother. As long as Crum does not consciously defy his mother, he can unconsciously experience her authority as his own.

But Crum is partly right: "The acquisition of consciousness is a crime, an act of *hybris* against the powers-that-be; but it is a necessary crime, leading to a necessary alienation from the natural unconscious state of wholeness. . . . in order to emerge at all, the ego is obliged to set itself up against the unconscious out of which it came and assert its relative autonomy by an inflated act" (ED, p. 24). Thus, the original, unconscious passive inflation of the child can be punctured, paradoxically, only by a half-conscious act of *hybris*. But this second "puffing up" has its own dangers, for it is a two-edged sword; on the one hand, a prerequisite for full consciousness and, on the other, a possibly double crime entailing very real punishment. The individual commits one crime in dissolving the original unity; he commits another and worse sin if, being now aware of his ego, he assumes that he alone is the image of God or God Himself, totally commanding the inner and outer worlds.

After losing an argument with his mother over kissing parties, Basil predictably commits his first, explicit inflated act by rightly but impudently questioning the competence of a mother figure, his teacher: " 'There's no use teaching us wrong.' " He is summarily informed that " 'What you think doesn't matter' " (B&J, p. 4) and that his parents will hear of his impertinence. Basil soon recovers an otherwise diminished ego by pummeling the more manageable Albert Moore, who has threatened to snitch to Basil's mother. Later at the kissing party, to keep the light of his consciousness aglow, Basil pushes into a dark closet the mother-obsessed, paralyzed, sightless, and tyrannical Carpenter Moore, another symbol of the unconscious with its crippling potential. While these inflated acts hardly constitute high crime, Basil still feels sinful, having in one day "committed insolence and forgery and assaulted both the crippled and the blind. His punishment obviously was to be in this life" (B&J, p. 14). Deflated by the actual and potential consequences of his assaults, Basil does not dare to assume God-like responsibility for Carpenter's "miraculous recovery" but rather views it somehow as punishment for laying his unsanctified hands on a tabooed object. Yet Basil intuitively senses the developmental value of his inflation when the elusive Dolly Bartlett, who had attended the party and "waited for some male to assert himself," phones this "lone wolf" who "possessed a romantic appeal for her" (B&J, p. 11).

Not all of Basil's assumptions of power can be so easily forgiven or characterized as merely the necessary means of asserting his relative autonomy. At times he appropriates full autonomy, seeking total ascendancy and control over others while failing to realize that "others had wills as strong as his, and more powerful" (B&J, p. 78). When he is thus inflated, he fails to use the individuation principle of combining the opposites of being an individual and being part of a group; he wants to be the only individual, with others being merely derivations or pale, inferior reflections of himself. But to be *united* to others, he must respect and nurture their otherness. Failing to see this, he watches the night fair with Gladys from her parents' box, where he is soon inflated with "a new wave of virtue" (B&J, p. 53) inspiring him condescendingly to repudiate Ripley's amorous adventures. Yet he quickly feels shameful and tries to discourage Mrs. Van Schellinger from "snitching" to Ripley's mother. As he grows older, however, Basil finds it increasingly difficult to deflate himself; for "fifteen years of thorough spoiling at home" had made him grow uselessly introspective [egocentric], and this interfered with that observation of others which is the beginning of wisdom" (B&J, p. 78). His mother's spoiling of him was calculated to keep him attached to her; yet he augments her inflation of him ultimately to rebel against her and the St. Regis population. While escaping the bounds of St. Regis, he simultaneously binds and confines others, only to earn the epithet "Bossy."

Basil's inflationary status as a bossy bad boy persists because he has long depended upon it to assert his selfhood. As a child he organizes a "gang" to, among other enterprises, waylay Hubert Blair and defy his parents. When the attack proves abortive and Hubert and his unknown enemies tell about his adventure, Basil and his gang talk "themselves into a state of considerable panic" (B&J, p. 34), believing that real kidnappers are in the vicinity. This is an example of how an inflationary role becomes bigger than life, frightening even its creator. Later at St. Regis, Basil in the bad boy role is accused of sins he has not committed and serves as the collective scapegoat, "The sponge which . . . seems to absorb all the others' fear" (B&J, p. 61). The sin of inflating one role at the expense of other traits is often punished by losing one's real face to a mask, by becoming merely an agent of a universal function. The inflationary role that was geared to create individuality becomes, if carried too far, the means of obliterating that identity.

While the bad boy role ostracizes Basil from most of society, it also serves to connect him with a small section of society, that is, with his band of fellow conspirators. When this use of the role is emphasized, Basil can be seen as creating one of his first personae or social masks that may help him to interact with others. But this persona is abortive because with its controlling quality it frustrates true relationship with others, and because it ignores the ideals of the larger society. Once Basil feels himself to be a pariah, he seeks to be nurtured by the societal reflection of the Self by adopting a mask more in keeping with collective norms. Fearing "being disqualified from achievement and power" (B&J, p. 125), he feels the need to make concessions to his status as part of a group. This need is reflected, for instance, in the way he and his gang, ensconced in their private and beloved clubhouse, struggle with the fact that the "centre of the world had shifted suddenly from the secret room to the little group outside" (B&J, p. 19), comprising Imogene Bissel and company.

Since the persona is "a compromise between individual and society as to what a man should appear to be,"[11] bad boy Basil listens with awe to John Granby, the voice of the perfect society, who evokes Basil's " 'power of influencing all these boys to lead clean, upright, decent lives' "(B&J, p. 123). Yet Granby qualifies his injunctions to Basil when he notes twice that every sin is " 'a little bit your responsibility' " (B&J, p. 124). In his subsequent moralizings to his "inferiors," including George and Jobena Dorsey, Basil magnifies "little bit" to "totally" and thus becomes unreal, inhumanly smiling benignly all of the time. Once again Basil inflates himself, this time with the more evident and thorough social role of the perfect man who tries to dissuade George and Jobena from the kissing and dancing he has forsworn. He thereby makes them into images of his own Godlikeness, fostered this time by society. As he represses his unacceptable rebellious role, his perfect persona hardens around him, making him into the typical " 'nasty little prig' " (B&J, p. 136). He becomes "a sort of counterfeit young man" (B&J, p. 79), a " 'boy in a false face' " (B&J, p. 27). Since he has surrendered his true sense of self that is nourished by an awareness of his capacity for evil, he can only feign individuality. He has failed to create a healthy persona which sanctions individuality when it can be used and withdrawn as a comprehensive examination of the situation directs.

During his youth, Basil assumes other personae, usually made manifest by clothing or physical mannerisms. We can see him frantically combing his hair and putting on a clean shirt of Joe's to prepare for a grand entrance at the kissing party. We see him donning "his favorite clothes—white duck knickerbockers, pepper-and-salt Norfolk jacket, a Belmont collar and a gray knitted tie" (B&J, p. 22)—to make still another flashy impression. And we see him proudly wearing a new suit of overalls for his "position with the railroad" (B&J, p. 179), only to have them stolen soon after he is fired. While these and other personae can hide the other, individualizing face of the ego, they can also help make him conscious of his true self by their ill-fitting nature. Without long pants, Basil "was cut off from his contemporaries, laughed at by a boy whom he had hitherto led" (B&J, p. 43); yet he rapidly perceived in his frustration with girls that the trousers cannot of themselves make

11. C. G. Jung, *Two Essays on Analytical Psychology,* in *The Collected Works of C. G. Jung,* ed. Sir Herbert Read et al., trans. R. F. C. Hull (Princeton, N.J.: Princeton Univ. Press, 1976), 7, p. 158; hereafter cited in the text as AP.

him a man. Later, enraptured by the universally admiring acceptance of Joe Gorman's singing, Basil "nourished a vague idea that if he got to know Joe Gorman very well he would get to sing like him" (B&J, p. 83); but it is a vague hope because Basil is lamentably aware that he himself "could not sing" " 'so people could stand it' " (B&J, p. 81). Basil likewise "wanted to learn from Hubert some of the graceful mannerisms that his contemporaries found so dazzling" (B&J, p. 34), and thus wears his hat in Hubert's jaunty manner and chuckles inanely like this versatile ham. Fortunately, Basil shortly abandons this inhibiting mask when he realizes that his friends "would never look at him as they had looked at Hubert" (B&J, p.35).

Basil's preoccupation with dressing for his parts accounts for his fascination with stage productions and actors and for his hidden collection of costumes and make-up, "all to be used when they decided what illegal enterprises to undertake" (B&J, p. 18). When Basil and his cronies costume themselves to waylay Hubert, their apparel constitutes personae which disguise and even repress their true intentions, for every persona is built up by shadowing certain once-conscious, individualizing traits unacceptable to a particular environment but necessary to the person's sense of wholeness. Unless these darker aspects that form the person's shadow reach the light of consciousness again, they will at least temporarily suffer the fate of the recorded misdeeds of Elmwood Leaming, which Basil, desiring but fearing to emulate them, notates with invisible ink in the Book of Scandal. Since these nefarious but growth-producing acts are imperceptible, they "were definitely entombed at last beneath a fair copy of Lincoln's Gettysburg Address" (B&J, p. 17), a symbol here of a stultifying persona. If the persona truly attempts interment of the shadow, the shadow will gain in force like steam in a sealed pressure cooker and eventually erupt violently, as does Mr. Rooney's when that moralist explodes into hedonism while in New York.

In a well-adapted individual, one's flexible, permeable persona mediates between one's shadow and the outside world, while the shadow, on the one hand, individualizes the persona and, on the other, helps to lead the outer-directed ego back to the inner depths, where it will hopefully one day directly meet the Self. In such an individual, sets of opposites (persona and shadow, individual and Self, individual and society, inner and outer worlds, etc.) are being continually recognized, and the components of each set are being differentiated and then united. "No adaptation," says Jung, "can result without concessions to both worlds," without "a union of opposites through the middle path" (AP, p. 205). When he is intellectually fashioning his perfect persona, Basil seems to make such concessions: "To be both light and dark. To harmonize this, to melt all this down into a single man—ah, there was something to be done" (B&J, p. 125). But when Basil then shadows and even tries to obliterate his fervent desire to kiss girls, he forgets that "the point is not conversion into the opposite, but conservation of previous values together with recognition of their opposites" (AP, p. 76).

For the shadow to be reconciled with the persona, this repressed dimension must be recognized. But, like the unconscious Self which cannot at first be directly faced, the shadow is often initially encountered indirectly through its projection upon someone whose behavior to some degree mirrors the projected quality. Since the individual, declares Jung, experiences his shadow always in a person of the same sex, Basil's benighted dimensions are cast onto a host of males who serve as his alter egos. But as long as Basil refuses to understand that what he sees in others is frequently, and to a large degree, also within himself, he will not be able to make use of his repressed qualities nor see others as they really are.

When he beats on Albert and Carpenter Moore, Basil is not only asserting his ego against agents of the mother but also trying *not* to face his own capacity for snitching and being inflated with the potentially crippling prerogatives of the Self. In Basil's view, these capacities are not in him but only in these brothers. He wants to spank the authoritative, demanding little boy at St. Regis but fails to see mirrored in the child his own unacknowledged bossiness. Yet the projected shadow is not always a negative attribute; when we are not living up to our potential, we unconsciously seek our positive dimensions in the other. "And then we admire him, love him, perhaps envy him or possibly hate him for having what we have not got."[12] "The person who carries the projection will seem to us to be 'always right,' able to do easily and well things that are difficult for us" (EH, p. 79). This description certainly characterizes several males as Basil sees them, such as Hubert Blair, "uninhibited by doubts or moods" (B&J, p. 23); Elwood Leaming, the "man of the world" (B&J, p. 38); Andy Lockhart, the "living symbol of the splendid, glamorous world of Yale" (B&J, p. 106); Ted Fay, "a legend, a sign in the sky" (B&J, p. 70); and John Granby, who easily "took the burdens of others upon his shoulders" (B&J, p. 124). When Basil cannot recognize even his bright projections, he either distances their carriers even further, as when he literally backs out of Elwood's group; or hates them, as when he plans to dump Hubert into

12. Esther Harding, *The 'I' and the Not-'I'* (Princeton, N.J.: Princeton Univ. Press, 1965), p. 75; hereafter cited in the text as EH.

a garbage can, "symbol of all that was repulsive" (B&J, p. 28); or copies them, as when he imitates the mannerisms of others instead of activating his own resources.

Occasionally, Basil half-consciously perceives that he is projecting. As he listens to a painful conversation between the apotheosized Ted Fay and a woman, Basil observes that Ted is not all Basil imaged him to be and that, consequently, he himself is not so distant from what Ted represents. Depressed by his constant struggling with his life, Basil now "gathered that life for everybody was a struggle, sometimes magnificent from a distance, but always difficult and surprisingly simple and a little sad" (B&J, p. 74). Like the stage curtain at the theatre where he sees Ted, Basil's image of him has "a curious sacredness, a prototype of the thing itself." When the projection and the curtain are lifted, they both become "waste paper to be dropped carelessly to the floor" (B&J, p. 70). By typing Ted with his projection, Basil had drawn a curtain between them which did not allow him to see the real Ted Fay, whom he resembles more than he had thought. Yet while Basil perceives that his projection of perfection does not quite fit Ted, he does not fully recall the image, for he still wants to resemble the man, even in his somewhat diminished state. Basil fares better when he makes the "startling discovery" that "he liked Hubert Blair" (B&J, p. 29), whom he had hitherto hated as another carrier of his bright shadow. Though he then tries to ape Hubert, Basil finally discerns that he can develop his own virtuosity in staging a play that to be successful does not require, as he once had thought, Hubert's participation.

This play, significantly titled *The Captured Shadow*, is largely a projection into the outer world of an unconscious drama produced within Basil's psyche. What goes on in the play, especially with regard to the male lead, is what Basil must consciously see as happening within him; his shadow must be captured and harmonized with the light of his persona. Projections are unhealthy only when they are *not* eventually recognized as such; as they give shape and illumination to what has been hidden in darkness, they create the opportunity for the individual to see himself from the outside, to say, "That figure is in a way really a part of me." This playwrighting exercise allows Basil later to project another drama in which a male figure, whom he immediately recognizes as himself, wants to hurt Jobena under the guise of protecting her (B&J, p. 138). Acquainted thus with his shadow, Basil tries to find another, less pejorative, way of helping her.

In conceiving *The Captured Shadow*, Basil half consciously brings his shadow into the light. While he has long cast his bright shadow of creativity onto the authors of the New York "crook comedies," he nevertheless retrieves his projection somewhat and resurrects his own creativity so that his play is not a mere imitation of those he loves. Furthermore, although he finds that his powers work most effectively when he is alone at night, he fears going crazy in the darkness and desires his play to see the light of day and be fully realized on stage with the help of his friends. And in refusing to harden in his persona of being " 'the best actor' " (B&J, p. 105), Basil gives up the male lead to one of his friends and brings back to the light his ability to "coach," discarded long ago when he had decided always to be in the limelight.

But it is in creating the figure of "the masked but well-groomed man in the dress suit and opera hat" (B&J, p. 54) that Basil comes closest to seeing what he must become to progress along the path of individuation. This character is the Shadow, otherwise known as the gentleman burglar. While this figure is modeled after the fictional Arsène Lupin, he is also the embodiment of Basil's hidden, more nearly complete self: " 'I am none other than that elusive gentleman, Basil Lee, better known as the Shadow' " (B&J, p. 55). Unlike Mr. Washington Square in another play Basil does not finish, the Shadow makes concessions to both the chthonic, essentially subversive region and the bright, clothes-conscious, socially appeasing sphere of the gentleman persona. Admired but feared by others, the Shadow seeks the light and assimilation into society; in short, he desires to be "a captured shadow."

Yet his allegiance to both worlds is probably a temporary one; for the Shadow is "really a young man about town doing it on a bet, and not really a burglar at all" (B&J, p. 105). This unfortunate conversion of one opposite into another, this failure to keep the values of both worlds at least relatively present presages Basil's own similar problem at the end of the performance. Applauded by one and all, Basil nonetheless "felt a great vacancy come into his heart" (B&J, p. 119); for he distances from his peers, his mother, and himself the dark knowledge of how he caused Evelyn Beebe's brother to contract the mumps in order to keep her in town and available for the female lead. He simply casts away his own shadowy selfish dimension onto others, lamenting that " 'nobody really cares . . . about anything' " (B&J, p. 120). Thus he alienates both a part of himself and a supportive society.

Even if Basil had fully recovered his shadow, he would have moved only a short way towards the ultimate goal of individuation: reconciliation with his deepest life, with the God within. He must be touched by an emissary or archetype of the Self. One of these archetypes, the anima, is the first to emerge in a male, arising to compensate his overly masculine orientation to life with the qualities of the eternal feminine dimension of the Self. Like all unconscious contents, the anima is usually not encountered at first directly as coming from within the male but rather indirectly as influencing him from without through projection upon a woman. These anima projections are harder to dissolve than those of the shadow because, unlike the contents of the shadow which are first known and then made unconscious, the anima is in the unconscious from the beginning of life. Hence, she is more alien and less accessible to the ego than the shadow; a male is more likely to recognize his shadowy masculine traits in another man than to see his own greatly more foreign contrasexual nature mirrored in a woman. Thus, anima projections are more resistant to dissolution and are shifted from one woman to another for a very long time.

According to Jung, "The first bearer of the [man's] soul-image [anima] is always the mother" (AP, p. 197). As previously noted, Basil's mother serves as a symbol or mirror of the total Self within him; however, she is especially reflective of the anima, the feminine aspect of his internal God, as she nurtures and consoles him. But as Basil grows older, he and his mother dimly realize that she is only an *image* of the Self's feminine side, which he needs to relate to directly. When he cannot allow her to comfort him after the play, she intuits his need to be touched by the Self and prays, " 'God, help him! help him . . . because he needs help that I can't give him any more' " (B&J, p. 120).

Though he gradually breaks away from his mother's influence, he merely shifts his projection of his anima from her to other females. His consequent failure to recognize his contrasexual dimension prompts his anima to take revenge by feminizing him, making him a sissy in football play, despite his wish to preserve his masculine persona. His repeated, painful analyses of himself are also caused by the ignored anima, the source of "bad mood, affects, phobias, obsessive ideas, backslidings, etc." (AP, p. 194). Denied her offer to serve him, Basil's anima activates her other, negative side until he acknowledges her.

Such acknowledgment is long in coming. Whenever Basil is overly occupied with "masculine activities" such as managing his gang, manipulating the arrival of his long pants, and trying to fit into one or another societal niche, he is usually sidetracked by irrepressible emotion and sensitivity which he experiences as inspired *not* by his deepest self but rather wholly by the girl before him: "warm freshets sprang up in his blood and he turned them, and with them his whole life, like a stream toward this girl" (B&J, p. 21). He must "perversely linger near" (B&J, p. 24) each girl because he is unconsciously and vainly seeking a part of himself in every one. As Jung points out, "Whenever an impassioned, almost magical, relationship exists between the sexes, it is invariably a question of a projected soul-image [anima]" (PT, p. 471).

Such a relationship exists, at least in Basil's eyes, between him and his first would-be girlfriend. Enrapturing to him, Dolly Bartlett "was not anyone he knew, certainly not the girl about whom he put his arms a week ago. He stared at her as at a spectre" (B&J, p. 8). As a figuration of his archetypal female soul that comes to soothe him after the kissing party debacle, Dolly is not to him, as she seems to "cooler observers," a particular little girl but rather "the essence of time and weather," of "elation," summer mystery, and inspiring music—in short, of all creation.

He later similarly endows Imogene Bissel "heavily from his fancy" (B&J, p. 24), as all the beauty of life and emotion "went into Imogene's face as she sat there looking up at him with a smile." Through Basil's encounter with her, "For the first time in his life he realized a girl completely as something opposite and complementary to him, and he was subject to a warm chill of mingled pleasure and pain." Though he now recognizes that there is a feminine element in life that can draw him out of his males-only clubhouse, he feels it only as an external presence: "the spell of her vitality crept over him suddenly" (B&J, p. 20). Only when Hubert and Imogene walk together away from him does Basil feel momentarily the beauty of life apart from her during a storm: "Imogene was gone. . . . A sense of extraordinary power welled up in him, until to leave the ground permanently with one of his wild leaps would not have surprised him." Yet it is doubtful that he is aware of being touched by his inner anima; for the source of his response may seem to him to be the feminine night and storm: "the change of weather had swept over his heart" (B&J, p. 26). In any case, he soon forgets Imogene and the moment in the storm as he engages once more in the "masculine" activity of managing his gang. After a week, "he saw only the familiar little girl he had always known" (B&J, p. 35). Basil does not here consciously withdraw his projection from Imogene; it simply drops because he is not ready to deal at length with his feminine side even in projection: "For a moment it was too much for him. He let it go . . ." (B&J, p. 20). "The ecstatic moment of that afternoon had been a premature birth" (B&J, p. 35); for at this point in his life, Basil's anima is not needed to correct an *overly* masculine conscious attitude— he is only beginning to manipulate his environment.

As he grows older, he continues unconsciously to seek the eternal feminine in women like Evelyn Beebe, who helped to inspire his creation of the play and in particular its female lead. Unlike the tomboy Margaret Torrence, "who had no terrors for . . .[Basil], and no charm" (B&J, p. 9), Evelyn is mysterious, emotional, unpredictable, and very disconcerting—a typical anima carrier. Chosen instead of Margaret for the feminine lead, Evelyn "compelled a breathless attention, and Basil recognized this by adding to her part" (B&J, p. 110) in his inner and outer drama. But he soon realizes that she is not what he is looking for, since "He could never please her"; "and from that moment, because they had no common ground even to quarrel on, they were friends for life" (B&J, p. 118). As the projection is dropped, Basil can relate to her as she really is.

Yet a few years later he once again unconsciously looks for his anima outside himself, this time in Jobena Dorsey, the first woman consciously to reject his anima projection. Though she has a penchant for "big sins," Basil nevertheless sees her as "the ideal girl that he would some day marry" (B&J, p. 135). But Jobena is disgusted by his perfect image of her, which hardly fits her sense of herself. When he overhears her mockery of his view of her, Basil begins to see her true nature and responds to it by boldly shutting off the light and kissing her. Jobena later helps him retrieve still another of his anima projections, this time from Minnie Bibble, the most significant of the anima women Basil encounters.

When he is with Minnie, he pieces "together all the shreds of romance" he knows to make a psychic garment for this figure who held "the promise that she could lead him into a world in which he would always be happy" (B&J, p. 160), a world he identifies at first with the external one of pomp and glory. Minnie is not like Dolly or Imogene, who are hardly conscious of their attractiveness to men and therefore cannot help them take back their projected dimensions; Minnie is all too aware of the control she has over Basil and others who have unwittingly surrendered a part of themselves to her. Unlike Jobena, who wants to appear as she really is and thus refuses Basil's projection, Minnie lures him into glorifying her so she may take advantage of him. Refusing to return to him what (his anima) is not hers to keep, "she alternately drew him toward her in her mind and let him go," but not too far. Though "so many men . . . wanted her so much" (B&J, p. 173), she must assure herself of Basil's being available when no one else is.

Like all anima women, Minnie does, at least inadvertently, furnish Basil with the positive chance to see his deeper soul mirrored in her. Through his anima projections, especially the one involving Minnie, Basil also moves out into the world to engage with women and so enlarges his experience: "It was written that in passage she would come to Basil as a sort of initiation, turning his eyes out from himself and giving him a first dazzling glimpse into the world of love" (B&J, p. 92). But Minnie's positive qualities as an anima woman are not consciously developed by her and are undercut by her negative dimension, by her refusal to let him finally realize that she is not the Goddess he myopically sees. Thinking that he is in control of himself, he is shattered when told that "she staged the whole thing from the beginning, even when you thought it was you" (B&J, p. 182). Basil is nevertheless partly to blame for his predicament, for he is "entirely unconscious" of her obvious habit of falling in love with the next man along, and feels, almost inexcusably at this time in his life, that he is "too small and impotent to seize the felicity he desired," ashamed as he is to inflict his "merely mortal presence on her" (B&J, p. 170).

But the day after this negative musing, he meets her "in a world that had shrunk back to reality, [where] things were more natural, but something was gone" (B&J, p. 170). And though he continues to tell himself and Minnie that all his accomplishments are " 'all for you' " (B&J, p. 175) instead of himself, he has a glimpse during football practice of the anima within him: "The quality of romantic speculation reawoke, and, listlessly at first, then with growing determination, he set about merging himself into this spirit which had fed his dreams so long" (B&J, p. 176). Scarcely brooding about her at all, he plays a brilliant, courageous game against the Princeton freshmen. Engaged in a public game requiring the use of his masculine faculties, Basil, "with his heart in a riot," is also inspired by his emotional anima; strangely, "it was someone else in his skin who called the first signals" (B&J, p. 178) and soothed his masculinity when he botched plays.

At a victory dance attended by Minnie, Basil asks Jobena Dorsey to help him disengage from his returned obsession with Minnie. She counsels him to show Minnie that he doesn't desire her so much, that " 'you don't care' " (B&J, p. 182). Basil had marshaled this indifference, which he had always admired in Hubert, only by accident a year earlier when he had attracted Minnie by having to ignore her to discharge his "duty" to his cousin. However, Basil can avoid "playing" at being indifferent only if he can stop his often frantic pursuit of Minnie by finding in himself what he seeks in her, by ceasing to see himself as a "lay figure" (B&J, p. 184) paling beside her sacred presence. It is only when he sees his possible future self in the lovesick, thoroughly Minnie-manipulated Littleboy Le Moyne that he can escape with his pride, strip Minnie of his projection, and see with the "practiced eye of the commander" that one star was "no longer there" (B&J, p. 185) in his starry sky, which continues to shine with unabated brilliance.

Despite this conscious dissolution of his anima projection onto Minnie, Basil will undoubtedly fail again and again to retain his new knowledge of his contrasexual nature. If, as Fitzgerald had tentatively planned, Basil was one day to encounter Josephine, the heroine of the companion stories, he might all too easily seek his feminine aspect in this extremely enticing and powerful negative anima figure. For at the end of his adolescent history, Basil is still experiencing considerable difficulty distinguishing his feminine dimension from his masculinity and then reconciling these complementary traits. His problem here is exacerbated by the fact that he has not been able to deal adequately with any set of psychic opposites; he has repeatedly failed to find the most healthy relationship between his individuality and his collective nature, between identification with his mother (and thereby with the Self) and alienation from her, between his ego inflation and deflation, and between his various personae and his shadow. Unless he can learn to accept all his dimensions, Basil will abort his individuation process and stagnate in a largely unconscious way of life.

3.

In any case, the "good material" Fitzgerald felt he had used in the Basil stories—which intervened between *Gatsby* and *Tender*—seems to have widened his understanding about crises of awareness in early youth and adolescence; these crises, if not properly resolved, could lead to a demise like that of Dick Diver or Jay Gatsby. Fitzgerald's growing sense of the predetermining nature of an individual's youth was evident in a peripheral way in the sixth chapter of *Gatsby*, which records James Gatz's meeting with the romantic Dan Cody, and in the concluding pages where Gatsby's father shows Nick the schedule for personal expansion which "Jimmy" had printed in his childhood copy of *Hopalong Cassidy*.

The Jay Gatsby who would come to believe, in his "overwhelming self-absorption," that "he was a son of God" had early on imagined and inflated himself, aided by his disciplined care of body and mind, with the attributes of the heroic, even Christ-like "Hoppy"—another "son of God" going "about His Father's business" (GG, p. 99) of righting wrongs done to ladies-in-distress like Daisy. Thus in Jungian terms, Gatsby, like Basil, later failed to distinguish himself both from the Divine and the material worlds which his "single dream" (GG, p. 162) had appropriated as his own. But, again like Basil, he ignored the relevance to his own life of what the figures of Hoppy and Cody—a modern analogue of Buffalo Bill Cody—might well have alerted him to: Hoppy as a glamorous figure dressed in *black* and riding a *white* horse and Cody as a "pioneer debauchee" (GG, p. 101) demonstrated that images of heroic or divine innocence and splendor seem inseparable from a dark aspect, and also that a persona always implies its inescapable, shadowy, and often repressed counterpart.

As a seventeen-year-old, Gatsby thus became a chaste teetotaler and later as an adult covered up his criminal activities with his pursuit of what was thereby a meretricious beauty found ultimately in Daisy. When as a young man he had first lost Daisy to Tom, Gatsby might thereby have recognized his human limitations and then sought to unite, rather than fuse with, an image of *inner* beauty—his anima—and one which, unlike Daisy, he could perceive immediately as *both* "light and dark." But his obsessive search outwardly for "some idea of himself . . . that had gone into loving Daisy" (GG, p. 111) kept him from embracing dimensions of his psyche that thus became destructive. Accordingly, when he loses Daisy a second time, he is destroyed in part by seeing through the beauty to "what a grotesque thing a rose is" and in part by "that ashen, fantastic figure gliding toward him through the amorphous trees" (GG, p. 162)—by Wilson, that image of the hidden Gatsby, the "proprietor" of a "road-house" (GG, p. 64).

Gatsby might well have avoided such a fate if he had adequately resolved the Basil–like crises of his youth. Ending *Gatsby* by directing the reader's attention to Jimmy's early years may have prompted Fitzgerald to look more closely into the psychology of youth before he could move on to complete with more subtlety and complication the story of Dick Diver. In *Tender*, little information is provided about Dick's childhood, yet it seems likely that in the little that is given, Fitzgerald had in mind once again the predetermining nature of early failures to differentiate one's individual self from the world and representatives of God, and to embrace the polarities of being. Two-thirds of the way through the novel, Dick's early posture as "all complete there" (TITN, p. 19), as "Lucky Dick" (TITN p. 116), as in short, a God-like figure of grace and discipline, has nearly shattered; after trying vainly to restore Nicole's innocence, he has attempted to recoup the consequent loss of his own image as savior by seeking in Rosemary's innocence that lost "idea of himself." He has ignored the darker, castrating aspects of both women and thus, even if he has tried to unite with his own inner feminine image, he has failed to see its dual nature. Moreover, because he has adopted the fairly rigid persona of the pure hero and savior, he has repressed, unlike Abe North and Tommy Barban, the undisciplined and instinctual aspects of his maleness.

At this point in the novel, his father dies and Dick recalls their early alliance. Dick had apparently fused with the image of his God-like father dressed in "beautifully cut clerical clothes. . . . He told Dick all he knew about life". . . (TITN, p. 203). The son had tried to act as his father might have, "from a good heart" with the " 'good instincts,' honor, courtesy, and courage" (TITN, p. 204); yet "not much but most" of what the clergyman told Dick were "true, simple things" that the man had derived from a limited range of experience (TITN, p. 203). Moreover, the father was " 'very much the gentleman, but not much get-up-and-go' " (TITN, p. 204). Thus, Dick had not only fused with a God-like figure but had also seen himself and his father as one-dimensional, as devoid of polarities, an action and perspective that determined his later demise.

4.

No doubt, Fitzgerald would not have used the terminology presented here to explain the process of early crises of awareness. Still, because so much of what Basil experiences is made coherent by Jung's conceptions, Fitzgerald's intuitive perception of the psychology of youth could not have been alien to Jung's.[13] Thus, if through the Basil stories Fitzgerald had indeed uncovered, with both empathy and critical detachment, the sources of potential adult horrors, then his return to the experiences of his youth was not an escape to the past from a difficult present; it was rather a movement back to the place where he had started in order to know it for the first time and thus perhaps to understand, if not change, the present and future of his characters and himself.

13. It is interesting to note that two of the settings of *Tender* are Vienna and Zurich, home bases for Freud and Jung, respectively. Both men are mentioned in the text; Jung, for instance, is called "the great Jung" (TITN, p. 195).

FITZGERALD'S SHORT STORIES AND THE DEPRESSION: AN ARTISTIC CRISIS

RUTH PRIGOZY

For the nation and for the majority of Americans, the year 1929 inaugurated a decade of struggle and despair. Among the many personal histories of suffering and tragedy that emerge out of the Depression years, few seem etched in more relentless misery than that of F. Scott Fitzgerald. At the top of the page in his *Ledger* devoted to the events of 1929, Fitzgerald wrote, "The Crash! Zelda and America!" (*Ledger*, p. 184). And indeed, from 1929 until his death in 1940, Fitzgerald's life seemed a peculiarly sensitive reflector of American society. The parallels between his life and American history continued with the national recovery and the author's artistic renewal, but Fitzgerald's physical resources were depleted and he died with his new novel incomplete and his fame far in the future.

Yet during the worst years of the Depression, despite personal anguish and insistent financial worries, Fitzgerald kept writing short stories and essays to support himself, his institutionalized wife, and his daughter, and to stave off bankruptcy. In the period from 1929 through 1935, when he was generally regarded as at his lowest creative ebb, he produced the novel many now acclaim as his greatest, *Tender Is the Night*, over forty short stories—two of which are acknowledged masterpieces—and several essays equal in quality to "The Crack-Up," which was hailed by many of Fitzgerald's contemporaries as signaling the return of his powers. To one biographer, they were "so different from the tired magazine stories he had been turning out, that it seems incredible they were written by the same person."[1]

Fitzgerald was the same person, but as a writer he was very different; he had emerged from six years of struggle, having faced a crisis that was at once personal, national, and artistic. In these years Fitzgerald's *Ledger* alternates notations of Zelda's periods of mental illness with statements about the progress of his short stories and his desperation at being unable to work on his novel. Personal and artistic concerns collided with traumatic severity in 1932 when Zelda collapsed, to be institutionalized for the second time, and in her novel, *Save Me the Waltz*, launched a thinly veiled, autobiographical literary attack on her husband, using the same materials he had been working into his own novel. At the same time, the national Depression worsened, a sense of economic desperation overtook even the equanimity of Maxwell Perkins, and Fitzgerald's drinking intensified. In November, 1932, he noted his "political worries, almost neuroses," and in December remarked, "Drinking increased. . . . Things go not so well." At the top of the page, as if to sum up 1932, he commented, "A strange year of work and drink. Increasingly unhappy—Zelda up and down. First draft of novel complete. Ominous" (*Ledger*, p. 187).

Small wonder that he had lost his taste for writing the stories of young love which had brought him to the top of the magazine pay-scale by 1929. His mind and spirit were occupied by other concerns, for as he said some years later, "I not only announced the birth of my young illusions in *This Side of Paradise*, but pretty much the death of them in some of my last Post stories like 'Babylon Revisited.' Lorimer seemed to understand this. . . . Nevertheless, an overwhelming number of editors continue to associate me with an absorbing interest in young girls. . . . So you see I've made a sort of turn" (*Letters*, p. 588). That turn was apparent by 1936, but the preceding six years, Fitzgerald's middle years artistically, were a time of trial and error, of struggle for the new style and new fictional forms that could accommodate the emotions, the needs, the ideas of a mature man and a tragic life.

Of the forty-two stories written during these six years, eight are part of two series devoted to Basil Duke Lee and Josephine Perry, drawing on autobiographical events and cultural attitudes that reflect the years from World War I through the 1920s. Five of the remaining stories are so trivial as to demand nothing but wonder that they managed to find

1. Henry Dan Piper, *F. Scott Fitzgerald: A Critical Portrait* (New York: Holt, Rinehart and Winston, 1965), p. 14.

their way into print.[2] With the publication of *The Price Was High* in 1979, all twenty-nine stories with which we are concerned here have been collected. They provide an important insight into Fitzgerald's artistic crisis when his subjects were as serious as his and the nation's trials demanded, but his plots were outworn, stale, mechanical—unintentional parodies of the exuberant accounts of young love and romantic longing that so captivated audiences during the boom years. These stories show Fitzgerald groping with painful subjects and achieving only intermittent success but on at least two occasions, with "Babylon Revisited" (1931) and "Crazy Sunday" (1932), producing masterpieces that incorporate the matter, if not the manner, of his more commercial contemporary work. In both of these stories, Fitzgerald was able to abandon the contrivances and rhetoric that for more than ten years were his hallmark; his style in both is nuanced and elliptical, the abundant romantic rhetoric singularly—and happily—absent. The following pages will show the nature of Fitzgerald's interests from 1929 through 1935 and his problems with plot and style, which he resolved by 1936 when the strict space regulations of *Esquire* coincided with his own need for a sparer style, thus resulting not only in the short, moving vignettes collected in *Afternoon of an Author* but in the ambitious new novel he was working on at his death.

One of Fitzgerald's most serious subjects was marriage—how two people can live together, retain at least some part of the initial feeling which united them, preserve individual freedom, and in addition communicate with one another when the stresses of daily life place a strain on marital intimacy. (Anyone even vaguely familiar with the Fitzgeralds' marital difficulties can see in the stories the extent to which he drew on his own problems in these years.) Of the five stories from this period dealing with marriage,[3] two are notably stronger than the others ("The Rough Crossing" and "One Trip Abroad") primarily because Fitzgerald was able to keep his focus on one issue—the deterioration of a marriage. Furthermore, he successfully employed one of his favorite techniques from the past, creating settings that function as symbolic reflectors of action. For example, in "The Rough Crossing" (1929), the complete deterioration of Adrian and Eva Smith's marriage is reflected in the gale outside, which grows into a storm that bursts upon the ship with a fury equal to the intensity of Eva's despair. Even more strik-

2. These include "The Passionate Eskimo" (1935), "Zone of Accident" (1935), "The Count of Darkness" (1934), "One Interne" (1932), "Indecision" (1931). They add little to our understanding of his artistic problems during the Depression.

3. "The Rough Crossing" (1929), "One Trip Abroad" (1930), "What a Handsome Pair!" (1932), "Two Wrongs" (1930).

ingly, in "One Trip Abroad" (1930)—from the ominous opening sentence, "In the afternoon the air became black with locusts, and some of the women shrieked, sinking to the floor of the motorbus and covering their hair with travelling rugs" (AA, p. 142), to the climactic storm which "came swiftly, first falling from the heavens and then falling again in torrents from the mountains, washing loudly down the roads and stone ditches. . . . the hotel crouched alone amid tumult and chaos and darkness" (AA, p. 163)—all nature seems to reflect the tumult and disorder of Nelson and Nicole Kelly's life together, suggests in fact a primordial force compelling and eventually engulfing them.

Finally, in these two stories, Fitzgerald retained enough rhetorical fluidity to capture the sense of loss that could always make even his least effort poignant. In "The Rough Crossing," Eva tries desperately to recapture the idyllic early years of marriage:

> There was the little villa in Brittany, the children learning French—that was all she could think of now—the little villa in Brittany, the children learning French—so she repeated the words over and over to herself until they became as meaningless as the wide white sky. The why of their being here had suddenly eluded her; she felt unmotivated, accidental, and she wanted Adrian to come back quick, all responsive and tender, to reassure her. It was in the hope that there was some secret of graceful living, some real compensation for the lost, careless confidence of twenty-one, that they were going to spend a year in France. (*Stories*, p. 261)

In a similar vein, in "One Trip Abroad," Nicole and Nelson make one last and perhaps hopeless effort to dispel the clouds that have darkened their marriage:

> Over the Dent du Midi, over a black bank of clouds that was the rearguard of the receding storm, the moon lifted itself and the lake brightened; the music and the far-away lights were like hope, like the enchanted distance from which children see things. In their separate hearts Nelson and Nicole gazed backward to a time when life was all like this. Her arm went through his quietly and drew him close.
>
> "We can have it all again," she whispered. "Can't we try, Nelson?"
>
> She paused as two dark forms came into the shadows nearby and stood looking down at the lake below.
>
> Nelson put his arm around Nicole and pulled her closer.

"It's just that we don't understand what's the matter," she said. "Why did we lose peace and love and health, one after the other? If we knew, if there was anybody to tell us, I believe we could try. I'd try so hard." (*AA*, p. 164)

None of the stories deal with the earliest years of a marriage. Fitzgerald's couples are past the flush of first love, finding all too frequently that their self-indulgence and superficial values have diminished not only them but their marriages as well. "The Rough Crossing," "One Trip Abroad," and "Two Wrongs" (1930) fall into this pattern. "What a Handsome Pair!" (1932) is a variation on the subject of marital values, competitiveness between partners, and compatibility, but it bogs down hopelessly under the weight of diverging themes: the nature of sportsmanship, the meaning of heroism, and the bases of male-female attraction.

Although perhaps the poorest story in the group, the most illustrative of Fitzgerald's problems is "The Intimate Strangers" (1935), based on an experience in the life of his friend Mrs. Nora Flynn. Perhaps because the narrative is so dull and unexciting, Fitzgerald dotted the tale with romantic clichés. The plot is simply a mass of barely-related details, the characters as wooden as any he had ever drawn, and even the settings—which ordinarily could compensate for a story's defects—are uninteresting. Yet the problem in the story is serious and central not only to Fitzgerald's personal life but to all marriages. Near the end of the story, Sara thinks about her marriage, "trying to accept the fact that a part of Killian and a part of herself would always be strangers. She wondered if that were especially her fate or if it were everyone's fate" (*Price*, p. 626). After an attempt to find a basis for communication in marriage, Fitzgerald implies that there are regions within the individual that should remain inviolate even from one's mate, that nothing destroys a marriage so much as the attempt by one member to enter completely into the other's private, personal world. It is sufficient, Fitzgerald indicates, that we retain the ability to communicate perfectly on even one level, as Killian and Sara do through their music. Sara struggles to draw closer to Killian than music and even sex allow, but he is unwilling to surrender to her the part of himself he regards as having died with his first wife. When Sara sees him at the latter's grave, she realizes that their own marriage can last only if she ceases her efforts to absorb him completely and allows him the freedom he—and by implication everyone—needs for maturity and the growth of responsibility.

In all of these stories, Fitzgerald has left the romantic antics of young lovers far behind and has moved well beyond the concerns of his bright young flappers and philosophers. However, the questions and problems in the stories, although approached seriously and sensitively, achieve genuinely artistic consummation in the novel Fitzgerald was writing at the same time, *Tender Is the Night*, where the Diver marriage serves as a symbolic representation of contemporary dissolution.

In the short stories of the 1930s, Fitzgerald returned to a subject that had always intrigued him but which now seemed tied to his comprehension of the events following the crash of 1929. He had always believed that struggle, particularly for control over oneself and against crushing social humiliation, resulted in heightened awareness, sensitivity, even vitality, and that conversely, easy and early acquisition of happiness and wealth led to passivity, inertia, and deadening satiety. Fitzgerald felt that the 1920s had exacted a national penalty and that those who were able to face the grim reality of their present lives, to retain their capacity to work, and to perform their required tasks professionally (similar to Hemingway's notion of "grace under pressure") would ultimately survive, not only economically but psychically as well. Thus many stories of this period[4] deal with struggle, with responsibility for others, with professionalism, and above all with that elusive trait character, which Charlie Wales ("Babylon Revisited") believed in so utterly: "he wanted to jump back a whole generation and trust in character again as the eternally valuable element. Everything else wore out" (*Stories*, p. 388).

"A New Leaf" (1931) is possibly the most representative of this group. It opens in the typical early Fitzgerald manner: the setting—Bois de Boulogne, an outdoor cafe, romantic music playing softly in the background; a lovely young girl and an adoring young man. Very quickly, however, Fitzgerald shifts the tone of the story as he introduces Dick Ragland, a handsome alcoholic whose past has been notorious for drink, women, jails, scandals, even a hint of manslaughter—a man generally regarded as lazy and worthless. Dick Ragland is a character out of Fitzgerald's middle years; he would not have existed as a romantic interest in a 1920s *Post* story. Like Dick Diver in *Tender Is the Night*, Dick Ragland has the ability to please people, but unlike Diver, Ragland lacks character. Given the opportunity to redeem himself, he fails without the immediate prop of his fiancée's presence. He might be Charlie Wales had Charlie taken the drink at the Ritz bar at the end of

4. Stories in this group include "No Flowers" (1934), "The Bridal Party" (1930), "I Got Shoes" (1933), "Family in the Wind" (1932), "Six of One" (1932).

"Babylon Revisited." "A New Leaf" shows Fitzgerald working with the same ideas but without the plot and language of "Babylon Revisited." Published in the same year, it differs in every way from the latter: the love story is hackneyed, the heroine unbelievable, the other suitor's nobility hollow, and Dick's death at sea—the inevitable plot twist—thoroughly unconvincing. The message, however, is clear—as Charlie Wales knew. Character is everything—and the ultimate sin is waste.

Another major concern in Fitzgerald's short fiction of the early 1930s was the erosion of old values, the gulf that had arisen between the generations during the boom, the new morality which appeared to lack definition or recognizable goals and he felt was reflected in the activities of corrupt and rootless Americans, sycophants of a decadent European aristocracy.[5] "The Hotel Child" (1931) is a satire about a modern Jewish Daisy Miller living in Europe among penniless European nobility, social climbers, and outright swindlers in a succession of luxurious hotels. The story is serious in its intent: an affirmation of American innocence, openness, and enthusiasm, but again it suffers from Fitzgerald's inability to create the plot and characters appropriate to his message.

For Fitzgerald, the lost generation was the one whose members came to maturity during World War I, were caught up in the pleasure-seeking of the 1920s, and merely "struck attitudes remembered from the past" (*Price*, p. 398) with no genuine principles on which to base their lives. "The Family Bus" (1933), with a mechanical wheel-of-fortune plot, derides the incompetent parents of the postwar world who failed to understand their society, their responsibilities, and their obligations as parents. Here Fitzgerald explores the world of established wealth, of the newly rich, and even the alternative of factory work for a young man who has lost his fortune. He criticizes the "thin, dehumanized level" of conversation among the wealthy, but as in so many of his early stories, he allows his young hero to regain his lost wealth in an Alger-like plot twist—to get the girl and, presumably, to live happily ever after.

Many of Fitzgerald's early short stories—even those dating as far back as 1920—explored the nature of unfulfilled lives, of the moment of beauty which passes so quickly that it is over before we realize its value, and the lifelong effort to recapture that evanescent encounter with bliss. Perhaps most touching about those youthful stories is the conjunction of ecstasy and melancholy, the slow drift toward death

5. "On Schedule" (1933), "A Freeze-Out" (1931), "The Family Bus" (1933), "The World's Fair" (posthumous, 1948), "The Hotel Child" (1931).

which begins at the moment we realize that the fleeting golden moment signals our own mortality. Even Fitzgerald's early heroes are filled with regret at opportunities lost, talents untapped, resources squandered. During the Depression years, Fitzgerald rarely touched on this theme,[6] probably because at least in this case he recognized that there was no way in which—even mechanically—he could realize a subject so close to his deepest, most immediate anxieties. Thus, only once does he recall (in "At Your Age" [1929]) in the old familiar style that

> the shop windows, glowing into the cold, the tinkling bells of a delivery sleigh, the white gloss left by shovels on the sidewalks, the enormous distance of the stars, brought back the feel of other nights thirty years ago. For an instant the girls he had known then slipped like phantoms out of their dull matronly selves of today and fluttered past him with frosty, seductive laughter. . . .
> "Youth. . . . I want it near me, all around me, just once more before I'm too old to care." (*Price*, p. 279)

The subjects discussed above are all concerned with human relationships on an intimate, personal level. The problems facing the nation in the Depression, however, stimulated Fitzgerald's use of communal social problems as subjects for fiction. We all know how successful he was as social historian in "Echoes of the Jazz Age" (1931), "My Lost City" (1932), and "My Generation" (published posthumously, 1973).[7] A number of the stories touch on the spectre of poverty, on class differences, on social snobbery, on the lust for money and power, and on the myth of success which took on greater significance than ever as the economic basis of the nation was being tested.[8] Undoubtedly, these are

6. "At Your Age" (1929) and "No Flowers" are two exceptions.

7. Fitzgerald has long been recognized as a brilliant social historian and critic. See histories of the 1920s by Malcolm Cowley, *Exile's Return* (New York: Viking, 1951), Allen Churchill, *The Literary Decade* (Englewood Cliffs, N.J.: Prentice-Hall, 1971), Elizabeth Stevenson, *The American 1920s* (New York: Macmillan, 1970 [published originally as *Babbitts and Bohemians*]), Ethan Mordden, *That Jazz!* (New York: G.P. Putnam's, 1978). Most historians quote Fitzgerald's "Echoes of the Jazz Age," finding in the account of his personal experiences during the decade a portrait of his generation and of American society as a whole. They also refer to his view of himself as "Dick Whittington up from the country" in "My Lost City" (C-U, p. 24) as symbolic of the way the decade and the excitement of New York City affected young men starting out to explore the possibilities of freedom and adventure that the years from 1920 to 1929 seemed to hold.

8. "The Rubber Check" (1932), "Between Three and Four" (1931), "A Change of Class" (1931), "Diagnosis" (1932), "Flight and Pursuit" (1932), "The Family Bus," "More than Just a House" (1933), "No Flowers."

the most interesting stories of the period, not the best necessarily but those which most reveal the direction Fitzgerald's fiction would take in his last years. "The Rubber Check" (1932), filled with the minutiae of class distinctions, provides a searing glimpse of the cruelty of the very rich. "Between Three and Four" (1931) captures the desperation and hopelessness of the city's mood, the "neurosis that gripped the nation":

> This happened nowadays with everyone somewhat discouraged. A lot of less fortunate spirits cracked when money troubles came to be added to all the nervous troubles accumulated in the prosperity—neurosis being a privilege of people with a lot of extra money. And some cracked merely because it was in the air, or because they were used to the great, golden figure of plenty standing behind them. . . . (*Price*, p. 339)

"A Change of Class" (1931), the clearest example of Fitzgerald's attempt to treat the Depression fictionally, takes its main character from 1926 through 1931, from working class to *nouveau riche* to small entrepreneur. There are several brilliant bits of social observation about the homelife of the barber, Earl Johnson, and his wife who "blundered into the Golden Age" on a stock tip, but Fitzgerald buries his astute insights, his extraordinary perception of the manners and morals of shifting social classes, beneath a flat and uninteresting love story, a collection of stereotyped characters, and a sub-plot that incorporates nearly every worn-out trick imaginable.

The accumulated pressures on the economy led Fitzgerald as well as many Americans in the 1930s to see the nation historically, to recover the values upon which the country had been founded, those which its citizens had always cherished—in name if not in deed. For Fitzgerald, the past had always given meaning to the present, but now he turned to it to interpret not merely an individual's life but the national experience as well. In several stories he asked what we were as a nation, what ideals were available in American history which we might rediscover to help carry us through the dark night of the nation's soul.[9] Often—and with usually maudlin or sentimental results—he sends a character back to the South, to find in the remnants (old houses particularly) of a once-flourishing region the traditions that had insured a graceful, stable life.[10] In "Six of One" (1932), the hero bemoans "all that waste at the

9. "New Types" (1934), "Six of One," "The Swimmers" (1929).
10. "Flight and Pursuit," "More than Just a House," "Diagnosis," "No Flowers."

top" of American life, but he has faith that "the republic would survive the mistakes of a whole generation" and regrets that he will not live long enough "to see great seriousness in the same skin with great opportunity—to see the race achieve itself at last" (*Price*, p. 381).

The 1929 story "The Swimmers" was regarded by Harold Ober as "the most thoughtful you have ever done," but to Fitzgerald it was the hardest he had ever written, "too big for its space and not even now satisfactory."[11] Both judgments are accurate. "The Swimmers" raises virtually every question Fitzgerald had ever asked about the relationship between Europe and America, money and power, waste and self-indulgence, character and responsibility, class and caste, incompatibility and adultery; but they are finally all subsumed under one passionate declaration of faith in America:

> . . . that under the ugly débris of industry the rich land still pushed up, incorrigibly lavish and fertile, and that in the heart of the leaderless people the old generosities and devotions fought on, breaking out sometimes in fanaticism and excess, but indomitable and undefeated. There was a lost generation in the saddle at the moment, but it seemed to him that the men coming on, the men of the war, were better; and all his old feeling that America was a bizarre accident, a sort of historical sport, had gone forever. The best of America was the best of the world. (*Bits*, p. 209)

The preceding pages have sought to identify Fitzgerald's interests during six critical years of his life, but the significance of these years of struggle to his artistic development must still be explored. Any reading of the stories I have cited reveals that Fitzgerald had not found a replacement for a love story to serve as the center of a work. He still relied heavily on the plot twist, the sudden reversal of fortune brought about by an external agent. He continued to pad lifeless plots with overblown romantic rhetoric, or by now hackneyed movielike scenic descriptions. And he could not create sympathetic and believable characters, only wooden stereotypes. The most serious problem was that his gift for narrative flow, the perfect distancing of author from subject, had virtually disappeared. In "The Swimmers," Henry Marston tricks his wife and her lover into signing a release for the children and an admission of fraud by telling them their boat is drifting out to sea.

---

11. *As Ever, Scott Fitz—: Letters Between F. Scott Fitzgerald and His Literary Agent Harold Ober 1919–1940*, ed. Matthew J. Bruccoli and Jennifer McCabe Atkinson (New York and Philadelphia: J.B. Lippincott, 1972), p. 142.

Later he miraculously encounters the young girl he had met in Europe years before who shared his passion for swimming; they go off together into the sunset. Completely unbelievable and forced, these twists undercut and cheapen the serious themes. The story is decidedly not a failure, but mechanical manipulation of plot mars its effectiveness, and a burst of patriotic rhetoric at the end cannot conceal its flaws.

"The Rubber Check," in many ways a very interesting story, suffers from Fitzgerald's over-identification with Val, the protagonist. The young man has been in attendance on the wealthy for years, the extra man at their intimate dinners, a charming but penurious hanger-on. After an incident in which he has self-protectively issued a rubber check which his wealthy mother refused to cover, he is subjected to scornful and abusive attacks by those whose dinner tables he had once graced: "He had been snubbed so often in the past months that he had developed a protective shell to conceal his injuries" (*Price*, pp. 429–30). Fitzgerald dramatizes every snub and rejection, abandoning plot lines to wallow in Val's misery. His identification with this outsider extends to a vicarious enjoyment of the hero's resurrection. Val's success is a veritable fairy tale; as abject as his humiliation had been, so glittering is his success:

> Regard him on a spring morning in London in the year 1930. Tall, even stately, he treads down Pall Mall as if it were his personal pasture. He meets an American friend and shakes hands, and the friend notices how his shirt sleeve fits his wrist, and his coat sleeve incases his sleeve like a sleeve valve; how his collar and tie are molded plastically to his neck. (*Price*, p. 432)

Although Fitzgerald's identification with Val is very close, Val himself has no distinction, strength, or solidity. Were it not for such an important lapse, the ending, wry, ironic, and honest, would prove more effective than it does:

> He had carried his essential boyishness of attitude into a *milieu* somewhat less stable than gangdom and infinitely less conscientious about taking care of its own. And they had set him planting cabbages. . . . Val Schuyler turned sadly back to his cabbages. But he was sophisticated now; he had that, at least, from his expensive education. He knew that Mercia would be back. (*Price*, p. 436)

Forced rhetoric cannot save the mechanically plotted "Six of One"; indeed, the last lines of the story are embarrassingly overblown:

> His own experiment—he didn't regret it, but he wouldn't have done it again. Probably it proved something, but he wasn't quite sure what. Perhaps that life is constantly renewed, and glamour and beauty make way for it; and he was glad that he was able to feel that the republic could survive the mistakes of a whole generation, pushing the waste aside, sending ahead the vital and the strong. Only it was too bad and very American that there should be all that waste at the top; and he felt that he would not live long enough to see it end, to see great seriousness in the same skin with great opportunity—to see the race achieve itself at last. (*Price*, p. 381)

In both "Between Three and Four" and "A Change of Class," the narrative falters, in the former through such stiff transitions as "Nevertheless, he had a vision, which is the matter of this story" (*Price*, p. 339), and in the latter through the ending which departs so completely from the tone of the story up to this point that it might almost seem that Ring Lardner had completed it for Fitzgerald: "The soul of a slave, says the Marxian. Anyhow that's the sort of soul that Earl has, and he's pretty happy with it. I like Earl" (*Price*, p. 368).

Despite their obvious flaws, these stories, as I have shown, are not "trash" (*Letters*, p. 481),[12] if only because they deal with matters as important as those found in any great work of literature throughout the ages. They represent, rather, Fitzgerald's last attempts to find fictional forms for the important matters that dominated his last years. We see the problem and the progress with startling clarity when we read "Babylon Revisited" (1931) and "Crazy Sunday" (1932) after reading the other stories from the same period. In both stories, plot—as Fitzgerald usually conceived of it, a series of actions, each culminating in either a moment of suspense, sudden reversal, intimation of disaster, or pitch of ecstasy followed by a series of complications (he referred to it as "plot business" in his outlines)—is by comparison with the above stories virtually absent. Charlie Wales is embarrassed by the intrusion of his former friends and is given a setback, but it is a single action that tells his story rather than multiple strands of action that converge at the end. In "Crazy Sunday," the plot is simple—but the one weakness

---

12. Fitzgerald often referred to his magazine stories as "trash," but the care he lavished on them suggests how seriously he regarded these efforts.

in this story is Fitzgerald's division of focus: Joel Coles is the central consciousness, Miles Calman the center of interest. When Fitzgerald introduces—however minimally—a love affair between Stella and Joel, he leads the reader away from Miles and Stella, and particularly from Miles as a fascinating representation of a Hollywood creative czar. But because his rhetoric never becomes strained or overblown, because he is content to suggest rather than exhaust possibilities, the story survives the lapse.

What emerges clearly in both stories is Fitzgerald's approach to scene and atmosphere: the nuanced line replaces the lengthy adjectival paragraph, and the atmosphere is always directly related to the meaning of the story. Particularly in "Babylon Revisited," atmosphere is related to Charlie Wales's memories of the past, contrasting with his sensitivity to the present and the changes wrought by time: "At noon he sat opposite Honoria at Le Grand Vatel, the only restaurant he could think of not reminiscent of champagne dinners and long luncheons that began at two and ended in a blurred and vague twilight" (*Stories*, p. 389). In "Crazy Sunday," too, Fitzgerald is acutely aware of the Hollywood ambience, its life almost independent of the throngs who pass through the city searching for fame. The lines describing the Calmans' house are among the best Fitzgerald ever wrote: "Miles Calman's house was built for great emotional moments—there was an air of listening as if the far silences of its vistas hid an audience, but this afternoon it was thronged, as though people had been bidden rather than asked" (*Stories*, p. 404). A brilliant passage, but no more so than the scene in "Winter Dreams" (1922) where Dexter Green lies on the raft in rapturous harmony with the world of the Sherry Island Golf Club—a scene so filled with color and sound that the moment of ecstasy glows beyond the printed page. Fitzgerald could not in the 1930s reach into his past to create such moods, as he admitted: "Whether it's something that happened twenty years ago or only yesterday, I must start out with an emotion—one that's close to me and that I can understand. . . . Plots without emotions, emotions without plots. So it goes sometimes" (AA, pp. 132, 134).

The emotions were there, but they were different from those that inspired "Winter Dreams." They were bound up with the needs and desires of a mature man facing artistic disappointments (Perkins was admonishing him to write more stories about America, less about Europe, warning that the magazines were threatening to reject his latest works—as they did by 1935), family crises, and physical debilitation. The stories of the Depression years show him dealing with these emotions but in mostly unsuitable fictional forms. He realized his problems, as his letters indicate, but not until after publication of "The Crack-Up" did he suggest that he would consciously try (albeit not eagerly) to find a fictional approach reflective of his "spiritual 'change of life'—a most unwilling one— . . . a protest against a new set of conditions which I would have to face and a protest of my mind at having to make the psychological adjustments which would suit this new set of circumstances" (*Letters*, p. 589).

The stories that he wrote for *Esquire* after 1935 are clearly out-growths of his struggles in the early 1930s. The last two successful stories that capture the old Fitzgerald mood are "The Last of the Belles" and "Majesty" (both 1929). The former is a touching reminiscence of the lovely Southern girl who frequented his early fiction. It is at the same time a lament for the passing of an age:

> And I can still feel that last night vividly, the candlelight that flickered over the rough boards of the mess shack, over the frayed paper decorations left from the supply company's party, the sad mandolin down a company street that kept picking *My Indiana Home* out of the universal nostalgia of the departing summer. The three girls lost in this mysterious men's city felt something, too—a bewitched impermanence as though they were on a magic carpet that had lighted on the Southern countryside, and any moment the wind would lift it and waft it away. We toasted ourselves and the South. (*Stories*, p. 248)

As the narrator and Ailie Calhoun grow older, the South of romance and youth becomes a memory, unrecapturable: "All I could be sure of was this place that had once been so full of life and effort was gone, as if it had never existed, and that in another month Ailie would be gone, and the South would be empty for me forever" (*Stories*, p. 253).

In "Majesty," he returns to the daring flapper whose chief delight is in shocking her sedate social-register family. Emily Castleton's indomitable spirit survives her existence as member of an impoverished royal family: "Then she looked at Emily—the same thick bright hair with sunshine in it, the eyes with the hint of vivid seas. Her face was faintly drawn, there were slight new lines around her mouth, but she was the Emily of old—dominant, shining, large of scale. It seemed shameful for all that beauty and personality to have arrived in a cheap boarding house at the world's end" (TAR, pp. 247–48). Emily's moment of triumph arrives finally, when as a queen she enters the palace in her carriage, part of "the gorgeous panoply" of resurrected royalty. Thus nostalgia in "The Last of the Belles" and a brief resurgence of enthusiasm for the iconoclastic debutante in "Majesty" are powerful enough to create the narrative flow and unity of vision that always insured a successful Fitzgerald story.

Through his efforts during the Depression, Fitzgerald had learned that, to paraphrase Wright Morris, he had plunged so often and so deep into the past that he had exhausted his imagination.[13] In the late 1930s, he continued to explore the themes and ideas described in this essay but so differently as to be almost unrecognizable as the Fitzgerald of the Jazz Age or of the early 1930s. To read "The Lost Decade," "Afternoon of an Author," or "News of Paris" is to see that he had indeed "made a turn," and that the years from 1929 to 1935 had not been wasted in an outpouring of "trash" but had established the basis on which he might start again.

The situation in "The Lost Decade" (1939) is simple: Orrison Brown, one year out of college and working for a magazine, is instructed by his boss to take a man, a visitor named Trimble who has been away for ten years, out to lunch. The rest of the story consists of their conversation and a series of clinically detached observations by Orrison, clues by which the enigmatic Trimble is finally revealed as a former drunkard who has lost ten years of his life in an alcoholic maze. The story achieves its effects through Orrison's curiosity about the visitor which we, through the young writer's eyes, share. The former's observations, youthful, intelligent, sympathetic, make the revelation of Trimble's secret poignant and unforgettable. Brief as it is, Orrison's shock at Trimble's tale is a fitting climax to the laconic but allusive dialogue on which the plot turns:

> "What do you want to see most?" Orrison asked, as they sat down.
> Trimble considered.
> "Well—the backs of people's heads. . . . Their necks—how their heads are joined to their bodies. I'd like to hear what those two little girls are saying to their father. Not exactly what they're saying but whether the words float or submerge, how their mouths shut when they're finished speaking. Just a matter of rhythm. . . . The weight of spoons . . . so light. A little bowl with a stick attached. The cast in that waiter's eye. . . ."(*Stories*, pp. 471-72)

In "News of Paris—Fifteen Years Ago" (1940), two brief lines, "It was quiet in the room. The peacocks in the draperies stirred in the April wind" (AA, p. 224), provide the perfect background for a haunting, retrospective account of dissolution, apathy, and tired sexuality in

13. Wright Morris, *The Territory Ahead* (New York: Atheneum, 1963), pp. 157–58.

the pre-Depression boom. In "Afternoon of an Author" (1936), the painful admission, "It was like in the beginning fifteen years ago when they said he had 'fatal facility,' and he labored like a slave over every sentence so as not to be like that" (AA, p. 181), is Fitzgerald's own judgment of his artistic struggle, expressed simply and briefly in this moving autobiographical sketch. Perhaps most representative of these works is "Author's House" (1936), where the author (Fitzgerald) surveys his youth, his illness, his mistakes and failures. All he has left is despair, knowing he can never dwell again in the turret of his symbolic house—that success, despite the "little while" he tasted it, has ultimately eluded him:

> "I lived up here once," the author said after a moment.
> "Here? For a long time?"
> "No. For just a little while when I was young."
> "It must have been rather cramped."
> "I didn't notice it."
> "Would you like to try it again?"
> "No. And I couldn't if I wanted to." He shivered slightly and
> closed the windows. (AA, p. 189)

The success of these stories does not mean that Fitzgerald was ever thoroughly comfortable with his new style, that he did not regret the waste of the many years that dried up his gift for romantic prose describable at its best as Keatsian. He renewed it once more—brilliantly. In the middle of the crisis, Fitzgerald wrote perhaps his most touching essay, "Sleeping and Waking" (1934). Feeling himself poised on the edge of an abyss, facing "the night after death," he again returns, in a dream, to those stirring days of early success, and in a passage equal to the best he had written in the early 1920s, he recalls "young and lovely people doing young, lovely things." After recording his jaunty poem, "In the fall of '16 in the cool of the afternoon/ I met Caroline under a white moon," he asserts, "Life *was* like that, after all; my spirit soars in the moment of its oblivion . . ." (C-U, p. 68). However successful he might be in the future, whatever he might accomplish artistically—and his accomplishment was considerable—Fitzgerald had buried a source of his artistry with the 1929 crash. I think his comeback would have been complete, that he had won his battle and would have added another masterpiece to his list with completion of *The Last Tycoon*. That he had come as far as he did, however, is testimony to the spirit of a courageous artist who, like *his* America, picked up the pieces and carried on.

HOLLYWOOD IN FITZGERALD:
AFTER PARADISE

ROBERT A. MARTIN

> As long past as 1930, I had a hunch that the talkies would
> make even the best selling novelist as archaic as silent pic-
> tures.
>
> —Fitzgerald, "Handle with Care"

When it became apparent in late April of 1925 that *The Great Gatsby*
was not going to become the immediate best-seller Fitzgerald had
hoped it would, he wrote a letter to Maxwell Perkins in which he
proposed a course of action that would influence his career as a writer
for the rest of his life. In debt (as usual) to Scribner's for advances
taken against future royalties, Fitzgerald planned to reduce his financial loss on *Gatsby* by publishing his third collection of short stories,
All the Sad Young Men, which he promised to deliver to Perkins by
June 1, 1925. Uncertain of his future as a writer of popular fiction, he
wrote Perkins on April 24 from "Marseille, en route to Paris":

> Now I shall write some cheap ones [short stories] until I've accu-
> mulated enough for my next novel. When that is finished and
> published I'll wait and see. If it will support me with no more
> intervals of trash, I'll go on as a novelist. If not, I'm going to quit,
> come home, go to Hollywood, and learn the movie business. I
> can't reduce our scale of living and I can't stand this financial
> insecurity. (*Letters*, p. 180)[1]

As one might suspect, the letter is signed, "Yours in great depression,
Scott." This in itself is not particularly indicative of anything, since

1. Aaron Latham in *Crazy Sundays: F. Scott Fitzgerald in Hollywood* (New York:
Viking, 1971), p. 49, confuses Fitzgerald's reference to "my next novel" with *The Great
Gatsby*.

127

novelists tend to rise and fall psychologically in direct ratio to the success or failure of their most recent work. In Fitzgerald's case, however, the second of two postscripts following the close is informative: "P.S. (2) Please refer any movie offers to Reynolds" [Fitzgerald's agent]. From this letter and its postscript, it is clear that three separate but related forces were at work on Fitzgerald early in his career: 1. his fear that he could not support himself as a novelist; 2. the assumption that he could always "go to Hollywood" and write for the movies; 3. the strong probability that a Hollywood producer would buy the screen rights to anything he wrote and save him from financial disaster brought about by his failure as a novelist.

Thus the pattern that was to haunt Fitzgerald for the rest of his life—artistic failure, debt, and Hollywood—was firmly established within the relatively short period of five years after the publication of *This Side of Paradise* in 1920. It is therefore not surprising that in December, 1935, following the failure of *Tender Is the Night*, his financial and emotional resources nearly depleted, his wife confined to a mental institution, Fitzgerald once again considered Hollywood as a way out of his numerous difficulties. It was not, however, until July, 1937, that he formally acknowledged his financial defeat as a novelist and short story writer and went to Hollywood as a screenwriter with a salary of $1,000 per week.

That Fitzgerald considered himself primarily a novelist who wrote short stories for the popular magazines to enable him to continue as a novelist is strikingly evident from his voluminous correspondence and from biographical accounts. This view—one that Fitzgerald himself encouraged and perpetuated throughout his life—is deceptive almost to the point of distortion. Now that Fitzgerald's *Ledger*[2] has been published, it is possible to see that his income from his novels (with the exception of the brief financial success of *This Side of Paradise*) did not meet his expenses at any time in his life. What the *Ledger* makes clear is that between 1920 and 1931, the years of his highest earnings, Fitzgerald's income was derived from three main sources: 1. from the short stories; 2. from advances from Scribner's against future novels; and 3. from Hollywood. His income from movie rights, titles, script work, and "treatments," plus the outright sale of novels and short stories *before* he went to Hollywood in 1937, was very substantial—so substantial that it is easy to see why Fitzgerald came to regard Hollywood as a source of perpetual income, marred only by the low esteem of screenwriting as a second-rate occupation for a genuine talent. Like

2. Financial data for Fitzgerald's income is taken primarily from his *Ledger*.

his later creation, Pat Hobby, Fitzgerald associated screenwriters and the movie industry in general with "as dismal a crowd of fakes and hacks at the bottom as you can imagine" (*Letters*, p. 278).

It is, then, not the popular view of the later "Fitzgerald-in-Hollywood" as screenwriter, lover and secret novelist that is accurate, as suggested by Sheilah Graham and Aaron Latham,[3] but the presence of "Hollywood-in-Fitzgerald" as theme and image that permeates his best short stories and novels. Though the "Fitzgerald-in-Hollywood" accounts are interesting biographically, they do little to explain Fitzgerald's work or the Hollywood theme in his work. Instead, they tend to perpetuate the widely held belief that Fitzgerald suddenly and belatedly seized upon the movie industry as the subject for his last, unfinished work, *The Last Tycoon*, instead of realizing that Hollywood and Fitzgerald were closely related throughout his entire career.

If, as he notes in his March, 1936, article "Handle with Care," Fitzgerald recognized that "the talkies would make even the best-selling novelist as archaic as silent pictures," he must have also recognized that between 1920 and 1931 a large portion of his income was the result of movie work, sales, and indirect sources of income related to Hollywood. For one example his much-heralded leap from an income of $879 in 1919 to $18,850 in 1920 following the publication of *This Side of Paradise* is often quite erroneously attributed to book sales, which in fact accounted for only $6,200 from *Paradise* and $500 from his first collection of short stories, *Flappers and Philosophers*. The remainder came from individual short story sales to magazines, amounting to $4,650 for eleven stories, and $8,750 for the film rights to three of his short stories ("Head and Shoulders," retitled *The Chorus Girl's Romance*, Metro: 1920; "Myra Meets His Family," retitled *The Husband Hunter*, Fox: 1920; and "The Offshore Pirate," Metro: 1921.) For these three story rights, Fitzgerald in 1920 received $2,500, $1,000, and $2,250 respectively, plus $3,000 from Hollywood for an "Option on my output" (*Ledger*, p. 52).[4]

Characteristically, Fitzgerald leaves the impression in his article "Early Success" that his first success financially came largely from *Paradise* sales. Moreover, the simile he uses is noteworthy:

> All in three days I got married and the presses were pounding out *This Side of Paradise like they pound out extras in the movies.* . . . [italics mine]

3. Latham; Sheilah Graham, *Beloved Infidel* (New York: Holt, 1958), *The Rest of The Story* (New York: Coward-McCann, 1964), *The Real F. Scott Fitzgerald* (New York: Grosset, 1976).

4. Michael Adams, "Fitzgerald Filmography," *Fitzgerald/Hemingway Annual*, 9 (1977), 101–2.

> In a daze I told the Scribner company that I didn't expect my novel to sell more than twenty thousand copies and when the laughter died away I was told that a sale of five thousand was excellent for a first novel. I think it was a week after publication that it passed the twenty thousand mark, but I took myself so seriously that I didn't even think it was funny. (C-U, p. 88)

Along with the heady business of selling *Paradise* and a collection of his short stories to Scribner's, plus three movie rights to Hollywood, Fitzgerald was also trying to win Zelda. As one way of impressing on her that he had arrived at a suitable position, Fitzgerald sent Zelda a telegram in March, 1920. It was obviously intended to impress her with his financial solvency, but it is so closely tied to Hollywood and the golden girl theme that it can also be seen more precisely as a metaphor reflecting Fitzgerald's lifelong preoccupation with Hollywood, Zelda, money, and his status as a successful writer:

> I HAVE SOLD THE MOVIE RIGHTS OF HEAD AND SHOULDERS TO THE METRO COMPANY FOR TWENTY FIVE HUNDRED DOLLARS. I LOVE YOU DEAREST GIRL.[5]

Following his marriage to Zelda in April, 1920, Fitzgerald began work on his second novel, *The Beautiful and Damned*. When in October, 1921, his daughter Frances Scott Key Fitzgerald was born, he sent Zelda's parents a telegram announcing the event, again using a Hollywood reference for news of major importance:

> LILLIAN GISH IS IN MOURNING CONSTANCE TALMADGE IS A BACK NUMBER A SECOND MARY PICKFORD HAS ARRIVED[6]

Although *The Beautiful and Damned* is generally considered an unsatisfactory novel, it nevertheless reveals a great deal about Fitzgerald's awareness of the movies as a popular form of entertainment. Published in March, 1922, it follows the decline of a young married couple, Anthony and Gloria Patch, through a study of moral decay and alcoholism among the very rich that would eventually find its fruition in *Tender Is The Night*. Two episodes illustrate Fitzgerald's use

5. Arthur Mizener, Introd., *Flappers and Philosophers* (New York: Charles Scribner's, 1959), p. 13.
6. Andrew Turnbull, *Scott Fitzgerald* (New York: Charles Scribner's, 1962), p. 127.

of the movies as background during his early career. Gloria, who is described as "a gorgeous girl of miraculous freshness," and Anthony are visited by Joseph Bloeckman soon after their marriage. Bloeckman offers to arrange a screen test for Gloria, who tells him that she wants to be " 'a successful sensation in the movies. . . . I hear that Mary Pickford makes a million dollars annually' " (B&D, p. 213).

> ". . . Any day next week," Bloeckman was saying to Gloria. "Here—take this card. What they do is to give you a test of about three hundred feet of film, and they can tell pretty accurately from that." (B&D, p. 214)

Following Bloeckman's departure, Anthony voices his objection to Gloria's forthcoming test because " 'it's so silly! You don't want to go into the movies—moon around a studio all day with a lot of cheap chorus people' " (B&D, p. 214). At the time *The Beautiful and Damned* was written, Fitzgerald had no direct experience with Hollywood and in fact was not even to visit there until 1927. But somewhere in the transition from New York to Hollywood as the center of the film industry in the early 1920s, Fitzgerald, either directly or indirectly, acquired a fairly specific knowledge of the mechanics and conventions of production. "Three hundred feet of film" was about the amount of footage allotted for a screen test in 1920–22, and Bloeckman's background and credentials as a producer are recognizable for many early film executives who began their careers in the days of silent movies:[7]

> Born in Munich he had begun his American career as a peanut vender with a travelling circus. At eighteen he was a side show ballyhoo; later, the manager of the side show, and soon after, the proprietor of a second-class vaudeville house. Just when the moving picture had passed out of the stage of a curiosity and became a promising industry he was an ambitious young man of twenty-six with some money to invest, nagging financial ambitions and a good working knowledge of the popular show business. (B&D, pp. 96–97)

Bloeckman is the owner of "Films Par Excellence" Studio and appears throughout Fitzgerald's work as the businessman-in-the-movies

7. For this and much of the following historical data on the film industry in the 1920s and 1930s, I am indebted to film critic and historian Professsor Hubert Cohen of the University of Michigan.

stereotype that Fitzgerald and literary people resented because they were gradually assuming control of a highly profitable industry in which the traditional arts and the traditional credentials of education, taste, and literacy were subordinate to power, money, and "cheap, trashy entertainment." This is why Anthony tells Gloria that she doesn't want to " 'moon around a studio all day with a lot of cheap chorus people' " and why Fitzgerald describes Bloeckman as a man who is more interested in the finances of films than in the artistic talents that create films. Needless to say, actors, actresses, and writers occupied an inferior position in the film hierarchy. But Bloeckman's ambition and his "good working knowledge" of popular entertainment place him squarely in the center (in Fitzgerald's view) of the one American industry that both demanded and rewarded ambition and knowledge of the sort Bloeckman possesses. He is one of the first tycoons.

If Fitzgerald understood the rising importance of movies as a popular medium using a new technique, he understood even more precisely what the movies could do for a novelist. In 1922 he sold *The Beautiful and Damned* to Warner Brothers for $2,500 and toyed briefly with the idea of calling his current collection of short stories *In One Reel*, subsequently published as *Tales of the Jazz Age*. Though the analogy between a one-reel film and a short story is a good one, it is interesting primarily as yet a further indication of his awareness of the medium as a widely understood form with its own terminology as early as 1922.

In "The Diamond as Big as the Ritz" (1922), published in *Tales of the Jazz Age*, Fitzgerald continued to play on the image of the movies as the creator of exterior extravaganzas by men who, like Joseph Bloeckman, had little personal vision, grace, or education. The Braddock Washington château, resting on a huge diamond in a Montana valley, was originally to have been designed by the joint efforts of "a landscape gardener, an architect, a designer of stage settings, and a French decadent poet left over from the last century," all of whom had been kidnapped by Washington and are representatives of the older, more traditional arts, encumbered by past conventions of style, form, and process. Though they had placed at their disposal any materials they might need and an unlimited work force, they were unable to come to any agreement, and all four "went mad early one morning after spending the night in a single room trying to agree upon the location of a fountain, and were now confined comfortably in an insane asylum at Westport, Connecticut" (*Stories*, p. 25).

If Fitzgerald is creating a fantasy with satiric overtones, it is of a highly unusual nature because of the implied criticism and perversely frank approach to the traditional arts (the East) versus the then new and untraditional film industry (the West). The traditional arts, having failed (gone mad), are unable to agree on a minor detail and are retired to an insane asylum in Connecticut. Undaunted, Washington engages the services of " 'a moving-picture fella,' " who manages to bring the château to completion. " 'He was,' " Percy Washington informs John Unger, " 'the only man we found who was used to playing with an unlimited amount of money, though he did tuck his napkin in his collar and couldn't read or write' " (*Stories*, p. 25). Though "Diamond" has been praised for its imaginative sweep and implied criticism of the materialism that underlies the American Dream, it is in the criticism of the traditional arts as "impractical" that Fitzgerald makes an equally strong and most damning indictment. While "the moving-picture fella" is illiterate and ill-mannered, he is unencumbered by tradition and able to use money imaginatively—at least he manages to build the château where the others failed, and he quite possibly left the valley alive. And like his fellows in Hollywood, he was catering in a direct way to his audience. If that audience demanded a dream world removed from reality, he knew how to deliver it.

If Braddock Washington's private diamond mountain in Montana can be equated with easily and immediately available wealth in the West, Fitzgerald's private diamond mine was the movie industry, also in the West. As early as December, 1920, Fitzgerald was dividing his working time between writing novels and writing for the movies. In a letter to Maxwell Perkins written on December 2, 1920, the pattern of artistic failure, debt, and Hollywood that I have suggested as forming the destructive triad of Fitzgerald's career is clearly in its early stages of formation. Though *This Side of Paradise* had done well financially, Fitzgerald was already drawing advances against his accumulated royalties. At the time, he was writing *The Beautiful and Damned* while living in New York City:

38 W. 59th St.
Dear Mr. Perkins:
    With the settlement still over a month away I'm begging for another thousand! This will still leave me with a balance of twenty-six hundred.
    I've taken two weeks out to write a scenario for Dorothy Gish on order—for which I hope to get a lot of money. So it sets my novel back until Jan. 1st.
    Can this nth advance be arranged?[8]

8. *Dear Scott/Dear Max: The Fitzgerald-Perkins Correspondence*, ed. John Kuehl and Jackson R. Bryer (New York: Charles Scribner's, 1971), p. 33.

Fitzgerald's diamond mine was becoming even more important to him as Hollywood rapidly began to increase its consumption of his material. In 1923 Fitzgerald's total income was $28,759.78, of which $7,492 came from writing seven short stories, $1,510 from book royalties, and $13,500 from "Movies" (*Ledger*, p. 55). Of his total movie income that year, he was paid $10,000 for a "treatment" of *This Side of Paradise*, which consisted of a ten-thousand-word condensation. The movie, however, was never made. The rest of the money came from the sales of film rights for "The Camel's Back" ($1,000); *Grit* ($2,000), based on an original story by Fitzgerald (unidentified); and $500 for what he entered in his *Ledger* as "Titles for Glimpses of the Moon." Altogether, seven Fitzgerald films were made during his lifetime, six of which were silent.[9] In addition to those already listed, *The Great Gatsby* was produced by Famous-Lasky-Paramount in 1926, for which Fitzgerald received $13,500 (*Ledger*, p. 60).

The movies attracted Fitzgerald both as a source of income and as an art form. In 1922, he wrote a piece on "Movies and the Publisher" (*Ledger*, p. 60), for which he received $5, and in 1923 he and Zelda collaborated on a short story titled "Our Own Movie Queen." Though Fitzgerald lists at one point in his *Ledger* (p. 7) that the story was "Two thirds written by Zelda. Only my climax and revision," in two other entries he notes that it was "half Zelda . . . half mine" (*Ledger* pp. 55, 143). When the story appeared in O'Brien's short story anthology for 1925, however, it did not list Zelda as co-author.[10] Whatever the division of authorship might have been, the story is a sympathetic portrayal of Gracie Axelrod, who sees her coronation as queen of her home town as the first step toward a career in the movies. As the queen of the city, Gracie is thrust into the role of "star" in the movie "New Heidelberg, the Flower City of the Middle West." The scenes of the actual filming are undoubtedly enhanced by Fitzgerald's revisions, even as the reactions of Gracie to later developments in the story are undoubtedly Zelda's.

On Gracie's first day on "the lot," she meets the director, who is standing on a platform "pacing nervously back and forth."

> Mr. Decourcey O'Ney had come early into the pictures and back
> in 1916 had been known as a "big" director. Then due to one of
> those spasms of hysteria which periodically seize upon the indus-

9. Adams, pp. 101–9.
10. Nancy Milford, *Zelda: A Biography* (New York: Harper and Row, 1970), p. 102. See also W. R. Anderson's "Rivalry and Partnership: The Short Fiction of Zelda Sayre Fitzgerald," *Fitzgerald/Hemingway Annual*, 9 (1977), 21–23.

try, he had found himself suddenly out of work. His acquisition by the "Our Own Movie" committee was especially played up by the New Heidelberg Tribune. (*Bits*, p. 97)

Even though O'Ney, like Gracie, is the subject of some gentle ridicule by the Fitzgeralds, he is described as a "good" but "raving crazy" director reduced to directing a small-town movie. O'Ney nevertheless insists on some small measure of professionalism by questioning Gracie's background as an actress:

> "Have you had any experience in pictures?" inquired Mr. O'Ney.
> "O, I seen a lot of 'em and I know just about how the leading lady ought to act."
> "Well," murmured Mr. O'Ney, alarmingly, "I think I'll have you gilded to start with."
> "Mr. O'Ney means he'll show you how to do," said Joe Murphy, hastily. (*Bits*, p. 98)

All this is rather amusing when taken in context and illustrates that one or both of the Fitzgeralds were aware of the various levels of professionalism within the industry. When Gracie's big opportunity finally arrives, she becomes the prototype amateur actress of silent films, emoting wildly without any meaning, hoping to substitute action for talent. Given even the slightest knowledge of production techniques during the 1920s, it is possible to see Director O'Ney, megaphone in hand, preparing his company for the final take:

> When the day came for the actual shooting she acted as she had never acted before. Entering the covered wagon, she violently elevated her eyebrows and crooked her little fingers into grotesque hooks. During the Indian attack she rushed about in the center of a blank cartridge bedlam, waving her arms and pointing here and there at the circling redskins as if to indicate startling tactical dispositions. At the end of the second day Mr. O'Ney announced that the shooting was done. (*Bits*, p. 99)

As Gracie learns at the premiere of the movie, more than one career has ended on the cutting room floor, and film can be spliced together in some curious ways. By the end of the story, her career as local movie queen is saved by the film's assistant director, Joe Murphy, Decourcey O'Ney has gone mad and is headed for "a nice quiet asylum," and

Gracie and Joe Murphy get married. As a spoof of small-town America's exuberant fascination with the power of a visiting film company to transform the boredom of its daily existence into something magical, the story succeeds in spite of its flaws. More directly, it reflects the growing fascination of the American public with the business of moviemaking. And if the home-town movie of the story did not quite catapult Gracie into the lights of Hollywood, it at least had a therapeutic effect on the career of director Decourcey O'Ney, who—after his release from the insane asylum—is immediately "engaged by 'Films Par Excellence,' at two thousand a week" (*Bits*, p. 110).

It is in fact the perfect ending, one that, appropriately enough, brings to mind one of Fitzgerald's favorite themes: the movie producer without taste or background who is in possession of "a good working knowledge of the popular show business." Joseph Bloeckman could not have thought of a better ending himself—an ex-proprietor of a second-class vaudeville house hires as a director of his film company an ex-lunatic whose most recent picture was a third-class Midwestern production of obscure origins starring no one in particular and with a cast of identical prominence. And it is perhaps of minor note but certainly no accident that in *Tender Is the Night*, Dick Diver, on his way to visit Rosemary Hoyt, tells the taxi driver: " 'I want to go to the Films Par Excellence Studio' " (TITN, p. 90), over which Joseph Bloeckman presumably still presides, grown even more rich and powerful but still lacking taste and artistic discrimination.

As Arthur Mizener has remarked in *The Far Side of Paradise*, the movies fascinated Fitzgerald, "as they must fascinate any artist, because, as a visual art, they have such exciting possibilities of greatness, for all their actual shoddiness, and because they offered Fitzgerald what always drew him, a Diamond-as-Big-as-the-Ritz scale of operation, a world 'bigger and grander' than the ordinary world."[11] According to Henry Dan Piper, scriptwriting offered little challenge to Fitzgerald, but "he had always been fascinated by the motion-picture industry as literary subject matter." This would have been especially true for Fitzgerald around 1924 since movies were not only becoming established as the popular medium of the day, they were also becoming an art form. Fitzgerald, says Piper, had foreseen the movies as art and at one time had suggested a film about the craft of moviemaking:

> As far back as 1920, so he said, he had tried unsuccessfully to
> persuade D. W. Griffith that the craft of movie making itself was

11. Arthur Mizener, *The Far Side of Paradise: A Biography of F. Scott Fitzgerald* (Boston: Houghton Mifflin, 1965), p. 180.

a wonderful subject for a picture. According to Fitzgerald, Griffith had laughed at him, but the success of *Merton of the Movies* not long afterwards proved Fitzgerald right.[12]

With the publication of *The Great Gatsby* on April 10, 1925, followed by its disappointing sales record, Fitzgerald would have had every reason to look toward Hollywood if his next novel would not support him. Although *The Great Gatsby* contains relatively few references to Hollywood and the movies, enough remain to suggest that Fitzgerald—even after three extensive revisions—was using the medium as a background reference for the novel. Gatsby's dream of Daisy is one that must be created out of myth and metaphor, and sustained, assembled, and directed much like a silent movie in which events and emotion are symbolized through mimicry. In one such scene, Gatsby uses a movie actress and her director to impress Daisy with his ability to collect the famous and the celebrated at his parties.

> "Perhaps you know that lady," Gatsby indicated a gorgeous, scarcely human orchid of a woman who sat in state under a white-plum tree. Tom and Daisy stared, with that particularly unreal feeling that accompanies the recognition of a hitherto ghostly celebrity of the movies.
> "She's lovely," said Daisy.
> "The man bending over her is her director." (GG, p. 106)

From Fitzgerald's correspondence with Harold Ober, it is clear that he was anticipating the movie sale of *Gatsby* as early as May 2, 1925. It is even possible that he wrote *Gatsby* with the intention of making it a filmable novel. On May 2, he wrote to Ober: "By this time next week . . . it'll be obvious both whether I was a fool not to sell it serially and also whether the movies are interested. The minimum price would be $5000.00. If it goes to say fifty thousand copies I should want at least $10,000, and for anything over that, in the best-seller class I think I should get $25,000.00. . . ."[13] Before the film rights were finally sold to Famous-Lasky-Paramount in late 1926, Fitzgerald received a telegram from Ober on April 16, 1926, concerning a possible offer:

12. Henry Dan Piper, *F. Scott Fitzgerald: A Critical Portrait* (New York: Holt, Rinehart and Winston, 1965), pp. 260–61.

13. *As Ever, Scott Fitz—: Letters Between F. Scott Fitzgerald and His Literary Agent Harold Ober 1919–1940*, ed. Matthew J. Bruccoli and Jennifer McCabe Atkinson (New York and Philadelphia: J. B. Lippincott, 1972), pp. 77–78.

GATSBY PICTURE POSSIBLE OFFER FORTY FIVE THOUSAND ADVISE AC-
CEPTANCE CABLE QUICK   OBER

On the same day Fitzgerald cabled his reply:

ACCEPT OFFER   FITZGERALD[14]

The $45,000 offer for film rights to *Gatsby* did not materialize, how-
ever; out of a total income for 1926 of $25,686.05, slightly more than
half ($13,500) came from the film rights to his most-praised novel. By
comparison, Fitzgerald's income from book sales for 1926 amounted to
$2,033.20.

As Matthew J. Bruccoli has detailed in his meticulous study, *The
Composition of "Tender Is the Night,"*[15] Fitzgerald had been working
unsuccessfully on his fourth novel since the late summer of 1925. In an
early version, dealing with matricide as a theme, Fitzgerald had attempted to portray a young motion picture filmcutter, Francis Me-
larky, who later evolved into Lew Kelly, a motion picture director. It
was not until sometime in 1930 that the novel's final version emerged
with Dick and Nicole Diver as the main characters and only Rosemary
Hoyt faintly reminiscent of the earlier versions and the Hollywood
connection. When the Fitzgeralds returned from Europe in December,
1926, Fitzgerald was offered a contract by United Artists to work on a
Constance Talmadge film titled *Lipstick*. Fitzgerald surprisingly accepted the offer, which involved rather minimal terms ($3,500 in ad-
vance and an additional $8,500 if the film was made).

Fitzgerald's sudden decision to go to Hollywood in January, 1927,
very likely served three purposes simultaneously. It provided an immediate addition to his dwindling finances; it would possibly help to solve
the writing problems of the Melarky-Kelly version of *Tender* by adding
authenticity through direct observation of the Hollywood scene that
Fitzgerald lacked; and it allowed him to take that first step after he
came home from Europe—to "go to Hollywood and learn the movie
business." Fitzgerald's script was rejected, and the movie was never
made. Nevertheless, his first trip to Hollywood brought him into the
studios through his acquaintances with a seventeen-year-old actress,
Lois Moran, with whom he fell in love, and Irving Thalberg, head of

14. *As Ever*, p. 88.
15. Matthew J. Bruccoli, *The Composition of "Tender Is the Night"* (Pittsburgh:
Univ. of Pittsburgh Press, 1963).

MGM. Both of them were to influence his future work, and both helped Fitzgerald to experience Hollywood firsthand. As a more immediate result of the trip, two short stories, "Jacob's Ladder" and "Magnetism," both written in 1927, are the first indications that Fitzgerald began to take Hollywood seriously as theme and subject. The 1927 trip was as much symbolic as substantive, and if not quite paradise, it did at least place Fitzgerald on the inside of the studio gates.

"Jacob's Ladder" and "Magnetism" deserve a higher place among Fitzgerald's short stories than has generally been accorded them by critics and scholars. "Jacob's Ladder" in particular is an important transitional story that remained uncollected until 1973, at which time it appeared in *Bits of Paradise*. To Robert Sklar, who saw the story's merit as early as 1967, it marked "Fitzgerald's new career as a professional writer of short stories . . . but it also squandered, by its very quality and breadth, nearly all of his newly acquired material." Sklar is impressed with "Jacob's Ladder" not only as a Fitzgerald story in itself but as representing through its main character, Jacob Booth, both an advance and an extension of Fitzgerald's previous protagonists. Jacob, Sklar notes, "is Fitzgerald's old hero in a new form; in a remarkable way he sets a *leitmotif* for the next seven years of Fitzgerald's fiction, culminating in *Tender Is the Night*." [16]

In his biography of Fitzgerald, Andrew Turnbull describes the brief romance that took place in Hollywood in 1927 between Fitzgerald and Lois Moran as "very pure and idealistic—never anything more than a delicate flirtation." At the time, Fitzgerald was thirty-one and Lois Moran was seventeen. Turnbull was apparently unaware of "Jacob's Ladder" and says that as a result of their flirtation, "Fitzgerald put his first emotion for her into a story called 'Magnetism,' where Lois is Helen Avery, the young movie star who causes the happily married George Hannaford to waver."[17] Although Sklar does not mention Lois Moran in his discussion of "Magnetism" and Turnbull does not mention "Jacob's Ladder" at all, the two stories actually derive from the same incident and emotion and should be viewed as early fictional harvests from Fitzgerald's first trip to Hollywood.

Both "Jacob's Ladder" and "Magnetism" were entered as "Stripped and Permanently Buried" in Fitzgerald's *Ledger* following their initial magazine publications, and passages from both appear in his later work, particularly in *Tender* during the Rosemary-Dick Diver scenes. Turnbull notwithstanding, it was not "Magnetism" wherein Fitzgerald

16. Robert Sklar, *F. Scott Fitzgerald: The Last Laocoön* (New York: Oxford Univ. Press, 1967), p. 229.
17. Turnbull, p. 170.

put his first emotion for Lois Moran but in "Jacob's Ladder," where Jacob Booth, a wealthy but bored New Yorker, meets Jenny Delahanty and decides to transform her into a movie star. After changing her name to Jenny Prince and introducing her to a movie director, he falls in love with her in a passive, romantically apathetic way, and when she becomes successful as an actress, she rejects him for an actor. Jacob is left with only her image on a movie screen. In one sense, the story is a modified version of *Pygmalion*, stripped down from Bernard Shaw's play and transferred to a new circumstance and Hollywood setting. In quite another sense, it is Fitzgerald using Hollywood as a metaphor for his own romantic attraction to Lois Moran (Jenny is sixteen when Jacob first meets her) and as a fictional equivalent for his own sublimated passion.

The first time Jacob kisses her, he hesitates tentatively and is "chilled by the innocence of her kiss, the eyes that at the moment of contact looked beyond him into the darkness of the night, the darkness of the world" (*Bits*, p. 167). Later, after her transformation into a professional actress, Jacob, who is now thirty-three, visits Jenny in Hollywood; she is now seventeen:

> But at seventeen, months are years and Jacob perceived a change in her; in no sense was she a child any longer. There were fixed things in her mind—not distractions, for she was instinctively too polite for that, but simply things there. No longer was the studio a lark and a divine accident; no longer "for a nickel I wouldn't turn up tomorrow." It was part of her life. Circumstances were stiffening into a career which went on independently of her casual hours. (*Bits*, pp. 171–72)

That Jenny Prince is modeled on Lois Moran is less important critically than her obvious reincarnation in Fitzgerald's later work as Helen Avery in "Magnetism," Rosemary Hoyt in *Tender*, and Cecilia in *The Last Tycoon*. On Sunday in "Jacob's Ladder," Jacob and Jenny go to three Hollywood parties because, as Jenny tells him, "that's what everybody does on a Sunday afternoon," thereby anticipating the theme and setting of "Crazy Sunday," which Fitzgerald would write in January, 1932, following his second trip to Hollywood as a screenwriter for MGM.

Among several other minor complications that Fitzgerald arranges for Jacob and Jenny, a shyster lawyer named Scharnhorst attempts to blackmail Jenny for $20,000 but is successfully disposed of through

Jacob's intervention. This is the same plot device that Fitzgerald uses in "Magnetism" and that he had outlined for a projected episode in *The Last Tycoon*,[18] in which Cecilia's father and Monroe Stahr are struggling for control of the studio. In this unwritten scene, Brady was to use his knowledge of Stahr's affair with Kathleen, while Stahr was to retaliate by threatening to reveal that Brady had arranged for the murder of his mistress's husband. Matthew J. Bruccoli, in his recent work, *"The Last of the Novelists": F. Scott Fitzgerald and "The Last Tycoon,"* comments perceptively on the implications of Fitzgerald's numerous drafts and revisions but sees only "Crazy Sunday" as forming immediate background material for *The Last Tycoon*. It is my belief that "Jacob's Ladder" and "Magnetism" form the nucleus of Fitzgerald's entire Hollywood theme and, along with "Crazy Sunday" and the early Melarky-Kelly versions of *Tender*, account for nearly all of the material, characters, and plot of *The Last Tycoon*.

In "Magnetism," for example, Fitzgerald made his story more integral to his theme by moving the setting to Hollywood entirely (as opposed to New York and Hollywood in "Jacob's Ladder") and by concentrating on the portrayal of George Hannaford, an actor who attracts women without effort or design. Many of Fitzgerald's first impressions of Hollywood appear in this story, and as George struggles to keep his marriage intact by fending off the unwanted attentions of several women, we see what Fitzgerald as novelist would have seen through intensely detailed scenes describing Hollywood and the movie studios. In the two passages below, Fitzgerald follows George Hannaford as he drives from his home to the studio. These passages are not only stylistically graceful, they reflect a detailed observation based on a strong sensory impression of atmosphere and place. They are as cinematically visual as anything Fitzgerald ever wrote.

> George left and drove out an interminable boulevard which narrowed into a long, winding concrete road and rose into the hilly country behind. Somewhere in the vast emptiness a group of buildings appeared, a barnlike structure, a row of offices, a large but quick restaurant and half a dozen small bungalows. The chauffeur dropped Hannaford at the main entrance. He went in and passed through various enclosures, each marked off by swinging gates and inhabited by a stenographer. (*Stories*, p. 222)

18. For a comparison of the blackmail episodes, see "Jacob's Ladder," *Bits*, pp. 179–81; "Magnetism," *Stories*, pp. 233–37; Matthew J. Bruccoli, *"The Last of the Novelists": F. Scott Fitzgerald and "The Last Tycoon"* (Carbondale: Southern Illinois Univ. Press, 1977), pp. 43–46, 104.

The studio is seen from without and within to form a complementary perspective of Hannaford in his life and work. Following his arrival at the office, he and Schroeder (a producer) walk to the studio to watch a movie in production. As they enter "a little door in the big blank wall of the studio building," they are absorbed "into its half darkness." Fitzgerald liked this passage so much that he incorporated it virtually intact into Chapter I of *Tender Is the Night* (TITN, p. 23):

> Here and there figures spotted the dim twilight, figures that turned up white faces to George Hannaford, like souls in purgatory watching the passage of a half-god through. Here and there were whispers and soft voices, and, apparently from afar, the gentle tremolo of a small organ. Turning the corner made by some flats, they came upon the white crackling glow of a stage with two people motionless upon it.
>
> An actor in evening clothes, his shirt front, collar and cuffs tinted a brilliant pink, made as though to get chairs for them, but they shook their heads and stood watching. For a long while nothing happened on the stage—no one moved. A row of lights went off with a savage hiss, went on again. The plaintive tap of a hammer begged admission to nowhere in the distance; a blue face appeared among the blinding lights above and called something unintelligible into the upper blackness. (*Stories*, pp. 223–24)

Edwin T. Arnold has noted that Fitzgerald gave Dick Diver "some of Jacob's more unfortunate characteristics" and that the title of "Jacob's Ladder" suggests a reexamination of Gatsby's ladder, which "foreshadows the theme's further development in *Tender Is the Night*."[19] In addition, Aaron Latham observes that when Rosemary Hoyt tells Dick Diver, "Oh, we're such *actors*—you and I" (TITN, p. 105), she is repeating precisely what Helen Avery tells George Hannaford in "Magnetism" (*Stories*, p. 228).[20] Hannaford and Helen Avery are so totally within the movie industry that the story and plot have no other significance. In placing "Magnetism" and "Crazy Sunday" entirely in Hollywood, Fitzgerald was writing not only about a profession and popular entertainment but about an entire way of life that could not possibly be overstated—one that both defined and created in its life and work the myths and illusions of American middle-class society,

19. Edwin T. Arnold, "The Motion Picture as Metaphor in the Works of F. Scott Fitzgerald," *Fitzgerald/Hemingway Annual*, 9 (1977), 51.
20. Latham, p. 84.

which in Fitzgerald's vision of America equals the American Dream itself.

By 1931, Fitzgerald's "next novel" was still unrealized, Zelda was in the midst of a serious mental breakdown, and America was in the midst of the Depression. His short story price had risen to $4,000, while his total income in 1930 had climbed to $33,090. Though his expenses were high, Fitzgerald's second trip to Hollywood, in November, 1931, cannot be said to have resulted from financial necessity. In 1929, his income had totalled $32,448, of which $27,000 came from writing short stories, $900 from "Talkie Rights" to *The Beautiful and Damned* and $31.77 from all his books. In 1930, his short story sales accounted for $25,200, while his income from all books was $99. In brief, it is necessary to look elsewhere for Fitzgerald's reason for returning to Hollywood in 1931 to work on a script for MGM for six weeks on a $1,200-a-week contract.[21]

During the four years since Fitzgerald had been there in 1927, the movies had changed from silents to sound. Given his 1936 statement in "Handle with Care" that "As long past as 1930, I had a hunch that the talkies would make even the best selling novelist as archaic as silent pictures," his trouble in writing the Melarky-Kelly version of *Tender* between 1926 and 1930, and his statement to Perkins that if his next novel would not support him he would "go to Hollywood and learn the movie business," his decision to return for a second try appears in a different perspective. In 1931, Fitzgerald would hardly have considered himself a "best selling novelist"; indeed, it is surprising that he could think of himself as a novelist at all, since the major source of his income after *Paradise* came from writing short stories for the "slicks" and from the sale of film rights and scripts to Hollywood. In that year, Hollywood needed writers who could write dialogue as well as continuity, and Fitzgerald's reputation as a popular writer was very high among producers and directors.

"Crazy Sunday" (written in January, 1932) is one of the finest stories Fitzgerald ever wrote and, like the earlier stories "Jacob's Ladder" and "Magnetism," was derived from his experiences during the six weeks he spent working for MGM and Irving Thalberg. The theme of the story derives from Fitzgerald's observation of the tragic potential that he saw existing beneath the glamor and publicity of the studios. His alter-ego, Joel Coles, is both observer and participant (as was Fitzgerald) in the story of Miles Calman, who is based on Thalberg. Joel Coles, again like Fitzgerald, is a recently arrived New York import to Hollywood

21. *As Ever*, pp. 178–80.

and is writing continuity at Calman's studio: "He was twenty-eight and not yet broken by Hollywood. He had had what were considered nice assignments since his arrival six months before and he submitted his scenes and sequences with enthusiasm. He referred to himself modestly as a hack but really did not think of it that way" (*Stories*, p. 403).

Like the Sunday afternoon parties in "Jacob's Ladder," which Hollywood people attend because "it's sort of the thing to do. . . . Otherwise you don't see anybody except the people on your own lot, and that's narrow" (*Bits*, p. 173), Joel Coles attends a party given by Miles and Stella Calman at which he makes a fool of himself, and is later drawn into the Calmans' social orbit and personal lives almost inadvertently. Fitzgerald's insight into the social and political undercurrents of Hollywood allowed him to merge the perceptions of a detached observer like Coles with the insider's view of Hollywood as an industry. In the two passages below, these dual perspectives flow in and out of the story to create not merely a point-of-view but a total effect, one in which Hollywood becomes not just a place but a microcosm of American society, morals, and manners. At the Calmans' party, Joel tells Stella:

"Everybody's afraid, aren't they?" he said. . . . "Everybody watches for everybody else's blunders, or tries to make sure they're with people that'll do them credit. Of course that's not true in your house," he covered himself hastily. "I just meant generally in Hollywood." (*Stories*, p. 404)

Between Sundays, however, which Fitzgerald says was "not a day but rather a gap between two other days," work in the studio continues in sharp contrast to the craziness of Sunday afternoon digressions into the "gossip and scandal" of Hollywood:

With Monday the week resumed its workaday rhythm, in sharp contrast to the theoretical discussions, the gossip and scandal of Sunday; there was the endless detail of script revision—"Instead of a lousy dissolve, we can leave her voice on the sound track and cut to a medium shot of the taxi from Bell's angle or we can simply pull the camera back to include the station, hold it a minute and then pan to the row of taxis"—by Monday afternoon Joel had again forgotten that people whose business was to provide entertainment were ever privileged to be entertained. (*Stories*, p. 411)

Thus the two Hollywoods, one composed of Sunday afternoons at Miles Calman's house—built, as Fitzgerald says, for "great emotional moments"—and the other of the Hollywood bourgeoisie of film technicians, craftsmen, and extras, are portrayed as mutually exclusive elements of the film industry. The "other" Hollywood of the story congregates for its emotional moments at the studio commissary during the week. Following his disgrace at the Calmans' party on Sunday, Joel enters the studio restaurant the following day:

> . . . he found a gloomy consolation in staring at the group at the next table, the sad, lovely Siamese twins, the mean dwarfs, the proud giant from the circus picture. But looking beyond at the yellow-stained faces of pretty women, their eyes all melancholy and startling with mascara, their ball gowns garish in full day, he saw a group who had been at Calman's and winced. (*Stories*, p. 408)

As intentionally grotesque as the group in this passage might appear, they are no less "sad" or "melancholy" than Stella Calman herself. Though Stella and Miles live in a Beverly Hills mansion looking "out toward the Pacific . . . the American Riviera and all that," Fitzgerald's criticism of Hollywood is not of an industry but of an attitude, a veneer of sophistication and acquired appearance that is fundamentally a fake. As Stella gradually reveals some embarrassing details of her life with Miles, Joel begins to see her insecurity and superficiality emerging during a conversation in her home:

> Under the high ceilings the situation seemed more dignified and tragic. It was an eerie bright night with the dark very clear outside of all the windows and Stella all rose-gold raging and crying around the room. Joel did not quite believe in picture actresses' grief. They have other preoccupations—they are beautiful rose-gold figures blown full of life by writers and directors, and after hours they sit around and talk in whispers and giggle innuendoes, and the ends of many adventures flow through them.
>
> Sometimes he pretended to listen and instead thought how well she was got up—sleek breeches with a matched set of legs in them, an Italian-colored sweater with a little high neck, and a short brown chamois coat. He couldn't decide whether she was an imitation of an English lady or an English lady was an imitation of her. She hovered somewhere between the realest of realities and the most blatant of impersonations. (*Stories*, p. 410)

"Crazy Sunday" is important not only for its realistic view of Holly-wood life but also because it anticipates *The Last Tycoon* through the character of Miles Calman, to reappear in altered form as Monroe Stahr in *Tycoon*, both of whom are variations on Irving Thalberg. Like Calman, Stahr was to be killed in a plane crash and similarly possesses "both an interesting temperament and an artistic conscience." Like Joel Coles in "Crazy Sunday," Cecilia Brady in *Tycoon* is "*of* the movies but not *in* them" (LT, p.138), which echoes closely Fitzgerald's description of Rosemary Hoyt in *Tender* when he says, "she was In the movies but not at all At them" (TITN, p. 31).

Fitzgerald received only $200 for "Crazy Sunday," as opposed to his usual price of $4,000. The story was turned down by *Redbook, Cosmopolitan,* and *Saturday Evening Post* "on the grounds that its publication might anger the movie studios and jeopardize these magazines' lucrative movie-advertising accounts."[22] After the story appeared, Fitzgerald received a letter from Edmund Wilson, who told him: "I thought your story in *The Mercury* was swell—wish you would do something more about Hollywood, which everybody who knows anything about it is either scared or bribed not to tell about or have convinced themselves is all right."[23]

"Crazy Sunday" was the last, certainly one of the best, Hollywood stories that Fitzgerald wrote until he began *The Last Tycoon* in 1939. As Matthew J. Bruccoli has written in his introduction to *As Ever, Scott Fitz—*, "It is impossible to understand Fitzgerald's career without understanding his feelings about money."[24] Numerous Fitzgerald critics have consistently overlooked this constant element in Fitzgerald's life and have attributed his final sojourn in Hollywood to a simple need for more money, an artistic retreat, or a depletion of the talent that had sustained him as a writer of popular fiction between 1920 and 1936. While there may be some validity in all of these views, Fitzgerald's own ledger is perhaps the most revealing source, together with his correspondence with Harold Ober, his literary agent. Between 1931 and 1936, Fitzgerald's income declined from an all-time high in 1931 of $37,599 to an all-time low in 1936 of $10,180.91. In 1931 he earned

22. Piper, p. 167.
23. Edmund Wilson, *Letters on Literature and Politics: 1912–1972*, ed. Elena Wilson (New York: Farrar, Straus and Giroux, 1977), p. 229. Wilson, whom Fitzgerald described as "my intellectual conscience" in "The Crack-Up," was interested in the movies as an art form and subsequently wrote *The Boys in the Back Room*, a study of nine authors who were associated with Hollywood and the movies or California. He also edited *The Last Tycoon* after Fitzgerald's death.
24. *As Ever*, p. xxi.

$31,500 from the sale of nine short stories and $5,400 (after commissions) from his work for MGM; his total income from book sales in the same year amounted to $100. By 1936, however, magazines such as *Saturday Evening Post* and *Collier's* were returning his short stories with the comment that they needed a different kind of story or that they were "too crazy . . . weak . . . and improbable." One editor suggested that a rejected story was not a typical "Fitzgerald piece," while another commented on a revision: "The new version of Scott Fitzgerald's story is a vast improvement over the first one. The writing has all the old Fitzgerald quality, but the plot values and the psychology are a bit hazy. For that reason, we must regretfully return the story."[25] One month later, in July, 1937, Fitzgerald left for Hollywood and $1,000 a week as a scriptwriter for MGM.

As I have suggested throughout this article, Fitzgerald always was a commercial writer and yet chose to think of himself as primarily a novelist. If his novels and short story collections did not meet his extravagant style of living, there was always another short story to write for the popular magazines or a quick movie script for Hollywood to make up the difference. After 1931, however, partly due to the Depression, partly due to his own inability to write stories the magazines wanted, and partly due to his own emotional depression, Fitzgerald's short story market simply disappeared. If he had become too closely identified with the Jazz Age or the persona of "The Crack-Up" articles (which he later disowned), the ultimate cause for his move to Hollywood was that as a writer he had no place else to go that would provide him with the income he thought he needed and deserved. The only place left was Hollywood, his third and final source of substantial earnings. By the time Fitzgerald settled in at the Garden of Allah hotel in Hollywood in July, 1937, his 1925 projection to Maxwell Perkins had come full circle. He had, indeed, discovered that not only would his "next novel" not support him, but that what he had earlier considered as "trash" in his short stories was no longer wanted either. He had at last gone to Hollywood "to learn the movie business."

Of the fiction written during his last years in Hollywood, *The Last Tycoon* and "The Last Kiss" (written in 1940, published in 1949— probably a rejected fragment from the novel), taken together with a handful of the Pat Hobby stories, clearly indicate that Fitzgerald *was* primarily a novelist and short story writer who had the misfortune to run out of money and material at the same time. Because of its recurring presence in Fitzgerald's work as myth and metaphor, Hollywood

25. Ibid., pp. 287, 303, 317, 318, 323-24.

is of primary importance in any critical assessment of his work. If Fitzgerald's life ended there on the far side of paradise, it is nevertheless Hollywood-in-Fitzgerald that helps to place his best fiction into perspective as contemporary chronicles of a particular time and place. As Henry Dan Piper has observed, "In Hollywood Fitzgerald, at any rate, had found his greatest theme."[26] This is quite possibly what Fitzgerald meant when he wrote in a letter to his daughter during the winter of 1939: "Sorry you got the impression that I'm quitting the movies—they are always there" (*Letters*, p. 48).

26. Piper, p. 280.

FITZGERALD AND *ESQUIRE*

JAMES L. W. WEST III

Most people who study F. Scott Fitzgerald's career as a writer of short fiction think of him as a *Saturday Evening Post* author. This idea is probably justified: Fitzgerald was proud of his standing as one of the *Post's* highest-paid writers during the late 1920s and early 1930s, and he tried to tailor most of the stories he wrote during that period to the *Post's* requirements. He appeared in the magazine no fewer than 70 times between 1920 and 1937, and he once even attempted to have the Internal Revenue Service consider him "virtually an employee" of the *Post*.[1] During the last six years of his life, however, Fitzgerald was not a *Post* author; rather, he was an *Esquire* author. Between 1934 and 1941 he appeared there 45 times, more than any other writer in the history of the magazine.[2] *Esquire* gave him an outlet for essays and short fiction during two of the most difficult periods of his life, the Baltimore/North Carolina years from 1934 until 1937 and the final Hollywood period from 1939 to 1940. *Esquire* was a more open and sophisticated magazine than the *Post*, and it placed few restrictions on its authors. Fitzgerald was able to give play to the

1. See *As Ever, Scott Fitz—: Letters Between F. Scott Fitzgerald and His Literary Agent Harold Ober 1919–1940*, ed. Matthew J. Bruccoli and Jennifer McCabe Atkinson (New York and Philadelphia: J.B. Lippincott, 1972), pp. 191–93. This particular quotation is from p. 193.

2. For a useful working bibliography of Fitzgerald's contributions to *Esquire*, see E. R. Hagemann and James E. Marsh, "A Check-list of Contributions of Literary Import to *Esquire* 1933–1958," an appendix to *The Armchair "Esquire,"* ed. Arnold Gingrich and L. Rust Hills (New York: G.P. Putnam's, 1958), pp. 1–24.

autobiographical and confessional impulses he felt during these final years, and in the process he produced some revealing essays and challenging fiction.

This essay presents an overview of Fitzgerald's relationship with *Esquire*. The first section treats Fitzgerald's professional dealings with the magazine and with its editor Arnold Gingrich. *Esquire's* early success and its importance in the magazine market during the 1930s are also examined. The second section concentrates on two pieces of fiction which Fitzgerald produced for *Esquire*, both of them "short short" stories. These two brief narratives—"Three Acts of Music" and "The Lost Decade"—employ a compressed, understated method which is quite unusual in Fitzgerald's fiction. They are among his best mature short stories and deserve our attention.

1.

The story of the inception and initial success of *Esquire* is fascinating in itself. The magazine grew out of *Apparel Arts*, a handsome "slick" which had been created by merchandiser David A. Smart for the men's fashion business. *Apparel Arts* was bought by high-class men's clothing stores and was then mailed *gratis* by them to regular customers and charge account holders. *Apparel Arts* was so successful that Smart decided to use the same idea with *Esquire*. Originally *Esquire* was to be a quarterly sold or given away mostly by clothing stores, with only incidental sales at newsstands or by subscription. However, the initial issue in autumn, 1933, was an instant hit at the newsstands, and Smart decided to turn the magazine into a monthly.[3]

Much of the appeal of that first issue and of subsequent issues can be traced to editor Arnold Gingrich, a man of ability, taste, and humor. From the beginning Gingrich decided that *Esquire* would be a showcase for the best contemporary writers, and he set about building an impressive stable. His biggest prize was Ernest Hemingway, who agreed to write a monthly letter for double the fee paid to the other *Esquire* writers.[4] Hemingway was cast as the magazine's star author—its lead-

---

3. A good account of the founding of *Esquire* is Arnold Gingrich's *Nothing but People: The Early Days at "Esquire"* (New York: Crown, 1971). For a briefer summary, see Theodore Peterson, *Magazines in the Twentieth Century* (Urbana: Univ. of Illinois Press, 1964), pp. 273–81.

4. Gingrich, *Nothing but People*, p. 86. Also see Gingrich's letter to Sister Richard Mary Grimes in her dissertation, "Ernest Hemingway: The *Esquire* Years," Ohio State Univ., 1965, p. 21.

off man—and much of *Esquire's* success was attributable to him. But there were other attractions: during the 1930s Gingrich featured writing by John Dos Passos, Dashiell Hammett, Theodore Dreiser, Conrad Aiken, Erskine Caldwell, Ezra Pound, Morley Callaghan, Stephen Vincent Benét, Thomas Wolfe, H. L. Mencken, George Jean Nathan, Ford Madox Ford, André Maurois, Aldous Huxley, William Saroyan, Bertrand Russell, Thomas Mann, Sinclair Lewis, Frank O'Connor, Langston Hughes, D. H. Lawrence, John Steinbeck, Waldo Frank, John Gould Fletcher, e. e. cummings, and many others—the most impressive array of talent in any American magazine of the time.

Esquire's masculine image also set it apart. At a time when nearly all mass-circulation magazines were geared for a female audience, *Esquire* was designed as a leisure magazine for men. The first issue proclaimed itself "the common denominator of masculine interests" and pledged itself to be "all things to all men."[5] *Esquire* was aimed at the well-to-do male: it was expensively printed on glossy paper in an oversized format and specialized in full-page illustrations and cartoons, many of them in color. The price was fifty cents per copy, high in the 1930s when comparably-sized magazines sold for a nickel or a dime. *Esquire* was racy and frank, but it always stayed within the bounds of good taste. Its advertisements were for better brands of clothing, accessories, automobiles, and liquor. That such a publishing venture could flourish during the darkest years of the Depression was remarkable. *Esquire's* circulation was around 130,000 when Fitzgerald began publishing there, and by his death in 1940 the magazine claimed over 468,000 readers.[6]

Fitzgerald, then, was publishing in a visible, lively, successful magazine which had an excellent group of writers appearing regularly in its pages. He was sometimes inclined to disparage his writing for *Esquire,* but his complaints were about the comparatively low fees, not about the quality of the magazine. Fitzgerald was publishing in good company, better than he had appeared with in the *Post*—and he knew it. Practically every important writer in his generation had appeared in *Esquire* or would publish there during his years with the magazine. Fitzgerald had to be on his toes in such a group.

Fitzgerald was directed to *Esquire* in the spring of 1934 by H. L. Mencken.[7] Mencken was a good friend to the magazine during its first

5. "As for General Content," *Esquire,* 1 (Autumn 1933), 1.

6. These circulation figures are taken from *N.W. Ayer & Son's Directory of Newspapers and Periodicals* (Philadelphia: N.W. Ayer, 1935, 1940). I am grateful to the reference staff at the University of North Carolina Library, Chapel Hill, for assistance in gathering these figures.

7. Gingrich, *Nothing but People,* p. 228.

few years; according to Gingrich, he brought many important writers
into the *Esquire* fold. Fitzgerald was living in Baltimore to be near
Zelda, who was under treatment at Johns Hopkins, and he was seeing
Mencken frequently.[8] As part of her therapy, Zelda was writing. One
of her productions, a long free-association catalogue of travel memories, seemed publishable to Fitzgerald, and he revised it and sent it to
Esquire under his and Zelda's names. Many years later Gingrich recalled the first manuscript and his subsequent wooing of Fitzgerald for
the magazine:

> He wrote me enclosing a script entitled " 'Show Mr. and Mrs. F.
> to Number—' " by Zelda and F. Scott Fitzgerald. And, since I was
> a great Fitzgerald fan from 1920 on (had read *This Side of Para-
> dise* in high school) I moved right in on him with long fan letters,
> and began an intensive correspondence and frequent exchange of
> phone calls, from February '34 onward.[9]

" 'Show Mr. and Mrs. F.' " was too lengthy for one appearance, so Gingrich divided it between two issues, May and June of 1934. Gingrich's
letters and calls also brought in another collaborative effort, titled "Auction—Model 1934," a listing of the memorabilia collected by the Fitzgeralds during their marriage. Gingrich published that manuscript in
July, 1934.

Fitzgerald did not send in a manuscript under his name alone for
several months, however. He was trying to recover from debts he had
incurred while writing *Tender Is the Night,* and *Esquire's* going rate of
$200 per item would have been of little help. Gingrich's attentions
were welcome, though, particularly at a time when the *Post* editors
were only giving Fitzgerald unsolicited advice about how to rewrite
the stories of young love he was trying so desperately to manufacture
for them. Some of Gingrich's fan letters survive, and they are eager
indeed. In one lengthy epistle he tells Fitzgerald that he has just finished rereading *This Side of Paradise*—and then proceeds to misspell

8. For information about Fitzgerald's friendship with Mencken during this period,
see James L. W. West III, "The Mencken-Fitzgerald Papers: An Annotated Checklist,"
Princeton University Library Chronicle, 38 (Autumn 1976), 21–45.

9. Gingrich to James L. W. West III, December 18, 1969. In 1969 and 1970 Mr.
Gingrich corresponded with me about his relationship with Fitzgerald. Quotations from
his letters are published in this essay with the kind permission of his widow, Jane Kendall
Gingrich.

Amory Blaine's name as "Emery" throughout the letter.[10] But Gingrich's enthusiasm appears to have been genuine, and Fitzgerald undoubtedly appreciated it.[11] In the late fall of 1934, he sent his first single-authored manuscript to *Esquire*; it was a curious little essay on insomnia called "Sleeping and Waking" which foreshadows the mood and subject matter of "The Crack-Up" series. Two brief stories followed—"The Fiend" (January, 1935) and "The Night before Chancellorsville" (February, 1935)—and Fitzgerald was on his way to becoming a regular *Esquire* contributor.

Gingrich learned early that one of the surest ways to bind authors to a magazine was by debt. In the spring of 1934, *Esquire* made an advance of $3,300 to Hemingway so that he could buy his deep-sea fishing cruiser *Pilar*.[12] Over the months that followed, each contribution from Hemingway simply reduced his debt to the magazine. Fitzgerald dealt with *Esquire* in somewhat the same way: Gingrich would send money to him in small amounts, and each manuscript, when it came in, would reduce his indebtedness by $250 (*Esquire*'s rate had gone up). Gingrich remembered the procedure clearly in 1970:

> The $250 we charged off against every accepted manuscript simply reduced by that amount his outstanding account with us which, while seldom much over a thousand dollars, never stayed much below that amount for very long either. The advances were made in dribs and drabs, as he would wire for them, sometimes at night and sometimes on holidays, and the money was usually wired to him, most often for fifty or a hundred dollars at a time.[13]

By the spring of 1935, however, Fitzgerald had managed to get fairly deeply in debt to *Esquire* and had sent no contribution to the magazine

10. Gingrich to Fitzgerald, May 1, 1935, F. Scott Fitzgerald Papers, Princeton Univ. Library, Princeton, N.J. A large file of Fitzgerald-Gingrich correspondence is housed at Princeton; Miss Jean F. Preston, Curator of Manuscripts there, very kindly made copies of these letters and telegrams available to me.

11. It is interesting to note that Gingrich was one of the earliest serious Fitzgerald collectors. He concentrated on Fitzgerald, Hemingway, and Dos Passos in his early book-collecting efforts; in fact, his initial meeting with Hemingway came through Captain Louis Henry Cohn, Hemingway's first bibliographer and the proprietor of House of Books, then and now one of the most distinguished dealers in modern first editions and manuscripts. See Gingrich, *Nothing but People*, pp. 84–86.

12. Carlos Baker, *Ernest Hemingway: A Life Story* (New York: Charles Scribner's, 1969), p. 259.

13. Gingrich to West, April 13, 1970. Fitzgerald always dealt directly with *Esquire* instead of going through his agent Harold Ober, who seems to have disapproved of the magazine's racy image. Ober probably also felt that it was not worth his time to handle an *Esquire* story for a 10 percent commission on a $250 fee.

for several months. Finally, according to Gingrich, "our auditors began asking about this non-writing writer who was getting more frequent advances than anybody else."[14] So Gingrich visited Fitzgerald in Baltimore and suggested that he write an essay about his inability to produce *Post*-style fiction.[15] The result was "The Crack-Up," Fitzgerald's best-known essay and a crucial document in understanding his disillusionment in the middle and late 1930s. *Esquire* published "The Crack-Up" in February, 1936, and the reaction from readers was immediate. In "Backstage with *Esquire*" Gingrich noted:

> We're seldom right but we were never wronger than when we told SCOTT FITZGERALD, upon receipt of his first article in *The Crack-Up* series, that we thought the whole idea of a series of self-revelatory sketches was lacking in general interest. Seldom has as much interest been aroused by anything printed in our pages. So there'll be some more soon.[16]

Much of the response was mixed or negative, but it was still a response. Letters in *Esquire*'s "The Sound and The Fury" section were scornful as well as sympathetic, but they were the first letters any Fitzgerald contribution to the magazine had drawn.[17] Comments on "The Crack-Up" appeared in several newspapers,[18] and the *New Yorker* ran a notice on the essay in "The Talk of the Town."[19] Many of Fitzgerald's old friends wrote concerned letters to him; he must have enjoyed the attention because his responses were generously long and detailed. It has often been assumed that "The Crack-Up" hurt Fitzgerald's reputation, but Gingrich—who was in a position to observe all reactions—thought otherwise:

> Can't feel that it did any damage. So it got him a brutal letter from Ernest Hemingway and a rather hoity-toity one from Dos

14. Gingrich, *The Armchair "Esquire,"* p. 92.

15. Gingrich, *Nothing but People*, pp. 241–43. See also Gingrich's letter in John A. Higgins, *F. Scott Fitzgerald: A Study of the Stories* (Jamaica, N.Y.: St. John's Univ. Press, 1971), p. 192, n. 45.

16. "Backstage with *Esquire*," *Esquire*, 6 (June 1936), 28.

17. For a negative letter, see Robert Alan Green, "Advice at Twenty," *Esquire*, 5 (April 1936), 8; for a positive letter, see Ernest A. H. Caverhill, "Esq's Advocate," *Esquire*, 6 (August 1936), 6.

18. Bibliotaph, "Tomes and Trifles," Providence (R.I.) *Journal*, January 26, 1936, Sec. 6, p. 8; James Aswell, "My New York," Burlingame (Calif.) *Advance-Star*, February 1, 1936, p. 8; Joseph Henry Jackson, "A Bookman's Notebook," San Francisco *Chronicle*, March 20, 1936, p. 11.

19. "Notes and Comment," *New Yorker*, 12 (March 14, 1936), 11.

Passos. And an interviewer for the *New York Post*, stimulated by it to look him up, did a nasty piece about him that Marjorie Kinnan Rawlings deplored. But don't forget, at this point, sixteen years after his first fame, a lot of people thought he was dead. So the publicity occasioned by the publication of the "Crack-Up" series undoubtedly reminded Hollywood that he was still around, and led either directly or indirectly to his getting his second chance out there, with his contract that took him out there in July of '37. At the "Crack-Up" stage nothing could harm his career—it could only help.[20]

Fitzgerald was so pleased by the wide response to his essay that he decided to explore the topic of his personal disillusionment further. Two sequels to "The Crack-Up," entitled "Pasting It Together" and "Handle with Care," appeared in the March and April, 1936, issues of *Esquire*. And a similar trio of semi-fictional sketches—"Author's House," "Afternoon of an Author," and "An Author's Mother"—was published in July, August, and September, 1936. During this period Fitzgerald also produced several short stories for *Esquire*. Nearly all of them are good; the two entitled "Three Acts of Music" (May, 1936) and "The Long Way Out" (September, 1937) are excellent. Whenever he tried to produce light, humorous fiction in his old manner, however, the results were unfortunate. Three such efforts ended up at *Esquire*— "The Ants at Princeton" (June, 1936), " 'Send Me In, Coach' " (November, 1936), and "The Honor of the Goon" (June, 1937).

Fitzgerald's first stretch as an *Esquire* writer ended when he went to Hollywood in July, 1937. He worked there under contract to Metro-Goldwyn-Mayer until January, 1939. Fitzgerald was handsomely paid during this eighteen-month period, and he had no need of money from *Esquire*. Most of his literary energies were being channeled into studio work in any case, and his writing for the commercial magazine market was limited to revising several already-written stories which had failed to sell. But after his contract with MGM was terminated, he once more turned to *Esquire*—and again the reason was debt. Fitzgerald had left North Carolina in July, 1937, still $200 in the red with *Esquire*. Gingrich wisely did not press for a manuscript right away; instead, he waited until Fitzgerald needed him again. On July 17, 1939, Fitzger-

20. Gingrich to West, December 18, 1969. The "nasty piece about him that Marjorie Kinnan Rawlings deplored" is Michel Mok's "The Other Side of Paradise: Scott Fitzgerald, 40, Engulfed in Despair," New York *Post*, September 25, 1936, pp. 1 and 15; republished in an abbreviated version in *F. Scott Fitzgerald in His Own Time: A Miscellany*, ed. Matthew J. Bruccoli and Jackson R. Bryer (Kent, Ohio: Kent State Univ. Press, 1971), pp. 294–99.

ald contacted Gingrich for an advance of $100 and shortly thereafter sent in two stories, "Design in Plaster" (November, 1939) and "The Lost Decade" (December, 1939).[21] Fitzgerald's account with the magazine was cleared, and he received a check for $200 besides.[22] To Gingrich's delight, Fitzgerald was coming back into the *Esquire* stable. Fitzgerald was still displeased about *Esquire*'s low fees, but the magazine provided him with more than money. The extra bonus was Gingrich himself, who was willing to pay attention to Fitzgerald and advance him funds on short notice. This role had been filled for many years by Harold Ober, Fitzgerald's literary agent in New York, but by the summer of 1939 that relationship had been strained by Ober's justifiable unwillingness to make further advances on unsold stories. Fitzgerald severed business relations with Ober completely in the late fall of 1939, and from that time on Gingrich (and to some degree Maxwell Perkins) functioned as his "handlers."[23]

In early September, 1939, Fitzgerald hit upon the idea of doing a series of stories for *Esquire* about an aging Hollywood hack named Pat Hobby. Writing a series was nothing new for Fitzgerald: he had done the Basil stories and the Josephine stories for the *Post* in the late 1920s and early 1930s. Those two ventures had been so successful that in 1935 Fitzgerald had tried to do a third series for *Redbook* about a medieval count named Philippe and attempted a fourth series for the *Post* in 1936 about an adolescent girl named Gwen. Both of these series were decidedly subpar, though, and neither was ever completed.

The Philippe and Gwen stories had been difficult for Fitzgerald to write, but the Pat Hobby sketches seem to have come easily to him. Between September 16 and November 13, 1939, he sent Gingrich seven stories for the series, and by the end of March, 1940, he had produced nine more. The final story, making seventeen in all, was in Gingrich's hands by late June.[24] But Gingrich had paid for each story as it came in, and Fitzgerald now found that he had saturated his market at *Esquire*. He therefore asked Gingrich to publish some of his other work

21. "Design in Plaster" was selected for Edward J. O'Brien's *The Best Short Stories 1940* (Boston: Houghton Mifflin, 1940).

22. Helene Richards (Gingrich's secretary) to Fitzgerald, July 24, 1939, Fitzgerald Papers.

23. Gingrich even had to see Fitzgerald through one of his periodic binges. For an account of the incident, see Sheilah Graham, *Beloved Infidel* (New York: Holt, 1958), pp. 206–10.

24. Gingrich tells the story of the inception and growth of the series in his Introduction to *The Pat Hobby Stories* (New York: Charles Scribner's, 1962). His comments are based on his correspondence with Fitzgerald and on *Esquire*'s record of when the various Pat Hobby stories arrived at the magazine.

under a pseudonym. Ideally *Esquire* would now publish two Fitzgerald stories in each issue, a Pat Hobby story under his real name and a "regular" story under his *nom de plume*. This plan would dispose of the backlog of Fitzgerald's stories in the *Esquire* files, double his market at the magazine, and make interesting literary news when he revealed himself as the author of the pseudonymous fiction. At best Fitzgerald might stir up attention and publicity as he had with "The Crack-Up" essays; at worst he could keep his identity a secret and pocket the money. He broached this idea to Gingrich in February, 1940, and, in July, Gingrich agreed to the scheme.[25] "On an Ocean Wave" appeared in February, 1941, under the fictitious name "Paul Elgin," but by that time Fitzgerald was dead. No other pseudonymous stories by him appeared in *Esquire*.

When Fitzgerald died in December, 1940, he was seven stories ahead with *Esquire*. Those stories were published in the months that followed, but Fitzgerald's association with the magazine did not end there. Gingrich had already written a tribute to Fitzgerald for the March, 1941, editorial page of *Esquire*,[26] and he printed letters from readers praising Fitzgerald's work as late as September of that year.[27] From 1940 to 1958, writings by Fitzgerald appeared in five of the popular *Esquire* anthologies;[28] and from 1951 to 1965 Gingrich published eight lengthy articles about Fitzgerald in *Esquire* by such writers as George Jean Nathan, Andrew Turnbull, and Vance Bourjaily.[29] Several previously unpublished pieces by Fitzgerald appeared in the mag-

25. Ibid., pp. xvi–xix.

26. Arnold Gingrich, "Salute and Farewell to F. Scott Fitzgerald," *Esquire*, 15 (March 1941), 6; republished in *F. Scott Fitzgerald in His Own Time*, pp. 477–81.

27. Mary Welsh, "Is This Just a Subtle Hint," *Esquire*, 15 (May 1941), 10; Jane Carter, "Keeping Scott's Memory Green," *Esquire*, 16 (September 1941), 10.

28. *The Bedside "Esquire"* (New York: Tudor, 1940) reprints "The Night before Chancellorsville"; *"Esquire's" 2nd Sports Reader* (New York: Barnes, 1946) reprints " 'Send Me In, Coach' "; *The Girls from "Esquire"* (New York: Random House, 1952) reprints "The Woman from Twenty-One"; *The "Esquire" Treasury* (New York: Simon and Schuster, 1953) reprints "Pat Hobby's Christmas Wish"; *The Armchair "Esquire"* (New York: G.P. Putnam's, 1958) reprints "Three Acts of Music."

29. Laurence Stallings, "The Youth in the Abyss," 36 (October 1951), 47, 107–11; George Jean Nathan, "Memories of Fitzgerald, Lewis and Dreiser—The Golden Boy of the Twenties," 50 (October 1958), 148–49; Frances Kroll Ring, "Footnotes on Fitzgerald," 52 (December 1959), 149–50; Budd Schulberg, "Old Scott: The Mask, the Myth, and the Man," 55 (January 1961), 97–101; Andrew Turnbull, "Scott Fitzgerald & Ernest Hemingway," 57 (March 1962), 110–24; Vance Bourjaily, "Fitzgerald Attends My Fitzgerald Seminar," 62 (September 1964), 111, 113, 193–96; Laura Guthrie Hearne, "A Summer with F. Scott Fitzgerald," 62 (December 1964), 160–65, 232, 236–37, 240, 242, 246, 250, 252, 254–58, 260; Frances Lanahan, "My Father's Letters: Advice without Consent," 64 (October 1965), 95–97.

azine,[30] and Gingrich helped keep interest in Fitzgerald active by writing articles about him and editing the Pat Hobby stories for Scribner's.[31] Clearly the *Esquire* connection was important to Fitzgerald during his life, and unquestionably it has been helpful to his reputation since his death.

2.

Critics have long recognized that Fitzgerald's *Esquire* fiction differs from his *Post* fiction. The *Esquire* stories are briefer, less romantic, more tightly structured, rougher in verbal texture—more Chekhovian and "modern" than his efforts for the *Post*. Aside from some general comments, however, virtually no penetrating criticism has been published about the *Esquire* stories.[32] No one has even examined such fundamental aspects as point-of-view, characterization, and theme. Nearly all of Fitzgerald's short fiction is neglected, to be sure, but the *Esquire* stories seem especially and unduly ignored. It is impossible here to deal with all 36 of Fitzgerald's *Esquire* stories, so I have chosen two of the best for discussion below. These two stories, "Three Acts of Music" and "The Lost Decade," are challengingly elliptical short stories with subtle narrative techniques and important themes. Perhaps these comments will suggest how fertile a field the *Esquire* stories are and will prompt other critics to examine this body of fiction in detail.

"Three Acts of Music" (May, 1936) tells the story of two unnamed lovers, a doctor from "a conservative old Vermont family" and a nurse from Yonkers. The lovers appear in only three brief scenes, and in each one they are in a bar where a small band is playing popular tunes. There is no transition between scenes; Fitzgerald simply presents three panels of action and dialogue and does not elaborate.

In the first scene the doctor is still an intern, and the nurse is just beginning her career. They are very much in love and seem to be on

30. F. Scott Fitzgerald, "Advice to a Young Writer," 50 (October 1958), 158–59; "My Generation," 70 (October 1968), 119, 121; "The Fitzgerald-Perkins Papers," 75 (June 1971), 107–11, 171, 174, 176, 178–80, 182–83; "Lo, the Poor Peacock!" 76 (September 1971), 154–58; "Infidelity," 80 (December 1973), 193–200, 290, 292, 294, 296, 298, 300, 302, 304; "On Your Own," *Esquire Fortnightly*, 91 (January 30, 1979), 56–66.

31. Arnold Gingrich, "Scott Fitzgerald's Forgotten Comedy," 58 (July 1962), 2; "Will the Real F. Scott Fitzgerald Please Stand Up and Be Counted?" 62 (December 1964), 8, 10, 12, 16; "Scott, Ernest and Whoever," 66 (December 1966), 186–89, 322–25.

32. The single exception is a dissertation by A. Bryant Mangum, "The Short Stories of F. Scott Fitzgerald: A Study in Literary Economics," Univ. of South Carolina, 1974. The comments on individual pieces by Higgins in *F. Scott Fitzgerald: A Study of the Stories* are routine and unimaginative.

the brink of marriage, though we sense that he is not entirely pleased with her background (he corrects her lower-class pronunciation, for example). This first scene breaks off, and we next see the couple several years later. They have not married. He has chosen to study medicine in Vienna, and she has moved up to a responsible and highly paid position in which she supervises interns and even surgeons. We learn that he did not marry her because his family disapproved of the match. The two lovers lament the passing of time and the loss of opportunity; she weeps, they dance, and the second scene ends.

In the third scene (or "act," if we follow the hint of the title) the man and woman are older still and it is "too late"; now they are both " 'fat and—sort of middle-aged.' " He is a well-known physician, and she is superintendent of a women's hospital. Both have traded love for professional success, but the woman regrets the emptiness of their emotional lives. " 'We never had much. Did we?' " she muses. And she wonders what it would have been like to "have married this man, borne him children, died for him." She also thinks "of how she had lived out of sordid poverty and education—into power—and spinsterhood" (*Price*, pp. 715–16). There the story ends.

This general plot line is quite familiar to readers of Fitzgerald's fiction. He was always fascinated by situations in which a person from a lower-class background falls in love with someone of higher social status. But this little plot is actually not very important in "Three Acts." In fact the story is not really about these two people. Instead, as Fitzgerald emphasizes twice in the text, it is about "music" and "tunes." In each scene, popular songs and lyrics drift through the dialogue; the man and woman hear "Tea for Two," "Always," "Blue Skies," "How about Me," "Remember," "All Alone," "Lovely to Look At," and "Smoke Gets in Your Eyes." In each scene the woman quizzes the man about the composers (Vincent Youmans, Irving Berlin, and Jerome Kern) who wrote these songs. By the end of the story we realize that she has used popular love songs as a substitute for actual love in her emotionally barren life. Her explanation is poignant: " 'It was all we had,' " she says, " 'everything we'll ever know about life' " (*Price*, p. 716).

Fitzgerald is making two related statements in the story. He is saying that most people possess the capacity to love but are unable to express their love in original or moving terms. It is therefore the role of the composer, musician, lyricist, or (by extension) writer to help other persons express love and pain. Popular music, though sometimes shallow and trivial, is one such medium of expression, and popular literature is another. The "public" artist has a function: he helps the inarticulate person speak and shows the undeveloped sensibility how to feel. As the woman in "Three Acts" puts it, " 'Your friend Mr. Berlin can talk better than we can. Listen to him' " (*Price*, p. 713).

The corollary is even more intriguing. Fitzgerald suggests in the last few paragraphs of the story that it is the duty of the popular artist to live through the experiences he writes about. If his songs (or stories) are to be genuine, if they are to arouse true emotion, then they must grow out of actual love and hurt. The artist cannot imagine these things—if he does, his work will be unconvincing. Again the woman hints at the idea: " 'All those people—that Youmans, that Berlin, that Kern. They must have been through hell to be able to write like that. And we sort of listened to them, didn't we?' " (*Price*, p. 716)

The story is almost an *apologia pro vita sua* for Fitzgerald himself. He reveals here his function as a popular artist and tries to explain something about his own tumultuous life. He also expresses the strange closeness he feels toward the thousands of unknown lovers whose emotions he must have moved over the years through his fiction. Fitzgerald is saying that many popular artists like Youmans, Kern, and Berlin must feel this same closeness.

Irving Berlin is especially important in "Three Acts." His name appears several times in the narrative, many of his songs are alluded to, and at four different points his marriage is mentioned. The woman in the story tells us that Berlin has "just married a society girl" and wonders if Berlin is "happy with this Mackay girl." The references are to Berlin's January, 1926, marriage to Ellin Mackay, daughter of Clarence Mackay, a Catholic millionaire and member of New York high society. Berlin, born Israel Baline, had risen from a Jewish neighborhood on the lower East Side to great success as a popular songwriter. He and Ellin eloped, and as a result her father severed all relations with her for five years. Berlin made use of these difficulties in his art, however. He wrote many of his most famous songs, including "All Alone" and "Always," for Ellin while they were first falling in love and seeing one another against her father's wishes. Berlin's biographer remarks, "It was a story that had all the elements of a fairy tale."[33]

The newspapers and gossip columns followed Berlin's romance closely through 1924 and 1925. Fitzgerald, as the author of "Winter Dreams" and *The Great Gatsby*, must have been fascinated by this real-life embodiment of his fiction. He uses Berlin's marriage thematically in "Three Acts" when the woman tells the man, with a touch of bitterness, that Berlin "married the girl—didn't he?" Of course the

---

33. For details about the Berlin-Mackay marriage see Michael Freedland, *Irving Berlin* (New York: Stein and Day, 1974), pp. 73 ff.

situation in "Three Acts" is different: Fitzgerald's *woman* is from a lower-class section of New York and his *man* is from an old and established family, but the parallel is still clear. The woman understands Berlin's music precisely because she and Berlin have lived through similar experiences, although her own love affair has ended sadly. It may even be that Fitzgerald, who liked to see himself as a poor boy who had pursued and won a rich, socially prominent girl, identified with Berlin. Irving Berlin's presence in the story reinforces its theme—that the popular artist must uˢ his own experiences, exploit his own pain, if he is to touch the hearts of his public.

"The Lost Decade" (December, 1939) is probably the best piece of short fiction that Fitzgerald published in *Esquire*. To understand the story fully, one should know the circumstances out of which it grew. No one has ever remarked on the fact, but "The Lost Decade" came from Fitzgerald's initial meeting with Budd Schulberg, and the story was more or less addressed to that writer. The Schulberg episode is familiar to students of Fitzgerald's Hollywood years. In November, 1938, Fitzgerald was hired to collaborate with Schulberg on a script about the Dartmouth Winter Carnival. Fitzgerald was selected for his experience with stories of college life; Schulberg, who was just beginning his literary and filmwriting career, was chosen because Dartmouth was his alma mater. When young Schulberg was told that he would be working with Fitzgerald, he said, "My God, isn't Scott Fitzgerald dead?"[34] Fitzgerald did not hear the remark, but obviously he sensed Schulberg's attitude toward him and restated it fictionally in "The Lost Decade."

The story is told from the point-of-view of a character modeled after Schulberg. He is a young fellow named Orrison Brown—"a curly-haired man who a year before had edited the Dartmouth *Jack-O-Lantern* and was now only too glad to take the undesirable assignments around the office" (*Stories*, p. 470). There can be no doubt that Orrison Brown is based on Budd Schulberg: in 1938 Schulberg, who has very curly hair, was less than three years out of Dartmouth where he had been associate editor of the *Jack-O-Lantern*, a campus humor magazine.[35]

The story takes place in New York City, where Brown is a sub-editor on a news weekly. One of his duties is to take visitors to lunch. His guest on this particular day is Louis Trimble, "a pale, tall man of forty

34. Arthur Mizener, *The Far Side of Paradise: A Biography of F. Scott Fitzgerald* (Boston: Houghton Mifflin, 1965), p. 315.

35. Telephone communication from Dartmouth College Archives, Hanover, N.H., August 22, 1978.

with blond statuesque hair and a manner that was neither shy, nor timid, nor otherwordly like a monk, but something of all three" (*Stories*, p. 470). Trimble's name evokes "some vague memory" for Brown, but he cannot place it and decides not to puzzle over it. Trimble is based on Fitzgerald.

Brown learns from his boss that " 'Mr. Trimble's been away a long time. Or he *feels* it's a long time—almost twelve years' " (*Stories*, p. 470). Brown is intrigued, and during lunch at a small restaurant he attempts to draw Trimble out and learn where he has been. Trimble responds to Brown's questions readily enough, but his answers are noncommittal. Brown asks, " 'You've been out of civilization?' " and Trimble answers, " 'In a sense.' " Brown wonders to himself whether Trimble "could have possibly spent the thirties in a prison or an insane asylum." Brown then asks Trimble, " 'What do you want to see most?' " and again Trimble's answer is cryptic:

> "Well—the back of people's heads. . . . Their necks—how their heads are joined to their bodies. I'd like to hear what those two little girls are saying to their father. Not exactly what they're saying but whether the words float or submerge, how their mouths shut when they've finished speaking." (*Stories*, pp. 471–73)

Brown, who is entirely literal-minded, assumes that Trimble has been *physically* absent for a decade. It therefore comes as a surprise to him when he learns that his guest had dinner in this same restaurant "last May." Brown also discovers that Trimble is an architect and that in 1928 he designed "the Armistead Building," a huge skyscraper in downtown Manhattan. Brown and Trimble walk to the building after lunch and have this revealing exchange:

> He paused by the brass entablature in the cornerstone of the building. "Erected 1928" it said.
> Trimble nodded.
> "But I was taken drunk that year—every-which-way drunk. So I never saw it before now."
> "Oh." Orrison hesitated. "Like to go in now?"
> "I've been in it—lots of times. But I've never seen it. And now it isn't what I want to see. I wouldn't ever be able to see it now. I simply want to see how people walk and what their clothes and shoes and hats are made of. And their eyes and hands." (*Stories*, p. 472)

Trimble of course has been neither intoxicated nor physically absent during the 1930s. Rather it is his spirit, his sensibility, his awareness of others which has been dormant and temporarily deadened. After twelve years of mental absence he is beginning to awaken again; his interest in the subtleties of human appearance and behavior is returning. He does not wish to examine past triumphs and accomplishments; now he is simply curious about people—their looks and speech, their clothes and shoes, their eyes and hands. He wants truly to *see* again. Brown, however, misses the point. At the end of the story Trimble leaves and walks down Fifth Avenue:

> Orrison looked after him when he started out, half expecting him to turn into a bar. But there was nothing about him that suggested or ever had suggested drink.
> "Jesus," he said to himself. "Drunk for ten years."
> He felt suddenly of the texture of his own coat and then he reached out and pressed his thumb against the granite of the building by his side. (*Stories*, pp. 472–73)

This last sentence ends the story, and it is a marvelously subtle touch. It shows that Brown and those like him are hopelessly rooted in the actual and will never understand what it is like to be spiritually dead for a time and then to reawaken. It is tempting to read "The Lost Decade" in terms of Fitzgerald's own life, or more specifically as a response to the callow Schulberg, but in a larger sense it is about any person of genius who abandons interest in life and becomes spiritually dead for a time, lost and unable to see. "The Lost Decade" is about the return of one such man to life and about the inability of most persons—particularly young persons—to understand where he has been and what has happened to him.

This story has an intriguing "architectural" dimension. Fitzgerald had a definite purpose in making Louis Trimble the designer of a famous skyscraper in New York City. The two best-known skyscrapers in New York, then as now, were the Chrysler Building and the Empire State Building, and Fitzgerald seems to have had both structures in mind as general models for Trimble's Armistead Building. Both the Chrysler Building and the Empire State Building were erected εᵗ the end of the 1920s. They were the final and most famous expressions of the brief, feverish skyscraper boom that took place in Gotham from 1925 to 1931. The Chrysler Building was begun in 1928 and completed in 1930; the Empire State Building was begun in 1930 and finished in

1931. Trimble's Armistead Building, like the Chrysler, was "erected" in 1928, but in the story it stands on Fifth Avenue—like the Empire State, which is on the southwest corner of Fifth Avenue and 34th Street. (The Chrysler is farther uptown at Lexington Avenue and 42nd Street.) Both buildings, particularly the Chrysler, are decorated with art deco embellishments—the characteristic architectural style of the late 1920s, also sometimes called "jazz modern."

Both structures became famous as expressions of the American desire to achieve, to rise, to better all previous accomplishments. The Empire State Building, in fact, was built in part simply to go the Chrysler Building one better, topping its altitude by two hundred feet. The craze for these marvelous towers of Babel and Babylon was killed off by the Depression, and Fitzgerald must have considered these two famous skyscrapers as final, end-of-the-decade expressions of the spirit of the 1920s. He must have seen them as architectural symbols of the extravagance, beauty, wealth, folly, and gaucherie of the period, just as he saw his own earlier writings as literary expressions of these same things. But now, ten years later, Fitzgerald's old novels no longer interested him, just as the Armistead Building no longer interests Louis Trimble. Like his creator, Trimble wants to look to the future, not at the past.

In this larger sense, Fitzgerald's story is about America, which was beginning to awaken from its own "lost decade" in 1939. Fitzgerald had long felt that the cycles of his own life paralleled the rises and falls of American society in the 1920s and 1930s. The twenties was his "boom" decade, a time of money, fame, and frivolity. But after Zelda's mental breakdown in the crash year of 1929, Fitzgerald's fortunes had plummeted, and the 1930s were for him "bust" years of remorse and regret, just as they were for America. Many of Fitzgerald's autobiographical heroes feel this same close identity with their times: Charlie Wales in "Babylon Revisited" (1931) and Dick Diver in *Tender Is the Night* are the two best examples. Louis Trimble should be added to their number. In "The Lost Decade" he is recovering from his own dark night of the soul at the same time that America is beginning to come out of the somber 1930s. Both the man and the country are reawakening, chastened by a decade of economic and spiritual depression, more mature and cautious than before. Fitzgerald is not insistent about this level of meaning—in fact, he underplays it—but it is still present in the story. "The Lost Decade" was published (perhaps coincidentally, perhaps not) in December, 1939, the final month of America's most sobering ten-year period. Anyone who read the story in *Esquire* surely knew what Fitzgerald was saying.

Why did Fitzgerald turn, late in his career, to the brief, tightly-structured understated short story form? He had for years produced longer and fuller stories, loose in structure and leisurely in pace, for mass-circulation magazines like the *Post*. In fact, about the only "short short" story that he wrote before 1934 was a charming little tale called "Outside the Cabinet-Maker's," which he published in *Century Magazine* in 1928. Do these late *Esquire* stories show Fitzgerald changing his artistic direction, venturing into the realm of the modern story where Anderson and Hemingway had held the field for so many years? Certainly one would like to think so, but Fitzgerald's real motivation was probably more mundane. The simple fact was that *Esquire* was going to pay him $250 no matter what the length of his contribution, and he had enough professional sense not to write 6,000-word stories for so modest a fee. If no other magazine would take one of these longer efforts, he would sometimes dispose of it at *Esquire*, but the stories he wrote specifically for *Esquire* were always brief and tight. Fitzgerald had decided to give *Esquire* only its money's worth, but a *good* money's worth—a string of well-crafted "short short" stories that would bring in money and keep his name visible on the New York magazine market. As is so often the case in literary studies, Fitzgerald's change in artistic direction seems to have been motivated more by the conditions of the marketplace than by his desire to break fresh ground.

But what a fortuitous circumstance that Fitzgerald should come to *Esquire* during these final years! Without *Esquire* we should not have "The Crack-Up" series or such fine stories as "Three Acts of Music," "The Long Way Out," "Financing Finnegan" (January, 1938), "Design in Plaster," "The Lost Decade," "Three Hours between Planes" (July, 1941), or "Dearly Beloved."[36] Nor would we have the Pat Hobby series, which is thin and often labored but which has its moments. It is even arguable that without *Esquire* to keep him writing and to provide him with money in tight spots, Fitzgerald would not have produced what we have of *The Last Tycoon*.

36. "Dearly Beloved" was not published in *Esquire*—in fact, it did not appear in print until after Fitzgerald's death—but he wrote it for *Esquire* and submitted it there in February, 1940. Gingrich, in one of his few errors in editorial judgment, turned the story down. See James L. W. West III, "F. Scott Fitzgerald to Arnold Gingrich: A Composition Date for 'Dearly Beloved,' " *PBSA*, 67 (Fourth Quarter 1973), 452–54. "Dearly Beloved" was first published in the 1969 *Fitzgerald/Hemingway Annual* and is most conveniently available in *Bits*, pp. 384–86.

Fitzgerald's *Esquire* stories are rich, virgin territory. These narratives represent his final work in the genre of short fiction, and many of them are among his best mature efforts. We need to examine these stories carefully in order to learn where Fitzgerald drew his material for them and how he composed them. Fitzgerald wrote seriously and well for *Esquire;* now it is up to us to study what he had to say.

INDIVIDUAL STORIES

PSYCHIC GEOGRAPHY IN "THE ICE PALACE"

JOHN KUEHL

Although in "Pasting It Together" Fitzgerald called his tendency to *become identified with the objects of my horror or compassion . . .* the death of accomplishment" (C-U, p. 81), it might be argued that to the extent such identification involved *public* phenomena, the texture of his work increased. Thus a subsequent comparison from the same essay, "my recent experience parallels the wave of despair that swept the nation when the Boom was over" (C-U, p. 84)—which suggests Fitzgerald's equation of autobiographical and historical events—led to the concept of emotional bankruptcy. But even more important than Boom and Depression or, for that matter, other temporal obsessions like the American Revolution and World War I, was the Civil War.

Fitzgerald's *Ledger* is filled with references to the last, a typical one being the observation of January, 1902: "He remembers Jack Butler who had two or three facinating books about the Civil War." Besides the play *Coward,* much early fiction (e.g., "A Debt of Honor," [1910], "The Room with the Green Blinds" [1911]) and late (e.g., "The Night at Chancellorsville" [1935], "The End of Hate" [1940]) treats that struggle. Moreover, having grown up in the Middle West and East, Fitzgerald attended the Southerner's Northern university, married a Southern belle, lived in various Southern locations, and was buried in Rockville, Maryland. Of nearby Baltimore, he said:

> I love [Baltimore] more than I thought—it is so rich with memo-
> ries—it is nice to look up the street and see the statue of my great

uncle [an approximate description of Francis Scott Key] & to know
that Poe is buried here and that many ancestors of mine have
walked in the old town by the bay. I belong here, where everything
is civilized and gay and rotted and polite. And I wouldn't mind a
bit if in a few years Zelda & I could snuggle up together under a
stone in some old graveyard here. That is really a happy thought
and not melancholy at all.[1]

Typically ambivalent, the statement, "I belong here, where everything is civilized and gay and rotted and polite," implies a private
conflict with consequences not unlike those Fitzgerald attributed to the
Civil War when he characterized it as the "broken link in the continuity of American life." On the one hand, Scott's father Edward "had
rowed Confederate spies across the river" and watched "Early's battal-
ions stream toward Washington in the last Confederate thrust." Edward's mother, Cecelia Ashton Scott, "was descended from Maryland
families that had figured prominently in the colonial legislatures and
on the governors' councils." Edward's great, great grandfather "was
the brother of Francis Scott Key, and Edward's first cousin was the
son-in-law of Mrs. Suratt, hung for complicity in the assassination of
Lincoln."[2] On the other hand, Scott's mother, born Mary McQuillan,
was the daughter of an Irish immigrant who had prospered in St. Paul
as a wholesale grocer. Her son defined his parental dilemma in a letter
of 1933: "I am half black Irish and half old American stock with the
usual exaggerated ancestral pretensions. The black Irish half of the
family had the money and looked down upon the Maryland side . . .
who had . . . 'breeding' " (*Letters*, p. 503). He connected the active
McQuillans with material success and the passive Fitzgeralds with
material failure but also made it clear through the remarkable document, "The Death of My Father," that though Edward "came from
tired old stock with very little left of vitality and mental energy," he
functioned as Scott's "only moral guide," thanks to "a good heart that
came from another America"—the America "of the generation of the
colonies and the revolution" (AF, pp. 67–68). Like Dick Diver, Scott
Fitzgerald inherited the manners and code of morality both associate
with the pre-Civil War South from an aristocratic but financially inept
sire.

His internal tensions, which were expressed by geographical as well
as historical analogues, sometimes took the form of Middle West versus

1. Andrew Turnbull, *Scott Fitzgerald* (New York: Charles Scribner's, 1962), pp.
266–67.

2. Ibid., pp. 5–6.

East. The Basil Duke Lee stories illustrate this. Published between April 28, 1928, and April 27, 1929, they focus on Fitzgerald's life from 1907 at age eleven in Buffalo to 1913 at age seventeen when he entered Princeton. Fundamentally a Midwestern boy, Basil regards the East as "the fabled world":

> Yale was the faraway East, that he had loved with a vast nostalgia since he had first read books about great cities. Beyond the dreary railroad stations of Chicago and the night fires of Pittsburgh, back in the old states, something went on that made his heart beat fast with excitement. He was attuned to the vast, breathless bustle of New York, to the metropolitan days and nights that were tense as singing wires. Nothing needed to be imagined there, for it was all the very stuff of romance—life was as vivid and satisfactory as in books and dreams. (B&J, p. 147)

Basil Duke Lee, like Nick Carraway and Jay Gatsby, is a Young Man from the Provinces come East to begin his conquest of "the successive worlds of school, college and New York" (B&J, p. 75). However, the chronologically earlier yet biographically later novel displays more ambiguity over the East-West polarity. Nick says *The Great Gatsby* is a "story of the West," and all the leading characters are Westerners who "possessed some deficiency in common which made us subtly unadaptable to Eastern life" (GG, p. 177). The East, then, destroys the older American qualities these Midwesterners have absorbed, qualities only he and Gatsby exhibit. The latter believes one may realize dreams, ideals, and illusions there, but Carraway asserts:

> He had come a long way to this blue lawn, and his dream must have seemed so close that he could hardly fail to grasp it. He did not know that it was already behind him, somewhere back in that vast obscurity beyond the city, where the dark fields of the republic rolled on under the night. (GG, p. 182)

For Gatsby and for America the transcendental, the spiritual, can be found solely in "towns beyond the Ohio," which because they are still located in a pastoral setting, are morally superior to the decadent East.

While significant, however, the East and West of Fitzgerald's psyche were probably not as crucial as the North and South. Nowhere does this become clearer than during "The Ice Palace" (1920), his initial Tarleton story. Its protagonist, Sally Carrol Happer, reappears in the other two—"The Jelly-Bean" (1920) and "The Last of the Belles" (1929)—though less centrally.

That Sally Carrol, like Daisy Fay, was based on Zelda Sayre is evident from the genesis of "The Ice Palace." Twin episodes, one involving a Northern girl and one a Southern girl, figured in the composition of the story:

> The idea of "The Ice Palace" (Saturday Evening Post, May 22d), grew out of a conversation with a girl out in St. Paul, Minnesota, my home. We were riding home from a moving picture show late one November night.
>
> "Here comes winter," she said, as a scattering of confetti-like snow blew along the street.
>
> I thought immediately of the winters I had known there, their bleakness and dreariness and seemingly infinite length, and then we began talking about life in Sweden.
>
> "I wonder," I said casually, "if the Swedes aren't melancholy on account of the cold—if this climate doesn't make people rather hard and chill—" and then I stopped, for I had scented a story.
>
> I played with the idea for two weeks without writing a line. I felt I could work out a tale about some person or group of persons of Anglo-Saxon birth living for generations in a very cold climate. I already had one atmosphere detail—the first wisps of snow weaving like advance-guard ghosts up the street.
>
> At the end of two weeks I was in Montgomery, Alabama, and while out walking with a girl I wandered into a graveyard. She told me I could never understand how she felt about the Confederate graves, and I told her I understood so well that I could put it on paper. Next day on my way back to St. Paul it came to me that it was all one story—the contrast between Alabama and Minnesota.[3]

Obviously, Montgomery-born Zelda represented only the most important autobiographical element in Fitzgerald's first complex treatment of the North-South dichotomy.

Anyone who remembers the confession, "I am half feminine—at least my mind is. . . . Even my feminine characters are feminine Scott Fitzgeralds,"[4] should not be surprised that the author projected his divided nature through a young woman in "The Ice Palace." Having explained, "I want to live where things happen," and having rejected Southern men as "ineffectual," Sally Carrol defines her split: "There's two sides to me. . . . There's the sleepy old side . . . an' there's a sort of energy" (Stories, p. 64). Unfortunately, the story, which begins and ends with images of inertia connecting heroine and landscape, lacks a credible psychological conflict because although "she liked all the winter sports" (Stories, p. 73), her "sleepy old side" completely dominates.

3. "Fitzgerald on 'The Ice Palace': A Newly Discovered Letter," Fitzgerald/Hemingway Annual 4 (1972), 59–60.
4. Turnbull, p. 259.

The iterative metaphor "home" thus becomes rationalization when applied to the North by Sally Carrol—whose previous excursions terminated in Asheville, North Carolina—but certitude when applied to the South.

A six-part narrative, "The Ice Palace" employs the quest-for-identity structure. However, since Sally Carrol's journey produces confirmation rather than transformation, it is circular, starting and stopping at Tarleton "in southernmost Georgia" (i.e., Montgomery, Alabama). Part III, after fiancé Harry Bellamy's visit to establish a March wedding date (in II), occurs on the transitional Pullman train, and Parts IV and V in the nameless Northern city that represents St. Paul, Minnesota. The first and sixth sections transpire during the summer and spring respectively, while the framed sections transpire during the fall and winter. Part VI repeats, sometimes verbatim, the introductory paragraphs of Part I.

If the South and its embodiment, Sally Carrol, are associated with inertia, the North and its embodiment, Harry Bellamy, are associated with energy. Therefore, enthusiastic Harry, who mentions " 'the pep in the air' " (Stories, p. 69) and claims " 'Everybody's healthy here' " (Stories, p. 74), ridicules small-town Southerners. He conversely praises the North as " 'a man's country,' " which has not only produced " 'the best athletes in the world' " but also John J. Fishburn, the " 'greatest wheat man in the Northwest, and one of the greatest financiers in the country' " (Stories, p. 70). The story's real conflict is cultural, then, for the antagonism between Sally Carrol and Harry Bellamy symbolizes a conflict between temperaments geographically determined. She makes this apparent to Roger Patton:

> "You see I always think of people as feline or canine, irrespective of sex."
> "Which are you?"
> "I'm feline. So are you. So are most Southern men an' most of these girls here."
> "What's Harry?"
> "Harry's canine distinctly. All the men I've met tonight seem to be canine."
> "What does 'canine' imply? A certain conscious masculinity as opposed to subtlety?"
> "Reckon so." (Stories, p. 72)

Sally Carrol's hostility toward Northern women or " 'glorified domestics' " like her future sister-in-law ("spiritless conventionality") and her future mother-in-law ("ungracious dumpiness of carriage") is unrelieved, whereas there are at least two exceptions among the men—Mr. Bellamy, because "he was born in Kentucky" and forms "a link between the old life and the new" (*Stories*, pp. 73–74), and Professor Patton, an Easterner with "blue eyes that had . . . some quality of appreciation" (*Stories*, p. 71). Perhaps this "Dangerous Dan McGrew," the man "she preferred," shares an attribute discussed by Edwin Moses:

> In a death-oriented society, the child-like has no place; thus, for instance, Harry's angry tirade on the subject of Southerners, who, according to him, have become lazy and shiftless like the colored people (those archetypes of the child-like nature) whom they live with. The attack on the child-like in Sally Carrol—that is, essentially, on her Southernness—extends even to her typically Southern double name: Harry's mother insists on calling her "Sally."[5]

Geographical antithesis, which poses masculine against feminine and grown-up against childlike, transcends national boundaries. When Patton asks Sally Carrol, " 'how's Carmen from the South?' " (*Stories*, p. 71), he anticipates other allusions involving Latin races. They are supposed to be "tragic," but actually it is the "Ibsenesque" Scandinavians, maintaining "the largest suicide rate in the world," that appear "gloomy," "melancholy," "righteous," "narrow," "cheerless" (*Stories*, p. 72). Drawn toward a similar fatal climate, "thousands of Swedes" have migrated and mingled there where Patton has taught French for ten years. These contemporary locals exhibit atavism during Part V, since then "the full-throated resonant chant of the marching clubs . . . grew louder like some paean of a viking tribe traversing an ancient wild" (*Stories*, p. 78). Moments after, Sally Carrol interprets their shout as "the North offering sacrifice on some mighty altar to the gray pagan God of Snow" (*Stories*, p. 79).

The snow god is opposed by the sun god in "The Ice Palace," whose images of heat and cold are even more pervasive than its related images of inertia and energy. Part I commences, "The sunlight dripped over the house like golden paint" (*Stories*, p. 61), and Part VI, "The wealth of golden sunlight poured . . . heat over the house" (*Stories*, p. 81), while Part II—outside the frame yet still inside Georgia—evinces a "cheerful late sun" (*Stories*, p. 65). An emblem of life, this god has created "tangled growths of bright-green coppice and grass and tall trees" (*Stories*, p. 64).

5. Edwin Moses, "F. Scott Fitzgerald and the Quest to 'The Ice Palace,' " *CEA Critic*, 36 (January 1974), 12.

Up North, however, the "summer child" will walk beneath a sun she will barely recognize, and first she must ride through "white hills and valleys and scattered pines" revealing occasional farmhouses, "ugly and bleak and lone." Each causes Sally Carrol "an instant of chill compassion for the souls shut in there waiting for spring" (*Stories*, pp. 67–68). The city—winter carnival notwithstanding—proves to be equally "dismal," "as though no one lived here" (*Stories*, p. 77). Yet, "here" seems hardly less loveless than lifeless, a condition Sally Carrol intuits when she asks Harry Bellamy, " 'I don't guess this is a very kissable climate, is it?' " (*Stories*, p. 70). Their ecstatic kiss of Part II in the South becomes the dispassionate kisses of Part III in the North, where his "icy-cold face kissed her" and "his cold lips kissed the tip of her ear" (*Stories*, pp. 68, 73). Thus we are prepared for Harry's symbolic desertion later.

Comments like " 'sometimes I look out an' see a flurry of snow, an' it's just as if somethin' dead was movin' " (*Stories*, p. 72) and phrases like "tombing heaps of sleet" (*Stories*, p. 77) echo James Joyce's most celebrated story. Though Fitzgerald possessed The Egoist Press 1922 edition of *Dubliners* (originally published in 1914), he may have read "The Dead" before he composed "The Ice Palace," since other early works were influenced by Joyce—*This Side of Paradise* by *A Portrait of the Artist as a Young Man*, "Absolution" by "The Sisters." Besides, Fitzgerald ranked *Dubliners* among the "great English classics" and in its Contents checked three stories, including "The Dead." There also, snow is associated with extinction:

> . . . snow was general all over Ireland. . . . It was falling, too, upon every part of the lonely churchyard on the hill where Michael Furey lay buried. It lay thickly drifted on the crooked crosses and headstones, on the spears of the little gate, on the barren thorns. His soul swooned slowly as he heard the snow falling faintly through the universe and faintly falling, like the descent of their last end, upon all the living and the dead.[6]

A real edifice supplied Fitzgerald with the physical model for the ice palace, his ultimate expression of death and frozen water:

> I had had the idea of using an ice palace in a story since several months before when my mother told me about one they had in St.

6. James Joyce, *Dubliners* (New York: Viking, 1967), pp. 223–24.

Paul in the eighties. . . . When I reached St. Paul I intrigued my
family into telling me all they remembered about the ice palace.
At the public library I found a rough sketch of it that had appeared in a newspaper of the period.[7]

Nevertheless, Hans Christian Andersen's "The Ice Maiden," containing
Swedes, journey, new home, and broken engagement, could have influenced him. The earlier ice palace resembles the "hard, glittering
crystalline object" John A. Higgins designates "a central symbol" of
"The Cut-Glass Bowl" (1920) and "The Diamond as Big as the Ritz"
(1922) as well as "The Ice Palace,"[8] which bears these two lines from
"Kubla Khan": "It was a miracle of rare device,/ A sunny pleasure-
dome with caves of ice!" Being lost and entombed in such a place is
prefigured by Andersen, too, for his "young hunters and young girls,
men and women who had been lost in the crevasses of the glacier,
stood there, lifelike, with open eyes and smiling lips; and far beneath
them arose from buried villages the church bells' chimes."[9]

Concerned about character and plot, Fitzgerald emphasized "lost"
over "entombed" during the genesis description:

I did the scene where the couple were approaching the palace in a
sleigh, and of a sudden I began to get the picture of an ice labyrinth so I left the description of the palace and turned at once to
the girl lost in the labyrinth.[10]

Fitzgerald's palace, Canuck-built and fortresslike in aspect, as the Viking invaders are hostlike, harbors many "labyrinths downstairs." After
Harry vanishes, Sally Carrol experiences characteristic confusion: "She
reached a turn—was it here?—took the left and came to what should
have been the outlet into the long, low room, but it was only another
glittering passage with darkness at the end" (Stories, p. 79). Her symbolic crisis terminates finally when Roger Patton, heralded by "a pale-
yellow sun," arrives. Both psychological and cultural dilemmas resolved,
Sally Carrol screams, " 'Take me home . . . tomorrow' " (Stories, p.
81).

7. "Fitzgerald on 'The Ice Palace,' " p. 60.

8. John A. Higgins, F. Scott Fitzgerald: A Study of the Stories (Jamaica, N.Y.: St.
John's Univ. Press, 1971), p. 55.

9. Frederick Jacobi, Jr., ed., Tales of Grimm and Andersen (New York: Random
House, 1952), p. 412.

10. "Fitzgerald on 'The Ice Palace,' " p. 60.

Still, the concept of entombment is *thematically* more important than that of bewildered estrangement. One "wide passage" was "like a damp vault connecting empty tombs" (*Stories*, p. 79). Then the protagonist "was alone with this presence that came out of the North. . . . It was an icy breath of death . . . rolling down . . . to clutch at her." She feels "damp souls . . . haunted this place," and, reminiscent of "The Ice Maiden," fears "she might . . . freeze to death and lie embedded in the ice like corpses she had read of, kept perfectly preserved until the melting of a glacier" (*Stories*, p. 80).

These ominous allusions are countered by a vision of dead Margery Lee, "with a young, white brow, and wide, welcoming eyes," and faded Tarleton "tombstones" (*Stories*, pp. 80–81), which precede Sally Carrol's deliverance in Part V but which derive from "one of her favorite haunts," the cemetery of Part II. This vision comforts partly because of climatic considerations: "Oh, if there should be snow on her grave! . . . Her grave—a grave that should be flower–strewn and washed with sun and rain" (*Stories*, p. 77).

However, it is the tie between the past and the Southern cemetery—a tie Fitzgerald would reforge personally and fictionally—that makes Sally Carrol happy and strong there. Margery Lee died young (1844–1873) yet continues to inspire romantic speculation: " 'And she was the sort of girl born to stand on a wide, pillared porch and welcome folks in. I think perhaps a lot of men went away to war meanin' to come back to her; but maybe none of 'em ever did.' " Those men might rest over the hill among the Confederate dead, whose inscriptions show "only a name and a date, sometimes quite indecipherable." Though obscure, they " 'died for the most beautiful thing in the world—the dead South' " (*Stories*, pp. 65–66).

The alive North, on the other hand, lacks tradition—a fact Sally Carrol notes when she compares "the battered old library at home, with her father's huge medical books, and the oil-paintings of her three great uncles, and the old couch that had been mended up for forty-five years and was still luxurious to dream in" to the Bellamy library, "neither attractive nor particularly otherwise . . . a room with a lot of fairly expensive things in it that all looked about fifteen years old" (*Stories*, p. 69). Harry claims he inhabits " 'a three-generation town,' " where " 'everybody has a father, and about half . . . grandfathers,' " but he must admit, " 'Back of that we don't go.' " Their " 'social model' " is, consequently, the daughter of " 'the first public ash man' " (*Stories*, p. 69). And their current ice palace, while impressive— " 'a hundred and seventy feet tall,' " " 'six thousand square yards,' " " 'walls twenty to forty inches thick' "(*Stories*, p. 78)—will be as temporary as the last one of 1885. Whatever history it connotes seems barbaric, foreign, vague.

According to Sally Carrol, there are people even now who embody the Southern past:

> "I've tried in a way to live up to those past standards of noblesse oblige—there's just the last remnants of it, you know, like the roses of an old garden dying all around us—streaks of strange courtliness and chivalry in some of these boys an' stories I used to hear from a Confederate soldier who lived next door, and a few old darkies." (*Stories*, p. 66)

That Fitzgerald intended his heroine to be the reincarnation of an archetypal predecessor becomes clear during two separate incidents where Sally Carrol invokes the archetype's ghost. At the cemetery, she says, " 'Dear Margery Lee. . . . Can't you see her?' " (*Stories*, p. 65) and, again, at the ice palace, " 'Why, it's Margery Lee. . . . I knew you'd come' " (*Stories*, p. 80). Reincarnation means the South achieves perpetuity through empathy, a sharp contrast to the North's preservation through refrigeration. As concomitant, Southern life-in-death represented by Sally Carrol, the resurrected antebellum woman, opposes Northern death-in-life represented by Harry Bellamy, the kiss of death. "Energy," which he relates to health, and "inertia," which he relates to degeneracy, are equally ironic states.

Nonetheless, the second 1920 Tarleton trilogy piece proves how critical Fitzgerald could be about the South even then. "The Jelly-Bean" begins, "Jim Powell was a Jelly-bean. . . . and he grew lazily all during Jelly-bean season . . . every season, down in the land of the Jelly-beans well below the Mason-Dixon line" (6TJA, p. 17), and ends, "In this heat nothing mattered. All life was weather. . . . Down in Georgia . . . this is the greatest wisdom of the South—so after a while the Jelly-bean turned into a pool-hall" (6TJA, p. 34). Furthermore, female antagonist Nancy Lamar drinks, gambles, drives carelessly, and runs off with a man she feels only indifference towards.

Describing what happened later, Scott Donaldson cites the third Tarleton story, "The Last of the Belles":

> The Southern belle that Scott Fitzgerald had bodied forth with the charming and vulnerable Sally Carrol in 1920 was transformed by 1929 into the vicious and cruelly aristocratic Ailie Calhoun. The girls come from the same town, they shop at the same drug store together, but there is a world of difference between them.

Donaldson, who argues Fitzgerald "was locked with his wife in a struggle for survival," finds the author's literary disenchantment over the South the result of personal experience. So Fitzgerald insisted their daughter attend Northern schools and forbade Southern boyfriends. He "dictated that Scottie should avoid the insidious appeal of warmer, softer climes and grow up tough and strong in a hardier region."[11] Zelda, the culprit, is frequently indicted—for example, in a letter of July 7, 1938:

> Then the dream divided one day when I decided to marry your mother after all, even though I knew she was spoiled and meant no good to me. . . . But I was a man divided—she wanted me to work too much for *her* and not enough for my dream. She realized too late that work was dignity, and the only dignity, and tried to atone for it by working herself, but it was too late and she broke and is broken forever. . . . We belonged to different worlds—she might have been happy with a kind simple man in a southern garden. She didn't have the strength for the big stage—sometimes she pretended, and pretended beautifully, but she didn't have it. She was soft when she should have been hard, and hard when she should have been yielding. She never knew how to use her energy— she's passed that failing to you. (*Letters*, p. 32)

Whereas his wife's indolence was willful—"never knew how to use her energy"—his father's had been inherited—"tired old American stock"—and thus Fitzgerald continued to love him. Edward died of heart trouble during January, 1931, an event Scott, having traveled from Europe to Maryland to attend the funeral, fictionalized in *Tender Is the Night*:

> For an hour, tied up with his profound reaction to his father's death, the magnificent facade of the homeland, the harbor of New York, seemed all sad and glorious. . . .
>
> Next day at the churchyard his father was laid among a hundred Divers, Dorseys, and Hunters. It was very friendly leaving him there with all his relations around him. . . .
>
> "Good-by, my father—good-by, all my fathers." (TITN, pp. 204–5)

Despite everything, the elder Fitzgerald and the South he personified remained for his son the source of those historical American values Dick Diver calls "honor, courtesy, and courage."

11. Scott Donaldson, "Scott Fitzgerald's Romance with the South," *Southern Literary Journal*, 5 (Spring 1973), 8, 10.

SEEING SLIGHTLY RED:
FITZGERALD'S "MAY DAY"

JAMES W. TUTTLETON

"May Day," a tale rich in social resonance, is authentic, vintage Fitzgerald. It flutters like a warning flag; it signals the locus of serious tensions and divisions in American society. It gazes with both bemusement and fascinated horror at the malaise of the time. It embodies the social sickness of the era in images of ennui, emotional deadness, complaisant self-indulgence, and in visions of the violence of accidental death, suicide, and anarchic riot. Yet the story vibrates just as resonantly with those very personal urgencies and intensities that always signal Fitzgerald's most autobiographical fiction. If, as John P. Marquand once claimed, a writer has only one story to tell and repeats it with variations throughout his career, "May Day" is a particularly apt, early formulation of the Fitzgerald "story." It combines with uncommon adroitness the social and the psychological, the public and private tensions of Fitzgerald the man and the historical moment, the year 1919. Very nearly all of the themes of the major and more mature stories are here, masterfully disposed, as Sergio Perosa has remarked, with "an economy of means that makes it possible for a vast frame of events to find its focus."[1]

As a very personal narrative, expressing Fitzgerald's analysis of his own emotional states, we may note the relation of his personal life to the facts of its composition. The tale was written in the early months of 1920 and published in July of that year in H. L. Mencken's the

1. Sergio Perosa, *The Art of F. Scott Fitzgerald*, trans. Charles Metz and Sergio Perosa (Ann Arbor: Univ. of Michigan Press, 1965), p. 33.

Smart Set.[2] Between Fitzgerald's departure from Princeton in 1917 and the composition of the story, he had gone through his army experience at Camp Sheridan in Alabama; he had met, fallen in love with, proposed to, and been rejected by Zelda Sayre, who thought him too poor to provide the life style they both wanted; he had rewritten, revised, and had accepted his first novel, *This Side of Paradise*; he had discovered Dreiser, Mencken, and Frank Norris; and he had shuttled back and forth between Montgomery and New Orleans, Princeton and New York in an effort, finally successful, to induce Zelda to marry him.[3] These experiences find their fictional transformation in "May Day."

Getting the "top girl" is of course a recurrent, even obsessive, aspect of the one story that Fitzgerald had to tell; and in the relationship of the struggling artist Gordon Sterrett and Edith Bradin, the "World's Worst Butterfly," aspects of the emotional history of Scott and Zelda in the immediate postwar years are intricately elaborated. As Fitzgerald later remarked in "My Lost City" in 1932, with reference to the four miserable months he spent living in the Bronx just before the publication of "May Day," "I was so entangled in life that a period of mellow monasticism in Washington Square was not to be dreamed of. . . . and in a haze of anxiety and unhappiness I passed the four most impressionable months of my life" (C-U, p. 25). Something of Sterrett's sensibility—as one rejected in love, failed in his art, and estranged from his wealthy former classmates—is also suggested in Fitzgerald's remark in "The Crack-Up" that New York City during those four months

had all the iridescence of the beginning of the world. The returning troops marched up Fifth Avenue and girls were instinctively drawn East and North toward them—this was the greatest nation and there was gala in the air. As I hovered ghost-like in the Plaza Red Room of a Saturday afternoon, or went to lush and liquid garden parties in the East Sixties or tippled with Princetonians in

2. Robert Sklar, *F. Scott Fitzgerald: The Last Laocoön* (New York: Oxford Univ. Press, 1967), p. 71.

3. Parts of the story appear to have been written in New Orleans during January, 1920, while Fitzgerald was living on Prytania Street. Twice during that month he went up from New Orleans to Montgomery to allay Zelda's anxiety about the marginality of his income and about their future together. Later that spring, back in Princeton, he wrote to Maxwell Perkins from the Cottage Club that he could not work there, "so have just about decided to quit work and become an ash-man. Still working on that Smart Set novellette ['May Day']," *Dear Scott/Dear Max: The Fitzgerald-Perkins Correspondence*, ed. John Kuehl and Jackson R. Bryer (New York: Charles Scribner's, 1971), p. 29. Very probably the tale was finished late that spring, while Fitzgerald was living in the Bronx and working for a Manhattan advertising agency.

the Biltmore Bar I was haunted always by my other life—my drab room in the Bronx, my square foot of the subway, my fixation upon the day's letter from Alabama—would it come and what would it say?—my shabby suits, my poverty, and love. While my friends were launching decently into life I had muscled my inadequate bark into midstream. . . . I was a failure—mediocre at advertising work and unable to get started as a writer. Hating the city, I got roaring, weeping drunk on my last penny and went home. (C-U, pp. 25-26)

Fitzgerald's attitude toward money—mingled envy and hatred of the rich man who might exercise a *droit de seigneur* and take away his girl—finds expression in Gordon Sterrett's ambivalence toward Phil Dean, whose Biltmore Hotel room is littered with silk shirts and expensive ties, while Gordon in a "faint gray" shirt frayed at the cuffs contemplates his own "faded and thumb-creased" necktie (*Stories*, p. 84). The scene at Brooks Brothers (here called Rivers Brothers), where Phil picks out a dozen neckties and laments the unavailability of the "Welsh Margotson" and the "Covington" collars while Gordon suffers growing panic over whether he will get a $300 loan, brings into sharp focus the emotional estrangement between the casual and careless rich man and the impoverished would-be artist.

Both Phil Dean and the top girl, Edith Bradin, emotionally withdraw from Sterrett because the stink of failure is on him. " 'I'm a failure,' " he tells Edith. " 'I'm poor as hell' " (*Stories*, p. 104). This equation of poverty and failure is endemic in all of Fitzgerald's most personal prose. As Gordon remarks, " 'I'm on my own now, you know, and Phil, I can't stand being poor.' " To Phil, Gordon seems to be "sort of bankrupt—morally as well as financially," with the effect that an aura of evil surrounds him. For Gordon, that "air of worry and poverty and sleepless nights" makes the two kinds of bankruptcy, moral and economic, " 'go together' " (*Stories*, p. 87).

Implicit in the fate of Gordon Sterrett, however, are two other considerations which bear remark. Sterrett is sometimes seen as an artist figure victimized by philistine American culture, which is said to destroy the man of imagination and talent. Sterrett pleads, " 'I've got talent, Phil; I can draw—but I just don't know how. I ought to go to art school and I can't afford it.' " He claims to be able to " 'draw like a streak' " but " 'half the time I haven't had the money to buy decent drawing materials—and I can't draw when I'm tired and discouraged and all in' " (*Stories*, pp. 87-88). But Sterrett hardly serves as a club to beat philistine America. He is too self-indulgent, too full of whining

184 / JAMES W. TUTTLETON

self-pity, as was his author sometime later, to merit much sympathy. His making " 'a hell of a mess of everything' " (*Stories*, p. 85) in the three short months since his discharge from the army seems less the consequence of the "dirty war" than of the continuous immediate postwar fun and games: " '. . . everybody began to come back from France in droves—and all I did was to welcome the newly arrived and go to parties with 'em. That's the way it started, Phil, just from being glad to see everybody and having them glad to see me' " (*Stories*, p. 86). If it is true, as Mizener remarks, that Sterrett is "Fitzgerald's exaggeratedly condemnatory portrait of himself," and if Gordon's suicide reflects "Fitzgerald's moments of acute despair over his financial situation,"[4] Sklar is undoubtedly right in remarking that "there is no evidence in the story that Gordon Sterrett is the victim of anything more than natural weakness; and his poverty is not a cause of his degeneration, but its result."[5]

Nor are we made to feel much sympathy for Sterrett in his relationship with Jewel Hudson. In the early part of the story, she is projected as a low, sexually corrupted woman who covets Gordon's money and social status. " 'She used to be "pure," I guess, up to a year ago,' " he tells Phil. " 'Lived here in New York—poor family. Her people are dead now and she lives with an old aunt' " (*Stories*, p. 86). As such, she might seem an effective foil to the top girl, the "pure woman" Edith Bradin, who sees "a quality of weakness in Gordon that she wanted to take care of," who thinks of herself as "made for love," and who in fact wants to get married. But like most of the fictional top girls, Edith is emotionally insincere and inaccessible, thoroughly trivial, and totally shallow. She mistreats Peter Himmel "because he had not succeeded in kissing her" (*Stories*, p. 100); fakes a friendliness with various shadowy men on the dance floor; and, after "falling in love with her recollection of Gordon Sterrett" (*Stories*, p. 98), cuts the real Gordon dead at the Delmonico dance. Jewel Hudson may be over-rouged and pulpy of lip, but marriage to her seems hardly a cause for suicide. And Fitzgerald is careful to establish the authenticity of her feelings for Gordon: " 'Haven't I just been saying that it [the money] doesn't matter? I wanted to see *you*, Gordon . . .' " (*Stories*, p. 56).

In several ways, then, the disintegration and suicide of Gordon Sterrett are less the consequence of philistine America or a gold-digging woman than the effect of a self-induced paralysis of the moral will. In the portrait of this psychic causation, Fitzgerald was immeasurably

4. Arthur Mizener, *The Far Side of Paradise: A Biography of F. Scott Fitzgerald* (Boston: Houghton Mifflin, 1965), p. 88.

5. Sklar, p. 77.

affected by two new overwhelming influences—Frank Norris and
H. L. Mencken. In a letter dated February 3, 1920, Fitzgerald told Maxwell Perkins:

> I've fallen lately under the influence of an author who's quite
> changed my point of view. He's a chestnut to you, no doubt, but
> I've just discovered him—Frank Norris. I think *McTeague* & *Van-*
> *dover* are both excellent. I told you last November that I'd read
> *Salt* by his brother Charles and was quite enthusiastic about it.
> Odd! There are things in "Paradise" that might have been written
> by Norris—those drunken scenes, for instance—in fact all the re-
> alism. I wish I'd stuck to it throughout! Another of my discoveries
> is H. L. Mencken, who is certainly a factor in present day litera-
> ture. In fact I'm not so cocksure about things as I was last sum-
> mer—this fellow Conrad seems to be pretty good after all.[6]

Norris was a postcollege discovery of Fitzgerald. In his years at
Princeton, he later complained, none of his English professors ever
remarked that books like Norris's had been or were being written: "The
realism which now walks Fifth Avenue was then hiding in Tenth Street
basements." But since then, he observed, "Brigadier General Mencken
has marshalled the critics in an acquiescent column of squads for the
campaign against Philistia."[7] To Fitzgerald's proposal that a special
edition of Norris's fiction be published, Mencken replied, "it goes without saying that I'll be glad to help it along."[8] From *McTeague: A Story*
of San Francisco, Fitzgerald may indeed have been inspired in "May
Day" "to try a more expansive social setting, to widen his range of
characters—in short to tell rather than to just imply the story of a place
and time," as Sklar observes. And it seems inescapably true that the
degeneration of Gordon Sterrett is derived from *Vandover and the*
Brute, which also portrays "an upper-class pseudo-artist who drank, let
his talent go, lost his money, and got in trouble with a girl." Sterrett's
death, as Sklar rightly remarks, is "simply the last step of an already
determined solution to a naturalistic equation. . . ."[9]
Yet Norris's influence is also to be seen in the characterization of the
soldiers Gus Rose and Carrol Key, who are called "human beings" but

6. *Dear Scott/Dear Max*, p. 28.
7. F. Scott Fitzgerald, review of *Brass* by Charles Norris, *Bookman*, 54 (November
1921), 253.
8. Quoted in John Kuehl, "Scott Fitzgerald's Reading," in *Profile of F. Scott Fitzger-*
ald, ed. Matthew J. Bruccoli (Columbus, Ohio: Charles E. Merrill, 1971), p. 50.
9. Sklar, pp. 73–74.

who are described as ugly, ill-nourished, and "devoid of all except the very lowest form of intelligence" (*Stories*, p. 91). Both incarnate the view, derived from Norris's *McTeague*, that certain individuals are biologically degenerate, or virtually subhuman, owing to hereditary atavisms induced by generations of ancestral alcoholism, syphilis, or other diseases. Indeed, if Key's name hints that "in his veins, however thinly diluted by generations of degeneration, ran blood of some potentiality," Key's face offers no "suggestion of either ancestral worth or native resourcefulness." Rose, the Jew with "rat eyes" and a "much-broken hooked nose," is a creature of the "world of snarl and snap" (*Stories*, p. 92). As animal-like incarnations of Norris's brand of naturalism, both are instruments and victims of the social disorder which erupts on May Day in the tale, Key plunging accidentally to his death from the office window of *The Trumpet* and Rose arrested and jailed for assault and battery upon Henry Bradin.

Mencken's influence is immediately to be seen in two aspects of the story: the theme of character in decay, and in the satiric treatment of socialism as a political ideology. The second of these themes will be discussed later on. Here it is sufficient to say that Mencken served as a powerful impetus to Fitzgerald's natural tendency to see something romantic in the touch of disaster befalling the decadent protagonist. Throughout his whole career Fitzgerald was fascinated with the deterioration of a man going gallantly to the devil. If, as Fitzgerald put it in "The Note-Books," "the very elements of disintegration seemed . . . romantic" (C-U, p. 206), Mencken's championing of realism served to put the theme in a new perspective. In both "May Day" and *The Beautiful and Damned* we are given realistic portrayals of character in decline; and it is well to remember that "May Day" was a discarded beginning to *The Beautiful and Damned*.

With remarkable prescience, Fitzgerald foresaw in 1920 the implications of the riotous events of May 1, 1919, as inaugurating a new historical era, the Jazz Age. He later told Max Perkins that "if Mark Sullivan is going on you might tell him I claim credit for naming it [the Jazz Age] & that it extended from the suppression of the riots on May Day 1919 to the crash of the Stock Market in 1929—almost exactly one decade."[10] In "Echoes of the Jazz Age" (1931), he observed that the Jazz Age began with the police riding down "the demobilized country boys gaping at the orators in Madison Square"—the sort of action

> bound to alienate the more intelligent young men from the prevailing order. We didn't remember anything about the Bill of

10. *Dear Scott/Dear Max*, p. 171.

Rights until Mencken began plugging it, but we did know that
such tyranny belonged in the jittery little countries of South Europe. If goose-livered businessmen had this effect on the govern-
ment, then maybe we had gone to war for J. P. Morgan's loans
after all. . . . It was characteristic of the Jazz Age that it had no
interest in politics at all. (C-U, pp. 13–14)

Yet more than gaping motivated the police charge on the mob of
servicemen, and "May Day" was not lacking in a political point of
view. The facts are these. On May 1, 1919, in several American cities,
including New York, mobs of soldiers and sailors attacked political
groups celebrating May Day, the traditional socialist holiday.[11] Several
factors made the 1919 holiday especially violent. The Socialists and
trade-unionists were protesting the imprisonment of Eugene V. Debs,
"Big Bill" Haywood, and Thomas J. Mooney for their political opinions. In the week before May Day, more than thirty homemade bombs
had been discovered in the United States Post Office, some of them
addressed to Mayor John F. Hylan of New York City, Judge D. C.
Westenhaver, who had sentenced Debs, and Judge Kenesaw Mountain
Landis, who had sentenced Haywood.

The soldiers and sailors who provoked the riots were animated by a
hatred of the Socialists' pacifist views during World War I, which they
equated with pro-Germanism, and by hatred of the Bolsheviks, who
had mounted the revolution in Russia in 1917, only two years before.
On this May 1, the eve of Attorney General Mitchell Palmer's "Red
Decade," a mob of about four hundred servicemen invaded *The Call*,
a Socialist daily with offices on Pearl Street. They also broke up a
reception of the board of directors at the new office of *The Call* at 112
Fourth Avenue. The New York *Times* reported that "one of the Call
stockholders, who was threatened by soldiers, ran to the rear of the
building and jumped from a window twenty-five feet above the
ground."[12] Another mob of soldiers and sailors, repulsed at the Madison
Square Garden concert arranged by the Amalgamated Clothing Work-

11. While May Day is a labor and socialist holiday, its other implications should not
be discounted. Its associations with various fertility festivals, indicated by dancing about
the May Pole and crowning the May Queen, may have an ironic bearing on the relationships of Edith Bradin and Jewel Hudson to Gordon Sterrett. That Edith might be so
regarded as the May Queen is intimated, perhaps, in the suggestive remarks of the
soldiers who invade *The Trumpet* office. In addition, the call "May Day" is a wireless or
radio distress signal, especially for aircraft and ships at sea—falsely derived, it would
seem, from the French *m'aidez*, "help me." As such, the urgency of the call in the
presence of disaster is particularly appropriate to the story.

12. "Soldiers and Sailors Break Up Meetings," New York *Times*, May 2, 1919, p. 3;
reprinted in *Fitzgerald and the Jazz Age*, ed. Malcolm and Robert Cowley (New York:
Charles Scribner's, 1966), pp. 57–59.

ers Union, marched down to the People's House at 7 East 15th Street and forced the Socialists to raise an American flag in front of the building. Another mob entered the Russian Workers' House at 133 East 15th Street, "trashed" all of the printed propaganda they could find, and forced those present to sing "The Star-Spangled Banner." Other Socialist groups were attacked at Webster Hall and at open-air rallies in Harlem, where resolutions were proclaimed calling for "the repeal of the espionage law, withdrawal of American troops from Russia, and the lifting of the postal ban on radical publications."[13]

There seems every likelihood that these were not spontaneous demonstrations but were secretly financed and well-organized attacks. In the repulsed assault on the Madison Square Garden concert, the soldiers—who claimed to be in search of "the German meeting"—arrived in a large white sightseeing bus and formed a phalanx when the bugle calls "Assembly" and "To Arms" were sounded. Sidney Hillman, president of the Amalgamated Clothing Workers Union, later absolved these "duped" servicemen of the attack and blamed "the Junker element," which he said was "attempting to destroy the labor movement."[14]

The tension between capital and labor in the story is neither merely historical nor incidental. And Fitzgerald's sympathy with the Socialists is not shallow. At Princeton Fitzgerald had been deeply influenced by Shaw, Wells, and the English Fabians. With his traumatic resentment of the very rich, he found a natural sympathy with the views of literary figures like Upton Sinclair, whose *The Jungle* had ended in a call for socialism. Sinclair Lewis, who had been with Upton Sinclair at Helicon Hall, a communitarian society, had also boldly proclaimed "The Passing of Capitalism" in *The Bookman* in 1914. Sherwood Anderson's "Why I Am a Socialist" is another of those formulations by literary figures who had a pronounced sympathy with the socialist political position.

In the decade between 1926 and 1936, Fitzgerald later confessed, "my political conscience had scarcely existed . . . save as an element of irony in my stuff" (C-U, p. 79). But this fact should not make us disregard the explicit "political content" of the fiction before 1926 or after 1936; nor should we be insensitive to its implicit ideology during that decade. A work contemporaneous with "May Day"—*This Side of Paradise*—ends with Amory Blaine's defense of socialism to the capitalist father of one of his former Princeton classmates. " 'This is the first

13. Ibid.
14. Ibid.

time in my life I've argued Socialism,' " Amory declares. " 'It's the only
panacea I know. I'm restless. I'm sick of a system where the richest
man gets the most beautiful girl if he wants her, where the artist
without an income has to sell his talents to a button manufacturer.' "
And he tells Jesse Ferrenby's father that he has " 'every reason to throw
my mind and pen in with the radicals' " (TSOP, pp. 277–78). Upton
Sinclair, Fitzgerald told Perkins in 1922, had led him to conclude that
"freedom has produced the greatest tyranny under the sun" in America. "I'm still a socialist," he wrote; but he said that he dreaded that
"things will grow worse and worse the more the people nominally rule.
The strong are too strong for us and the weak too weak" (*Letters*, p.
154).

The Great Gatsby is pervaded with, if not revolutionary fervor, at
least deep-seated resentment of the careless and irresponsible affluent
class produced by capitalism. And it is well to remember that *Tender Is
the Night*, in its outline form, identifies Dick Diver as a communist
who will at the end of the novel send his son to Russia for the right
kind of education. Between 1932 and 1934, in fact, Fitzgerald even
"let 'La Paix' be used for meetings organized by local Communists."[15]
He had great trouble, he told Ceci Taylor at this time, in reconciling
his "double allegiance to the class I am part of, and the Great Change
I believe in" (*Letters*, p. 417), and he broke with the Communists in
1934 only because of their meddlesomeness in his art and their repre-
hensible position on the Negro question. Yet toward the end of his life,
he reaffirmed to his daughter Scottie that he did not believe that "the
system that produced Barbara Hutton [a millionaire playgirl] could
survive more than ten years, any more than the French monarchy
could survive 1789" (*Letters*, p. 36). He said that "most questions in
life" had an "economic basis (at least according to us Marxians)" (*Letters*, p. 47), and he reminded Scottie that if she read "the terrible
chapter in *Das Kapital* on 'The Working Day' " she would never be
"quite the same" (*Letters*, p. 102). Finally, to Perkins just before his
death Fitzgerald observed that Spengler and Marx were "the only
modern philosophers that still manage to make sense of this horrible
mess . . ." (*Letters*, p. 290).

I have gone somewhat afield from "May Day" in order to accent
what I believe to be a lifelong sympathy with the ideology of socialism.
It is doubtless true that Fitzgerald was an individualist, hustling with
the best of the entrepreneurs to make a dollar—in his case from fiction.

15. Henry Dan Piper, *F. Scott Fitzgerald: A Critical Portrait* (New York: Holt,
Rinehart and Winston, 1965), pp. 175–76.

And it is unarguable that his views were sketchy and based more on feeling than on dialectical materialism. But his socialist sympathies color his fiction and should not be lightly regarded by those who would grasp the ideological subtext of his work.

In "May Day," however, the treatment of socialism is a rather confused and ambivalent affair. On the one hand, we are made to sympathize with the Socialists as idealistic victims of the mindless mobs which rove the streets. The man on Sixth Avenue who is beaten up for haranguing the crowd on J. P. Morgan's and John D. Rockefeller's war beautifully adumbrates the fate of Henry Bradin, who is assaulted in his office by Rose, Key, and the mob. The mindless chant, "Kill the Bolsheviki—We're Americuns," is artfully satirized as the raving of those who have already been shown to be less than fully human.

Yet the Socialists presented here are not wholly noble political standard-bearers of the brotherhood of man. Something of Fitzgerald's own American nativism is suggested in the language describing the street-corner orator as a "gesticulating little Jew with long black whiskers" (*Stories*, p. 93); *The Trumpet* office worker Bartholomew, described as giving "the impression of a Middle-Western farmer on a Sunday afternoon," is called "loosely fat" (*Stories*, p. 112). And before we ever meet him, Henry Bradin is described by Gordon Sterrett as "sort of a socialistic nut" (*Stories*, p. 90); we later learn that he has left a Cornell instructorship in economics to come to New York in order, in Fitzgerald's words, "to pour the latest cures for incurable evils into the columns of a radical weekly newspaper" (*Stories*, p. 100). A member of the upper class, given to radical chic, Bradin is described as dissociated from the working class he presumes to help. Twice he is described as having "far-away eyes" that seem "always fixed just over the head of the person to whom he was talking" (*Stories*, p. 111); and when the soldiers break into the newspaper office and he declaims his propaganda with his "far-away eyes fixed over the heads of the crowd" (*Stories*, p. 115), it is no wonder that they break his leg. As a visionary idealist, he cannot establish any human connection with those for whom socialism was supposed to be the only panacea.

Why should Fitzgerald here have satirized those with whom he would normally have sympathized? He may of course have wished to explore what Henry James had called "the possible other case"; that is, he may have wished to lay bare another dimension of his political subject, the artist's natural wish to deepen the complexity of his material. And it is true that Fitzgerald always projects something of a double point of view toward the moral character of the social classes produced by capitalism. But the peculiar quality of his treatment of the Socialists is in part to be explained, I think, by the sudden influence of Mencken, who warped him out of his natural orbit. Mencken's various essays in the *Smart Set* and elsewhere shocked Fitzgerald into perceiving, among other things, the impractical dreaminess of many of the liberals and the mindlessness of the populace. Fitzgerald's image of "the people," the bedrock on which liberal society was to be based, is faithful to Mencken's notion of the "lower orders" as "inert, timid, inhospitable to ideas, hostile to changes, faithful to a few maudlin superstitions."[16] Mencken's *A Book of Prefaces* (1917) and like works are full of witty and withering satire on the "American booboisie," the "democratic fustian," and the "truculent and mindless plutocracy." Like many of the avant garde young of the time, Fitzgerald was drawn under the spell of Mencken's free-wheeling satirical style and became something of a debunker himself, both of liberal socialist theoreticians and of the people themselves.

Mencken's influence extends even into the texture of the style of "May Day." The prologue, which has the flavor of Stephen Crane's ironic phrasing, broadens revealingly into the coarser satiric style of the Baltimore sage. It describes a set of armistice attitudes keyed to peace and prosperity, to victory and consumer goods. But even the Menckenesque, dead-giveaway phrasing of the prologue[17] should not obscure for us its function. In its avoidance of the specific indices of time and place, Fitzgerald's generalized introduction—like the image of Columbus discussed below—is meant to offer a context applicable to every American postwar experience, against which will be measured the experience of specific soldiers (like Sterrett, Key, and Rose) who returned from World War I, and those young women (like Edith and Jewel) who awaited them. Fitzgerald's prologue emphasizes the concurrence of the "many adventures that happened in the great city," and he remarks that "of these, several—or perhaps one—are here set down" (*Stories*, p. 83).

There is no doubt that Fitzgerald saw the diverse simultaneous experiences of his several characters as composing a single story. The tale has eleven parts, very nearly each one explicitly specified as to time and place, with the effect that the simultaneity of the actions and the

16. H. L. Mencken, "The National Letters," in *Prejudices: Second Series* (1920); reprinted in *The Vintage Mencken*, ed. Alistair Cooke (New York: Vintage, 1955), p. 100.

17. I have in mind the hyperbole, the high-flown rhetoric, and the archaisms put to the service of satiric deflation in a sentence like ". . . all exulted because the young men returning were pure and brave, sound of tooth and pink of cheek, and the young women of the land were virgins and comely both of face and figure" (*Stories*, p. 83).

interconnectedness of the characters and the settings fuse the parts into a single experience. Clearly this was Fitzgerald's intention, for as he later remarked in his Preface to *Tales of the Jazz Age*, although the events in life "were unrelated," he had tried, "unsuccessfully I fear, to weave them into a pattern."[18] His modesty is engaging here, but in this instance he may have builded better than he knew, Perosa rightly remarking that "there are no loose ends, no incongruous parts in the story. . . ."[19] The focus of these diverse experiences, the pattern, comes down to Fitzgerald's attempt to characterize the American social order, at a particular moment in time, as a complex interaction of economics (wealth and poverty), social dislocation (caused by the war), and collapsed personal values (leading to hedonism and mindless violence). Throughout, Fitzgerald interconnected the several parts through a network of interlacing adumbrations and recurrences so artfully disposed that they unify the work. They all bear upon the principal image of the dawn sun striking the statue of Columbus, which elevates to the dignity of an artistic theme the notion of the decline of potentiality implied in the discovery of the New World:

> A fresh argument ensued at the cashier's desk, where Peter attempted to buy another dish of hash to take with him and throw at policemen.
> But the commotion upon his exit proper was dwarfed by another phenomenon which drew admiring glances and a prolonged involuntary "Oh-h-h!" from every person in the restaurant.
> The great plate-glass front had turned to a deep creamy blue, the color of a Maxfield Parrish moonlight—a blue that seemed to press close upon the pane as if to crowd its way into the restaurant. Dawn had come up in Columbus Circle, magical, breathless dawn, silhouetting the great statue of the immortal Christopher, and mingling in a curious and uncanny manner with the fading yellow electric light inside. (*Stories*, p. 120)

Sklar has remarked that this dawn passage at Columbus Circle is charged with an irony that undercuts its putative transcendental significance. He calls attention to "an advertisement for 'Edison Mazda' light bulbs painted by the artist Maxfield Parrish, which appeared in *Ladies' Home Journal* for January, 1918. In the painting dawn is rising over a mountain lake. A lightly-clad, golden-haired beauty of nature sits on a

18. F. Scott Fitzgerald, *Tales of the Jazz Age* (New York: Charles Scribner's, 1922), p. viii.
19. Perosa, p. 33.

rock in the center foreground, watching with sublime awe as golden
dawn strikes the mountainside, driving back the 'deep, creamy blue' of
a Maxfield Parrish moonlight, quite as Fitzgerald has described it."
Sklar does not venture to say that Fitzgerald knew of this advertisement, but it leads him to argue that "such 'magical, breathless' dawns
are false and sentimental dawns, and that if nature produces dawns
equally as beautiful as a commercial artist can, they are equally to be
distrusted." For him, "this passage is not an evocation of romantic
wonder, but a heavily ironic deflation of it."[20]

We owe Sklar a debt in calling our attention to this advertisement,
but the inference he draws from it in interpreting the scene is almost
exactly wrong. It is entirely possible that Fitzgerald did see the advertisement. Maxfield Parrish was a well-known illustrator, no mere hack
commercial artist as Sklar's remark implies. (He was well known to a
number of novelists of the period, whose works he illustrated—for
instance, Edith Wharton's *Italian Villas and Their Gardens*.) If Fitzgerald did see the advertisement, it more probably struck him just
as did the dust jacket of *The Great Gatsby*, with its picture of the eyes
of Dr. T. J. Eckleburg—a pictorial image to be put to the service of a
deeper symbolism in the story. Certainly no one would want to err by
reading into "May Day" a sophisticated prototype of Fitzgerald's mature symbolic technique. Yet, like *The Great Gatsby*, where the Dutch
sailors gaze in breathless romantic wonder at the "green breast" of the
New World, this dawn image of romantic possibility is suffused with
the style of lyrical enchantment utterly free, as I read it, of ironic deflation. Moreover, like the green breast of the New World, this image
of romantic possibility is shown as tawdrily betrayed in the actual
condition of society represented by the rich and poor, the privileged
and the dispossessed, as well as by the merchants whose life-denying
materialism is suggested by their stores—which, covered at night by
"great iron masks," are "shadowy tombs of the late day's splendor"
(*Stories*, p. 111). Surely the tale's pattern of light imagery (darkness,
yellow and kaleidoscopic artificial lights, and dawn sun) supports Edwin Fussell's claim that the image of Christopher Columbus, the
"Christ-bearer," offers Fitzgerald the means of expressing "the behavior
and attitudes of the Lost Generation with a symbol of romantic wonder extensive enough to comprehend all American experience, as far
back as 1492. . . . What Fitzgerald is almost certainly trying to say

20. Sklar, p. 78. This advertisement is reproduced in *"The Ladies' Home Journal"
Treasury*, ed. John Mason Brown (New York: Simon and Schuster, 1956), p. 30.

with this image is: we are at the end of Columbus's dream, and this is our brave new world."[21]

Of the radical disparity between the ineffable romantic promise implied by Columbus's discovery and the tawdry actualities of the Jazz Age, two episodes are particularly striking. The first is the orchestra at the Gamma Psi dance, which is "headed by a famous flute-player, distinguished throughout New York for his feat of standing on his head and shimmying with his shoulders while he played the latest jazz on his flute" (*Stories*, p. 107). For pure inanity, Fitzgerald could not have improved on this choice example of contemporary idiocy—except in the case of Mr. In and Mr. Out. This transient pair is ironically introduced as having no identity in the social order:

> You will search for them in vain through the social register or the births, marriages, and deaths or the grocer's credit list. Oblivion has swallowed them and the testimony that they ever existed at all is vague and shadowy, and inadmissible in a court of law. Yet I have it upon the best authority that for a brief space Mr. In and Mr. Out lived, breathed, answered to their names and radiated vivid personalities of their own. (*Stories*, pp. 120–21)[22]

Their drunken search for more liquor, the satire on Yale and Sheffield students, and their vaudeville clowning convey more than just Princeton undergraduate hijinks. A deeper meaning is suggested in the pattern of physical movement, both circular and vertical, that pervades the story. Toward the end of the tale, when Mr. In and Mr. Out observe Rose arrested in the lobby of the Biltmore as they enter the elevator, Fitzgerald writes:

21. Edwin Fussell, "Fitzgerald's Brave New World," *ELH*, 19 (December 1952), reprinted in *F. Scott Fitzgerald: A Collection of Critical Essays*, ed. Arthur Mizener (Englewood Cliffs, N.J.: Prentice-Hall, 1963), p. 46.

22. While their identities are obscure in the tale, Phil Dean and Peter Himmel were suggested by Fitzgerald's own experience with his Princeton classmate Porter Gillespie. Mizener remarks that after the interfraternity dance at Delmonico's in May of 1919, Fitzgerald went to the Child's restaurant on 59th Street and proceeded to mix up "hash, dropped eggs, and catsup in his companion's derby. When he was interrupted he insisted on climbing on a table and making a speech, and after he had been dragged from the table and out of Child's he wanted to explain to everybody that the facade of the buildings around Columbus Circle does not really curve; it only seemed to because he was drunk. Later he and a college friend, Porter Gillespie, returned to the party at Delmonico's and played their game of Mr. In and Mr. Out. Well into the next morning they breakfasted on shredded wheat and champagne, carrying the empty bottles carefully out of the hotel and smashing them on the curb for the benefit of the churchgoers along Fifth Avenue" (Mizener, pp. 88–89).

> . . . the stout person made a sort of lightning-like spring toward the short, dark soldier, and then the lobby closed around the little group and blotted them from the sight of Mr. In and Mr. Out.
>
> But to Mr. In and Mr. Out this event was merely a particolored iridescent segment of a whirring, spinning world.
>
> They heard loud voices; they saw the stout man spring; the picture suddenly blurred.
>
> Then they were in an elevator bound skyward.
>
> "What floor, please?" said the elevator man.
>
> "Any floor," said Mr. In.
>
> "Top floor," said Mr. Out.
>
> "This is the top floor," said the elevator man.
>
> "Have another floor put on," said Mr. Out.
>
> "Higher," said Mr. In.
>
> "Heaven," said Mr. Out. (*Stories*, p. 126)

This passage has been called "a parody of the Ascension" which serves comically to express "the materialistic hedonism, along with its traditional counterpart, a vulgar idealism, which Fitzgerald is already identifying as his culture's fatal flaw."[23] But this movement upward should also be seen in the light of the aimless circular drift of several of the characters (for example, the dancers on the dance floor) and of the mob (which circles about the city). It should also be seen as the counter-symbol of the descent of both Carrol Key and Gordon Sterrett.

In Key's case it is a literal fall from an upper-story window at *The Trumpet* that causes his death: "He had fallen thirty-five feet and split his skull like a cracked cocoanut" (*Stories*, p. 118). This death is anticipated in the violence offered to the street-corner orator and is alluded to several times in the Mr. In and Mr. Out episode (although it is clear that Phil Dean and Peter Himmel could not have known about Key's fall). The idea of the waiters objecting to their having champagne for breakfast seems " 'mortifying' " to the pair, and "they collapsed into laughter, howled, swayed, rocked back and forth in their chairs, repeating the word 'mortifying' over and over to each other—each repetition seeming to make it only more brilliantly absurd" (*Stories*, p. 124). Later, "either of them had only to mention the word 'mortifying' to send them both into riotous gasps." The play on the words *mortifying* and *riotous* has a double function: it directs the reader backward and forward along the narrative. Key's death calls into focus the riotous violence that smolders in the hearts of the economically dispossessed. His death is compounded in irony by the fact that Key and the

---

23. Fussell, p. 45.

mob offer violence to the very ideologists who are committed to alle-
viating their lot in life but have that violence turned against them by
the counter-violence of the Socialists and the police.

Descent and mortification of another kind are figured in the social
decline of Gordon Sterrett, which also ends in death. Sterrett is no
different from the rest of the Yale boys, except that once the prop of
money is removed, his feeble moral will and incapacity for resolute
action make him a prey to depression and whining self-indulgence.
Marriage to a social inferior as an adequate cause for suicide is an
outdated theme and is not, as I suggested earlier, the central point of
Sterrett's death. What is at issue here is the terrifying fluidity of the
American social organization, which, with its emphasis on wealth,
carries morally weak individuals up and down with irrational power.

The twin aspects of this theme of social mobility—first, character in
decay (or a man going to the devil) figured as social descent; and
second, the upward aspiration of the *nouveau riche* outsider—are also
a constant in the one story Fitzgerald had to tell. The personal urgency
of this theme, however, found a powerful expression in Fitzgerald's
new discovery, H. L. Mencken. In *The American Credo*, Mencken had
pointed to this terrible fluidity in remarking that "such a thing as a
secure position is practically unknown among us. There is no American
who cannot hope to lift himself another notch or two, if he is to keep
on fighting for whatever position he has; no wall of caste is there to
protect him if he slips. One observes every day the movement of individuals, families, whole groups, in both directions." And he concluded
that "it is this constant possibility of rising, this constant risk of falling,
that gives a barbaric picturesqueness to the panorama of what is called
fashionable society in America."[24]

Lacking "interior security," however, Fitzgerald could not take a
satirist's mere amusement in the picturesqueness of that panorama. He
wanted to be one of the beautiful, moving upward, rather than one of
the damned. But living in the Bronx in early 1920, struggling with his
failure in love and literature and meditating on the strengths and
weaknesses of his own character, he inclined toward the view—ambi-
valently expressed in "May Day"—that perhaps only a socialism adequately grounded in the pragmatics of the redistribution of wealth
could create a more stable social order. Mencken's forceful debunking
of visionary egalitarianism briefly deflected Fitzgerald from his own
point of view, for in the end his sympathy for socialism was sentimen-

24. H. L. Mencken and George Jean Nathan, *The American Credo* (New York:
Knopf, 1920), pp. 30, 32.

tal. Nevertheless, this sympathy was a sufficient enough constant in his thought to constitute one of the emotional subtexts of his greatest work. In the 1930s it brought him to the point of saying that "to bring on the revolution it may be necessary to work inside the Communist party" (C-U, p. 126). Fortunately, that double point of view, that attraction-repulsion, that ambivalence about "the panorama of what is called fashionable society in America," prevented him from taking an ideologist's narrowly didactic approach to his materials. "May Day" may not be his best work, but it richly demonstrates how Fitzgerald could tap and organize his own inner conflicts in order to produce a vision of the troubled complexity of American social interrelationships.

"WINTER DREAMS" AND SUMMER SPORTS

NEIL D. ISAACS

"Winter Dreams" appeared first in 1922 in the *Smart Set* and then in the 1926 collection *All the Sad Young Men*. It has more than satisfied Fitzgerald's own requirements that he should "write for the youth of his own generation, the critics of the next, and the schoolmasters of ever afterward."[1] The story has been praised by critics of his own and succeeding generations, and it continues to be enjoyed by each generation of American youth.

As for the schoolmasters, they have perpetuated the popularity of the story because they have seen it to be, in the self-damning phrase of the profession, an eminently teachable story. It supports any number of exemplary critical or pedagogical approaches, yet the enduring power that "Winter Dreams" has for contemporary American readers seems to elude explanation through traditional classroom lesson-plans.

Practitioners of point-of-view analysis, for instance, see "Winter Dreams" as a neat example of third-person restriction, with occasional shifts to omniscient commentary. All the action is seen through Dexter Green's eyes, all the emotion felt through his heart, all the nostalgic attitude toward youth perceived from his mature vantage. Yet Fitzgerald intrudes with such direct reminders to the reader as: "Remember that—for only in the light of it can what he did for her be understood" (*Stories*, p. 138), and:

1. *F. Scott Fitzgerald in His Own Time: A Miscellany*, ed. Matthew J. Bruccoli and Jackson R. Bryer (Kent, Ohio: Kent State Univ. Press, 1971), p. 164.

> This story is not his biography, remember, although things creep
> into it which have nothing to do with those dreams he had when
> he was young. We are almost done with them and with him now.
> (*Stories*, p. 143)

Standing behind this kind of analysis is a perceived identity of Fitzgerald and Dexter Green that justifies the shifts and allows the apparent
inconsistencies to be reassessed as appropriate to the story's generic
nature as exemplum. Either technical curiosity or a taste for exempla
will make such an approach valuable, but it cannot account for the
broad appeal.

Similarly, tonal analysts have ample grist for their mill (though there
is hardly a mass demand for tone-pieces). Fitzgerald pretends a clinical
dispassionateness in "Winter Dreams," posing as a narrator who is, as
he claims his protagonist to be, "at bottom hard-minded." Yet the
emotions run as deep in the narrator as in Dexter Green, from the
class-ist cynicism to the romantic angst. The poor are typed with "a
neurasthenic cow in the front yard," and the rich are characterized
with the blustery vapidity of Mr. T. A. Hedrick or with a precarious
peddling of bonds, a precarious investing of patrimonies.

More than a minimum daily dosage of irony is supplied by the story.
Some is conscious, as when the glamorous creature, the object and
symbol of all Dexter's craving for "the glittering things themselves"—
Fitzgerald's prescient vision of Ali MacGraw—is given the sublimely prosaic name of Judy Jones. And some is unconscious, as when Fitzgerald protests for Dexter (and himself) that there is nothing "merely
snobbish" in him. After all, that unattainable, illusory American
dream, chased by Dexter and Gatsby and Diver and Stahr, is perhaps
nothing so much as the attainment of an elitist stature that can support
an ultimate snobbism.

Indeed, the aesthetic employment of Fitzgerald's snobbism is what
makes "Winter Dreams" suitable for pedagogical anatomizing of tex-
tures in the names and allusions. With an artistic restraint appropriate
to what Dexter has acquired—"that particular reserve peculiar to his
university, that set it off from other universities" (*Stories*, p. 134)—
Fitzgerald doesn't even name the university. The text is not overloaded
with the local color of a generation, but the occasional Pierce-Arrow
and "Chocolate Soldier" and Hot Springs do their job. The evocation
has all the vivid and ephemeral, sharp and gauzy quality of dreams.

The allusions also harmonize with the thematic burden of the story,
in which Fitzgerald's notion of the American dream and Dexter's winter dreams cluster around the dialectic of illusion and reality so dear to

the hearts of both structuralist and interpretive critics. And speaking of clusters, Fitzgerald's use of imagery in this story is so painstaking and striking as to command the attention of any reader with half an eye open to colors, or half an ear open to the favorite method of whole generations of schoolmasters. Neatly, almost too neatly, do the images fall into categories. There are the brilliant, the gay, the shining, the gleaming, the colors of summer, the dreams, the illusion, love, the richness of life, youth. And there are the dreary, the icy, the white and black and mostly gray, the winter, the reality, the loss beyond grief; and in maturity, "the gray beauty of steel that withstands all time" (*Stories*, p. 145).

One could go on. "Winter Dreams" provides clues for the critical detective of any persuasion, an answer for any scholarly paranoia that asks Oedipa Maas's existential question, "Shall I project a world?" The Freudian can revel in the ambivalence of attraction and fear, the lure of the unattainable and forbidden, not to mention the symbolic function of cars, golf clubs, swimming, and diving; the myth-hunter in the analogues of Lilith, Aphrodite, Parsifal, male Cinderella; the ritualist in the series of initiations, challenges, and rejections; et cetera.

The point has already been made that a capacity to support prevailing critical approaches is a story's best hope for continued success. A corollary point is that while such approaches may illuminate intrinsic excellences in the story, they tell more about the criticism, more about the critical climate, than about the author and his audience. The counterpoint, which will serve to introduce the rest of this essay, is this: we must look through, around, or above such techniques to discover in the story the basis for its continued appeal for a large American audience.

None of these preliminary remarks should be taken as deprecating the special insights of any critical analysis. Indeed, that the story has been illuminated for us thereby is a tribute to its textural wealth. Nor should the following discussion be mistaken as a claim to the one-reading-that-binds-them-all. Yet I find, in an area often neglected by aestheticians and cultural historians alike, a potential clue to an enriched understanding of the story, to an appreciation of part of its continued appeal to a large audience, and to some notion of its possible centrality in Fitzgerald's work.

"Winter Dreams" shares with much of Fitzgerald's work an attitude he implicitly shared with most of his society. America of the early 1980s retains this given of Fitzgerald's America of the 1920s: its sportsmindedness. Perhaps such a generalization may seem irrelevant, but the fact that it "goes without saying"—for Fitzgerald as for most of us—does not exclude its relevance. I submit that a common frame of reference that provides a channel for almost universal communication cannot be totally irrelevant either to literary critic or to social historian.

Fitzgerald, like most contemporary Americans, found his heroes primarily in sports. There was "the romantic Buzz Law" whom he remembered in his 1927 "Princeton" essay as having "last seen one cold fall twilight in 1915, kicking from behind his goal line with a bloody bandage round his head" (AA, pp. 72–73). There was Sam White, who scored the winning touchdown for Princeton against Harvard in 1911, a brilliant individual effort that made Fitzgerald, who saw the game, choose Princeton, as he was fond of confessing. And above all there was the legendary Hobey Baker, called by Arthur Mizener the "Sir Philip Sidney or . . . the Major Robert Gregory of his age" and compared by Al Lang to "Sir Galahad, Richard the Lion-Hearted and even Paul Bunyan."[2]

Baker, the Princeton football captain in 1913 and an even more outstanding hockey player, was killed just before the armistice in 1918, gallantly flying an unnecessary mission. But his immortality was assured by Fitzgerald, who borrowed his second name, Amory, for the protagonist of *This Side of Paradise* (1920) and explicitly modeled the character of Allenby on him. Football images are prominent in that first novel, especially near the end when Amory thinks,

> Life was a damned muddle . . . a football game with every one off-side and the referee gotten rid of—every one claiming the referee would have been on his side. . . . (TSOP, p. 265)

Life properly, apparently, should be a football game played properly, as Hobey Baker would have played it and lived it. Through worshipful eyes, Amory sees Allenby in an image that is an epiphany for him:

> There at the head of the white platoon marched Allenby, the football captain, slim and defiant, as if aware that this year the hopes of the college rested on him, that his hundred-and-sixty pounds were expected to dodge to victory through the heavy blue and crimson lines. (TSOP, p. 42)

The cultic attitude toward football was not invented by Fitzgerald, but it persists in his work far beyond 1920. (And in such disparate novelists as Walker Percy, Don DeLillo, James Whitehead, and Fred-

2. John D. Davies, *The Legend of Hobey Baker* (Boston: Little, Brown, 1966), pp. vii, 114.

erick Exley, it yet survives unabated.) As late as 1935, with the publication of *Taps at Reveille,* he can use a two-word sentence—"Football weather"—to sum up the protagonist Charlie Wales's whole perception of an environment in the story "Babylon Revisited." And it may be accurate to say that it is clearer in the texture of his fiction than in that of other contemporary writers. But it is also important to understand that football had been mythologized to such an extent in his culture that the romanticized attitudes toward it were taken for granted. Doctorow's narrator in *Ragtime* observes that "football players in their padded canvas knee pants and leather helmets . . . were the [leading] glamour personages. . . ."[3]

Fitzgerald, however, recognized the dark side of the myth, its dangerous implications of brutality and its elevation of sophomoric values. Nick Carraway's first reference to Tom Buchanan in *Gatsby* reads:

> . . . among various physical accomplishments, [he] had been one of the most powerful ends that ever played at New Haven—a national figure in a way, one of those men who reach such an acute limited excellence at twenty-one that everything afterward savors of anticlimax. (GG, p. 6)

The cultic attitude was not limited to football. If we take *Gatsby,* as we fairly may, as a basic chart both of American attitudes of the time and of Fitzgerald's preconceptions, we find what amounts to a cult of all sports. Gatsby himself, fashioning the pattern of his success, included fifteen minutes of "dumbbell exercise and wall-scaling" at the beginning of his crowded daily schedule and left a half hour in the afternoon for "baseball and sports." Having scaled every wall but one toward his dream, Gatsby has had his picture taken at Oxford with a cricket bat in his hand, introduces Tom Buchanan as "the polo player," and says to Nick about Jordan, " 'Miss Baker's a great sportswoman, you know, and she'd never do anything that wasn't all right' " (GG, p. 72).

Carraway doesn't share Gatsby's pure naivete. He has heard rumors about Jordan, how at her first big tournament, she "had moved her ball from a bad lie in the semi-final round." But Nick, too, is a devotee of the cult. He casts an aura of glamor and elegance around women in terms of summer sports:

3. E. L. Doctorow, *Ragtime* (New York: Random House, 1975), p. 128.

> there was a jauntiness about her movements as if she had first
> learned to walk upon golf courses on clean, crisp mornings. (GG,
> p. 51)

> all I could think of was how, when that certain girl played
> tennis, a faint mustache of perspiration appeared on her upper lip.
> (GG, pp. 58–60)

> her voice came over the wire as something fresh and cool, as if a
> divot from a green golf-links had come sailing in at the office
> window. (GG, p. 155)

Nor are the associations limited to women. His reaction to Meyer
Wolfsheim, "who fixed the World Series in 1919," is especially revealing: "It never occurred to me that one man could start to play with the
faith of fifty million people" (GG, p. 74). It would never occur to
Fitzgerald to question the faith of fifty million Americans in their
sports.

The large-scale, though understated and taken-for-granted preoccupation with sports in *Gatsby* carries over substantially to *All the Sad
Young Men*, which followed it into print by less than a year in 1926. In
some stories it is only remotely present, as in "Absolution," where little
Rudolph Miller's ambition to be a baseball player seems the most
casual and obligatory of references; or in the marvelously clinical presentation of "The Rich Boy," where allusions to "the locker-room over
at the Links" and to the many men gone up to New Haven for "the ball
game" are only the most perfunctory of details. But in others it comes
sharply to the fore, as in "Winter Dreams."

Dexter Green begins, in Fitzgerald's portrait, as a caddy. His family
name refers to the game of golf as well as to his youth, while his given
name gives obvious attention to athleticism. His early dreams are conceived as he skis over snow-covered fairways of the golf course, and
they are fantasies of success—social, economic, personal—projected
precisely in athletic terms:

> He became a golf champion and defeated Mr. T. A. Hedrick in a
> marvellous match played a hundred times over the fairways of his
> imagination, a match each detail of which he changed about
> untiringly—sometimes he won with almost laughable ease, some-
> times he came up magnificently from behind. Again, stepping
> from a Pierce-Arrow automobile, like Mr. Mortimer Jones, he
> strolled frigidly into the lounge of the Sherry Island Golf Club—or
> perhaps, surrounded by an admiring crowd, he gave an exhibition
> of fancy diving from the spring-board of the club raft. (*Stories*, p.
> 128)

The exhilaration of these fantasies alternates with a "profound melancholy," stemming from the "enforced fallowness" of the links during
the long season, a dreariness from the "desolate sand-boxes knee-deep
in crusted ice," where "gay colors fluttered in summer" on the tees
(*Stories*, p. 127). Thus the prevailing sets of contrasting imagery are
introduced in a sporting context.

Dexter abruptly quits, though he is the best caddy at the club, after
his first humiliation by Judy Jones. Eleven years old, at the course first
thing in the morning with five small new golf clubs in a white canvas
bag and with her white linen nurse, she is by turns sophisticated,
haughty, infantile, violent, coy, and imperious. Yet she arouses a mixture of strong emotions in Dexter and from the narrator words of praise
for the "almost passionate quality of her eyes" and her "vitality" which
is seen "shining through her thin frame in a sort of glow" (*Stories*, p.
128). Rather than caddy for her, Dexter quits, and with the end of his
caddying comes the end of Part I of a six-part story.

In Part II he returns in modest triumph to play the course, not as a
champion but as a successful young businessman with a respectable
golf game. Just two years out of college, his success in the laundry
business began when he

> made a specialty of learning how the English washed fine woolen
> golf-stockings without shrinking them, and within a year he was
> catering to the trade that wore knickerbockers. Men were insisting
> that their Shetland hose and sweaters go to his laundry, just as
> they had insisted on a caddy who could find golf-balls. (*Stories*, p.
> 131)

During the round, Judy Jones, perhaps as outrageous *mutatis mu-
tandi* as nine years before, carelessly plays through his foursome (including Hedrick). Her beauty is remarked upon, of course, but her
quality is characterized by the way she plays the game. And that same
evening, on the lake, Dexter falls in love with her, with her "sinuous
crawl" in the water, with her widespread arms on the surfboard and
her dark eyes lifted toward the moon. The section ends with her casual
invitation to dinner the following night.

The brief third part sketches in that evening. There are no explicit
references to sports, but the men who have preceded Dexter in Judy's
life are generalized with "the deep tan of healthy summers." More
important, he sees that,

> in one sense, he was better than these men. He was newer and strong. Yet in acknowledging to himself that he wished his children to be like them he was admitting that he was but the rough, strong stuff from which they eternally sprang. (*Stories*, p. 134)

The athletic grace of the rich—the sort of romantic appeal that drew Fitzgerald, like Dexter, to the Eastern Ivies—was intrinsically weaker than the rugged newness of the "West." Its strength, however, lay in its nostalgic power. Remember that by the time of the action of this story, and particularly by the time of its composition, even the aristocratic game of college football was no longer dominated by Yale, Harvard, and Princeton, or even Cornell and Penn, but had been taken over by the rough, strong young men of Chicago, Wisconsin, Michigan, Minnesota, Illinois, and Notre Dame.

The fourth and fifth parts, the longest and shortest of the story, narrate the incidents of Dexter's engagement to Irene Scheerer and his breaking it off for a last one-month fling with Judy Jones. On the eve of a golf date with Irene and just a week before the announcement of their engagement, Dexter drives Judy home from a dance and stays with her. He is startled by the solidity of Mortimer Jones's house, its "great white bulk . . . somnolent, gorgeous, drenched with the splendor of the damp moonlight." It is there, he feels, to contrast with the slightness of her beauty, "as if to show what a breeze could be generated by a butterfly's wing" (*Stories*, p. 142).

There follows the hurt—to Irene, to her parents, deeper for him when Judy's "flare for him" lasts only a month. And then the war releases him from "webs of tangled emotion." Yet the "deep happiness" that "he had tasted for a little while" (*Stories*, p. 143) prevents him from ever regretting his decision. That beauty, transient and ephemeral as youth, as a butterfly, as a moment of glory in a winning race, as a laurel "garland briefer than a girl's," is the stuff of the winter's dreams of summer, the essential element of Fitzgerald's most compelling constructs.

The imagery of these sections is not explicitly athletic. I have extrapolated and translated, perhaps overstating what I see as an implicit connection. And yet in the final part of the story, Fitzgerald gives substance to my subjection. Seven years later, Dexter has news of Judy Jones at twenty-nine (he insists she is twenty-seven), and finally, "The dream was gone" (*Stories*, p. 145).

In his anguished realization of irreparable loss, Dexter calls up images not only of "gingham on the golf-links" but also of Judy's kisses and eyes and "freshness like new fine linen in the morning"—less a laundry image than a faint echo of "the tees where the gay colors fluttered in summer." The "thing" that "is gone" from Dexter, the dream with all its colors "in the country of illusion," is his youth (*Stories*, p. 145). And Fitzgerald, in his Jazz Age depiction of a sports-minded America, presaged the mass-age youth cult that is inextricably wound up with athleticism in contemporary culture.

"Winter Dreams" retains its appeal for audiences largely because Fitzgerald's perceptions—whether prominent, subdued, or totally submerged—of the significance of sports in our society's attitudes touch our conditioned responses. In the jargon, we *relate* to the ways people and types and classes are characterized in their sports, to the ways beauty is glimpsed in association with sports, and to the ways dreams are set in the arenas of sports.

Now it would be foolish to assert that "Winter Dreams" can be satisfactorily explained only in this way, just as foolish as the exclusive application of any *one* of the pedagogical approaches I mocked earlier. Yet I submit that this approach tells us something that is central to Fitzgerald's work in general and that it is a primary element in accounting for the persistence of his strong following among young contemporary audiences.

Further, I venture to predict that his popularity will continue as long as American sportsmindedness retains its hegemony among our prominent cultural attitudes—or until, in Robert Coover's words,

> . . . we have passed, without knowing it, from a situation of sequential compounding into one of basic and finite yes-or-no survival, causing a shift of what you might call the equilibrium point, such that the old strategies, like winning ball games, sensible and proper within the old stochastic or recursive sets, are, under the new circumstances, *insane*![4]

And even then, in some mad cybernetic topology of sport-as-ritual, Fitzgerald's "Winter Dreams" will have a place in the new sets of meanings and patterns beyond conjecture, as dreams of ineffable summers and their untimed sports may properly be.

4. Robert Coover, *The Universal Baseball Association, Inc., J. Henry Waugh, Prop.* (New York: New American Library, 1971), p. 148.

"ABSOLUTION": ABSOLVING LIES

IRVING MALIN

1.

Many Fitzgerald critics view him as a social observer of his times, as a "realist." They neglect the fact that he is often concerned with the unseen, spiritual dimensions of life—that he is a religious writer. Although *The Great Gatsby*, for example, is about Nick's and Gatsby's attempts to get ahead in *this* world, the novel subtly suggests that they dream of invisible transformations of substitute realms of faith. I do not mean here—or in the close analysis which follows—to suggest that Fitzgerald believes in orthodox religion; I do imply, however, that he can never completely remove himself from the Catholicism of his youth.

"Absolution" (1924) is a complex story because it dramatizes the various conflicts in Fitzgerald's fiction. We can read the story as a literal narrative of a boy's introduction to the deceits of this world, or as a sharp rendering of the "madness" and disappointment of a lonely priest. But if we read the story closely enough, we perceive "the added dimension." "Absolution," as its title suggests, is about the attempt to escape from this world, to transform routine experience and to enter other, complete worlds. Thus the story is built on structural (and thematic) opposition. Fitzgerald doesn't commit himself to orthodox religion—or to art—as salvation. There is great irony present. This story asks a fundamental question overlooked by many critics of Fitzgerald who offer the usual remarks about the American Dream, etc. It asks whether art itself—that is, imagination, dream, romance—can be as sufficient, helpful, and necessary as religious belief. Is faith in the other world enough to help us live here and now? What is the connection between artistic "lies" and religious "truths"?

Fitzgerald opens with a brilliantly phrased sentence: "There was once a priest with cold, watery eyes, who, in the still of the night, wept cold tears" (*Stories*, p. 159). The words move slowly—perhaps like the still night?—until they sharply end with "cold tears." The rhythm is haunting; it alternates, as does the entire story, between slow thoughts and sudden actions. But Fitzgerald is also careful about the tone of the sentence. He sets the scene as a kind of "fairy tale" or "legend"—the opening words are, "there was once." We expect anything to happen; we are surprised by the "tears"—they seem out-of-place, swift, *real*. Thus the tonal alternation parallels the rhythmic one. Both, however, underline tension, stress, and oddity.

The next sentence emphasizes the "weeping," which is a result of incomplete "mystical union." Although we do not know yet the reasons for the missing union, we understand that unlike the writer, the priest cannot *accept alternation and use it for his own ends.*

When Fitzgerald mentions the "rustle" of the Swedish girls and their "shrill laughter," the sounds startle us. We have been lulled by the absence of noise in the first two sentences. The weeping was silent, contemplative, and comfortable. Now with the sudden introduction of voices, we can appreciate the "terrible dissonance" the priest finds. We are, however, still troubled: why should he, and we in turn, be assaulted?

The rest of the paragraph suggests that the priest cannot function in the world. Lights seem to disturb him; the smell of soap is oppressive. His senses are almost *enemies*. We have moved from the stillness of night into anxiety-provoking daylight, and like the priest, we want to scream or to retreat—we also hope for another kingdom in which we can remain pure, virginal, peaceful.

But the priest cannot move. He sees his doom in the "grotesque labyrinths" of the wheat, and the fact that he projects his inner "dissonance" upon nature suggests his unbalanced, self-centered state. It is not the wheat or the sun who are enemies; it is, to use Fitzgerald's word, the "unavoidable" self which creates tension.

The priest is "run down"—like an "old clock." He is somewhat crazy. But only he knows about his condition. He cannot reveal his problems to anyone; he cannot, for the time being, confess. He must continue to function, to "act" his role. (We can see that the priest makes believe; the fairy-tale quality of the opening sentence has been reinforced by the psychic unrealities—and vice versa.)

Rudolph Miller is a "beautiful, intense little boy of eleven." He enters the priest's study—is there a pun on "study"?—and sits down in "a patch of sunshine." It is interesting to note that the boy is linked to light (and beauty); he is a source of terror for the priest because he resembles, metaphorically, the wheat and the girls and the sun. Even the boy's eyes are "gleaming points of cobalt light" (*Stories*, p. 159).

We learn that the priest's name is "Father Schwartz" (possible darkness?). Although he is terrified by the boy, he understands that Rudolph is also terrified. There is a strange bond, a "reflection" of sorts. And when the boy maintains that he's committed a "terrible sin," the words seem to apply to both of them.

The first section of the story ends with an odd mixture—one we have met before—of "union" (the priest and the boy as anxious souls) and "incompletion." The boy's words lead back to his father's, " 'Don't come back till you go . . . ' " (*Stories*, p. 160). The first sentence of the section was peacefully closed; the last is open. Again there is structural opposition. We need only see the ellipsis in the father's remark to note the incompletion, the suspension; the ellipsis combats the circling closure of "fears."

2.

The second section of the story begins with "dismal creases," an "old man's old shoe" (*Stories*, p. 160). Darkness dominates the scene (as it did at the beginning of the story). Nothing can be perceived behind the confessional curtain; the only "exposed" thing is the shoe. (The story itself is about exposure, revelation, vision.)

Fitzgerald moves from "vision" to "sound." He writes "sound began" in an almost biblical way, and his underlying rhythm hints at the presence of higher meanings. Are the priest (Father) and boy *more* than specific "characters"? Do they stand for creatures of other realms? The questions provoke us, but they cannot be answered yet.

Rudolph has "switched places" with the priest. *He* is looking at the confessional curtain; *he* tries to overhear the words; *he* longs for meaning. When he tells himself to be prepared for his turn in the confessional, he cannot really get rid of his tension and like the priest, he feels that he is going "mad"—he is "partially possessed" by a "demoniac notion." Rudolph is dirty; he is oppressed by whispers, darkness, and indeed by all the objects around him. He fears and yearns for an *end* to crisis, a death if you will. Thus Fitzgerald uses such phrases as the "large coffin set on end" (the confessional), the boy's face "sinking precipitately into the crook of his elbow," and the "fallen slide" of the confessional (*Stories*, p. 161).

The words of Rudolph and Father Schwartz in the "confessional" are clichés because they do not return to individual sources, anxious roots. There is a subtle kind of irony. When we read between the lines of the role-players, we see more lingering dissonance. Father Schwartz interrupts "sharply"; Rudolph says he does not lie while he lies. Perhaps Fitzgerald implies here that sin occurs when we—and the priest and the boy who represent us—refuse to be open and face our private demons. Rudolph feels relief in coming "from the muggy church into an open world of wheat" (*Stories*, p. 163)—the reverse movement of Father Schwartz's—but even celebrating openness, he feels uneasy. The boy is still trapped by self-centeredness; he is in a "corner." He is—to use the death metaphor—buried like his priest.

3.

The third section is in certain ways a climax. Fitzgerald switches again; we now have the father, Carl Miller, as center of consciousness (at least at the opening). Like Rudolph and Father Schwartz, he is "mad"; he is full of "fear and trembling"—to use Kierkegaard's phrase—because he cannot accept his position in the world. He is "continually dismayed." He misses the "balance of any single thing" (*Stories*, p. 164).

The fact that Fitzgerald subtly moves from Father Schwartz to son to father Miller is of great interest. He unbalances us; he does not let us rest, thereby placing us on the edge (as he does his characters). But at the same time we see the ties between us *and* the three, and we seek relief, peace, absolution from severe unbalance.

Carl Miller is overly alert. He is disturbed by the "shrill birds," the "whirring movement" of chickens, and the "furtive sound" coming from the kitchen (*Stories*, pp. 164–65). He is so uneasy that he breathes heavily.

When Carl Miller confronts his son at the sink, they are briefly a study in contrasts—Rudolph is almost asleep; his father is wide awake—but we soon view them both as extremists. They are as "disturbed" as the faucet which has just been used by Rudolph.

The action takes place in daylight. We are told that the "kitchen was garnished with sunlight which beat on the pans and made the smooth boards on the floor and table yellow and clean as wheat" (*Stories*, p. 165). The symbolic sentence suggests that the "light" which has been used throughout the story is extreme, blinding, and apparently "evil." "Wheat"—the word makes us remember Father Schwartz's vision of the terrifying patterns of grain. Therefore the comforting shelter—we may call it the "father's house"—is suddenly transformed into a *haunted* one. We are again in an "enchanted" world in which unpredictability triumphs.

There is a confession in the scene. Rudolph lies about drinking the water; he decides not to tell all to his father because he fears "savage ferocity"; he does not want to be beaten. But he cannot escape the "dull impact of a fist" (*Stories*, p. 166). After he is wounded, he laughs hysterically; he recognizes that there is no escape.

As the section ends, father and son walk "along the road toward the Catholic church" (*Stories*, p. 167); they seek salvation there from their craziness. In an ironic way they care less about sanctity than mental health!

4.

The "uneven breathing" of Rudolph disturbs the "Sunday silence" (*Stories*, p. 167), and this very unevenness forces us once more to think of an unbalanced, crooked pattern throughout the story. Carl and Rudolph are solitaries in an alien environment. The matter is, of course, more complicated because as we learn from the next descriptions of words and deeds, father and son are estranged from *each other*; each sees only his own heartfelt needs.

Rudolph confesses inside the church that he has missed his morning prayers. He hides his *other* sins—and his feelings about his father. He buries another part of himself. When Fitzgerald describes Rudolph's confession, he informs us that the boy has crossed "an invisible line":

> Hitherto such phenomena as "crazy" ambitions and petty shames and fears had been but private reservations unacknowledged before the throne of his official soul. Now he realized unconsciously that his private reservations were himself—and all the rest a garnished front and a conventional flag. (*Stories*, p. 167)

These sentences are shrewdly offered to show us that Rudolph has unearthed some of his buried life—he has done so by telling lies and recognizing them *as such*. Perhaps it is too much to suggest that he resembles Fitzgerald himself—the storyteller who lies in order to create truth? Picasso once called art a "lie like truth." Rudolph is reaching toward the same goal; he apparently accepts the creative quality of

214 / IRVING MALIN

make-believe while he sees its "irreligious"—or at least unorthodox—
style. Therefore he tastes the "consciousness of a sharp, subtle revenge"
(*Stories*, p. 168) not only against his father but against the church
itself. He looks "coldly" at the collection box.

Rudolph cannot control his shifting moods. He quivers at Communion time; he soon perspires. He is "alone with himself, drenched with
perspiration and deep in mortal sin." His temporary rebellion and
victory as "artist" taste like "dark poison." And his anxiety rises to the
surface, compelling him to hear "sharp taps of his cloven hoofs" (*Stories*, p. 169).

5.

In section five we are brought back to the present; we remember that
Rudolph is expressing the events of the last few days. We are somewhat
startled—Fitzgerald again unbalances us!—because we have been so
caught in his narration that our sense of time has been suspended. I
believe that we are supposed to see the cycle of life asserting itself.
Rudolph is caught by history, family, existence—only when he (re-)
creates stories (lies) can he breathe fresh air.

Rudolph is sitting in the "square of sunshine" (*Stories*, p. 169). He
still desires security, believing that if he can continue to stay in the
room, he can keep breathing and gain absolution from his demons. He
waits for the answer, the cure, the magical transformation.

Father Schwartz is also waiting for a sign. His mind is fixed, however, on the other patterns, figures in the carpet. He sees "pale echoes
of flowers" and "flat bloomless vines"; he feels trapped by meaningless-
ness, dimness, sterility. The sounds are also disturbing—they are hammering or ticking insistently. Father Schwartz is even, if possible, more
doom-conscious than previously; his rosary beads crawl and squirm
"like snakes" (*Stories*, p. 169) upon the table top—they are curiously
alive.

He reaches out to Rudolph. He tries to look at the "beautiful eyes"
(*Stories*, p. 169) because they are so pure. He almost *worships* them.
He is, of course, guilty of idolatry. The matter is more complex. Although we can sense a sexual tone in the description, we should note
that Father Schwartz is not a mere pederast (or a would-be one). He
sees symbolic light in Rudolph, a "glimmering" of innocence. What
irony! The boy *knows* at this very instant that he and the priest are
decidedly corrupt, dark, "crazy."

Now Father Schwartz is caught by his visions. His words are addressed to himself; he re-creates parties, "best places"—social *heavens*—and he sees these as dream "stars" (*Stories*, p. 170). He enchants himself with giddy lights.

The description builds to a climactic one of an "amusement park" in which light is tempting, warm, *not* evil (at least from a distance): " 'Go to one at night and stand a little way off from it in a dark place— under dark trees. You'll see a big wheel made of lights turning in the air. . . . It will all just hang out there in the night like a colored balloon—like a big yellow lantern on a pole.' " Father Schwartz cannot completely let go; he wants to watch the park lights from a "dark place"—he cannot bear " 'the heat and the sweat and the life' " (*Stories*, p. 171). He confesses his fear of this world.

Rudolph at first feels enchanted by the magical world of light. He uses his imagination—he sees his soul as "radiant" (despite his sins), and like the priest, he believes in "silver spurs," dreams of glory, "stars of lights" (*Stories*, p. 171). But he cannot submit entirely. He also recognizes his foolishness. He sees *through* the vision. It is not surprising that as he matures, he perceives the horror of Father Schwartz's own vision. He cannot, therefore, remain calm and brave—he panics in the face of the priest's craziness—and he runs from the study; he does not recognize that he will have to live with horror in a state of continual *non-absolution*.

Although the story began with the priest and the night, it ends with stirrings and "exciting things." The world has won in a strange way; Schwartz and Rudolph disappear. We see the "girls with yellow hair"; we hear their "exciting" and innocent words (*Stories*, p. 172). (Fitzgerald again stresses sight and sound.) Although these normal girls are warmly alive, they do not impress us as much as does Father Schwartz—they are, finally, silly creatures who are unaware of demons, anxieties, the soul's need for grace. In an ironic way we feel pity for them—they are surely not prepared for the oncoming "night."

I suggest that Fitzgerald is a conscious, disarming ironist; he makes us dislike Father Schwartz and Rudolph and Carl Miller—how can we, after all, be sympathetic toward "madmen"?—but at the same time he presents their needs in such a way that we oddly admire their search for absolution. It is unfortunate that the "trinity" is never really explored. We do not, for example, understand the reasons for their actions (except in stereotyped ways), although we *feel* their madness. Perhaps Fitzgerald cannot understand his main characters because he cannot explore his own conflicts between "romance" (magical transformation) and absolution. But this very conflict effectively dramatizes the events.

Earlier I mentioned symbolic realms. I do not want to view Father Schwartz as more than what he is—an anxious priest—but I can see other readers labeling him a symbolic authority or even deity. Fitzgerald does not work in lofty symbolic ways; he remains close to the ground, the farms, the *heartland*.

Despite my reservations, I believe "Absolution" is a wonderfully designed story, one which captures Fitzgerald's characteristic divisions of soul and demonstrates clearly that he is a religious writer. He may give us the "moon" and "hot fertile life"—these are, however, simply part of his sense of wonder at man's and Christ's spiritual complexities.

There is an absence of any "final solution" in the story. Throughout "Absolution," Fitzgerald has been offering "alternatives" (light and dark, youth and maturity, earth and Heaven, lie and truth), suggesting thereby that daily life—as recounted here—is a *double-edged* source of uncertainty. We cannot be very sure of motivations, roles (father, priest, son), rituals. But at the same time Fitzgerald—like his characters—yearns for some promised end, some resolution, some vision in which wounds are healed, souls united, and lies transformed into truths. If "Absolution" were merely to talk about these subjects—largely "alternatives" and "marriages" ("unions")—it would be mere propaganda, simple sermon. But the fact that the story embodies its thematic tensions in the subtle, "overlooked" patterns of imagery—we need only look at the patterns of light—makes it a satisfying labyrinth, a religious (and artistic) triumph which *contains* contraries.

"NO AMERICANS HAVE
ANY IMAGINATION":
"RAGS MARTIN-JONES
AND THE PR-NCE OF W-LES"

VICTOR DOYNO

Is "Rags Martin-Jones and the Pr-nce of W-les" (1924) mere fluff? After a cursory reading, an immediate reaction would be to dismiss the story as an insignificant little tale told with easy charm and wit, an airy bit of froth. Most critics have ignored the story or omitted detailed commentary.

But reflection and rereading permit a different evaluation to emerge, an understanding that the story is paradoxically both atypical and quite revealing. Because no standard approach shapes opinion about this story, we may examine it freshly, introducing and suggesting approaches which may be appropriate for this or other stories. We may, in this brief consideration, use stylistic, folkloristic, thematic, structural, genetic, and contextual critical methods. Each casts a distinct light, illuminating different facets of the story. What had been regarded as fluff may turn out to be—albeit small—a diamond.

The stylistic critic, for example, would observe precisely how the teller has created an unreal world of exaggeration and sophistication. From the first paragraph the narrator offers descriptions and elaborate sustained comparisons which are ostentatiously witty:

> The *Majestic* came gliding into New York harbor on an April morning. She sniffed at the tugboats and turtle-gaited ferries, winked at a gaudy young yacht, and ordered a cattle-boat out of her way with a snarling whistle of steam. Then she parked at her private dock with all the fuss of a stout lady sitting down, and

announced complacently that she had just come from Cherbourg
and Southampton with a cargo of the very best people in the
world. (ASYM, p. 133)

The storyteller expects agreement with his evaluations and acceptance
for his metaphors; moreover, while he usually speaks confidently to his
readers, making us his equals, he speaks condescendingly and mock-
ingly about his subjects. The hidden message seems to be, "You and I
know how boring the world is, if described somberly, and it is so much
more fun, and so easy, of course, to be witty and moderately disjunc-
tive."

The concluding reference to "the very best people in the world"
becomes increasingly—more obviously—ironic by repetition as the second paragraph specifies a portion of the passengers:

The very best people in the world stood on the deck and waved
idiotically to their poor relations who were waiting on the dock
for gloves from Paris. Before long a great toboggan had connected
the *Majestic* with the North American continent, and the ship
began to disgorge these very best people in the world—who turned
out to be Gloria Swanson, two buyers from Lord & Taylor, the
financial minister from Graustark with a proposal for funding the
debt, and an African king who had been trying to land somewhere
all winter and was feeling violently seasick. (ASYM, p. 133)

By now the narrator's tone is a bit puzzling because there is no attitude
of approval; the arriving passengers behave idiotically while their relations wait as beggers in expectation of token gifts. Pleasantly surprising
descriptions flash by, such as "a great toboggan"; but even this metaphor is incongruous because the visual similarity of an angle of descent
quarrels with the inappropriateness of a static bridge described as a
moving vehicle. There is also a striking contrast in scale. Throughout
the story there are numerous verbal devices such as metaphor, meton-
ymy, and synecdoche used to change the normal perception of size and
the normal relation of part to whole. The results are pleasure and
surprise, which are central to the charm of the story. Within this
disorientation most readers do not notice the anticlimactic ordering, or
the connection between an object and a human, as in the ship which
disgorged a violently seasick person. The irony is all-pervasive; the
scorn all-encompassing.

We learn from the opening that the narrator expects us to recognize
certain categories, such as "poor" or "Middle Westerners," and also to

agree with his unstated attitudes and consider these groups automatically uninteresting, worthy only of rapid dismissal. Such assurance plays off against mounting confusion because the metaphoric complexity of the story increases as people are presented as their objects:

> The deck gradually emptied, but when the last bottle of Benedictine had reached shore the photographers still remained at their posts. (ASYM, p. 134)

Momentarily we wonder. Does the bottle of Benedictine refer to a gift, a gift-bearer, or to a drinker? We may begin to accept as a characteristic of the narrative technique some distortion in the part-whole relationship. Miss Rags Martin-Jones is first described as "something that might have been a pile of gorgeous silver-fox fur," and we learn that she "was half a girl and half a flower" (ASYM, p. 134). Her actual arrival on shore presents a world of sophisticated exaggeration:

> Tap! Her one hundred and five pounds reached the pier and it seemed to sway and bend from the shock of her beauty. A few porters fainted. A large, sentimental shark which had followed the ship across made a despairing leap to see her once more, and then dove, broken-hearted, back into the deep sea. Rags Martin-Jones had come home. (ASYM, p. 135)

The careful and deliberate achievement of this special, whimsical style creates a world of wit and sophistication, distortion and exaggeration. The trick of the story, as shall become clear, is to see the illusions sympathetically and with penetration, realizing that the irony about "the very best people" will gradually become dominant.

If we adopt, instead of the stylistic method, the approach of a folklorist, we would observe quite different yet complementary ideas. Obviously the story involves the familiar motif of mutual testing of two lovers and the resolution in their proposed marriage. Fitzgerald noted that he had been "struck by personality of girl just home from Europe and hating America. Also gossip about Prince of Wales. Invention."[1] The conflict involves a cosmopolitan flapper, Rags Martin-Jones, and an apparent dullard, the overeager John Chestnut. The heroine is an orphan of great wealth who has spurned other suitors and is deciding

---

1. *F. Scott Fitzgerald in His Own Time: A Miscellany*, ed. Matthew J. Bruccoli and Jackson R. Bryer (Kent, Ohio: Kent State Univ. Press, 1971), p. 175.

about John. We have some indication of her worthy character, despite her frivolous mannerisms, in that her parents preferred to remain together on the *Titanic* rather than separate. Rags is herself to be tested in an elaborate artifice, and she reveals herself to be surprisingly loyal and devoted when she thinks John is a fugitive murderer.

On the opposite side of this misalliance, the story involves a hero who appears to the woman as an unimaginative, dull bumpkin actually arranging an elaborate entertainment to sweep her off her feet. He exploits her desire for romance and excitement while revealing the illusory nature of her thinking. After Rags condescends to go with John to the rooftop night club in hope of seeing the Prince of Wales, she is invited to the royal table because of her striking beauty. When Rags asks John's permission to visit the Prince's table, John nods agreement, and after her departure he seems rejected but is actually in complete control. Rags believes in all the illusions, including the Prince of Wales and the charge that John is a hunted criminal. It is significant that John feigns drunkenness when at the apparent nadir of his fortunes. Rags behaves like a heroine of romance fiction and uses her acquaintance to ask the Prince of Wales for help. She explains her need to sneak John across the border to Canada by saying with a blush, "Why—it's a runaway marriage." After a staged police raid and gun battle, Rags is understandably confused when John congratulates everyone for acting the parts well. She mistakes John's revelation of the illusion for madness, and some first-time readers may be momentarily confused—duplicating Rags's situation.

The congruence—the fit—of the reciprocal testings indicates that Fitzgerald's story is as well-plotted as John Chestnut's deception. Actually John not only sweeps Rags off her feet; he has also used the opportunity to make a business deal with a restaurateur, converting the illusion of a novel rooftop club into, we assume, a tidy profit. The overall conflict is resolved when the sophisticated, cosmopolitan Rags acts obediently toward the all-controlling American and agrees to marry.

Thematically the story is hardly impenetrable, being instead quite obvious about themes of European sophistication versus American ingenuity and romantic illusion opposed to humorous manipulation. Shortly after Rags's arrival in America, she whimsically desires to return to Europe. John's request that she stay and get to know him better elicits this reply:

> "Know you!" Her tone implied that he was already a far too open book. "I want a man who's capable of a gallant gesture."

"Do you mean you want me to express myself entirely in pan-
tomime?"

Rags uttered a disgusted sigh.

"I mean you haven't any imagination," she explained patiently.
"No Americans have any imagination. Paris is the only large city
where a civilized woman can breathe." (ASYM, p. 139)

John manages, of course, to have enough imagination to create
elaborate illusions of romance, complete with a pretended Prince of
Wales, a fugitive, and a staged police raid. Accepting Rags's challenge,
John becomes in fact the imaginative manipulator of romance and its
attendant illusions.

The clear, almost schematic, opposition in values appears as Rags
explains why she wishes to return to Paris:

"It isn't just you," she said in a softer voice. "Dull and uninspired
as you are, I care for you more than I can say. But life's so endless
here. Nothing ever comes off."

"Loads of things come off," he insisted. "Why, to-day there was
an intellectual murder in Hoboken and a suicide by proxy in
Maine. A bill to sterilize agnostics is before Congress—"

"I have no interest in humor," she objected, "but I have an
almost archaic predilection for romance. Why, John, last month I
sat at a dinner-table while two men flipped a coin for the kingdom
of Schwartzberg-Rhineminster. In Paris I knew a man named
Blutchdak who really started the war, and has a new one planned
for year after next." (ASYM, p. 141)

At the conclusion the cultural dominance has shifted; the American is
no longer measured by European standards because he has mocked the
veneration of those standards and, moreover, controls or employs all
the Europeans Rags had idolized. John achieves this feat by a clever
combination of imagination and financial power.

After the denouement, the theme of control by finances is made
more explicit as we watch John take charge of the "real" world. He
explains that he was able to sell the idea of the night club. Furthermore, we realize that John, who had earlier described himself as not
very rich, is able to control not only the very men who had impressed
Rags in Europe by their manipulations but is in fact also able to control
a country by setting the price of the currency. Accordingly, the repeated reference to "a bazaar of love" is an assimilation of the appeal

of love within the real power of an American merchant prince. At the conclusion:

> John Chestnut began rubbing his hands together in a commercial gesture.
> "Patronize this place, lady," he besought her. "Best bazaar in the city!"
> "What have you got for sale?"
> "Well, m'selle, today we have some perfectly be-*oo*-tiful love."
> "Wrap it up, Mr. Merchant," cried Rags Martin-Jones. "It looks like a bargain to me." (ASYM, pp. 159–60)

The difference in the wealth of each person is now insignificant; in Fitzgerald's "Marxian" view, the man of affairs who controls the market place is now on at least an equal footing with the *haut monde*. Moreover, the use of a word like "bargain" by Rags implies, within the shared playfulness, a new realism in her attitude toward the world.

What is interesting about these themes, despite their obviousness, is how neatly these treatments differ from Fitzgerald's usual presentations. It is almost as if the author deliberately created a counterpoint by reversing some of his motifs. In this case the man is not flawed but totally self-sufficient; his drunkenness is a sham, and he is without illusions about the woman. She, on the other hand, is a *femme fatale* who is herself manipulated. Moreover, her great wealth is not a limiting factor but becomes irrelevant. Most strikingly different, she is not destructive but devoted and loyal to the man who loves her when he is apparently down-and-out. Fitzgerald, in a letter to Maxwell Perkins, called the story "fantastic jazz," and we notice, with sadness, how the meanings of *exaggeration* and *nonsense* are each conveyed in *each* word. It is touching that Zelda's favorite story was the thematically similar "The Offshore Pirate" (1920), in which the man courts and wins the willful woman by an elaborate deception.

A structural approach to this apparently frivolous story would discover a pattern of real action followed by a duplication as a symbolic event. For example, the tale opens with the arrival of a real ship named the *Majestic*, and later a pretended majesty, connoting romantic illusions, arrives at the nightclub. Similarly, John's actual fall off the pier is repeated symbolically as Rags's loss of illusion. When she learns that the person she had admired as the Prince of Wales is actually John's British elevator boy, John instructs him to slow the elevator, saying, "Not so fast, Cedric. This lady isn't used to falls from high places"

(ASYM, p. 159). John's final attitude is a combination of compassion and irony.

The most significant parallel is the metafictional relationship between John Chestnut—devoted suitor, writer, and manipulator of illusion—and F. Scott Fitzgerald. Both John Chestnut and his creator have made a grand gesture and revealed that Americans do indeed have imagination, including the creativity necessary to penetrate the illusory nature of romance.

The genetic critic can reveal, by a comparison of the manuscript, magazine, and final versions, precisely how Fitzgerald carefully crafted his story. From the numerous changes Fitzgerald made while revising the story, we may choose several examples; for instance, our attention may return to the opening of the story. In the version published in the July, 1924, issue of *McCall's*, we find that "the very best people in the world" on the *Majestic*

> turned out to be movie queens, missionaries, retired jewellers, British authors, musical comedy twins, the Duchess Mazzini (nee Goldberg) and, needless to add, Lord and Lady Thingumbob, of Thingumbob Manor.

The tone is uncertain, and the catalogue seems unfocused. Fitzgerald's revision for *All the Sad Young Men* makes the description more specific and more emblematic, with references to romance, finances, and satirized royalty. The revised passenger list

> turned out to be Gloria Swanson, two buyers from Lord & Taylor, the financial minister from Graustark with a proposal for funding the debt, and an African king who had been trying to land somewhere all winter and was feeling violently seasick. (ASYM, p. 133)

This version gives the narrator more knowledge and in addition has a progression of conventional putative prestige as well as a decline in actual control or power. This catalogue also contributes to the themes of the story.

The magazine text described Rags's arrival by saying:

> She came slowly down the gangway. Her hat, an expensive, inscrutable experiment, was crushed under her arm so that her scant, French-bobbed hair tossed and flopped a little in the harbor wind. Her face was like seven o'clock on a summer morning . . . .

But the final text changes the description to: "her scant boy's hair, convict's hair, tried unsuccessfully to toss and flop a little in the harbor wind." Did Fitzgerald make the change to keep up with the fashion world, or to characterize her with a different immediately recognizable trait? The description of her face like a "summer morning" Fitzgerald also changed, instead likening it to a "wedding morning," obviously telegraphing the conclusion.

Similarly, the careful writer touched up his first presentation of John Chestnut: "he was already talked of as a risen star in Wall Street. . . ." The magazine version revealed John's financial power at the outset, diminishing much of the suspense. While revising for the collection, Fitzgerald substituted a vague indication of fame: "he had already written the story of his success for the *American Magazine* . . ." (ASYM, p. 136). Both the nationalistic and the metafictional strands of the story receive some emphasis by such careful revision.

The genetic approach may also lead to some inferences concerning the author's expectations about his different audiences. Fitzgerald tended to break the magazine text into shorter paragraphs for book publication; the final text seems more emphatic, but we could suppose that Fitzgerald perhaps anticipated a less literate, more flippant audience.

Several final questions remain, and they may be explored by using contextual criticism. Does a change in meaning occur when Fitzgerald decided to include the story—originally written in December of 1923 and published in *McCall's*, July, 1924—in the 1926 volume *All the Sad Young Men?* We may wonder what meanings would exist if Fitzgerald had simply reprinted the 1924 version in the collection instead of revising as he did, or what changes if any were forced by the decision to fit the story into a collection. Further, we may speculate whether Fitzgerald achieved any aesthetic effect by revising his original plan for the volume, shifting his table of contents to have this story occupy the midpoint in the nine-tale collection. The first four stories, "The Rich Boy," "Winter Dreams," "The Baby Party," and "Absolution," conclude with the young male protagonist sadder, more knowledgeable about this fallen world. And the same condition exists for the young men of the three stories which follow "Rags Martin-Jones and the Pr-nce of W-les," "The Adjuster," "Hot and Cold Blood," and " 'The Sensible Thing.' " As Fitzgerald had planned in the letter to Perkins, seven stories in the volume would "deal with young men of my generation in rather unhappy moods" (*Letters*, p. 189). Only in "Rags Martin-Jones and the Pr-nce of W-les" and in "Gretchen's Forty Winks" does the young man not appear to be sad. However, in both stories this condition is avoided only by staging an elaborate deception which momentarily fools the woman. Fitzgerald, who could write so evocatively of moods and moments and emotions, who could create iridescent phrases, seems to be stating that the adequate man must be both sensitive to the appeal of the illusion and able to control and direct that illusion. (The counterpoint to *Gatsby* seems obvious.) Because the deception of drugging the wife is done cold-heartedly in "Gretchen's Forty Winks," the volume accordingly ends on a note of callous cynicism. But "Rags Martin-Jones and the Pr-nce of W-les" provides a light version of this serious insight, and the story thus assumes in the revised table of contents a position of special significance as the keystone of the arch of *All the Sad Young Men.*

The interaction of these critical approaches creates possibilities for interpretation in even an apparently slight Fitzgerald story which seem if not endless, certainly attractive. As scholar-critics explore Fitzgerald's short stories, we may be reasonably confident about finding brilliant objects. Whether the discoveries are in fact diamonds or zircons created by modern high pressure technology can be determined, as can most critical questions, by a careful rereading of the primary text.

FREEDOM, CONTINGENCY, AND ETHICS IN "THE ADJUSTER"

CHRISTIANE JOHNSON

"The Adjuster" was written in December, 1924, one month after F. Scott Fitzgerald finished *The Great Gatsby*. It was published in *Redbook* in September, 1925; in 1926, Fitzgerald chose to put it in his collection *All the Sad Young Men*. This book includes some of the writer's best stories, such as "The Rich Boy," "Winter Dreams," and "Absolution," but also some mediocre or flatly didactic ones, such as "Gretchen's Forty Winks" or "Hot and Cold Blood." One of the lesser-known stories in this collection, "The Adjuster," is not devoid of interest; it is concerned with several typical Fitzgeraldian themes and deserves a careful reading.

The story begins like one of the flapper stories which gave Fitzgerald his popular success at the beginning of his career and which dealt with young girls eager to escape the stifling world of conformity around them. Those girls are generally depicted as selfish but charming, and their revolt as justified. The author shows definite indulgence toward them. They belong to that generation at the beginning of the 1920s which revolted against its Victorian parents and claimed the privilege of freedom. Fitzgerald began his career as its spokesman, but having encouraged that revolt, he appeared to realize soon that there was a generation left with nothing to replace the values it was rejecting and to feel it his duty to provide them with an ethic, after all. By the time he wrote *The Great Gatsby* and "The Adjuster," he was no longer so indulgent; he blamed Daisy Buchanan and Jordan Baker severely. In 1924 and 1925, Fitzgerald, by then a father himself, wrote several essays dealing in essence with the lack of values and the irresponsibility of the younger generation: "What Kind of Husbands Do 'Jimmies' Make?," " 'Wait Till You Have Children of Your Own!'," and "What Became of Our Flappers and Sheiks?"[1] In these essays, freedom is shown no longer as the positive but instead as the negative pole.

Contrary to other stories of that period, "The Adjuster" takes the same stand as the essays. One critic writes that "it marks Fitzgerald's first explicit exorcizing of his flapper creation."[2] Luella Hemple, the protagonist of the story, is no longer depicted as charming and irresponsible, or charming because irresponsible; on the contrary, she is severely judged. But this is a magazine story, and she must turn out all right in the end; thus she learns a lesson and becomes a better person. In most of Fitzgerald's magazine stories, the happy ending is achieved through a clever twist. That is not the case here and William Goldhurst is incorrect when he calls the last sentence "a crowning implausibility."[3] The ending is the logical outcome of a definitely didactic story. But the lesson learned is complex and perhaps a little confused.

1.

Luella Hemple appears to be a very self-centered person, and to emphasize her self-centeredness, most of the story is told from her own point of view, with a few intrusions of the omniscient author. In the first four parts, the world is seen through her eyes, and it is her own limited world; we hear her talk, and her thoughts are expressed in free indirect speech. Only in the last part is there a sudden shift of point of view—a changed Luella is seen from a distance, and the shift makes that change all the more remarkable.

Luella belongs to a very wealthy class and seems to have all that one can wish. Her wealth, however, is taken for granted; it is not the core of the problem. She herself attributes it to "fate," ignoring the fact that it is the result of her husband's work. We enter her interior world from the very start: she is described in a tone of affected sophistication, in the appropriate background of the elegant Ritz and at the appropriate

1. "What Kind of Husbands do 'Jimmies' Make?," " 'Wait Till You Have Children of Your Own!'," "What Became of Our Flappers and Sheiks?," in *F. Scott Fitzgerald in His Own Time: A Miscellany*, ed. Matthew J. Bruccoli and Jackson R. Bryer (Kent, Ohio: Kent State Univ. Press, 1971), pp. 186, 192, 202.

2. Robert Sklar, *F. Scott Fitzgerald: The Last Laocoön* (New York: Oxford Univ. Press, 1967), p. 203.

3. William F. Goldhurst, *F. Scott Fitzgerald and His Contemporaries* (Cleveland and New York: World, 1963), p. 199.

time of day, which Fitzgerald calls "the singing decorative part of the day" (6TJA, p. 140). Appropriately, she is having tea and chatting with a friend. All she wants is to talk about herself, and she does not require much prompting to go on with her "confession"; her friend need only suggest, " 'It may be because you don't love Charles,' " or simply, " 'Go on. . . . Tell me more' " (6TJA, p. 141), and the self-centered Luella is ready to offer the whole story.

The story concerns her reactions to the role of housewife and mother, a role which she feels is expected of her by a constraining society. Viewing that role as an obstacle to her desire for freedom, she revolts, obviously intending to create a sensation—and she does. Speaking of her child, she is aware that she should have another attitude yet cannot help admitting how much he bores her. She cannot stand having to care for him very long, and she delegates her functions to a paid nurse. Her visits to the nursery are brief, and she utters vacuous words: " 'Well, aren't you a smart boy!' " For Luella, her son is "a dear little rose" (6TJA, p. 145)—which is affected and meaningless but does convey the idea that to her he is no more than an object for her own gratification. Even when the child is sick, the thought that occurs to Luella is "how much he resembled the incredible cherub in the 'Lux' advertisement in the bus" (6TJA, p. 152). He is little more than an ornament, and, incapable of giving him any of herself, Luella lends him her beads, another ornament. Only at rare moments does she feel intensely about him: "His face was the same shape as hers; she was thrilled sometimes, and formed new resolves about life when his heart beat against her own" (6TJA, p. 145). What thrills her is the narcissistic satisfaction of finding that he looks like her. But she is incapable of accomplishing the routine tasks implied in having a child—she does not know how to cook his food; she cannot discern his temperature.

Just as she leaves the care of her child to a nurse, Luella leaves the care of her house to servants, who are also nothing more for her than convenient objects. Even though she herself admits to total incompetence, she feels the right to find the servants annoying and incompetent. And when she decides to fire them, she leaves that chore to her husband. Pretending to be fair and see other people's point of view, she overwhelmingly imposes her own: "It was hard to do with only a single servant when things were so complicated" (6TJA, p. 150). She acts insensitively toward the cook, Mrs. Danski, and loses control when the latter suggests that things are too complicated for her, protesting, " 'I've got my own health to think of,' " and, " 'I've got my own children to think of, just like you' " (6TJA, p. 151). After having been callous to Mrs. Danski, refusing to pay her, Luella complains of "the sudden callousness of the world" when she realizes that her sick husband can be "neither a reference nor a refuge any more" (6TJA, p. 153).

In her relationship with her husband, she does not care much for him as a human being either. Feeling " 'a good sport,' " she callously states to her friend, " 'I'd rather he'd be unhappy than me' " (6TJA, p. 142). When she comes back home from the Ritz, she observes him from a distance, and for her the man who looks romantic to other women is only a nervous and tired person whose habit of rubbing his face irritates her tremendously. Later, when Charles has a breakdown, she cannot wait until a trained nurse arrives; she expresses her annoyance at having to cook his food.

From all that Luella says grows a strong impression that nothing is allowed to stand between her and her pleasure. Like the previous flappers, she wants to do only what she likes. Housework is particularly irksome to her, as it is to the young girls of Fitzgerald's early work. Rosalind, in *This Side of Paradise*, announces, " 'I like sunshine and pretty things and cheerfulness—and I dread responsibility. I don't want to think about pots and kitchens and brooms' " (TSOP, p. 196). Gloria, the married flapper of *The Beautiful and Damned*, refuses to have a child and wants to be "taken care of." In this story, however, Fitzgerald makes a moral issue out of such selfishness. What made the early flappers charming is here either reversed or deemphasized with Luella. Even her beauty is mentioned in terms of narcissism only.

To clarify his judgment of Luella, the author says, "If she had been a pioneer wife, she would probably have fought side by side with her husband. But here in New York there wasn't any fight. They weren't struggling together to obtain a far-off peace and leisure—she'd had more of either than she could use" (6TJA, p. 142). Fitzgerald is often nostalgic about that period of the American past when qualities of energy and character were necessary, and he mentions by contrast the softness of the younger generation in his essays or in letters to his daughter.

Having nothing specific to do, Luella looks for excitement, and in her impatient quest for pleasure, she needs more and more excitement. The test with her husband at the beginning of the story is " ' an interesting engagement, a supper after the theatre to meet some Russians, singers or dancers or something' " (6TJA, p. 143). She has reached a point when she must go out for the sake of going out, no longer using her judgment, not really knowing what she is going to see. Later, in an outburst to Doctor Moon, she takes up the same theme: " '. . .everything seems as if it's going on forever and ever? I want excitement; and

I don't care what form it takes or what I pay for it, so long as it makes my heart beat. . . . If I'm one of those women who wreck their lives for nothing, then I'll do it now. . . . in five minutes I'm going out of this house and begin to be alive' " (6TJA, p. 147–48). Unthinkingly, she declares she is ready to sacrifice everything to her craving for excitement, which she calls being alive.

To be alive for Luella is to be free from the drudgery of everyday life. Escape is a recurrent motif in the story. On a literal level, all along Luella feels the urgent desire to walk out. The theater she loves so much is also a way of escaping. Even going to Europe, it is suggested, can be nothing more than an escape. The Hemples went to Europe for their honeymoon, and they needed a purpose—buying objects—for what would otherwise have been an aimless trip. All through Fitzgerald's work, the lure of the East has replaced the lure of the West. The East is where the excitement is, and Europe—merely farther East—is not a different culture one might want to know; it is simply a place where people like the Hemples go in their restlessness, in search of more adventure, more stimulation, more agitation.

The absolute freedom that Luella so impatiently wishes for proves impossible. She will gradually become aware of contingency in her life. The catastrophes that she experiences in the first half of the story are shown as the consequences of her craving for pleasure and freedom. Her husband breaks down under the strain of having to provide for her and live her kind of life in addition to his work. Her troubles with servants get worse. And the death of her baby, it is suggested, might not have occurred if she had not entrusted him to a nurse who didn't " 'know her business.' " But even though these crises are brought upon Luella by herself, she still views them as outside events and does not realize her share of responsibility.

The baby's death is a climactic moment in the story. Having lost him, Luella is forced to redefine her role. Not having a child anymore, she thinks she can go back to the freedom of her youth: " 'Life has given me *back* freedom, in place of what it took away from me' " (6TJA, p. 155; italics mine). She thinks she has a choice. Haunted by the desire to be "free as the wind," she does not weigh the consequences of her acts. Just what is she free from? She expresses it under the vague concept of "life." What she tries to escape is all that hurts her and opposes her search for pleasure—"she musn't linger even a minute, or Life would *bind* her again and make her suffer once more" (6TJA, p. 155; italics mine).

In fact, she has no choice. Deliberately Fitzgerald does not even suggest that she could be running away to another man, even though this could have been a possible outlet for her craving for excitement. She has no job, no special talent; no family background is mentioned. How can she live the comfortable life she needs and is used to if she leaves Charles? She needs to be shown her foolishness, to be shown that she has no choice; and this is where Doctor Moon enters the narrative.

2.

Doctor Moon is an enigmatic character termed a psychoanalyst by some critics.[4] In fact, in the story he protests against being called that; he even adds, " 'I am not a specialist, nor, I may add, a faddist of any sort' " (6TJA, p. 146). Doctor Moon never acts like a psychoanalyst. A psychoanalyst encourages patients to talk, but mainly listens; a psychoanalyst helps people discover their own problems and figure out their own answers. Analysts rarely interfere; they never use authority. Doctor Moon acts with Luella in precisely the opposite way: he dictates the answers and prescribes her conduct to her. He compels her to stay when she wishes to go out; in the end he teaches her a thorough lesson. Psychoanalysis explores the past and the subconscious; Doctor Moon forces Luella to face the present, and his appeals are to her conscious will.

At the end of the story, when Luella asks Doctor Moon who he is, he answers, " 'I am five years.' " We must accept the writer's intention of having him represent Time. His name evokes the succession of the months, the waxing and waning of the moon. It might also be intended to give a certain cosmic dimension to the story, but Doctor Moon falls very short of this function. In fact, if we do not entirely agree with Arthur Mizener's opinion that "only the handling of Doctor Moon spoils a fine account of suffering and maturity,"[5] we are forced to admit that the intrusion of the would-be supernatural in a realistic story is one of its weak points. It is confusing and mars "The Adjuster"; and most of the time Doctor Moon is too didactic to be an acceptable symbol. However, interesting consequences follow if we accept him as Time.

The story is definitely about the passage of time. In most of his work, Fitzgerald is concerned with this theme. *The Great Gatsby* is written with an accompaniment of calendars, schedules, and clocks. In this

4. Sklar, p. 203; John A. Higgins, *F. Scott Fitzgerald: A Study of the Stories* (Jamaica, N.Y.: Saint John's Univ. Press, 1971), p. 91.

5. Arthur Mizener, *The Far Side of Paradise: A Biography of F. Scott Fitzgerald* (Boston: Houghton Mifflin, 1965), p. 214.

story, it is first felt and expressed by Luella herself: " 'I've been married three years' " (6TJA, p. 140) are her first words to her friend; and to Doctor Moon she talks of the impression that everything is " 'going on forever and ever' " (6TJA, p. 147). This realization is the cause of her strong frustration. Another important point is that the story is told from the vantage point of five years later (even though the anonymous narrator who stresses this soon disappears). At the beginning, the emphasis is on Luella's youth. She is called "young Mrs. Charles Hemple" and is compared to "English country *girls*" (6TJA, p. 140; italics mine). She and her friend are said to be twenty-three. The fear of aging is a frequent concern in Fitzgerald's work, which is not surprising from an author who wrote to his editor a year after the publication of "The Adjuster": "You remember I used to say I wanted to die at thirty— well, I'm now twenty-nine and the prospect is still welcome."[6] In "Winter Dreams" (1922), he called a woman of twenty-seven "faded." No wonder the importance of the five years over which this story extends should be emphasized; it explains the description of Luella at twenty-eight as a mature woman. The fear of aging is very present in Luella's remark, " 'I told Charles frankly that I was *still* young enough to want some fun' " (6TJA, p. 142; italics mine); it expresses the need of a young wife to be reassured after her first child. Luella's youth seems to be what appealed to her husband: "Luella's selfishness existed side by side with a childish beauty" (6TJA, p. 148). Luella still betrays the impatience of youth when after her baby's death, she wants to leave " 'this house of death and failure!' "—to which exclamation Doctor Moon answers, " 'You haven't failed yet. You've only begun' " (6TJA, p. 157). When Doctor Moon tries to help her and she wants to see the results immediately, his answer is, " 'It takes time' " (6TJA, p. 150). But in the end, he can go away—" 'You don't need me any more. . . . You don't realize it, but you've grown up' " (6TJA, p. 158).

The change in Luella due to her having grown up is shown as very meaningful. She changes from a spoilt, superficial, and irresponsible young socialite to a mature and responsible woman. This change is illustrated by the last scene, which is completely antithetical to the first one. Luella is no longer in the Ritz, no longer chatting idly; she is in her own home, not alone but with her husband. They form a genuine couple; they are going to the nursery to give the children an expected goodnight. Her face is no longer described as artificially made up but it has "lines around her eyes" and "a mature kindness" (6TJA, p. 159).

6. *Dear Scott/Dear Max: The Fitzgerald-Perkins Correspondence*, ed. John Kuehl and Jackson R. Bryer (New York: Charles Scribner's, 1971), p. 126.

The change is complete, and it is attributed above all to biological time: we grow up and we are bound to change. In fact, the contingency of time is emphasized by the technical handling of point of view previously mentioned. During the first four parts, we look forward with Luella, and there seem to be choices open to her. But in the last part, we look backward with the author and are left with the conviction that things could not have been otherwise.

The ideal of the mature woman—which Luella is the first Fitzgerald heroine to illustrate, and which Fitzgerald opposes to the many women who have not been able to grow and acquire control and a sense of responsibility—is to be found later in his work in definitely older women: Mrs. Speers in *Tender Is the Night*, and in the same novel the gold-star mothers, about whom he says, ". . . in their happy faces, the dignity that surrounded and pervaded the party, he perceived all the maturity of an older America" (TITN, pp. 100–1). We are a long way from the ideal of the flapper, and "The Adjuster" points to the transition.

All through the story, Luella is made to perceive time as compelling, contingent. When Doctor Moon first talks to her, he bends her will and her mind, and she says things she had not intended to say; because of this, she is afraid of him. When she says she is going out, he authoritatively answers, " 'I'm quite sure you're not going out' " (6TJA, p. 148). Gifted with a sort of clairvoyance, he seems to have realized what was taking place when Charles broke down: "he raised his head as if he were listening to something that was taking place a little distance away" (6TJA, p. 148). Moon says, " 'I do not act as a free agent' " and talks to her "as though she were not a free agent either" (6TJA, p. 147). The climax comes when, after the death of her child, Luella tries to escape to the vague freedom she thinks life has given back to her; at that moment, the shadow of Doctor Moon prevents her from passing: " 'Let me pass.' 'No.' Abruptly she gave way, as she always did when he talked to her," and she had "the conviction that her spirit was broken at last" (6TJA, p. 157).

It is under the strong guidance of Doctor Moon, which she is unable to escape, that Luella changes. From each catastrophe, she learns—however unwillingly. After Charles breaks down, she stays at home and faces the managing of her house. Doctor Moon congratulates her for that, but she is not quite ready yet; she interprets her difficulties as "the callousness of the world." The next step is when she faces her baby's death, the one after that when she takes her husband for a drive. Curiously, this starts a new chain of habits, breaks the vicious circle of the old self-centered attitudes. "But as the days passed, she found herself doing many things that had been repugnant to her before"; after having refused to supervise the servants, "she visited the kitchen every day, and kept an unwilling eye on the house, at first with a horror that it would go wrong again, then from habit" (6TJA, p. 157). In his last message, stressing the new attitudes she must acquire to become really adult, Doctor Moon uses the expression, " 'you've got to' " (6TJA, p. 158), thus showing that some outside force compels her. The final scene is introduced by the words "as usual." Luella has done all these things until they have become natural to her. A behaviorist approach is suggested here: the process of growing up is equivalent to the acquisition of new attitudes and sets of habits. But it is not clear whether behavior modification is the cause or the effect of growing up, whether growing up is achieved through, or results in, changed habits.

In the story, besides changing, growing up also implies facing life, facing the truth, and this too Luella learns from Doctor Moon. He forces her to admit that her baby is dead; he forces her to look at the reality of life, the reality of death, the reality of aging, to face these rather than to try to escape from them, which is what Luella is tempted to do. " 'I am leaving my mistakes behind,' " she says, but Doctor Moon answers, " 'You're trying to leave yourself behind, but you can't. The more you try to run away from yourself, the more you'll have yourself with you' " (6TJA, p. 157). A few months before "The Adjuster," Fitzgerald wrote in an essay entitled "How to Live on Practically Nothing a Year": "We were going to the Old World to find a new rhythm for our lives, with a true conviction that we had left our old selves behind forever,"[7] but he was soon to learn that this is impossible. This is why he makes Luella realize that she cannot leave her old self behind, that the past cannot be ignored, that the process which made her what she is cannot be forgotten. Only by facing the truth can she begin to build something; and this is what she does, step by step. In the end, Doctor Moon makes her look at herself in the mirror, which is an important symbolic gesture. No longer narcissistic, she looks at herself and sees lines, but she does not mind; she accepts them. She has become reconciled with the passage of time.

Only thus could Luella learn the ambivalence of time which is suggested in the story. After her baby's death, Doctor Moon is on the point of revealing to Luella something "at once brutal and kind" (6TJA, p. 155). Time seems to go on inexorably, but it also teaches; it can be lived as intolerable boredom, but it solves problems eventually. Time

---

7. F. Scott Fitzgerald, "How to Live on Practically Nothing a Year," *Saturday Evening Post*, 197 (September 20, 1924), 17.

causes suffering and cures suffering; it brings lines, but it also heals. This is why Luella no longer grieves for her baby, no longer is concerned with the lines in her face. But this is a difficult knowledge to acquire: "it was something he kept telling her about life, or almost telling her, and yet concealing from her, as though he were afraid to have her know" (6TJA, p. 157). And Doctor Moon is weary; this is stressed all along in the story. What he is trying to teach Luella has to be taught all over again to each new generation; it is a never-ending task.

3.

If Doctor Moon teaches Luella that she cannot ignore the passage of time, that time imposes changes upon her, he also goes beyond that; he teaches her the consequences she must draw from that knowledge. If she accepts the fact of growing up, she must accept its consequences—that is, the responsibility involved: " 'We make an agreement with children that they can sit in the audience without helping to make the play,' he said, 'but if they still sit in the audience after they're grown, somebody's got to work double time for them, so that they can enjoy the light and glitter of the world' " (6TJA, p. 158). The stress on responsibility is to be found throughout Fitzgerald's writing; it is one of his dominant themes, which he will develop especially in *Tender Is the Night*. It is also one of the main points he will emphasize in his correspondence with his growing daughter.

In "The Adjuster," this lesson comes as a conclusion to Luella's experience. If she remains a child, a passive spectator, and refuses to accept certain responsibilities, then others—her husband, her child—are bound to suffer. The toll exacted by people like her from other people is heavy—" 'somebody's got to work double time for them.' " This is precisely what happens in Luella's relationship with her husband, even though he is partly responsible. He accepts her selfishness, which has "an irresistible appeal" to him, and shows only devotion to her; he does not encourage her to change but takes on alone the responsibility for their situation. Fitzgerald qualifies Charles's attitude as "unhealthy," and says that because of this, "his mind had sickened" (6TJA, p. 148), causing him to break down. On the other hand, Luella's strength and vitality seem to have been the measure of her selfishness.[8] In the end, Luella is said to be "more noticeably changed" than

8. I do not agree with Higgins, who sees in Charles's sickness a prefiguration of the theme of transference of vitality used in *Tender Is the Night* (Higgins, p. 91).

Charles. This may seem a surprising statement since we have just been told that Charles's hair had become "dead white." But the reason for her greater change is that she started as much more immature and irresponsible than he.

" 'We make an agreement with children,' " says Doctor Moon, and the interesting notion of agreement implies some sort of social contract. There is a basic role for each generation, and only thus can society function. The children watch the play, the adults make the play; the two have completely different roles. Fitzgerald seems to suggest that the child is not "father to the man"; there is no continuity, no slow evolution but instead a break.

Because each generation has its role, Fitzgerald insists—here and all through his career—on the value of work and achievement. That is part of the contract. Freedom is not a value but is the lack of one; later, in *Tender Is the Night* or in his correspondence, Fitzgerald will severely condemn freedom by calling it self-indulgence. Children can only be passive because they have no skills; they cannot achieve. Adulthood, on the other hand, is active, and with it goes the learning of skills. After having lived as if she could have a husband and child without having to work, Luella must learn the necessity of achievement. She must learn how to supervise the servants and make her house function; she must learn how to take care of her husband and her children. She especially must learn to cook; this is her basic role—she must be the purveyor as well as the provider of life. Food is a recurrent motif in the story. It is about food and cooking that Luella first complains to her friend; the kitchen does not interest her, and she refuses to look into the icebox. Perhaps because of her attitude toward food, it is food that Charles throws all over the kitchen when he has his breakdown. Later, cooking for her child and her invalid husband seems to be an impossible task for Luella, and she has more difficulty with the cook than the other servants. When she accepts the facts and the truth they reveal, she can look unmoved at the little pans in which the baby's food was cooked. In the end, when she begins to take things in hand, she can bring herself to visit the kitchen every day and to look into the icebox.

Does that mean that Fitzgerald sees cooking and children as the only roles of the mature woman? In that respect, the story would appear quite conventional: the basic unit is the family, and to grow up is mainly to please a husband and take care of children. In this age of feminism, we could have sympathized with Luella at the beginning of the story and chosen to see her as suffering from an understandable *mal du siècle*. But in Fitzgerald's day, the growing woman did not have much of a choice. We noticed that Luella, having no job and no particular talent, had no other alternative. However, Fitzgerald does not want to have her become a perfect housewife; he wants her to become a better person. This is what Doctor Moon tells her, sketching a fine portrait of the mature woman:

> "It is your turn to be the centre, to give others what was given to you for so long. You've got to give security to young people and peace to your husband, and a sort of charity to the old. You've got to let the people who work for you depend on you. You've got to cover up a few more troubles than you show, and be a little more patient than the average person, and do a little more instead of a little less than your share." (6TJA, p. 158)

What is demanded of her is not conventional, it is expressed in much more subtle terms. By being the center, she will no longer be a satellite, one of the many Fitzgeraldian young women who put a strain on their husbands because they expect and demand everything and give nothing in exchange; she will have something to give that is appropriate to each one close to her.

But why does she have to do more than her share? Fitzgerald had by then become very aware of the irresponsibility of the rich, which is such an important aspect of *The Great Gatsby*. In one of the essays mentioned earlier, he demonstrates that on the contrary the rich, because they are privileged, have more responsibilities than others: ". . . the American 'leisure class' . . . has frequently no consciousness that leisure is a privilege, not a right, and that a privilege always implies a responsibility."[9]

Doctor Moon is an "adjuster" when he makes Luella become aware of her responsibilities toward others whom she has been ignoring. The word "to adjust" has many meanings, but the broader and subtler meaning of it is a now commonly accepted definition: "to achieve mental and behavioral balance between one's own needs and the demands of others."[10] This is demonstrated in the story, the ending of which suggests that such a balance has been achieved. But the concept of adjusting also implies time; this is why time is the adjuster in Luella's tale.

In the end, when Doctor Moon is on the point of leaving, his face dissolves into as many faces as there are months in five years, "three-

9. "What Kind of Husbands Do 'Jimmies' Make?," in *F. Scott Fitzgerald in His Own Time*, p. 188.
10. *Webster's New Collegiate Dictionary*, s.v. "adjust."

score," "each one different yet the same—sad, happy, tragic, indifferent, resigned" (6TJA, p. 159). These are the moods we go through with
the passing of time. It is interesting to see that the list concludes with
the word "resigned." Is, then, the ultimate lesson resignation? Doctor
Moon says to Luella that if she makes the choice to accept the passage
of time and with it her responsibilities, she will find whatever happiness
there is in the world. This is how he expresses that happiness: " 'Happy
things *may* come to you in life, but you must never go seeking them
any more' " (6TJA, p. 159; italics mine). Fitzgerald comments, ". . . if
the world seemed less gay and happy to her than it had before, she
experienced *a certain* peace, *sometimes*, that she had never known"
(6TJA, p. 157); and later: ". . . she was *still* lovely" (6TJA, p. 159;
italics mine), "still" being the admission that Luella had not lost everything. It is obvious that there is a great reserve in this expression of
happiness; it is a modest happiness. Resignation is indeed necessary.

In spite of the positive things in Luella's life at twenty-eight, there is
a sad mood in the ending. That sadness seems due to the implicit
admission that something is lost when you grow up, even though
something else is gained—and the loss seems greater than the gain. The
children watch the show and enjoy "the light and glitter" of the world.
These two metaphors, here only suggested, appear frequently in Fitzgerald's work, and they are used in contexts that make them positive
and desirable. In "Absolution" (1924), the lights of the amusement park
suggest to the young Rudolph a fuller and more beautiful life than that
imposed by his rigidly religious father. *The Great Gatsby* is a novel of
lights—light of wealth, light of entertainment, light of conviviality and
gaiety, but above all light of dreams and wonder. Many of the earlier
stories literally use some sort of show which is being put on; Gatsby as
party-host organizes a show for his guests; and later, in *Tender Is the
Night*, the show will express Dick Diver's attempt to make the world
brighter and reality more beautiful for his friends. In "The Adjuster,"
these metaphors are present, but their implications are not developed.
There is simply a faint regret permeating the ending, as if with adulthood a whole world were lost, the world of the imagination, the world
of wonder so very present in *The Great Gatsby* but only alluded to
here. Luella says, " 'I want the light and glitter,' " and Doctor Moon
answers, " 'The light and glitter of the world is in your hands' " (6TJA,
p. 158). With these words, through a reversal of terms which comes
out almost like a trick, Fitzgerald expresses the acceptance of that loss,
although it is not very convincing.

Going further, he associates light with warmth: " 'The household
here is in your keeping. . . . If there is any light and warmth in it, it

will be your light and warmth.' " Doing this, he adds a notion to the word "light" which no longer means the same. It becomes a completely different metaphor with completely different connotations—warmth provided by the mother, warmth of the hearth, warmth of the home. And when he concludes, " 'It is your turn to make the fire' " (6TJA, p. 159), we no longer have the "light and glitter."

In Fitzgerald's fiction, the exuberance of the tone connotes the search for happiness which is often expressed by the metaphor of "light and glitter." But "The Adjuster" is toned down; the diffused regret which can be felt at the end expresses faintly—as it does more clearly in other works by Fitzgerald—a feeling of being torn between the search for ethics and the search for happiness. An important dimension of Fitzgerald's writing is that the search for ethics, the heritage of Puritanism and at the same time of the Catholicism in which the author was brought up, often runs counter to the search for happiness, the heritage of the American dream. This struggle gives to his finer fiction an ambivalence which is its greatness. In "The Adjuster," however, the search for ethics prevails, and the story does not have the complexity of contemporaneous stories such as "Absolution" or of *The Great Gatsby*, in which the moral awareness is delicately balanced by a strong sense of wonder. This story, dealing only with moral issues, is deprived of the ambivalence of the novels.

In spite of the relative simplicity of its theme, "The Adjuster" does not have a clear focus. Freedom is opposed both to the contingency of time and to the sense of responsibility. Doctor Moon is a rather confused representation. Intended to be a symbol, he simply appears to be a *deus ex machina*. He is meant to represent Time, but at the same time he is the mouthpiece of Fitzgerald the moralist. The fact that there is more than one focus weakens the impact of the story and its use of symbolism. The passage of time, which stresses contingency, is contradictory to the ethical view of responsibility which implies a certain amount of free will. Finally, there is something contrived in the conclusion suggesting that we must accept the fact that life is determined, that we must freely choose to face the inevitable because this is the only way to find some sort of happiness.

But, as we have seen, the main interest of "The Adjuster" does not lie in its actual lesson; it lies in all that is suggested. The story touches on most of the themes dear to the author and foreshadows concerns that he developed in his later work, especially in *Tender Is the Night*.

FACES IN A DREAM: INNOCENCE PERPETUATED IN "THE RICH BOY"

PETER WOLFE

A writer who can reinforce his statement of narrative intent with memorable phrasing will seize the reader's attention and win his confidence. The third paragraph of "The Rich Boy" (1926) begins with Fitzgerald's most famous pronouncement: "Let me tell you about the very rich. They are different from you and me" (*Stories*, p. 177). Through the career of the story's main character, Anson Hunter of New York City, Fitzgerald spells out the difference that both charmed and beredeviled him throughout his adult life: the rich believe that the prizes they possess and enjoy early are theirs by right. No process of logic has convinced Anson Hunter of his superiority. Privilege has accompanied him from the start; he has never doubted his claim to it, nor will he let it go away. But what does it consist of? And what price must he pay for it?

A rarely challenged truism of our consumer-industrial urban state decrees that riches buy happiness. To accept this nostrum is to invite its corollary. If the rich man basks in happiness, then the rich boy is twice blessed; for he can enjoy the privileges that money brings without having to justify himself. He can make his own rules. Because the middle-class virtue of moral consistency doesn't apply to him, he can carouse all night, go home for a cold shower and a change of clothes, and then teach Sunday school with stony-jawed piety. Time has given him opportunities to develop his foibles and eccentricities. No wonder Paula Legendre, the only woman Hunter ever loved, thinks of him as a dual personality. Wearing the stripes of the dissolute and the conservative, he alternates recklessness and control.

At a deeper level, his princely code rules out adult actions like getting married or even acting decently and responsibly in personal relationships. Hunter's life is a calculated smash-and-grab raid on the hearts of others. In his younger and more vulnerable years, he had everything he wanted. Freed from the middle-class urge to get ahead, he now summons all the force of his forceful personality to keep and even build on his advantage. The effort entails denying the reality of other persons as independent centers of significance. After his military discharge removes the barrier of distance between him and Paula, he doesn't know how to act with her, his confusion stemming from a need to protect himself. His preference for conducting intimacies through the mail rather than in person conveys his fear of commitment. The first-hand and the immediate threaten him. Only a boy, he hasn't learned to share. He deems it safer to pine for someone he can't have than to work at a relationship with somebody available and at hand. As can be expected, Paula's value for him increases as she moves away from him. By stages, their broken romance, her marriage, and finally her death enrich the rosy hues of an attachment whose main ingredient consists of apartness rather than union. Maintaining his identity as rich young prince always wins his first priority. Thus every stage of his adult life (we know him from ages twenty-one to thirty) shows Hunter displaying photographs taken at an earlier time and living emotionally through them.

Hugging a reconstructed, idealized past denies his truest self in other ways, too. In what is perhaps a legacy from his favorite writer Keats, the Fitzgerald of "The Rich Boy" believes that a romantic relationship can attain a flame-tip of psychic intensity, during which the emotion-charged lovers both see that the moment has come for a declaration of mutual commitment. Fitzgerald also believes that if the moment isn't seized and shared, it will probably vanish forever. Anson Hunter attains this sort of romantic crescendo with Dolly Karger in Port Washington, Long Island, when a glimpse at Paula Legendre's picture cools his ardor and sends him from Dolly's bedroom with a nasty remark. (A more vibrant example of the crescendo, or shared epiphany, occurred a few years earlier when he visited Paula in Florida, presumably to propose marriage.) Looking at Paula's picture while embracing Dolly gives him the courage to do what he has wanted to do all along. His conduct with both women reflects both the impudence and the arrogance of power. The interlude with Paula also shows that a calculating lover is no lover at all. His need for her, great as it is, falls short of his need to sustain his princely self-image. Shrinking from a marriage proposal he knows will be accepted, he tries instead to impose a less binding tie:

> They embraced recklessly, passionately. . . . Then Paula drew back her face to let his lips say what she wanted to hear—she could feel the words forming as they kissed again. . . . Again she broke away, listening, but as he pulled her close once more she realized that he said nothing. . . . Humbly, obediently, her emotions yielded to him and the tears streamed down her face, but her heart kept on crying: "Ask me—oh, Anson, dearest, ask me!"
>
> "Paula. . . .*Paula!*"
>
> The words wrung her heart like hands, and Anson, feeling her tremble, knew that emotion was enough. He need say no more, commit their destinies to no practical enigma. . . .
>
> He had forgotten that Paula too was worn away inside with the strain of three years. Her mood passed forever in the night. (*Stories*, pp. 186–87)

As her passing mood shows, Paula won't play by his rules. Like Dolly after her, she recovers from her setback, outgrows him, and marries another man when Hunter squanders their moment of deep physical and psychic communion. That she has already outpaced him shows in the moral gamble she took for his sake: Paula risked losing Lowell Thayer, her future husband, who was playing bridge with her and Hunter at the time she left the table without excusing herself to join Hunter for a walk on the moonlit beach. Such spontaneity and moral courage discomfits Hunter, with his meager powers of commitment. Predictably, he goes back to New York the very next morning.

This haste typifies him. If the American South represents softness and drowsy, easygoing charm for Fitzgerald, then Hunter has the energy, aggressiveness, and determination of the practical-minded industrial North. No brooding isolato he. Even though responsibility and authority are thrust upon him by the accident of being the eldest of six children whose millionaire parents both die before he is thirty, he warms to the challenge. His set ideas about right and wrong banish any pangs of self-doubt. These ideas he applies to others as strictly as to himself. When Dolly Karger tries to end her romance with him, ironically at the same time he wants to break with *her*, he refuses to walk away. His sense of superiority must not be tampered with; she must suffer for presuming to control the romance, even for sparing him the trouble of instigating an action agreeable to him. Paula, too, has felt the weight of his cold, strong will. In her last meeting with him, seven years after their romantic heyday, she explains, "I was infatuated with you, Anson—you could make me do anything you liked. But we wouldn't have been happy" (*Stories*, p. 205).

She argues well. His fear of impulse and commitment shows frontier energy fighting itself in the age of the closed frontier. Hunter mixes memory and desire with strong lashings of money, social rank, and vanity. Yet every exercise of his powerful will diminishes him rather than confirming his preeminence. An excellent example of the slamming recoil caused by his bullying comes after his discovery of his aunt's love affair. Hunter, it is seen here, lives at a great moral distance from himself. So alien is he to emotion that when he sees it, he crushes it; perhaps sexual commitment in any form, even that of others, threatens him so much that he must stamp it out. Of little import to him is the fact that in the process of stepping between his uncle's wife and her lover, he wrecks a few lives—including his own. Invoking the creed of family honor, he breaks up the affair. (His aunt's first response to the moral lecture he gives her, "Edna stood up, leaving her crab-flake cocktail untasted," has the same perfection of detail as Tom and Daisy Buchanan's conspiratorial supper of cold chicken and ale the night of Myrtle Wilson's death in *Gatsby*.) But his meddling creates other, unexpected changes. Edna's lover kills himself, and Anson stops receiving invitations to his uncle's home.

The act he performed in the name of solidarity has proved, ironically, divisive. Another irony inheres in the timing of his self-righteous act, which comes at a stage of his life when he most needs the security and warmth represented by the family. Modifying Gatsby's belief that the past can be relived is his conviction that it can be prolonged. "The Rich Boy" tallies the high cost of trying to maintain the status quo. Though he lives amid fast change, Hunter won't alter the basic realities governing his life. Leaning on his tie with Yale, he helps his former classmates find jobs, women to date and marry, and places to live. But playing the busybody with ex-classmates helps him no more than it did with Edna. Like his women, his college friends outgrow their dependence on him—moving to the suburbs, becoming absorbed by their new marriages, and sometimes going to Hollywood to write for the movies. At thirty, he is trapped by a past he can never revive. The sight of a new desk clerk at the Plaza makes him wince; so remote is the past he constantly invokes that the exchange of a phone number he dials in order to beat back loneliness no longer exists. The atavistic associations called up by his last name hearken to primitive cultures in a manner befitting his persistence in dredging up the past.

What this modern caveman proves is that Eden lies beyond recovery, especially by money or power. He misreads and mistreats the past throughout. His strongest link to a living past, namely the family, he forfeits by trying to control Edna (whose name and harmless affair both recall Eden, together with the idea of self-renewal through sexual love). Fitzgerald believes in the value of family, money, and even power. But he also believes this value to be instrumental rather than absolute: Nick Carraway's solid midwestern family strengthens him for the ordeal of coping in a fast-moving, competitive society, but it doesn't ensure his success. Any virtue prolonged or extended to the point where it rules people loses its value, like southern Georgia's drowsy charm in "The Ice Palace" (1920) and, more hauntingly, Braddock Washington's stupendous castle in "The Diamond as Big as the Ritz" (1922). Wealth must be shared rather than hoarded. Characters less favored by birth than Anson Hunter have put this lesson to work in the Fitzgerald canon. Dexter Green, for instance, amasses money and status to impress his *princesse lointaine*, Judy Jones, in "Winter Dreams" (1922), just as Gatsby believes that winning a fortune, however dishonestly, will also win him Daisy's love. The Midwesterners Gatsby and Green surpass the New York blueblood Hunter in their purity of motive; however wrongheaded their methods, they want to marry and serve the women they love. Their goal is one of sharing. Hunter, on the other hand, wants a chorus of admirers, and he wants them at a safe distance; he uses his money to boost his ego. Since the reassurances he buys count more to him than those who reassure him, he is really buying what he fears most and wants least—loneliness.

Self-distrust runs high with him, as befits a hunter whose arrows usually miss their mark. Both his love for Paula Legendre and his later elevation of her to near-legendary grandeur take root in self-distrust, perhaps even self-dislike. If love is to have a place in his life, let it be safe and tame rather than stormy. Thus his courtship of serious, gentle Paula has a solemn, nervous tone he has substituted for passion. Yet Paula's choice of passion over safety puts her beyond his control during their last meeting. His final words to her, four successive yesses, show that while he has remained a boy, she has grown into a woman— another sign of which is her heavy pregnancy. Overmatched, he can only agree and consent. Yet this biddable boy once came close to marrying Paula. His choice of Dolly Karger as a major romantic involvement—the only one Fitzgerald dramatizes after Paula—shows how much Paula frightened him. So well does he know what excites him in a woman that, in Dolly, he deliberately selects one who falls short of those things. And she fails to meet his standards of human decency and dignity more vividly than he himself does. His female mirror-image, Dolly resembles Anson Hunter as strikingly as Paula, who comes from a more prominent family, differs from him. Whereas Paula is repelled by his hard drinking, Dolly hopes to profit from it. This "gypsy of the unattainable" also yearns for the men she can't have rather than trying to build a relationship with one within reach. So close is she in spirit and purpose to Hunter that they write each other identical letters at precisely the same time on the same subject—the wisdom of ending their relationship. His similarity to her disturbs as well as comforts Hunter. Angered that she should presume to take charge of her relationship with him, he concocts an elaborate scheme to punish her. His inability to revise the scheme in the face of change— the sudden romantic glow he ignites with her—spells out his rigidness. Both he and Dolly suffer from his failure to cope with change and chance. As the episode with Edna showed, the crime of resisting his mental concepts carries stiff penalties for all.

As usual, the stiffest penalties are suffered by him. Did he know that Paula's picture was in the bedroom before he put Dolly there? Nobody less than Paula, herself a victim of his romantic fears, could dim the glow created by their being alone together. The way he used Dolly shows how far he has regressed since the night on the Pensacola beach. Whereas he wasted his moment of shared intensity with Paula by neglecting to act on it, some cruel words shatter Dolly's romantic hopes. He now fights love with elaborate strategies instead of resisting it. He would never have dismissed Paula as rudely as he does Dolly.

Paula's centricity in his life is conveyed by narrative structure. "The Rich Boy" has two competing designs. In the first, Part I is a prologue, written as a narrative, and Part VIII is a dramatic epilogue; the action extends from Part II to Part VII. The competing design, breaking the story at its halfway point at the end of Part IV, introduces moral commentary. Each of the story's two halves ends with a combined birth and death. At the end of Part IV, Hunter has just heard of Paula's engagement to Lowell Thayer, some two months after Pensacola. For three days after hearing the news, he cries unpredictably. The melting into life implied by his involuntary tears and the symbolic three-day crying period both prime him for rebirth. But, as he did in Pensacola, he lets the breakthrough moment pass him by without acting on it. The meaning of his failure hits home in Part VIII, a coda or reworking of earlier elements in his wasted life. This reworking gives the combined birth-and-death of Part VIII much more force than that of Part IV, which occupied but two paragraphs. In Part VIII, Hunter learns of Paula's death in childbirth, significantly three days before his trip to

Europe. Even in death, she reproaches him morally. Just as she had risked alienating Lowell Thayer by leaving him to go out with Hunter, so does Hunter's last visit with her in Part VII—coincidentally seven years after the fated moonlight walk—reveal her outpacing him in pep and resiliency. Unwisely, she married Thayer on the rebound from her setback with Hunter. But she fought back from this bad marriage to marry a man she loves—only to die bearing his child. Like her brave life, her tragic death gives her a stature that belittles rich, vain Hunter.

The last part of the story shows a nerve-frayed Hunter sailing to Europe aboard a passenger ship; the American male defines himself in action. He also can't bear to sit still, do nothing, and face himself. As with the Jamesian pattern of European travel in works like *Daisy Miller* and *The Golden Bowl*, Hunter has used up his American social options. But he leaves the domestic front as a casualty, not as a star. Rather than coping with the horror of being alone, he goes looking for self-confirmation. As always, the search sends him back into himself. The story ends with his ship on the ocean, the universal symbol of motherhood. Further proof of his reversion to infancy is his creating an admirer of another passenger, known to us only as the girl in the red tam. His being literally at sea chimes with his loss of moral control. Like an unsure child, he needs the approval of others to carry on. As such, he defines himself once again as Paula's opposite number. Whereas Paula blossomed into adulthood but died before she could savor it (another Keatsian motif), Hunter survives as an emotional infant, preying on the susceptibilities of others.

His story reaches us through the narration of a contemporary, a fellow New Yorker and Ivy Leaguer who did not attend Yale. The nameless narrator has known Hunter for about eight years, i.e., during the time of the recorded action. That he is also with him at the end indicates that the men are well enough acquainted to sail together on an ocean cruise. The fellow passengers team well artistically: Hunter needs an audience to play to, and the narrator is content to stand back. If bullying, badgering Hunter resembles Tom Buchanan, the self-effacing narrator recalls Nick Carraway's quiet stability. His lack of a name reflects his willingness to let life happen to him instead of imposing himself. Only in Part I, the prologue, does he state opinions about Hunter. And even here, he is providing a moral context for what will happen rather than judging. Nor does he complain at the end, when Hunter deserts him aboard ship to spend time with the girl in the red tam. This likeable, trustworthy man makes good company as well as providing a good foil to the bully whose tale he tells. First, his well-bred reticence tones down the hectic pace created by Hunter's anxiety.

Next, his long personal tie with Hunter fends off dryness and cold. It is material that he holds the stage alone in the story's first part, only mentioning Hunter by name in the next-to-last sentence. Besides wanting his moment of glory, he also knows that he must grab it quickly. Once introduced, Hunter will dominate. The burden of the story consists of the rich boy's need to extend and solidify his self-importance. In the last section, though, the narrator comes forth as more of a person than a device or disembodied voice. A well-to-do man and not a rich boy, he feels lucky that he hasn't been tempted as Hunter has; the blessings that came to Hunter at birth have blocked the latter's growth. On the other hand, the narrator reacts to Hunter personally as well as socially; as he said in his opening monologue, Hunter is more of an individual than a type. And his personal behavior has given the narrator plenty to resent. Hunter forgets about the narrator for years at a stretch; he only phones him on the Saturday he happens upon Paula Legendre Hagerty because, for once, he has nothing to do and nobody to be with. Hunter discards him aboard the *Paris* the first day out in favor of the girl in the red tam, having already made sure that she is traveling alone.

In view of these slights, why aren't the tone and the thesis of "The Rich Boy" both bitter? First, the narrator sees Hunter as a victim. The depression Hunter has suffered in recent months and his sharp attraction to the girl in the red tam, even though Paula died only three days before, both show his helpless addiction to female approval. His job is an incidental in his life. Were he able to certify his self-being through the world of work and men, he'd not have needed the European vacation his colleagues forced upon him. Also tempering the narrator's harsh judgment of Hunter is the suspicion that love can kill: Paula dies delivering the baby of the only man she ever loved, and the middle-aged passion of Edna and Cary Sloane has created a contagion of physical and moral death. The narrator has seen this wreckage. Presumably lacking a rich private life of his own (and a career as well, judging from his ability to leave New York for three to six months in order to go to Europe with Hunter?), he won't censure Hunter directly for shrinking from the dangers of love. Better half a life than none. If this tame, bystanderish behavior indicates a different half from that of the predatory Hunter, it infers no moral superiority. And the narrator knows it. He has also reached the age—i.e., thirty—where he cannot lie to himself. Failing to live at full stretch, he can't attack Hunter. Besides, the rich boy has always gladdened the hearts he shatters. Nor was the shattering permanent, Paula and Dolly both benefiting from his negative example to marry other men. The narrator has probably never made such an impact upon a woman.

No drab factual report, "The Rich Boy" resembles a moral parable channeled through the media of escapist psychology and urban social history. The passage of years creates changes in the lives of various privileged New Yorkers, during which time Hunter fights change and growth. The absence of a concluding judgment of his immaturity, a function of the narrator's restraint and moral malaise, promotes narrative economy. It also reflects artistic self-confidence. Fitzgerald revealed Anson Hunter and his biographer so well that he didn't need to explain them.

"THE SWIMMERS":
PARIS AND VIRGINIA RECONCILED

MELVIN J. FRIEDMAN

"The Swimmers," published originally in the October 19, 1929, *Saturday Evening Post*, may be said to belong to a literary sequence which starts with Edgar Allan Poe and carries to Yves Berger and William Styron. When the young Poe moved to Richmond, Virginia, and settled into his career as a writer, he left an indelible impression on literary history. He was perhaps the first responsible for what Harry Levin aptly called a "transatlantic refraction." Levin went on to characterize Poe's special position in France: "More than his work, the legend of his life made him a generic literary hero, gallicized and virtually canonized. . . ."[1] A succession of French Symbolist writers and musicians, which included Baudelaire, Mallarmé, Valéry, and Debussy, performed miracles in their renderings of the author of "Annabel Lee" and "The Fall of the House of Usher." The "French face" of Poe (as one critic described it) is disturbingly more prepossessing than his American one. Poe completed the terms of the Franco-American exchange by occasionally choosing Paris as the setting for his stories.

Julien Green, a member of F. Scott Fitzgerald's generation, offers another kind of "transatlantic refraction." He was born of American parents in Paris in 1900, with establishment Virginia credentials hauntingly in the background. Henri Peyre put the matter eloquently: "Most of all, his mother's teaching permeated him with Southern traditions. He never saw the American South as a child, but he was convinced of

---

1. Harry Levin, *"France-Amérique:* The Transatlantic Refraction," *Comparative Literature Studies*, 1 (No. 2, 1964), 87–92; quotation from p. 88.

the superiority of the Southern culture that the victors in the Civil War
and the carpetbaggers who followed them had wrecked. It was early
impressed upon him that he belonged to a vanquished nation."² Green
partly accommodated himself to his ancestry by attending the University of Virginia and writing several novels with Virginia backdrops,
such as *Mont-Cinère* (1926; translated as *Avarice House*) and *Moïra*
(1950). The latter, set in Charlottesville, seems to offer twisted reminders of Green's earlier years at the university. Later in his career,
when Green turned to playwrighting, he entitled his first dramatic
work *Sud* (1953).

This title may indeed have inspired Yves Berger's novel *Le Sud*,
which appeared nine years later. It is clear, in any case, that there is a
strong connection between Julien Green and the twenty-nine-year-old
author of this compelling first novel, as Harry Levin has already suggested. *Le Sud*, translated into English as *The Garden*, has as its real
setting France, but it is mythically haunted by a utopian dream of
nineteenth-century antebellum Virginia (the date 1842 recurs). An in-
tentional bit of confusion, which reinforces Berger's symbolic design, is
that the heroine's name is Virginie; thus we have this coupling: ". . .
Virginie, Virginia, they are inside me," they argue, quarrel, they put
forward words, raise pictures. . . ."³ Susan Sontag, in her review of
The Garden in *Book Week*, expressed all of this in the most lucid terms:

> But M. Berger goes the American Southern writers one better.
> For him, America, the American South, becomes literally an item
> of the imagination. Virginia is not a place, but an idea, upon
> which a mad provincial French family immolates itself. The pub-
> lic myth of America as the land of revivifying contraries (of youth
> and materialism, of innocence and brutality, of virgin forests and
> the asphalt jungle) has been refined . . . into the study of a cancer-
> ous private myth of America.⁴

A Virginia-born novelist who seems tuned into the same frequency is
William Styron. He might be characterized as a Julien Green or an
Yves Berger in reverse. He looks across the ocean from Virginia, which
is a very real presence in his fiction—not the "item of the imagination"

2. Henri Peyre, *French Novelists of Today* (New York: Oxford Univ. Press, 1967), p.
197.
3. Yves Berger, *The Garden*, trans. Robert Baldick (New York: New American
Library, 1964), p. 142.
4. Susan Sontag, "Virginia is a State of Mind," *Book Week*, 1 (September 15, 1963),
28.

it is for Green and Berger. One of the characters in Styron's *Lie Down in Darkness* (1951) is warned by his father about his Virginia inheritance: ". . . the ground is bloody and full of guilt where you were born and you must tread a long narrow path toward your destiny."[5] The reality of the Virginia soil is even more palpable in *The Confessions of Nat Turner* (1967). The only one of Styron's novels which has something directly and explicitly of Levin's "transatlantic refraction" is *Set This House on Fire* (1960). This book moves freely back and forth across the Atlantic, with Virginia as an important landmark. The principal European setting, where the violence occurs, is the Italian village of Sambuco, but there is also a brief Parisian interlude which is given special emphasis. One is strongly reminded of the hymnal quality at the end of *The Great Gatsby* in reading the final pages of *Set This House on Fire*:

> "Then you know, something as I sat there—something about the dawn made me think of America and how the light would come up slowly over the eastern coast, miles and miles of it, the Atlantic, and the inlets and bays and slow tideland rivers with houses on the shore. . . . And I kept thinking of the new sun coming up over the coast of Virginia and the Carolinas, and how it must have looked from those galleons, centuries ago, when after black night, dawn broke like a trumpet blast, and there it was, immense and green and glistening against the crashing seas."[6]

Set This House on Fire is indeed a book much indebted to F. Scott Fitzgerald.

Which brings us to "The Swimmers," with its restless movings between Paris and Virginia. It seems to me to be part of that literary cycle which I have sketched in above. Its hero, Henry Clay Marston, is not a literary person, but he seems to be sensitive to the same mythical and historical cadences. He is a businessman blessed with certain of the sensibilities and caprices of the poet. Like the narrator of Berger's *The Garden*, Marston is haunted by his special view of Virginia—particularly when living in France. Like Poe, Green, and Joseph Day (the main character of *Moïra*), he attended the University of Virginia.

At the beginning of the story, the thirty-five-year-old Marston, living in Paris with a French wife and two sons, experiences "a black horror"

5. William Styron, *Lie Down in Darkness* (New York: New American Library, 1960), p. 69.

6. William Styron, *Set This House on Fire* (New York: Random House, 1960), pp. 499–500.

which seems to presage a nervous breakdown. The breakdown itself properly begins later in the day when he arrives home to discover "a man's hat and stick on the hall table and for the first time in his life he heard silence . . ." (*Bits*, p. 190). His wife's "certain indiscretion," as she delicately describes it, seems to bring on something which had been building up for some time with this expatriated Virginian ("the kind who are prouder of being Virginians than of being Americans" [*Bits*, p. 191]).

To hasten his recovery from the breakdown, Marston and his family vacation at a beach resort, St. Jean de Luz. A kind of Joycean epiphany occurs for Marston as he, a non-swimmer, attempts to rescue a drowning girl—herself an accomplished swimmer. This eighteen-year-old girl, who remains an unnamed but central presence in the story, teaches Marston to swim. After he acquires the rudiments of this new art, he returns with his family to Virginia.

We next find Marston "almost three years later" working for the Calumet Tobacco Company in Richmond. His wife's new infidelities have finally convinced him that he wants to return to France and leave her behind with her new lover. The point of contention is custody of the two sons. Marston, his wife, Choupette, and her lover go out in the latter's motorboat to discuss the matter. After a predictable series of events, which underscores the lover's underhandedness and Marston's coolness and composure under pressure, the father gains custody of the sons and then leaves by himself for Europe. On the boat he encounters the unnamed girl for the third time (the second had been on a Virginia beach when he discovered, delightedly, that she was Virginian like himself). These two "swimmers," we seem to be told, can successfully negotiate the transatlantic crossing while Choupette and her lover cannot.

This brief outline scarcely does justice to the twists and turns of the plot. Much goes on in this twenty-three-page story, which not only takes Henry Marston from nervous breakdown to complete renewal and revitalization but also affords Fitzgerald a showcase for some striking, almost hymnal passages extolling Virginia and America.

The few critics who have discussed "The Swimmers" have somewhat different notions of its worth. Matthew J. Bruccoli, in his thoughtful preface to *Bits of Paradise*, suggests that "despite its over-plotting and unlikely climax, [it] may well be the most significant of the heretofore buried stories" (*Bits*, p. 10). Kenneth Eble, after commenting on the extent to which it resembles a Henry James story, offers a compromise somewhat akin to Bruccoli's but more restrained: "Though the story ends with a desperate contrivance, it is worth reading if only for its style and for its skillful contrasts between two cultures."[7] Robert Sklar gives the most detailed analysis anywhere in print (three pages!). He begins by speaking of it as "a neglected, undervalued story"[8] and then proceeds to a convincing, full-scale interpretation—with Spengler's *Decline of the West* as an accompanying text. Finally, John A. Higgins considers "The Swimmers" as being "of negligible worth," with a "rickety plot" redeemed only by "a number of significant passages." He ends by saying: "Significant themes are wasted on poor form in 'The Swimmers' . . . and good symbolism is wasted. . . ."[9]

None of these critics suggests that "The Swimmers" is vintage Fitzgerald, of the order, say, of "The Diamond as Big as the Ritz" (1922) and "Babylon Revisited" (1931) (a story it occasionally resembles). Yet all feel that there is something compelling about it, that at least its failures are interesting ones. Its themes, symbols, and stylistic felicities seem partly to redeem it despite the contrivances and structural deficiencies.

Kenneth Eble, I think, comes closest to explaining the strength of "The Swimmers" when he points to "its skillful contrasts between two cultures."[10] It somehow becomes a better story when viewed in terms of its "transatlantic refraction," when seen as part of that literary genealogy which carries from Poe to Yves Berger and Styron.

To play a bit on the word "genealogy," which seems to me central to the story, Marston is haunted by his, especially during his Paris interlude: "His seven generations of Virginia ancestors were definitely behind him every day at noon when he turned home" (*Bits*, p. 189). Virginia and his proud forebears seem infinitely exciting to him from his expatriated vantage point. Henry Marston, like Alex Haley more recently, is intensely preoccupied with his "roots." In a *New Yorker* piece concerned with the television dramatization of "Roots: The Next Generations," Michael J. Arlen made much of "the fantasy or dream of Going Home." Arlen accumulated a series of turns of phrase which apply very well to Marston's situation: "mysterious difficulty in Going Home," "fantasies of the returning voyagers," "the returning-voyager myth," "remote and golden past."[11] All of these phrases have a compel-

---

7. Kenneth Eble, *F. Scott Fitzgerald*, rev. ed. (Boston: Twayne, 1977), p. 121.

8. Robert Sklar, *F. Scott Fitzgerald: The Last Laocoön* (New York: Oxford Univ. Press, 1967), p. 236.

9. John A. Higgins, *F. Scott Fitzgerald: A Study of the Stories* (Jamaica, N.Y.: St. John's Univ. Press, 1971), pp. 113–14.

10. Eble, p. 121.

11. Michael J. Arlen, "The Air: The Prisoner of the Golden Dream," *New Yorker*, 55 (March 26, 1979), 115–25.

ling bearing on Marston's removal of his family from Paris to Richmond, Virginia, and his own subsequent return to Europe.

The mysterious, the fantastic, the mythical comfortably control his
view of Virginia as long as he remains abroad—as long as he indulges
his imagination. The actual return proves disappointing, shades perhaps of Thomas Wolfe's "you can't go home again." Marston indeed
encounters the "mysterious difficulty in Going Home." He somehow
figures that his wife's infidelity will be cleansed by the pure Virginia
air, by "his ever-new, ever-changing country" (*Bits*, p. 195). This proves
emphatically wrong. All his high-sounding phrases and sentiments retreat in the face of the actual Virginia. The Paris Marston saw at the
beginning of "The Swimmers," with the "suspended mass of gasoline
exhaust cooked slowly by the June sun" and the "roads choked with the
same foul asthma" (*Bits*, p. 187), is not unlike his newly-regained
Richmond, Virginia, dominated by the Calumet Tobacco Company.
Not only does Choupette commit adultery in Richmond but, significantly, we are told that this French woman "might have passed for an
American. Southernisms overlay her French accent with a quaint
charm. . . ." (*Bits*, pp. 198–99). Choupette, ironically, has managed
the settling into Virginia life more smoothly than the Virginian Henry
Clay Marston. One might conclude from all this, echoing Susan Son-
tag's remark about *The Garden*, that Virginia has more vitality for
Marston as an idea, "an item of the imagination," than an actual place.
His systematic attempts at recovering his "roots" prove both futile and
frustrating.

Yet as I have suggested above, "The Swimmers" is all about Marston's renewal and revitalization. His seeming failure to adjust to Richmond is viewed as being far more positive than negative. Fitzgerald
makes this clear indirectly when he speaks of his wife's "adjustment":
"Divorced from her own country, Choupette had picked the things out
of American life that pandered best to her own self-indulgence" (*Bits*,
p. 208). Negative words like "divorced," "pandered," and "self-indulgence" forcefully anchor this sentence. We connect more positive words,
many associated with swimming, with Henry Marston. Thus we have
the following:

> For three years, swimming had been a sort of refuge, and he
> turned to it as one man to music or another to drink. There was a
> point when he would resolutely stop thinking and go to the Vir-
> ginia coast for a week to wash his mind in the water. Far out past
> the breakers he could survey the green-and-brown line of the Old
> Dominion with the pleasant impersonality of a porpoise. (*Bits*, p.
> 201)

It is the eighteen-year-old Virginia girl who first makes the connection between swimming and getting clean. She appears three times in the story. (The number three probably has some importance in "The Swimmers," although it is not the same *passe partout* as in the New Testament, the Cid poem, or in Dante.) Her function seems more symbolic than anything else. She is never given a name and turns up conveniently at crucial moments in Henry Marston's life: she teaches him to swim before his return to Virginia; she reinforces his desire on the Virginia beach to return to France and maintain the custody of his sons; she is present aboard ship at the end when his convictions about his country and his family are at their firmest. Water is of course present on each occasion, and swimming suggests the metaphor for their almost fairy tale relationship. Water is as central to this story as snow is to "Babylon Revisited."

Even John A. Higgins, who offers the most negative view of "The Swimmers," points to its "good symbolism." Symbolic detail abounds here and reinforces the real settings of France and Virginia at every turn. The naming of the characters, for example, carries certain properties of suggestion. Marston was named after Henry Clay, the Virginia-born statesman whose life was filled with frustration because of his failure to reach the presidency and whose political career was repeatedly linked with thoughtful and aggressive compromise. The connection between Marston and the American statesman may be inexact, but these two Virginians have in common a sense of the "indomitable and undefeated" and the assurance that "the best of America was the best of the world" (*Bits*, p. 209).

Choupette is another name with suggestive possibilities. *Chou* literally means cabbage, but in a figurative sense means dear or darling. A term of endearment in French is *mon petit chou*. At one point in the story, when Henry regains his bearings following his breakdown, Choupette comforts him in surprisingly unidiomatic English: " 'Sleep, male cabbage' " (*Bits*, p. 190). She is obviously translating the first part of her name into its literal rather than its figurative meaning. Aside from this lapse, Choupette seems to get on very well in her adopted tongue (even if it is occasionally a bit stilted), especially after her three years in Virginia when "she might have passed for an American" (*Bits*, p. 198). This one slip, however, seems to tell us important things about her. Just as she cannot manage the correct term of endearment, so there is nothing especially endearing about her. All of Fitzgerald's descriptions of her accent the negative or at least compromise the positive; thus we view "Choupette, frightened, defiant and, after her fashion, deeply sorry" (*Bits*, p. 190). The name Choupette, then, carries with it a certain irony; while it suggests fondness and affection, her person emphatically does not.[12]

The judge who tempts Marston with a lucrative position in Richmond and fondly urges him on, " 'Come home, boy' " (*Bits*, p. 188) has the surname Waterbury. This name would seem to have consequence in a story which uses water as a central symbol and offers burying the past as a significant theme.

These names may not have quite the suggestive ring as, say, Honoria in "Babylon Revisited" (1931) or Carrol Key in "May Day" (1920). Yet they do add to the symbolic design of the story. "The Swimmers," which leaps so elliptically across time and space, needs these *points de repère* to anchor the events and the characters. Or to put it another way, this crowded twenty-three-page story turns about five or six scenes—which occur on two continents marked by a considerable passage of time—and hence requires these *ficelles* (Henry James's word) to tighten the seams and the joints of the narrative.

Another structuring device is the series of hymnal passages which punctuate the story. These are rather artfully spaced and thrive on a rhetoric which has usually been associated with the American South. Just after Marston arrives at St. Jean de Luz, we have this bloated sentence: "That mighty word printed across a continent was less to him than the memory of his grandfather, who freed his slaves in '58, fought from Manassas to Appomattox, knew Huxley and Spencer as light reading, and believed in caste only when it expressed the best of race" (*Bits*, p. 191). Several pages later, just after a crucial conversation between Marston and the unnamed girl, we are told of "his ever-new, ever-changing country" (*Bits*, p. 195). An interesting contrast between England and America, written in the same epigrammatic way, is offered during the beach scene in Virginia: "In England property begot a strong place sense, but Americans, restless and with shallow roots, needed fins and wings. There was even a recurrent idea in America about an education that would leave out history and the past, that should be a sort of equipment for aerial adventure, weighed down by none of the stowaways of inheritance or tradition" (*Bits*, p. 201).

These passages seem to offer a stylistic foreshadowing of the final section of the story which intones a kind of hymn to America (rather like the ending of Styron's *Set This House on Fire*): ". . . he had a sense of overwhelming gratitude and of gladness that America was there,

---

12. *Choupette* is actually a French word which means either a tuft of baby hair tied in a bow or a special bow used for a baby's hair. This seems to have no particular relevance to the character of Choupette in "The Swimmers."

that under the ugly débris of industry the rich land still pushed up, incorrigibly lavish and fertile, and that in the heart of the leaderless people the old generosities and devotions fought on, breaking out sometimes in fanaticism and excess . . ." (*Bits*, p. 209). After a paragraph of this kind of writing, there is a final brief exchange between Marston and the girl and then a final paragraph which features this sentence, "France was a land, England was a people, but America, having about it still that quality of the idea, was harder to utter—it was the graves at Shiloh and the tired, drawn, nervous faces of its great men, and the country boys dying in the Argonne for a phrase that was empty before their bodies withered" (*Bits*, p. 210).

Matthew Bruccoli, in his Preface to *Bits of Paradise* (p. 10), describes this section as being an "eloquent coda." It is certainly consistent in every way with those earlier passages which extolled the virtues of America, usually at a comfortable remove from its shores. Marston is one of those "Americans who go abroad only to rediscover themselves."[13] He lives out a legend like the narrators of Berger's *The Garden* and Styron's *Set This House on Fire*. His life, like theirs, is balanced precariously between Europe and America. The heightened diction of these set pieces which thread their way through the narrative of "The Swimmers" mirrors the grandeur of these conceptions.

The symbols and the hymnal passages, then, reinforce the sense of Marston as dreamer and unconscious mythmaker. The unnamed girl—who reminds one of another unnamed girl appearing at the end of the fourth chapter of *A Portrait of the Artist as a Young Man*—has a curative effect. Her own restlessness and uprootedness, as she moves from one beach resort to another, offer Marston a paradigm for his behavior. His freedom, gained at a fairly high cost, permits him to traverse the Atlantic with a clear conscience. Robert Sklar puts the matter accurately, although in somewhat different terms, when he says: "By solving the crisis in his life Henry does not simply restore his old order, he builds a new one" (p. 256). Swimming has won out over the sedentary activity of moneymaking.[14] The pride of being a Virginian has given way to a mobility and flexibility which allow for a more intriguing transatlantic perspective.

The story clearly has its defects. Kenneth Eble and John A. Higgins point to the contrivances and coincidences. Higgins bemoans the fact

13. Levin, p. 88.

14. Money is obviously a central concern of this story, as virtually every critic has pointed out. Marston is a true Fitzgerald character when he makes the following high-sounding pronouncement just before returning to America: " 'American men are incomplete without money' " (*Bits*, p. 196). Although he is forcibly reminded of the "power" of money in a later part of the story, he comes finally to reject this position.

that "significant themes" and "good symbolism" are wasted on faulty technique. One can even say that perhaps form and content seem often at odds with each other. But "The Swimmers" dares where many other Fitzgerald stories fear to tread. Bruccoli tells us that "Fitzgerald described it as 'the hardest story I ever wrote, too big for its space + not even now satisfactory' " (*Bits*, p. 10). Its bold conception and intricate symbolic pattern were obviously too large for its slender twenty-three-page frame, but "The Swimmers" survives handsomely as a contribution to a Franco-American dialogue initiated by Poe and carried on by Green, Berger, and Styron.

19. RICH BOYS AND RICH MEN: "THE BRIDAL PARTY"

JAMES J. MARTINE

> If he needs a million acres to make him feel rich, seems to
> me he needs it 'cause he feels awful poor inside hisself,
> and if he's poor in hisself, there ain't no million acres
> gonna make him feel rich. . . .
>
> —John Steinbeck, *The Grapes of Wrath*

The debate about how different the very rich are was to be ignited in a 1926 Fitzgerald story and explode almost exactly a decade later in a famous reference in Hemingway's "The Snows of Kilimanjaro." This was followed by a celebrated letter from Fitzgerald to his friend Hemingway and then by Max Perkins's letter to Fitzgerald (September 23, 1936), which placed Fitzgerald "many miles away" when that "reference was made to the rich and the retort given." Arthur Mizener's interesting 1946 note that as a joke Hemingway's reply is clever, but as a reply to a serious observation, it is "remarkably stupid"[1] may lead eventually to a fresh consideration of a little commented-upon Fitzgerald short story, "The Bridal Party" (1930).

But to see what Fitzgerald has effected there, we would do well to examine that story in context with two others, "May Day" (1920) and "Magnetism" (1928). All three stories contain blackmail attempts, and the way in which these attempts are handled suggests something about how the rich may be, indeed, different from you and me, and the way Fitzgerald's vision matured in the dazzle of that decade which separated the earlier story from the later. This essay does not pretend that "The Bridal Party" is a better story than the earlier "May Day." It is

---

1. See Maxwell Perkins's letter to Fitzgerald in *Dear Scott/Dear Max: The Fitzgerald-Perkins Correspondence*, ed. John Kuehl and Jackson R. Bryer (New York: Charles Scribner's, 1971), p. 232; letter from Fitzgerald to Hemingway in *The Letters of F. Scott Fitzgerald*, ed. Andrew Turnbull (New York: Charles Scribner's, 1963), p. 311; and Arthur Mizener, "Scott Fitzgerald and the Imaginative Possession of American Life," *Sewanee Review*, 54 (January-March 1946), 86n.

not. Yet the author's understanding of the rich, the human situation, and the processes of male maturity—at least as reflected in these two stories—changed and perhaps deepened between their writing.

First of all, it must be allowed that "May Day" is not, after all, simply a story about Gordon Sterrett but is a significant attempt to capture within the scope of an exact twenty-four hours—from 9 a.m., May 1, 1919, to 9 a.m., May 2—the ambience of New York City immediately after the war and the opening of the Jazz Age. Also, as some critics have pointed out, the story is an exaggerated expression of personal and artistic concerns plaguing Fitzgerald at the time.[2] In addition, the author uses the city of New York as a microcosm in an effort to portray the mood of the entire nation. Even as the story succeeds on all levels, particular attention to the character of Gordon Sterrett will serve as the focus of our present discussion.

Maxwell Geismar calls Sterrett "the outcast of Gamma Psi."[3] What has to be noted here, however, is not the ways in which Sterrett is cast out but what is in him, or, more properly, what is lacking in him. One critic has noted:

> There is something pathetic about Gordon Sterrett's suicide only because it was accomplished in self-pity and resulted merely from his coming up against forces with which his naive early faith in his own talent could no longer cope.[4]

Another critic points out,

> It has sometimes been argued, for example, that Gordon Sterrett is the victim of society and of poverty. But there is no evidence in the story that Gordon Sterrett is the victim of anything more than natural weakness; and his poverty is not a cause of his degeneration, but its result.[5]

2. See, for example, Kenneth Eble, *F. Scott Fitzgerald* (New York: Twayne, 1977), p. 53; Charles E. Shain, *F. Scott Fitzgerald* (Minneapolis: Univ. of Minnesota Press, 1961), pp. 27–28; Arthur Mizener, *The Far Side of Paradise: A Biography of F. Scott Fitzgerald* (Boston: Houghton Mifflin, 1965), p. 88; Andrew Turnbull, *Scott Fitzgerald* (New York: Charles Scribner's, 1962), p. 95; K. G. W. Cross, *F. Scott Fitzgerald* (New York: Grove, 1964), pp. 43–45.

3. Maxwell Geismar, "F. Scott Fitzgerald: Orestes at the Ritz," in *The Last of The Provincials: The American Novel, 1915–1925* (New York: Hill and Wang, 1943), p. 318.

4. Ray B. West, Jr., *The Short Story in America, 1900–1950* (Chicago: Henry Regnery, 1952), p. 67.

5. Robert Sklar, *F. Scott Fitzgerald: The Last Laocoön* (New York: Oxford Univ. Press, 1967), p. 77.

This second view is closer to the truth and suggests possibilities for further development. Sterrett could, for example, be profitably compared with George Hannaford in Fitzgerald's "Magnetism" and both Michael Curly and Hamilton Rutherford of "The Bridal Party." Taking all three stories together, we become aware of what Fitzgerald is indicating about people and qualities he admires other than those contingent upon wealth. If Fitzgerald's work and temperament reveal "the strain of the outsider," as Geismar suggests,[6] it is not merely the possession of money or the lack of it that marks those people whom the mature Fitzgerald finds attractive. There is also a quality, a confidence that characterizes admirable men, at least to the Fitzgerald who wrote short stories. The very rich, then, are different, and it is not the fact of having more money that makes them so. Consider Hamilton Rutherford, George Hannaford, and Gordon Sterrett and the way each handles attempts at blackmail.

Sterrett succumbs to the overrouged Jewel Hudson's blackmail, wakes from a drunken stupor to find himself "irrevocably" married to her, and fires a cartridge into his head just behind the temple. Had Philip Dean given him the money, it would have made little difference; Dean, after all, gives him almost a third of what Sterrett requested. It is not merely his lack of money that causes Sterrett to be cast out and to kill himself. It is a lack of internal qualities of which he is guilty—caused perhaps by assumptions bred into the rich or qualities that aid in the acquisition of wealth. Also and perhaps most important, Sterrett's vision, like that of many early Fitzgerald heroes, is terribly romantic. His dreams and expectations of and his relationship with Edith Bradin make that very clear.

George Hannaford in "Magnetism," on the other hand, who does not fully understand the attraction he holds for women, accepts his magnetism and strives to place things in the perspective of reality in the unreal world of Hollywood. Thus when Margaret Donovan, a friend of many years, attempts to blackmail him, he confronts her gently but directly, defuses the attempted blackmail, and *she* is the one who attempts suicide. As her romanticism leads her to an ambulance and the hospital, his ability to deal forthrightly with the romantic enables him to escape tragic (or at least pathetic) consequences and leads to an effective reconciliation with his wife. Although he is characterized as a "romantic man," there is enough of the straightforward, confident, realistic man to handle successfully his wife's sentimental notions about Arthur Busch, Margaret's blackmail attempt, the blatant over-

6. Geismar, p. 318.

tures by Dolores the domestic, and insure a relatively happy ending. The requirements of the *Saturday Evening Post* aside, this conclusion suggests that Hannaford's sense of himself is a thing apart from what women think of him.

The best examples of the pragmatic man and the romantic one are, however, Hamilton Rutherford and Michael Curly in "The Bridal Party." Curly is the romantic who believes that it is money that makes the very rich different and a man successful. Curly, like so many heroes in Fitzgerald, loved a young girl and then lost her—lost her, he believes, because he had no money. His loving and losing Caroline Dandy leaves him with the fear that he will never be happy. Like a more famous example from the Fitzgerald canon, he feels he needs this woman to complete his conception of himself. Rutherford, on the other hand, who has begun in 1920 with $125,000 of borrowed money, knows better. He is no romantic, and the attempt by Marjorie Collins to blackmail him is handled in a cool rational manner, almost coldly, and finally most effectively. His summoning of the Sûreté Générale man is the act of a calm, deliberate, practical man. Following this, it is learned Rutherford has lost all his money in the crash, and Curly has magically become rich by a *deus ex grandfather* inheritance. But Caroline Dandy does not change husbands, or fiancés, in mid-engagement. Money or good looks are not what makes the desirable man; Rutherford is "not handsome like Michael, but vitally attractive, confident, authoritative . . . " (*Stories*, p. 272). Rutherford has tried to prepare and instruct poor Curly, whose "profound woundedness" and excess romanticism are more of a disqualification, and more readily visible, than his shabby clothes. Though Rutherford is not as handsome or—suddenly—as rich as Curly, he remains vitally attractive because of his very confidence and authoritative bearing which are evident throughout the story. He warns and finally teaches Curly that his affair with Caroline was based on sorrow, an adolescent and romantic sorrow for one another, while his own relationship with her is based on hope and something more secure than a fairy's wing. Rutherford is very pleasant, but he tells Curly:

> "And since you've brought it up, let me say that if you and Caroline had married, it wouldn't have lasted three years. Do you know what your affair was founded on? On sorrow. You got sorry for each other. Sorrow's a lot of fun for most women and for some men, but it seems to me that a marriage ought to be based on hope." (*Stories*, p. 278)

Following the double reversal in fortunes, Curly romantically persists in believing that now Caroline Dandy will certainly belong to him. After learning that his grandfather's death has brought him a legacy of a quarter of a million dollars, Curly whispers:

> "Well, I won't give up till the last moment. . . . I've had all the bad luck so far, and maybe it's turned at last. One takes what one can get, up to the limit of one's strength, and if I can't have her, at least she'll go into this marriage with some of me in her heart." (*Stories*, p. 274)

But the pragmatic and realistic Rutherford is never in doubt. He knows—and so does Caroline; she, of course, will remain with him. The text at the moment of choice reveals the attitude of both men and suggests the reason Caroline chooses to remain with Rutherford: "Two pairs of eyes were regarding her—Rutherford's noncommittal and unrequiring, Michael's hungry, tragic, pleading" (*Stories*, p. 282).

In the story's final section, at the wedding, the reader learns that Rutherford has been offered a good job and will regain his social position, and presumably begin the process of the restoration of his wealth. Evaluating both the elaborate quality of the wedding and the character of Rutherford, George Packman tells Curly enthusiastically:

> "It's amazing, . . . This show will cost Ham about five thousand dollars, and I understand they'll be just about his last. But did he countermand a bottle of champagne or a flower? Not he! He happens to have it—that young man. Do you know that T. G. Vance offered him a salary of fifty thousand dollars a year ten minutes before the wedding this morning? In another year he'll be back with the millionaires." (*Stories*, p. 285)

While Curly's inheritance is a stroke of romantic good fortune that stretches credibility for a reader, the sense of the final reversal for Rutherford causes no such pause. It is credible, for it is the result of that set of internal qualities that clearly indicate Rutherford will certainly achieve success—" 'He happens to have it—that young man.' " But these qualities are not of the romantic, Horatio Alger variety. Rutherford is no dreamer—of wealth or of women. He accepts what he is, what he has, and what he can rightfully expect. He is calm, cool, and, yes, rich—and the fact of his having or not having money seems almost accidental to his wealth.

This strain of the realistic and pragmatic man ending happily and the romantic always left yearning is also contained, aside from Fitzgerald's most famous examples, in stories such as "The Love Boat" (1927), "Two for a Cent" (1922), "John Jackson's Arcady" (1924), "Diagnosis" (1932), and even "Flight and Pursuit" (1932), most often relating the yearning for the past to a romantic nature. These stories suggest as well that wealth does not guarantee happiness if the longing characteristic of the romantic is tied to it.

Finally, however, dating the three stories considered here will give some clue to potential sources for the change in their characters and Fitzgerald's attitude toward them. The romantic Sterrett appears in "May Day," published in the *Smart Set* in July of 1920. Gordon Sterrett is "about twenty-four"; Fitzgerald would be twenty-four in September of that year. "Magnetism" appeared in the *Saturday Evening Post*, March 3, 1928. Its hero, George Hannaford "was thirty"; Fitzgerald at the time was thirty-one. "Magnetism" is a part of a second group of stories, post-*Gatsby* and pre-Depression, and illustrates Fitzgerald's famous double vision. Hannaford is both a romantic and realistic hero; his handling of Margaret Donovan's blackmail attempt and his wife's brief romance reflect that.

"The Bridal Party," published in the *Saturday Evening Post*, August 9, 1930, and suggested by Powell Fowler's famous wedding, demonstrates the atmosphere of pre-October, 1929, the *milieu* of the crash, and also indicates that Fitzgerald was up to more than merely keeping the pot boiling. In this story two heroes appear, the romantic hero and a hero of another sort. Just as Hemingway had by that time published stories and a novel with both the romantic hero and what is now called his "code hero," Fitzgerald here lets us compare the romantic Curly with the contrasting Rutherford. It might be too much, of course, to suggest that Fitzgerald was directly influenced by the master tough guy's vision of manhood or that, lacking grace under pressure—this time financial—borrowed that vision. But certainly Rutherford identifies his manhood as a thing apart from women—"noncommittal and unrequiring." The fact that Caroline tells Rutherford that at one time she cared "an awful lot" for Curly does not worry him. In fact, in his way he tries to assist Curly when he tells him:

> "Sensitive? Women aren't so darn sensitive. It's fellows like you who are sensitive; it's fellows like you they exploit—all your devotion and kindness and all that. . . ." (*Stories*, p. 277)

And again:

"This all sounds pretty crude to you, Mr. Curly, but it seems to me that the average man nowadays just asks to be made a monkey of by some woman who doesn't even get any fun out of reducing him to that level. . . ." (*Stories*, p. 278)

Just as Robert Cohn and Pedro Romero illustrate Hemingway's conception and treatment of two kinds of heroes in the novel upon which Fitzgerald exercised some now-renowned editorial influence, the two men here suggest something of the same sort.[7] Clearly, Rutherford has a confidence apart from his wealth or lack of it, and, like Romero's, his manhood is a thing independent of women. The former's handling of the affair with Marjorie Collins and his relationship with Caroline illustrate this. He is a man, with or without women. Curly, treated much differently by Fitzgerald than Cohn is by Hemingway, is a romantic who needs Caroline to complete his image of himself as a man.

In conclusion, however, Fitzgerald may not have needed the lesson of the romantic hero and the code hero from Hemingway, nor did he really need *The Sun Also Rises* to influence him. His own life—from the 1920 of "May Day" and Gordon Sterrett to 1930 and Hamilton Rutherford in "The Bridal Party"—might have taught him that a man must be prepared in some ways to be ready to accept a life without *the* woman. For eventually, "The Bridal Party" must be seen as an initiation story, the initiation of Michael Curly. He has grown not just rich but, by the story's conclusion, toward an awareness; suddenly it seems that the loss of the romantic notion is a condition necessary for the Fitzgerald male to grow. It is as though this tyro Michael Curly has learned something from the tutor Hamilton Rutherford. His initiation leads him beyond the trap of an overly romantic nature, which is made clear in the opening of the story's final paragraph:

Michael was cured. The ceremonial function, with its pomp and its revelry, had stood for a sort of initiation into a life where even his regret could not follow them. . . . he walked forward to bid Hamilton and Caroline Rutherford good-by. (*Stories*, p. 286)

Curly no longer needs the tutor or the girl of his dreams. The party in "The Bridal Party" begins as a celebration of the wedding of Caroline

7. The concept of the various heroes in Hemingway's novel appears in Mark Spilka, "The Death of Love in *The Sun Also Rises*," in *Twelve Original Essays on Great American Novels*, ed. Charles Shapiro (Detroit: Wayne State Univ. Press, 1958), pp. 238–56.

and Rutherford and ends as a metaphorical *bar mitzvah* for Michael Curly. He is cured, but was his creator? Completely? Babylon was yet to be revisited. Six months after the appearance of "The Bridal Party," the same *Saturday Evening Post* would publish the results of that journey back, and it would begin: " 'And where's Mr. Campbell?' Charlie asked."

The rich may or may not be different. Like all generalizations, that one needs refinement. For they are different, as different from one another as they are from you and me. After all, then, it is not a matter of money that makes us rich, as Steinbeck's Jim Casy observes in his astute analysis of the very rich which serves as the epigraph for this essay. Romantic rich boys are rich, but they are boys. Men are men, rich or poor. Manhood is a function of the process of maturing. Stories such as "The Bridal Party" suggest this; had their creator been able to accept it, perhaps his suffering might have been lessened. But it is part of the human dilemma that we often *know* things and continue to act as though we do not know them. Fitzgerald's humanity, poor Scott and rich, made him like the rest of us—often knowing something yet unwilling or unable to act upon what we know.

WHEN THE STORY ENDS:
"BABYLON REVISITED"

CARLOS BAKER

> A kind of change came in my fate,
> My keepers grew compassionate,
> I know not what had made them so.
> They were inured to sights of woe.
> And so it was:—my broken chain
> With links unfastened did remain
> And it was liberty to stride
> Along my cell from side to side.
>
> **—Byron, "The Prisoner of Chillon"**

Fitzgerald once called "Babylon Revisited" a magnificent short story (*Letters*, p. 64). The adjective still holds. It is probably his best. Written in December, 1930, it was first published February 21, 1931, in the *Saturday Evening Post,* whose editors must have recognized its superior qualities, well above the norm of the stories from his pen that this magazine had been publishing for the past ten years. Collected in *Taps at Reveille* in 1935, it stood proudly at the end of the volume, a memorable example of well-made short fiction.

The epigraph from Byron bears upon the story for many reasons, not least because "The Prisoner of Chillon" was the first poem that Fitzgerald ever heard, his father having read it aloud to him in his childhood, a circumstance that he recalled in a letter to his mother in June, 1930, when he paid a tourist visit to "Chillon's dungeons deep and old" while staying at Ouchy-Lausanne in order to be near Zelda, who was desperately ill in a nearby sanatorium (*Letters*, p. 495). The story he wrote six months afterwards might have been called "Chillon Revisited," involving as it does the double theme of freedom and imprisonment, of locking out and locking in. For although Charlie Wales seems to himself to have redeemed his right to parenthood and to have regained his proper freedom, the links of his fetters are still visible when the story ends. And we, the keepers, inured as we are to sights of woe both inside and outside Fitzgerald's life and works, cannot help feeling compassion for this fictive prisoner, who tries so hard to measure up, only to be defeated by a past that he can never shed.

From the triple nadir of the Wall Street crash, months of recupera-
tion from alcoholism in a sanatorium, and the death of his wife,
Charlie Wales has now rehabilitated himself as a successful man of
business in Prague, Czechoslovakia, and has returned to Paris in the
hope of taking custody of his nine-year-old daughter Honoria, who has
been living in the care of her aunt and uncle since her mother's death.
He feels ready for the responsibility, since he has made another kind of
comeback, having staved off drunkenness for a year and a half by the
simple expedient of rationing himself to one whisky a day. All those sins
of commission which led to the débâcle are now, he is sure, behind
him. He recognizes that while he was flinging away thousand-franc
notes like handfuls of confetti, even the most wildly squandered sum
was being given "as an offering to destiny that he might not remember
the things most worth remembering, the things that now he would
always remember" (*Stories*, p. 389): Honoria taken from him and
Helen buried in Vermont.

Two motifs stand opposed in the story. One is that of Babylon,
ancient center of luxury and wickedness in the writings of the Fathers
of the Church. The other is that of the quiet and decent homelife that
Wales wishes to establish for his child. He defines the Babylon motif as
a "catering to vice and waste" (*Stories*, p. 389). It is what used to
happen every afternoon in the Ritz bar when expatriated Americans
like himself systematically hoisted glasses on the way to the ruin, moral
or physical or both, that besets so many of them now. More spectacu-
larly, it is places of decadent entertainment like the Casino where the
naked Negro dancer Josephine Baker performs "her chocolate ara-
besques" (*Stories*, p. 388). It is squalidly visible along the streets of
Montmartre, the Rue Pigalle and the Place Blanche, where nightclubs
like "the two great mouths of the Café of Heaven and the Café of Hell"
(*Stories*, p. 389) used to wait, as they still do, to devour busloads of
tourists, innocent foreigners eager for a glimpse of Parisian fleshpots.

Fittingly enough, it is in the Ritz bar that the story opens—and
closes. The place is nothing like it used to be. A stillness, "strange and
portentous," inhabits the handsome room. No longer can it be thought
of as an American bar: it has "gone back into France" (*Stories*, p. 385).
All the former habitués are absent—Campbell ailing in Switzerland;
Hardt back at work in the United States; and Fessenden, who tried to
pass a bad check to the management, wrecked at last by shame and
obesity. Only Duncan Schaeffer is still around Paris. Swallowing his
loneliness, Charlie Wales hands the assistant bartender a note for
Schaeffer including the address of his brother-in-law in the Rue Palatine. It is his first mistake. A key clicks in the prison door. Although he

does not know it yet, Schaeffer will twice seek Charlie out, only to lock him into loneliness again.

At the outset Fitzgerald alternates interior and exterior scenes, with the obvious intent of providing the Babylonian background against which the principal dramatic scenes are to occur. While Charlie is on his way to the Peters's apartment in the Rue Palatine, he is most impressed by the nocturnal beauty rather than the wickedness of Paris. Bistros gleam like jewels along the boulevards, and the "fire-red, gas-blue, ghost-green signs" blur their way "smokily through the tranquil rain" (*Stories*, p. 386). By contrast, the livingroom at his brother-in-law's place is "warm and comfortably American" (*Stories*, p. 387), with a fire on the hearth and a pleasant domestic bustle in the kitchen. Although Honoria is well, and happy enough with her small cousins, she is plainly overjoyed to see her father again. At dinner he watches her closely, wondering whom she most resembles, himself or her mother. It will be fortunate, he thinks, "if she didn't combine the traits of both that had brought them to disaster" (*Stories*, p. 388).

Marion Peters has no doubt as to whose traits must be guarded against. Between Charlie and his sister-in-law an "instinctive antipathy" (*Stories*, p. 387) prevails. In her eyes he can do nothing right. When he says how strange it seems that so few Americans are in Paris, she answers that she's delighted: " 'Now at least you can go into a store without their assuming you're a millionaire.' " But Charlie replies that it was nice while it lasted. " 'We were a sort of royalty, almost infallible, with a sort of magic around us. In the bar this afternoon,' "—and here he stumbles, seeing his mistake—" 'there wasn't a man I knew.' " Marion looks at him keenly: " 'I should think you'd have had enough of bars' " (*Stories*, p. 387–88).

In Marion's mind the reference to bars has no double significance; she means only those places where drinking is done. But to the eyes of the reader, aware of Charlie's prisonlike predicament, the word might well carry an ulterior suggestiveness. For he has had enough of bars in both senses, longing instead for the freedom to live a responsible domestic life and "more and more absorbed," as he thinks next day, "by the desire of putting a little of himself into [Honoria] before she [has] crystallized utterly" (*Stories*, p. 391) into maturity.

The bars of his incipient prison move closer on the following afternoon when he takes Honoria to lunch and afterwards to a vaudeville matinée at the Empire. That morning he has awakened to a bright fall day that reminds him, as it so often reminded Fitzgerald, of football games. Charlie is naturally optimistic, sanguine by temperament, at least in the mornings. The gloom closes in when two ghosts from his past—Duncan Schaeffer and Lorraine Quarrles—intrude on the father-daughter colloquy, first at the restaurant and then at the theater. He puts them off as well as he can: they are the counterforce to all he now longs for. Going home in the taxi, Honoria says firmly that she wants to live with him. His heart leaps up. When he has delivered her to the apartment, he waits outside for her to show herself at the window. She appears, warm and glowing like an image of domesticity, and throws him a kiss in the dark street where he stands.

On his return that evening, Marion meets him with "hard eyes" (*Stories*, p. 393). She is wearing a black dinner dress that faintly suggests mourning, possibly for her dead sister. Although he understands that he will "have to take a beating," Charlie supposes that if he assumes "the chastened attitude of the reformed sinner" (*Stories*, p. 393), he may be able to carry the day and win the right to his daughter, despite Marion's legal guardianship. But she remains obdurate. Never in her life, she tells him, can she forget that early morning when Helen knocked at her door, " 'soaked to the skin and shivering' " (*Stories*, p. 394), with the news that Charlie, in drunken and jealous anger, had locked her out in the snow, where she had been wandering in slippers, "too confused to find a taxi" (*Stories*, p. 396).

Once again the imagery of keys and locks and doors rises into view. Seeing that Marion has "built up all her fear of life into one wall and faced it toward him" (*Stories*, p. 395), Charlie can only swallow his protestations. When he points out in a dull voice that Helen, after all, " 'died of heart trouble,' " she picks up and echoes the phrase as if—unlike her earlier reference to "bars"—this one of " 'heart trouble' " has "another meaning for her." But she has reached the end of her tether. " 'Do what you like!' " she cries, springing from her chair. " '. . . You two decide it. I can't stand this. I'm sick. I'm going to bed' " (*Stories*, p. 396).

Next day when Charlie lunches with Lincoln Peters, he finds it difficult "to keep down his exultation" (*Stories*, p. 397). The two men agree to a final conference that evening to settle all details. But Charlie's past cannot be shed so easily. Back at his hotel he finds a *pneu* from Lorraine Quarrles, reminding him of their drunken exploit in stealing a butcher's tricycle and pedalling round the Étoile until dawn. " 'For old time's sake,' " she urges him to meet her at the Ritz that afternoon at five (*Stories*, p. 398).

Lorraine as temptress has lost her charm for Charlie. At five he leaves instead for the Rue Palatine for what will amount to the obligatory scene of the story. Honoria, who has been told that she is to go with her father, can scarcely contain her delight. Even Marion seems at last to have "accepted the inevitable" (*Stories*, p. 398). Charlie nods to Peters's offer of a drink: " 'I'll take my daily whisky.' " The wall that Marion erected against him has fallen now. The apartment is warm— "a home, people together by a fire" (*Stories*, p. 399), the ideal of domesticity that Charlie would like to establish on his own for his child.

At this point comes the long peal at the doorbell and the sudden intrusion of Duncan Schaeffer and Lorraine, drunken, word-slurring, "hilarious . . . roaring with laughter" (*Stories*, p. 399). When Charlie introduces his old friends, Marion freezes, drawing back toward the hearth, her arm thrown defensively around her daughter's shoulders. After he has gotten rid of the intruders, Charlie notices that she has not moved from the fire. Both of her children are now standing in the maternal shelter of her arms. Peters is still playfully "swinging Honoria back and forth like a pendulum from side to side" (*Stories*, p. 400)—a gesture to which Fitzgerald plainly attaches symbolic significance and one that even echoes, though doubtless by chance, the very words of the prisoner of Chillon. Once more, in a telling repetition of first effect, Marion rushes from the room. She is in bad shape, as Peters returns to say. Dinner is out of the question and Charlie must go.

> Charlie got up. He took his coat and hat and started down the corridor. Then he opened the door of the dining-room and said in a strange voice, "Good night, children."
> Honoria rose and ran around the table to hug him.
> "Good night, sweetheart," he said vaguely, and then trying to make his voice more tender, trying to conciliate something, "Good night, dear children." (*Stories*, p. 401)

The story returns to its opening locale. In the grip of his anger, Charlie hopes to find Lorraine and Duncan at the Ritz bar. But they have done their sorry work and vanished from his life. He orders a whisky and chats idly with the bartender about times past. Once more the memory of those days sweeps over him like a nightmare—the incoherent babbling, the sexual advances, "the women and girls carried screaming with drink or drugs out of public places," or the men like himself "who locked their wives out in the snow" on the theory that "the snow of twenty-nine wasn't real snow. If you didn't want it to be snow, you just paid some money" (*Stories*, p. 402).

Another lock-out is imminent, which will also amount to a locking-in. When Charlie telephones, Lincoln Peters is compassionate but firm:

" 'Marion's sick. . . . I know this thing isn't altogether your fault, but I can't have her go to pieces about it. I'm afraid we'll have to let it slide for six months.' " Charlie returns to his table. Although he tells himself that "they couldn't make him pay forever," he knows he must serve a further sentence in the prison of his days. But he is "absolutely sure that Helen wouldn't have wanted him to be so alone" (*Stories*, p. 402).

In the spring of 1940 Fitzgerald returned finally to Babylon, at least in memory and imagination, when he began negotiations for a screenplay based upon his nine-year-old story. A producer named Lester Cowan bought the property for "something over $800.00" (*Letters*, p. 287), which Fitzgerald rightly thought to be very little as Hollywood prices were going at the time. But he accepted the pittance out of sheer desperation, having to support an ailing wife and an undergraduate daughter. His hopes rose a month later when Cowan proposed that he undertake the screenplay himself. This meant that Columbia Pictures would pay him for eight weeks' work at a salary equivalent to $287.50 per week. Disgusted though he was by the penuriousness of this advance, he could still anticipate a considerably larger sum if the producer and the company should decide to carry the film to completion (*Letters*, pp. 68, 288).

He began the task on April 12. The work went well and his spirits were generally high. "I've written a really brilliant continuity" (*Letters*, p. 116), he told Zelda on May 11, and on June 7 he declared the job finished (*Letters*, p. 77). About mid-June he seems to have been assured that while the picture would definitely be made, it would have to be postponed until the completion of another in which Laurence Olivier was to appear (*Letters*, p. 80). Meantime there was the possibility that Shirley Temple, the child star, might be induced through her mother to play the role of Charlie Wales's daughter. On July 11, in pursuit of one more hope, Fitzgerald spent the day with Shirley and her mother. "She really is a sweet little girl," he told his daughter Scottie, "and reminds me of you at 11½" (*Letters*, p. 84). Thereafter, although he continued to tinker with the final draft of the script and to dream that Miss Temple might take part in it, the film was never made (*Letters*, pp. 601–2, 86). *Cosmopolitan*, which was the third of his working titles, seems to have been the last of his screenplays.[1] Before the end of that parlous year, Fitzgerald was dead.

1. Further allusions to Fitzgerald's work on the three versions of his script appear in the *Correspondence of F. Scott Fitzgerald*, ed. Matthew J. Bruccoli and Margaret M. Duggan (New York: Random House, 1980), pp. 587, 589, 593, 599–600, 602, 604, 608. The most extensive study of the scripts, which were named *Honoria, Babylon Revisited*, and *Cosmopolitan*, is that of Lawrence D. Stewart, *Fitzgerald/Hemingway Annual*, 5

Apart from the pleasure it gave him, the metamorphosis of "Babylon Revisited" from story to filmscript opened vistas into his past that enabled him to comprehend, with characteristic honesty but also with a sinking heart, the shape his career had taken over the past twenty-five years. The little girl whom Gerald Murphy had nicknamed Scottina on the Riviera in 1925 was now a young woman in her nineteenth year, already showing signs of a developing literary talent and devoting some of her energies at Vassar to the writing of a musical comedy. Her father was fearful: "You are doing exactly what I did at Princeton," he told her.

> I wore myself out on a musical comedy there for which I wrote book and lyrics, organized and mostly directed while the president played football. Result: I slipped back in my work, got T.B., lost a year in college—and, irony of ironies, because of the scholastic slip I wasn't allowed to take the presidency of the Triangle. From your letter I guess that you are doing exactly the same thing and it just makes my stomach fall out to think of it. . . . *Please, please, please* . . . keep your scholastic head above water. To see a mistake repeated twice in two generations would be just too much to bear. This is the most completely experienced advice I've ever given you. (*Letters*, pp. 69–70)

Two months later he returned to the topic. "I don't doubt your sincerity about work. I think now you will always be a worker and I'm glad. Your mother's utterly endless mulling and brooding over insolubles paved the way to her ruin. . . . She was a great original in her way, with perhaps a more intense flame at its highest than I ever had, but she tried and is still trying to solve all ethical and moral problems on her own, without benefit of the thousands dead" (*Letters*, p. 78). It seemed to him that Scottie's resemblance to himself was greater than hers to Zelda. "Doubt and worry—you are as crippled by them as I am by my inability to handle money or my self-indulgence of the past. . . . What little I've accomplished has been by the most laborious and uphill work, and I wish now I'd *never* relaxed or looked back" (*Letters*, p. 79).

(1971), 81–103. Stewart finds in the various treatments "all the myopia which characterized" Fitzgerald's later work. An earlier study by Robert Gessner concluded that "the slight drama is overburdened by narrative ideas" and that the script reveals "the frenetic state of mind of the exhausted author" (*The Moving Image* [New York: E. P. Dutton, 1968], pp. 240–248).

But he was looking back still, not only to the ruination of his Princeton career but also to the time in the summer of 1924 when he had first met Gerald and Sara Murphy. "There was many a day," he told them in February, 1940, "when the fact that you and Sara did help me in a desperate moment . . . seemed the only pleasant human thing that had happened in a world where I felt prematurely passed by and forgotten. . . . So you were never out of my mind" (*Letters*, p. 428). He went on to say that the child heroine of the film on which he was about to start work was named Honoria and added, almost defiantly, "I'm keeping the name" (*Letters*, p. 429).

He clung to it as if it had been a kind of talisman, a means of reentering a past epoch of pleasant human things. In the same way he was somehow reassured by the image of Scottie as a child—the model, as he told her twice, for the nine-year-old daughter of Charlie Wales in the story (*Letters*, pp. 64, 78). It may even be a legitimate surmise that her affectionate greeting after long separation, "Oh, daddy, daddy, daddy, daddy, dads, dads, dads," was a direct transcript of one by Scottie at some reunion in the late 1920s.

Both the Murphys and their Honoria were much in his mind in those Hollywood days. "I wish very much you would call on the Murphys during your spring vacation," he wrote his daughter. "If there is any way in which you could help Honoria—to a date, for instance—I think it would be mutually very advantageous. . . . I know it is difficult to pick up an old thread after an interval but it would please me immensely if you could at least pay a call there" (*Letters*, pp. 66–67). In June he repeated the suggestion: "Please go in to see Gerald Murphy at Mark Cross in passing thru N.Y. this summer" (*Letters*, p. 79).

Yet this picking up of old threads was precisely what his filmscript was compelling him to do. The warp and woof of two whole decades appeared in the ironic chronology he sent to Zelda that June: "Twenty years ago *This Side of Paradise* was a best seller and we were settled in Westport. Ten years ago Paris was having almost its last great American season but we had to quit the gay parade and you were gone to Switzerland. Five years ago I had my first bad stroke of illness and went to Asheville. Cards began falling badly for us much too early" (*Letters*, p. 119).

These four straightforward sentences, and particularly the second, about the necessity of leaving Paris for the gray prison of Switzerland, show clearly enough that 1930 stood in Fitzgerald's mind as the watershed or turning point of his career and of that of his wife. For it was then that the onset of Zelda's illness started them both on the downgrade from which, despite the most valiant of efforts, neither of them ever wholly recovered. Another of his letters, written the summer before, summarized the crucial change. "I not only announced the birth of my young illusions in *This Side of Paradise* but pretty much the death of them in some of my last *Post* stories like 'Babylon Revisited' " (*Letters*, p. 588).

Although his memory deceived him somewhat, since more than twenty of his stories had appeared in the *Post* after the publication of "Babylon Revisited," this one plainly stood out in his mind as a fictional embodiment of the great shift from false romanticism to a firmer realism in his life as a writer. Arthur Mizener states the situation exactly and eloquently:

> Very gradually, under the pressure of great personal suffering, out of the toughness of his Irish determination not to be beaten, with the help of the New England conscience he had developed in Minnesota, Fitzgerald achieved a kind of acceptance of this state of "lost illusion." It is impossible to say that he ever accepted it as necessary: he seems always to have felt that unnecessary personal failures were really responsible for it. But at least he learned how to live with it. Out of this attitude came the theme of his last stories with their marvelous and subtle balance between an unquestioned acceptance of what he and his world are and an acute awareness of what they might be and, indeed, in some respects at least, once were.[2]

2. Arthur Mizener, *Afternoon of an Author* (New York: Charles Scribner's, 1958), p. 10.

THE SANE METHOD OF
"CRAZY SUNDAY"

SHELDON GREBSTEIN

Precise factual information which aids the reader to place an artist's work securely into a biographical-historical context is always welcome. Such information establishes a sound foundation for critical analysis and enhances our appreciation of the artist's achievements. Fortunately, any student of Fitzgerald's brilliant story "Crazy Sunday" (1932) finds an abundance of data already provided by Arthur Mizener, Dwight Taylor, Andrew Turnbull, Kenneth Eble, Henry Dan Piper, and Aaron Latham, among others.[1] Accordingly, no further evidence is needed to prove that in writing "Crazy Sunday," Fitzgerald chose a phase of recent experience in which he suffered disappointment and disgrace, then deliberately exploited it as the basis for the story's locale, major characters, and precipitating episode. Few examples of Fitzgerald's work better illustrate the intimate yet complex relationship between his life and his art. In this instance, an unsuccessful screenwriting stint in California during the fall of 1931 and a drunken episode at a party given by the Thalbergs were soon after transformed into a work of fiction that still endures, after almost half a century, as perhaps the best American short story about Hollywood.

But if the biographical basis is manifest, what of the art? Here one

1. The fullest account of Fitzgerald's misadventures in Hollywood during the fall of 1931 appears in Dwight Taylor, *Joy Ride* (New York: G. P. Putnam's, 1959), pp. 234–50. In some respects Taylor is the prototype for Joel, perhaps even the inspiration for the incongruous "cow-brown" eyes. Summary accounts, bibliographical information, and additional detail appear in the other works mentioned, all well known to any student of Fitzgerald.

can perhaps offer a contribution, for to this point there has been surprisingly little aesthetic discussion of the story. The treatments that do exist pay insufficient attention to the work's subtle and controlled method.[2] My essay will attempt just that.

As its most obvious theme or subject, "Crazy Sunday" contrasts the physical beauty, charisma, or talent of its major characters—Joel, Stella, Miles—with the element of instability, weakness, or tendency toward self-destruction which seems to coincide, even be necessary, to their beauty and talent. Joel drinks to excess. Miles is exhausted, marked for death. The alluring Stella is emotionally fragile, subject to hysteria. What Joel first says to Stella as a conversational gambit—" 'Everybody's afraid, aren't they?' " (Stories, p. 404)—becomes a portentous cue to this dimension of character.

The story's atmosphere and action are thus intensely psychological, not only in the specifically psychiatric sense conveyed in Miles's talk of his psychoanalysis and personal troubles, but more important in that the narrative emphasizes states of feeling and the impressions people make upon one another from moment to moment. In this, Fitzgerald expresses his vision of one aspect of the Hollywood milieu which differentiates it from the run of common life: there the most private matters—marital infidelity, sexual problems—are discussed as though they were public knowledge. Relationships that would take months, even years, to develop in "real" or "normal" life are accelerated, foreshortened, developed in one or two brief encounters. In this concentration and distillation of experience, Fitzgerald both exercises the economy of the short story form and evokes the method of a film scenario.

2. Other than biographically-based critical approaches, the most intensive aesthetic analyses of "Crazy Sunday" appear in Sergio Perosa, The Art of F. Scott Fitzgerald, trans. Charles Metz and Sergio Perosa (Ann Arbor: Univ. of Michigan Press, 1965), p. 99; John A. Higgins, F. Scott Fitzgerald: A Study of the Stories, (Jamaica, N.Y.: St. John's Univ. Press, 1971), pp. 152–54, and Kenneth G. Johnston, "Fitzgerald's 'Crazy Sunday': Cinderella in Hollywood," Literature and Film Quarterly, 6 (Summer 1978), 214–21. I disagree with Perosa's negative assessment of the story's treatment of character motivation and relationships. Perosa also faults the structure. Higgins's brief but astute reading notes the dependence upon the three Sunday scenes, praises the narrative perspective, cites the function of dialogue, but questions the focus on character. Although my own observations coincide with Higgins's in some major points, I arrived at them independently. Kenneth Johnston's essay is the most extensive discussion of the story to date. He adheres closely to the narrative and offers the stimulating suggestion that "Crazy Sunday" depends upon the Cinderella motif. However, I am fundamentally at variance with Johnston's main thesis, that the story is really about Joel Coles's failure of perception: "Although alcohol is a contributing factor, Joel's inability to distinguish between appearance and reality is primarily the result of having lived and worked too long in a world of make-believe" (Johnston, p. 220).

The story's title alerts us to its psychological focus, although it is also deliberately ambiguous. "Crazy" applies less obviously to the day than to the characters. Sunday is celebrated because it represents a release from the confines of work, but as Fitzgerald suggests throughout the story, work is really the basis of sanity for everyone in the film industry.

Among the reasons we come to believe most in Joel's probity, the truth and reliability of his perspective, is that we actually witness him at work. We may accept that Stella is a movie star and Miles a famous producer; we view the result of their success in their impressive house. Miles's achievement and ability as producer are asserted repeatedly. But unlike Joel, their professional skills are not *demonstrated* to us. Even in the one encounter between Joel and Miles at the studio (on Wednesday, not Sunday), Miles is depicted as confused, jealous, wavering—a creature wholly concerned with his personal afflictions and in the grip of his fluctuating moods, rather than as a keen, tough, decisive film executive. Although Sunday is defined in the story's opening paragraph as a time for relaxation, pleasure—"individual life starting up again"—it functions most tellingly as the time for self-disgrace, self-revelation, breakdown.

Appropriately, the emphasis on the psychological dimension is reinforced by the story's dramatic stucture. This structure basically depends not upon the five formal sections into which Fitzgerald has overtly divided it, although these are important as phases in the action, but upon three crazy Sundays. In turn, each of these Sundays serves as the occasion for the exposure and humiliation of each of the main characters.

Joel, of course, is the first to crash when, pumped up by drink and the silly desire to impress the glittering array at the Calman party, he foolishly performs a skit which inherently mocks the business they all depend on. This performance, "Building It Up," betrays the worst side of him: the hired writer who professes to despise the crass elements of the film industry yet courts its favor. Despite the cruelty of his audience of celebrities, he deserves their rebuff. If he is "not yet broken by Hollywood," he certainly has been infected by it. The one saving element in the occasion is the attraction that arises between Joel and Stella.

But on the next Sunday, as the guest had humiliated himself before the host, the host now takes a tumble before the guest. Joel enters another party, only to find himself immediately embroiled in the chaos of the Calmans' marriage and made confidant to Stella's bitter recounting of her husband's just-exposed adultery. In this scene the reader actually meets Miles for the first time. On the first Sunday he had been a remote, offstage but nevertheless awesome, presence; here he is precipitously lowered, immediately introduced to us as "not a well man": an involuntary philanderer, a helpless public target of his wife's rage, and in general deeply troubled. For Joel the effect of the second Sunday is to banish his awe of Miles and confirm his desire for Stella.

On the third Sunday, Stella falls. While it is still Saturday, she can set up a seduction scene for her own purposes, lead Joel on but still keep control and hold back at the crucial moment. Joel cannot break through her composure or allegiance to her husband. However, when the first minute of Sunday tolls and with it arrives the message of Miles's death, she collapses and pleads for the consummation she had only minutes earlier resisted. And as the story concludes, with Joel's realization that he will indeed return to take advantage of Stella's vulnerability and participate in her emotional attempt to resurrect Miles, there is the promise of yet other crazy Sundays to come.

Inextricably intertwined with the "crazy" motif, and equally important as a thematic and structural element, is the story's emphasis upon the artificiality and theatricality of this microcosm and the conduct of its inhabitants. This motif of frenetic make-believe is rendered both metaphorically and as direct exposition. It begins at once in the simile of the characters as enchanted puppets infused temporarily with life. It is soon reinforced by the description of the producer's home as a vast theater or auditorium: "Miles Calman's house was built for great emotional moments—there was an air of listening, as if the far silences of its vistas bid an audience" (*Stories*, p. 404). With this image the stage is prepared, not only for Joel's catastrophic performance at the Calman party but also for the significant action of the other "Crazy Sunday" scenes I have just summarized. The theatricality of the house is perfectly congruent with the intrinsic melodrama of the characters' behavior. Their extravagance and self-consciousness require a large arena: "Under the high ceilings the situation seemed more dignified and tragic" (*Stories*, p. 410). Even nature seems sensitive to the histrionic conduct of these Hollywood people, for in each of the major scenes the condition of sea or sky collaborates with the Calman house or some other extreme feature of the California setting to supply a fittingly cinematic backdrop for the plot. In the first Sunday scene, "the Pacific, colorless under its sluggish sunset," conveys an ominous mood which presages the nasty reception the unwitting Joel is about to elicit. As background for Stella's irresistible beauty and outpouring of emotion on the second Sunday, nature offers "an eerie bright night with the dark very clear outside" (*Stories*, p. 410), which highlights both the bizarre nature of the Calman marriage, as it is now revealed to Joel, and Joel's sharp realization of his attraction to Stella. Finally, preparatory to the invitation-seduction involving Joel and Stella on the third Sunday, there is Fitzgerald's most openly stated California make-believe metaphor: "the full moon over the boulevard was only a prop, as scenic as the giant boudoir lamps of the corners" (*Stories*, p. 414). The pseudo-romantic moon and the sexy streetlights combine to anticipate the action and, in retrospect, to offer an ironic commentary upon it.

Within this prevailing context of theatricality, each of the main characters appears both genuine and artificial. Stella seems especially at home in the melodramatic mode and glows as the story's most vivid incarnation of the enchanted puppet motif. A creation of Miles Calman—perhaps Miles's most successful production, " 'a sort of masterpiece' " (*Stories*, p. 418)—it is almost impossible to tell what is hers and what his. Despite the depth of the feelings she exhibits as the narrative progresses, including pain, anger, and grief, Joel persists in thinking of her as an actress: "She hovered somewhere between the realest of realities and most blatant of impersonations" (*Stories*, p. 410). In accordance both with the norms of her Hollywood status and to enhance further our sense of the theatrical, Fitzgerald usually presents Stella to us in vibrant color and exquisite clothing or, said otherwise, in the suitable make-up and costume for her role.

As actor in his own life story, Miles Calman creates almost as much fantasy and melodrama in his career and marriage as in the films he produces. Miles's spontaneous public revelations of private matters hint that despite his show of regret and anguish at his tangled emotional condition, he secretly relishes its complications as "good material." The series of telegrams he sends Stella, culminated by a message from others announcing his death, would work splendidly in a film script as a kind of *montage*. Because Fitzgerald is pursuing personality above all, the story presents Miles with a minimum of detail about his appearance. Unlike Stella, Miles is depicted almost wholly in black and white. However, upon our first direct encounter with him there is a brief but striking passage emphasizing Miles's eyes and the incongruous juxtaposition of "curiously shaped head" and "niggerish feet" (*Stories*, p. 408–9). This peculiar description does not, I believe, suggest only a heaven-earth or brain-body dichotomy as intrinsic to the artistic personality, but also transmits Fitzgerald's reliance upon the racial stereotypes of Negro and Jew and their supposedly inborn traits and talents as exhibited in show business. In this he was imitating a technique prevalent in Hollywood films until very recently.

Joel as performer is rendered most indirectly and tacitly of all. His overtly histrionic behavior diminishes as the story proceeds. Even so, in his carefully selected wardrobe for the second Sunday and in the calculation of his moves during the attempted seduction, he remains something of an actor almost to the very end.

I venture one final observation on the theme of theatricality and its relationship to the story's dramatic structure. Although Joel, Stella, and Miles all participate as players in the story's three big scenes, the size and nature of their roles shift significantly. Each, as it were, has the opportunity to lead, yet each in turn takes a subordinate or minor part. In the first scene, Joel plays the lead, Stella a highly visible but nevertheless supporting role, and Miles the smallest part. His presence is important; we know he stands in the background as one of the crowd, but we do not observe him directly or hear him speak. He really serves as audience or witness. In the second scene, however, Miles and Stella are co-featured, with Joel relegated to the role of audience or witness. The final scene casts Joel and Stella together again, this time as co-stars but with Stella's lines and action paramount. As in the first scene, Miles again functions as distant onlooker; indeed, even though he is physically absent, he exists more than ever as a dominant presence in the minds of the others. Note also that the varying interplay of the three characters, staged primarily in the Calman house in each of the three "Crazy Sunday" scenes, occurs at equivalent intervals in the story's formal divisions, Sections I, III, and V, and provides an unobtrusive but pleasing structural symmetry. Moreover, the placement of the Joel-Stella scenes at the beginning and end of the story works as a form of closure. Interspersed with these major scenes and temporarily to relieve their focus on the leading characters, there are a number of quick, sharp glimpses at others: Nat Keogh, a group of bit players at the studio, the passing crowd outside a theater. Such sidelights help to create a fullness of vision, an entire ethos.

Fitzgerald's treatment of character in "Crazy Sunday," provokes some of the same tantalizing questions we ask of *The Great Gatsby.* Although the story seems to be *about* Miles Calman, is he truly its hero or protagonist? I think not. Essential as Miles is to the situation, the significant change happens to Joel. Admittedly, if Joel is too much the opportunist to win our full approval or admiration, nevertheless in comparison to Miles and Stella he does emerge as the story's most credible and thoroughly developed character. Despite his participation in all the crazy Sundays, he overcomes his initial lapse and gains authority as the story progresses. Certainly his emotional status at the end of the story is markedly improved over his condition at the beginning. We recall his unwittingly significant remark: " 'Everybody's afraid, aren't they?' " (*Stories*, p. 404). I agree with Robert Sklar that Joel belongs to that class of Fitzgerald protagonists who illustrate that fate (or history) rather than free will controls man's destiny, yet I would also insist that by the third crazy Sunday he is clearly far saner, more aware, more in command than on the first.[3] Initially an insecure and obsequious outsider, self-consciously flattering his hostess and straining to make conversation, he moves quickly into the deepest lives of Hollywood's great. In contrast, the concluding scene reveals him speaking and behaving with considerable poise and acuity: protecting Stella from the consequences of her hysteria and himself from an impossibly awkward entanglement. Still susceptible to her beauty, he at least has the presence of mind to realize her motives and to choose a more advantageous time—in short, to operate by some of his own terms. After all, what Fitzgerald hero can permanently resist a beautiful woman? In short, Joel is neither lovable nor virtuous, but we do get to know him, understand him and most important, to trust his perceptions to a considerable degree. This evolution in Joel's character from weakness toward strength is clearly evident by a simple comparison of his conduct and speech in Section I with that of Section V. As soon as he learns about Miles's death, his speech becomes terse, direct, functional. It employs the syntax of command: " 'I want the name of your doctor,' he said sternly" (*Stories*, p. 416). Likewise, his actions exhibit the same assurance: "Resolutely Joel went to the phone and called a doctor" (*Stories*, p. 417). Joel's self-control in this final scene is emphasized all the more by Stella's hysteria.

The development of Joel's sanity, as overtly demonstrated by action, exposition, and dialogue, is subtly corroborated throughout by the story's narrative perspective. The choice of narrative viewpoint or voice could, as we know, pose problems for Fitzgerald, but in this case both the selection and execution are wholly felicitous. Almost instantaneously the authorial perspective merges with that of the protagonist, producing a single unified voice and consciousness.

Although the first page conveys the quality or mood of editorial omniscience, with a detached author making statements about who the characters are and what they think, the mode quickly becomes selective omniscience—the limited focus upon the sensibility of a single character. (One key phrase in the story's second sentence cues the

3. Robert Sklar, *F. Scott Fitzgerald: The Last Laocoön* (New York: Oxford Univ. Press, 1967), pp. 256–57.

selective mode and distinguishes it from the editorial: "for all of them."
The "them" really functions as would "us" in an I-narrative.) Indeed,
after Joel is introduced in the story's second paragraph, nothing that
happens from that point is, or would be, beyond his knowledge or
witness—including the analysis of the thoughts and motives of Miles
and Stella. What occurs, then, as intrinsic to the selective-omniscient
mode when properly rendered, is a merging of the writer's voice and
vision with those of his central character. The story is told in the third
person, but it assumes the impact and the immediacy of a first-person
narrative. The third person voice also retains the author's flexibility to
provide appropriate stage directions and to probe into his characters'
psyches. This merger of external and internal perspectives is further
enhanced by the story's increasing emphasis on dramatic scene and
dialogue as it proceeds. Virtually all of Sections IV and V are dialogue,
interrupted only by brief passages of exposition. The natural impact of
dialogue, the "dramatic" effect, even carries over into the exposition so
that it registers as internal monologue. Note this passage as an example:

> Joel thought of Miles, his sad and desperate face in the office two
> days before. In the awful silence of his death all was clear about
> him. He was the only American-born director with both an inter-
> esting temperament and an artistic conscience. Meshed in an
> industry, he had paid with his ruined nerves for having no resili-
> ence, no healthy cynicism, no refuge—only a pitiful and precar-
> ious escape. (*Stories*, p. 416)

With only minimal editorial revision—merely change Joel to "I"—the
passage could easily be transmuted into an I-narrative.

Concomitant with the story's portrayal of film people and its dramatic structure, much of its aesthetic method depends upon the *visual*,
both as the reader's attention is focused upon the characters' eyes and
in the visual exchanges among the characters. With the exception of a
few bright splashes of color—especially the red-gold and ice-blue associated with Stella—the story's most vivid imagery is reserved for eyes.
I count about forty direct references in the story either to eyes or to
actions of sight: seeing, looking, watching, staring, etc. Whatever the
clothing, manners, physical structure, or presence of the characters,
their *eyes* betray the deepest truth about them.

Joel is initially described as "a handsome man with . . . pleasant
cow-brown eyes" (*Stories*, p. 403), but these are soon to be shadowed
by "dark circles of fatigue" (*Stories*, p. 408). This indication of stress

belies the cheerful and dashing clothes Joel has donned for the occasion. Only one small imperfection mars Stella's beauty, "the tired eye-lid that always drooped a little over one eye" (*Stories*, p. 405), but this functions subliminally as the physical blemish which foreshadows her later psychic collapse. Similarly, the reader's first sight of Miles Calman shows him with "the unhappiest eyes Joel ever saw" (*Stories*, p. 408). In the next look at Miles, a few pages later, the extent of his weariness— a premonition of his death—is defined as "life-tired, with his lids sagging" (*Stories*, p. 412). Most vivid of all are the two images used to describe the hostility of Joel's audience at his disastrous parlor game. As he begins, "the Great Lover of the screen glared at him with an eye as keen as the eye of a potato," and as he concludes in failure, "the Great Lover, his eye hard and empty as the eye of a needle, shouted 'Boo! Boo!'" (*Stories*, p. 406-7). Another, more sympathetic, evocation of movie people is conveyed by the depiction of bit-players, "the yellow-stained faces of pretty women, their eyes all melancholy and startling with mascara" (*Stories*, p. 408). Compositely, what Fitzgerald saw in the eyes of these Hollywood folk was indeed depressing.

As one aspect of its style that I find reminiscent of Hemingway in such stories as "Hills Like White Elephants," some passages of "Crazy Sunday" also take such words and phrases as "look," "look out," "see," and "eyes" and build them into unobtrusive little runs of incremental repetition, playing off on the varying usages and shadings of meaning inherent in the colloquial language. The first party scene is one such. It happens again early in the attempted seduction scene, as Joel is initially encouraged to approach Stella by a visual transaction in the theater: "Once he turned and looked at her and she looked back at him, smiling and meeting his eyes for as long as he wanted" (*Stories*, p. 413). As the scene progresses, it continues to utilize the visual dimension with unusual emphasis:

> On into the dark foliage of Beverly Hills that flamed as eucalyptus by day, Joel saw only the flash of a white face under his own, the arc of her shoulder. She pulled away suddenly and looked up at him.
>
> "Your eyes are like your mother's," she said. "I used to have a scrap book full of pictures of her."
>
> "Your eyes are like your own and not a bit like any other eyes," he answered.
>
> Something made Joel look out into the grounds as they went into the house, as if Miles were lurking in the shrubbery. (*Stories*, p. 414)

Clearly, Joel's attraction to Stella depends not on what she is but upon what he sees, a combination of visual appeal and sexual desire, epitomized in this: "Still as he looked at her, the warmth and softness of her body thawing her cold blue costume, he knew she was one of the things he would always regret" (*Stories*, p. 415).

I find another Hemingwayesque touch in the deliberate omission of action which is then cued by the dialogue. The first example is visual, capitalizing on a look in Joel's eyes and a facial expression that Stella sees but we do not:

> There she was, in a dress like ice-water, made in a thousand pale-blue pieces, with icicles trickling at the throat. He started forward.
> "So you like my dress?" (*Stories*, p. 413)

The second delicately omits certain physical details and gestures of the failed seduction:

> "Come sit beside me." Joel urged her.
> It was early. And it was still a few minutes short of midnight a half-hour later, when Joel walked to the cold hearth, and said tersely:
> "Meaning that you haven't any curiosity about me?"
> "Not at all. You attract me a lot and you know it. The point is that I suppose I really do love Miles."
> "Obviously."
> "And tonight I feel uneasy about everything." (*Stories*, p. 415)

Between "early" and "And," thirty minutes' worth of important but undescribed activity and conversation occur yet are not communicated explicitly to the reader. Fitzgerald trusted our imaginations. Reinforcing the dialogue and its conspicuous omission, there is the striking objective correlative "cold hearth," should anyone have missed the point. Apparently there is neither a fire in the fireplace of the Calman mansion at this precise moment during the California Christmas season nor for Joel a sufficiently warm response from his ravishing hostess.

The story's demands upon our sensitivity and capacity for attention characterize Fitzgerald's most serious and accomplished work. However, as an artistic performance, "Crazy Sunday" does not immediately impress us as a spectacular or dazzling work of fiction. Stylistically, even its most eloquent passages fall well short of the bravura effects of *The*

Great Gatsby or *Tender Is the Night*. It lacks the complex symbolism and intricate stucture of "Absolution" (1924), the poignancy of "Winter Dreams" (1922), the elegant grace of "The Rich Boy" (1926). Its language is unlyrical, taut, compressed, sometimes harsh; its imagery is spare. Because of its unobtrusive method and its apparent dependence upon the verisimilitude of time, place, and character, only with difficulty does one break free of the temptation to read "Crazy Sunday" as disguised autobiography or embellished case history—and all the more when so full a dossier is available on the story's genesis and real-life prototypes. For example, Dwight Taylor's generally affectionate reminiscence of Fitzgerald in Hollywood concludes with a brusque but temptingly persuasive summary of the story which derives from his knowledge of Fitzgerald's personal tragedy and how the writer had manipulated actual events. Taylor says: "The truth is turned topsyturvy, as in *Alice Through the Looking-Glass*. . . . Just as Jupiter is said to have taken on a variety of disguises . . . in order to gain access to a woman, so did Scott project himself into the skin of others in an attempt to enjoy himself without the concomitant of guilt."[4] Psychologically, this analogy may be true in part about Fitzgerald the man. It may even apply to some phases of the mysterious process by which life is "projected" into art. But it assumes insanity or illness or atavistic impulse as the motivating force.

I would argue to the contrary. Whatever its primal or subconscious sources, Fitzgerald's best fiction demonstrates not his illnesses and failures but the manner in which he overcame them. Certainly for the reader the triumph of "Crazy Sunday" finally does not consist of its success in exorcising particular demons of bad behavior or memory but rather in its sanity as art: the craft, economy, and symmetry of the whole. Finally, the story reminds us that perhaps of all American writers F. Scott Fitzgerald best exemplifies Heine's dictum, *"Aus meinen grossen Schmerzen/Mach ich die kleinen Lieder."*[5]

4. Taylor, pp. 249–50.
5. "From my great wounds I make little songs." Heinrich Heine, *Buch der Lieder*, "Lyrisches Intermezzo," No. 36.

TWO SETS OF BOOKS,
ONE BALANCE SHEET:
"FINANCING FINNEGAN"
GEORGE MONTEIRO

Fitzgerald's "Financing Finnegan," a late story, appeared in *Esquire* in January, 1938. The same issue contained as well a non-fiction piece by Hemingway. In an editorial note the magazine informed its readers that publication of the latter brought to an end the hiatus initiated by the farewell Hemingway had bade *Esquire* with the publication of "The Snows of Kilimanjaro" in August, 1936.[1] The magazine's editors did not mention Fitzgerald on this occasion, although had they had the gift of prescience, they could have as readily announced that after "Financing Finnegan," Fitzgerald would himself disappear from the pages of *Esquire* for nearly two years. Indeed, that story turned out to be the only one of Fitzgerald's to appear in print in the whole of 1938, a fact resonant with import for the writer whose stories had once commanded the best prices from America's highest-paying magazines.

It was fitting that having failed to place the story elsewhere, Fitzgerald was compelled to sell "Financing Finnegan" to *Esquire*, for the story can be read satisfactorily as Fitzgerald's qualified "answer" to Hemingway's "Snows" in much the same way the latter constituted Hemingway's sniping "answer" to Fitzgerald's original "Crack-Up" pieces, also published in *Esquire*.

In a fine phrase, though one that is now somewhat shopworn, Fitzgerald had referred obliquely to Hemingway as his "artistic conscience" (C-U, p. 79). It was that role Hemingway had performed, not entirely unwittingly, when he chastised Fitzgerald for the irresponsibility,

1. "Autobiography of a Four-Year-Old," *Esquire*, 9 (January 1938), 5.

weakness, and pusillanimity he displayed in publishing his apologia for his near-collapse. Indeed, not content with the harsh if private words he committed to paper in his letters to their shared editor at Scribner's, Maxwell Perkins, and in letters to Fitzgerald himself, Hemingway felt compelled to go public on the matter of Fitzgerald's situation in the mid-1930s. He did so in the famous reference in "Snows" to "poor Scott Fitzgerald." That the remark hit home, perhaps even more keenly than Hemingway had anticipated and despite his having assigned it to a persona—an apostate writer—is obvious from Fitzgerald's touching complaints to Perkins and to Hemingway himself, exacting from the latter a promise to excise Fitzgerald's name from all reprintings of the story and then enlisting Perkins's aid in keeping Hemingway to his word. When Hemingway reprinted the story in October, 1938, he did of course drop the *direct* reference to Fitzgerald, thereby fulfilling the letter of his uneasy promise. But even then he would not entirely abandon his attack on his friend and fellow author, for with sly diminishment he substituted *Julian* for *Scott*. It seems most unlikely that it would not have occurred to the well-read Fitzgerald, a lapsed Catholic, that Hemingway was now referring to an earlier apostate, the emperor who had tried and failed to reestablish paganism. If, by November, 1937, Fitzgerald talked about seeing old friends again, and being "friends again with Ernest,"[2] as late as December, 1939, he lamented to Perkins that "Ernest's crack in *The Snows*" had turned them into "something less than friends."[3]

What Fitzgerald did not entirely perceive at the time, however, was that if he saw Hemingway as his "artistic conscience," Hemingway had in turn cast him, consciously or not, as a personal scapegoat. Indeed when one thinks about it, it is evident that Hemingway's reaction to Fitzgerald's "Crack-Up" pieces was really an obvious overreaction. Fitzgerald had confessed to aesthetic and personal failings that Hemingway feared he too might share. That Hemingway would never directly face his own apostasy as Fitzgerald had is suggested not only by the way that the former distorted the "rich are different from us" anecdote to tell it at Scott's (Julian's) expense, but also by the way he distanced himself from his protagonist, the dying writer who would make amends for having betrayed his talent and his trust.[4] Actually,

2. *Correspondence of F. Scott Fitzgerald*, ed. Matthew J. Bruccoli and Margaret M. Duggan (New York: Random House, 1980), p. 483.
3. *Dear Scott/Dear Max: The Fitzgerald-Perkins Correspondence*, ed. John Kuehl and Jackson R. Bryer (New York: Charles Scribner's, 1971), p. 261.
4. That the butt of the original anecdote was Hemingway himself and not Fitzgerald is established in Matthew J. Bruccoli's *Scott and Ernest: The Authority of Failure and the Authority of Success* (New York: Random House, 1978), pp. 4, 130–33.

Hemingway's relationship to his persona in "Snows" is somewhat complicated. The author is both repelled by his creation and attracted to him. He seems to deplore his past and present weaknesses—selling himself a bill of goods about the land of the Philistines and his writer's responsibility to record the ways of the rich, thereby living an apostate's life—but seems ultimately to applaud the way in which his mind and sight clear to the point that he will not ruin his death, the last great experience life holds for the writer. Seen this way, "Snows" is Hemingway's "Crack-Up" performance, distinguished most tellingly from Fitzgerald's pieces in that while the vulnerable Scott stands nakedly before his readers, the canny Ernest disappears behind his persona.

With the publication of "Snows," the fictional lessons of conscience and scapegoatism were fully available to Scott. Hemingway's bullish public presence and headline bravura did not fool Fitzgerald. He saw clearly that in the mid-1930s his friend was as troubled as he was, perhaps even more so. To Perkins's detailed account of Hemingway's rather silly fracas with Max Eastman over the latter's published insinuation that Hemingway was less in control of his emotions and psyche than the public Hemingway was wont to claim, Fitzgerald replied keenly and with generosity. From Hollywood he wrote in September, 1937:

> I was thoroughly amused by your descriptions, but what transpires is that Ernest did exactly the same asinine thing that I knew he had it in him to do when he was out here. The fact that he lost his temper only for a minute does not minimize the fact that he picked the exact wrong minute to do it. . . .
> He is living at the present in a world so entirely his own that it is impossible to help him, even if I felt close to him at the moment, which I don't. I like him so much, though, that I wince when anything happens to him, and I feel rather personally ashamed that it has been possible for imbeciles to dig at him and hurt him. After all, you would think that a man who has arrived at the position of being practically his country's most imminent [eminent] writer, could be spared that yelping.[5]

But Fitzgerald's insight into the sources of Hemingway's harried and boorish behavior was not entirely a new thing. In September, 1936, for example, he had distinguished acutely between himself and Heming-

5. *Dear Scott/Dear Max*, pp. 240–41.

way, finding that Hemingway was "quite as nervously broken down" as he was himself but the fact manifested itself in "different ways." Hemingway's inclination was "toward megalomania" and Fitzgerald's "toward melancholy" (Letters, p. 543). "Financing Finnegan" was written in June, 1937. It has customarily been read as a narrowly autobiographical piece, "admittedly a self-critical bit of slightly disguised autobiography,"[6] in which Fitzgerald reveals himself in the comic, ironic voice of an unnamed narrator who is merely one-half of himself, the other half being the title character, a second writer.[7] And indeed there is some merit in that view. He did refer, in 1939, to "the semi-crippled state into which," he admitted, "I seem to get myself sometimes (almost like the hero of my story 'Financing Finnegan')," but he qualified the identification with the telling "almost."[8] But that Finnegan was "an exaggerated portrait of Fitzgerald himself,"[9] down to the details of the swimming pool accident Fitzgerald suffered in 1936, as has been proposed, is only partly true.[10] For a writer, as Fitzgerald reminded us, is "many people, if he's any good" (C-U, p. 177). And one of those "many people," in Fitzgerald's case, was his "artistic conscience," the eminent (or forever imminent?) Hemingway. To say this is not to gainsay that at times the experiences attributed to Finnegan correspond in detail to Fitzgerald's but rather to call attention to the important idea that Fitzgerald has cast those details upon Finnegan, a public figure of bravado and derring-do. If the high point of Fitzgerald's misfiring adventures in the 1930s was perhaps his boorish revelry at the Dartmouth winter carnival, Hemingway had successfully brought off a well-publicized African safari. If Fitzgerald ended up in Hollywood hoping to recoup his fortunes by hammering out screen scripts, Hemingway, having gone off to war-ravaged Spain, was flamboyantly raising funds among Hollywood's moneyed elite for the Spanish ambulance corps.

6. Milton Hindus, F. Scott Fitzgerald: An Introduction and Interpretation (New York: Holt, Rinehart and Winston, 1968), p. 95.
7. See Sergio Perosa, The Art of F. Scott Fitzgerald, trans. Charles Metz and Sergio Perosa (Ann Arbor: Univ. of Michigan Press, 1965), pp. 143–44; Robert Sklar, F. Scott Fitzgerald: The Last Laocoön (New York: Oxford Univ. Press, 1967), p. 315; and John A. Higgins, F. Scott Fitzgerald: A Study of the Stories (Jamaica, N.Y.: St. John's Univ. Press, 1971) pp. 167–68.
8. As Ever, Scott Fitz—: Letters Between F. Scott Fitzgerald and His Literary Agent Harold Ober 1919–1940, ed. Matthew J. Bruccoli and Jennifer McCabe Atkinson (Philadelphia and New York: J.B. Lippincott, 1972), p. 403.
9. Henry Dan Piper, F. Scott Fitzgerald: A Critical Portrait (New York: Holt, Rinehart and Winston, 1965), p. 243.
10. Dear Scott/Dear Max, pp. 230–31.

Fitzgerald was of course never entirely taken in by Hemingway's public self. In "Financing Finnegan," instead of having him go on an African safari or to a civil war fought on an international scale, Fitzgerald has Finnegan concoct a harebrained scheme to explore the Arctic wastes of the North Pole in the company of three Bryn Mawr anthropologists, three "girls," we ultimately learn. When he is told that out of that trip, whatever Finnegan will write is going to be "pure white—it's going to have a blinding glare about it" (*Stories*, p. 452), the reader will perhaps recall that Hemingway's "Snows" is replete with memories and illusions involving snow and ice—from Harry's memories of skiing in Austria to the blinding whiteness of his final illusion of a journey toward the house of God on Kilimanjaro.

Fitzgerald and Hemingway, like the narrator and Finnegan, shared the same publisher, Scribner's, located as in the story on New York's Fifth Avenue, and the same editor, Maxwell Perkins (Jaggers, in the story); if they did not share the same literary agent, Harold Ober, they had once come close to sharing him. It was certainly not Fitzgerald's fault that Ober and Hemingway, after considerable negotiation, had failed to come to terms. But for the purposes of his story, Fitzgerald makes Cannon (Ober) both the narrator's and Finnegan's agent. In neither case is the portrayal detailed or particularly significant, for the two are merely *ficelles*, to adopt Henry James's term, and as such are useful only insofar as they help the author get his story told. And that story is not merely Finnegan's, nor is it primarily that of Fitzgerald's otherwise Jamesian narrator. It is on one level the story of the contrasting lives of two practicing writers, and it is on the second level the fanciful and wishful playing-out of the Fitzgerald-Hemingway literary competition. On the first level, "Financing Finnegan" is a Jamesian tale of the responsible writer working hard and honestly at his trade but achieving only modest critical and popular support. The nature and extent of his professional reputation are defined and put into perspective when seen in the context of conflicting facts and fictions behind Finnegan's enormous public reputation. It is a Jamesian tale, along the lines of "The Next Time," its diction and sentential rhythms recalling the master himself in referring to the career of the "distinguished author," who " 'can do anything when he puts his mind to it. There's never been such a talent' " (the agent's words), "had started brilliantly and if it had not kept up to its first exalted level, at least it started brilliantly all over again every few years. He was the perennial man of promise in American letters"—(the narrator's words) (*Stories*, pp. 448–49). (Perhaps in the letter to Perkins quoted above Fitzgerald did indeed intend to call attention to Hemingway's "imminence.") But it is a Jamesian tale about Fitzgerald and Hemingway, one in which Fitzgerald has rearranged facts, swapped around episodes, and allocated fancies to work out his reply to those veiled charges in Hemingway's "Snows" that Fitzgerald saw aimed at himself.

In "Financing Finnegan," I would suggest, Fitzgerald was setting Hemingway up as his own scapegoat. This is particularly evident in his attributing to Finnegan the autobiographically based swimming pool accident and in the observations that Finnegan's (Fitzgerald's) way "with words was astounding, they glowed and coruscated—he wrote sentences, paragraphs, chapters that were masterpieces of fine weaving and spinning" but which, when written down " 'plain,' " one poor screenwriter insisted, " 'it's like a week in the nut-house' " (*Stories*, p. 449). Moreover, if the biographical Hemingway's major books were all being turned into Hollywood movies, the fictional Finnegan's are not. While Hemingway not only worked on novels, stories, and a play but brought them to completion and publication, it is perhaps nothing more than a rumor spread anxiously by his agent that Finnegan " 'may be bringing a manuscript. He has a novel he's working on, you know. And a play too . . . or maybe a short story' " (*Stories*, p. 448). While Hemingway in the 1930s was making a great deal of money from his writing and making a great deal of it for his publishers as well, Finnegan is living on advances. If the truth about Finnegan is that he has " 'been in a slump, he's had blow after blow in the past few years' " (*Stories*, p. 450), the parallel is again not entirely with Hemingway. The closer parallels by far in these instances, of course, are with Fitzgerald himself. But that is not to say that Fitzgerald saw mostly himself in Finnegan. His fictional (and psychological) strategy was to load up Hemingway-Finnegan with his own deficiencies and failures, thereby perhaps getting deeply beneath the facade of Hemingway's superficial personality.

With considerable acumen, he sees his Finnegan-Hemingway as a schemer. On the small scale, Finnegan works on his publisher for favors. Although he has a rule against author's advances, Finnegan's publisher admits waiving it " 'once in the last two years and that was for a woman who was having a bad struggle—Margaret Trahill, do you know her? She was an old girl of Finnegan's, by the way' " (*Stories*, p. 453). In early 1937, shortly before Fitzgerald wrote "Financing Finnegan," Hemingway had "tipped Max Perkins off about the possibility of publishing Martha Gellhorn," the novelist and reporter who would become Ernest's third wife. She had recently written a story entitled "Exiles," which, as she and Ernest had hoped, was bought for

Scribner's Magazine.[11] Fitzgerald never did approve of Martha as a wife for Ernest. "It will be odd to think of Ernest married to a really attractive woman," he wrote to Perkins; "I think the pattern will be somewhat different than with his Pygmalionlike creations."[12]

On a grander scale, the schemer Finnegan persuades his publisher to bankroll the hijinking trek into the Arctic wilderness. Perhaps Fitzgerald knew that it was his second wife's uncle, and not Hemingway, who had paid for the African safari that resulted in *Green Hills of Africa*, "The Short Happy Life of Francis Macomber," and, of particular significance for Scott, "The Snows." With considerable prescience Fitzgerald imagines both the disappearance and assumed death of the literary lion and his equally remarkable reappearance. Just as Finnegan-Hemingway had "walked off into a snowstorm when the food supply gave out" (*Stories*, p. 453) only to reappear sometime later in Oslo, so too would Hemingway, years later, "die" in Africa (twice in a matter of days) only to come walking out of the jungle large as life. To anyone familiar with Hemingway's telegraphic epistolary style, moreover, Finnegan's cablegram from Oslo, unlike the telegram that materializes early in the story (which is vintage Fitzgerald) is pure Hemingway:

> *Am miraculously safe here but detained by authorities please wire passage money for four people and two hundred extra I am bringing back plenty greetings from the dead.* (*Stories*, p. 454)

If Finnegan brings back "plenty greetings from the dead," what he doesn't bring back, as it turns out, is much material for his writing, for as the narrator notes rather ungenerously, "so far there's only been a short story about the polar expedition, a love story" (*Stories*, p. 455). Out of the Spanish Civil War, on the other hand, Hemingway would get a play, some stories, and a major novel—yet one that, interestingly enough, was also something of a love story.[13]

11. A. Scott Berg, *Max Perkins: Editor of Genius* (New York: E.P. Dutton, 1978), p. 323.

12. *Dear Scott/Dear Max*, pp. 266–67.

13. The "Arctic business" had considerable significance for Fitzgerald. In the late 1930s, after many years of loyal support, Harold Ober finally began to turn down Fitzgerald's requests for money. Fitzgerald's description of his reaction to Ober's denials and his own subsequent behavior echoes, interestingly enough, the Arctic motif he had used in "Financing Finnegan." "The situation resolves itself into this," explained Fitzgerald, "it is as if a man had once trekked up into the Arctic to save a partner and his load, and then when the partner became lost a second time, the backer was not able or willing to help him get out. It doesn't diminish the lost man's gratitude for former favors, but rather than perish, he must find his own way out" (*As Ever, Scott Fitz—*, p. 403). Ober was not the only one to "fail" Fitzgerald at this time. Hemingway was another denier, of course. Hence the deep logic of Fitzgerald's use of the Arctic analogy as late as 1939.

What was Fitzgerald's subconscious working out in "Financing Finnegan"? It was in part at least taking an inventory of Fitzgerald's and Hemingway's careers, and it was fictionally assigning and reassigning details and episodes. When Fitzgerald suffered his freak swimming pool injury, the accident was publicly seen as characteristic of his overall fatuity; when Hemingway, with a propensity for suffering accidental hurt, broke his arm and smashed his shoulder in a Montana automobile accident, it was publicly seen as still another occasion for the durable hero to display his characteristically stoic heroism. As Finnegan's agent says admiringly, the injury did not keep him from practicing his trade. Though he did have " 'to write on the ceiling . . . he didn't give up writing,' " he emphasized; " 'he has plenty of guts' " (*Stories*, p. 449).

Out of all this double-entry bookkeeping of literary and personal accounts comes Fitzgerald's view of Fitzgerald and Hemingway. At undoubtedly a low point, Scott had once written that while he wrote with "the authority of failure," Ernest wrote with "the authority of success" (C-U, p. 181). It was not in that mood, however, that Fitzgerald wrote "Financing Finnegan." As Fitzgerald saw it, the true Hemingway of the late 1930s was far more like the public's image of Fitzgerald as pathetic, fatuous, and predictably unreliable than anyone would admit. Concomitantly, the real Fitzgerald, if the truth were known, was the one who genuinely embodied some of the more admirable qualities so publicly granted to the "distinguished author." At the end of "Financing Finnegan" it is the narrator-Fitzgerald who, having earned his thousand-dollar advance, is ostensibly at honest work on a Hollywood venture, while it is Finnegan-Hemingway who, when the movies get around to taking "a good long look at him" (*Stories*, p. 455), will find that the burden for coming through at last will be squarely upon his shoulders.

Exasperated, Fitzgerald's narrator at one point calls Finnegan a " 'four-flusher' " (*Stories*, p. 451). In a notebook entry Fitzgerald would similarly imply that Hemingway was something less than the real thing. "Contrary to popular opinion, he is not as tall as Thomas Wolfe, standing only six feet five in his health belt," he wrote. "He is naturally clumsy with his body, but shooting from a blind or from adequate cover, makes a fine figure of a man" (C-U, p. 189). When Hemingway turned his 1920s memories into the manuscript that was ultimately published in 1964 as *A Moveable Feast*, he observed of Fitzgerald that "when he sat down on one of the bar stools I saw that he had very short legs. With normal legs he would have been perhaps two inches taller."[14] The local coloration was different, but the hard malice was the same.

14. Ernest Hemingway, *A Moveable Feast* (New York: Charles Scribner's, 1964), p. 150.

Appendix
Contributors
Index

THE SHORT STORIES OF
F. SCOTT FITZGERALD:
A CHECKLIST OF CRITICISM

JACKSON R. BRYER

This checklist is modeled to a great extent on the extremely useful listing in Jackson J. Benson's *The Short Stories of Ernest Hemingway: Critical Essays* (Durham, N.C.: Duke University Press, 1975). Minor modifications in Benson's bibliographical style have been made; and a section listing the contents of books including several Fitzgerald stories has been added. Explanatory notes precede each section.

Sections include:

    I. Collections Containing Fitzgerald Short Stories
    II. Books on Fitzgerald's Work Containing Discussion of the Short Stories
    III. Dissertations Containing Discussion of Fitzgerald's Short Stories
    IV. General Books Containing Discussion of Several Fitzgerald Short Stories
    V. General Articles Containing Discussion of Several Fitzgerald Short Stories
    VI. Reviews of Fitzgerald Story Collections
    VII. Criticism, Explication, and Commentary on Individual Stories, Listed by Story—Including Specific Articles, Segments from Books on Fitzgerald's Work, and Segments from General Books

I. Collections Containing Fitzgerald Short Stories

Listed in this section are volumes in the English language which include short stories by Fitzgerald and are primarily or entirely composed of material by him. In listing the contents of each title, only the short stories by Fitzgerald in the book are included. Paperback reprintings of hardcover originals are listed only when such reprintings include material not in the originals. The abbreviations listed following each title are those used in Sections II, IV, VI and VII of the checklist.

Flappers and Philosophers (F&P). New York: Charles Scribner's, 1920. The Offshore Pirate, The Ice Palace, Head and Shoulders, The Cut-Glass Bowl, Bernice Bobs Her Hair, Benediction, Dalyrimple Goes Wrong, The Four Fists.

Tales of the Jazz Age (TJA). New York: Charles Scribner's, 1922. The Jelly-Bean, The Camel's Back, May Day, The Diamond as Big as the Ritz, The Curious Case of Benjamin Button, Tarquin of Cheapside, "O Russet Witch!," The Lees of Happiness, Mr. Icky, Jemina.

All the Sad Young Men (ASYM). New York: Charles Scribner's, 1926. The Rich Boy, Winter Dreams, The Baby Party, Absolution, Rags Martin-Jones and the Pr-nce of W-les, The Adjuster, Hot and Cold Blood, "The Sensible Thing," Gretchen's Forty Winks.

Taps at Reveille (TAR). New York: Charles Scribner's, 1935. The Scandal Detectives, The Freshest Boy, He Thinks He's Wonderful, The Captured Shadow, The Perfect Life, First Blood, A Nice Quiet Place, A Woman with a Past, Crazy Sunday, Two Wrongs, The Night of Chancellorsville, The Last of the Belles, Majesty, Family in the Wind, A Short Trip Home, One Interne, The Fiend, Babylon Revisited.

The Last Tycoon (LT). New York: Charles Scribner's, 1941. May Day, The Diamond as Big as the Ritz, The Rich Boy, Absolution, Crazy Sunday.

The Portable F. Scott Fitzgerald (*Portable*). Selected by Dorothy Parker. New York: Viking Press, 1945. Absolution, The Baby Party, The Rich Boy, May Day, The Cut-Glass Bowl, The Offshore Pirate, The Freshest Boy, Crazy Sunday, Babylon Revisited.

The Diamond as Big as the Ritz and Other Stories (*Diamond*). New York: Editions for the Armed Services, 1946. The Diamond as Big as the Ritz, Babylon Revisited, May Day, The Rich Boy, Crazy Sunday, Winter Dreams, The Adjuster, Hot and Cold Blood, "The Sensible Thing," Gretchen's Forty Winks.

Borrowed Time (BT). Selected by Alan and Jennifer Ross. London: Grey Walls Press, 1951. The Cut-Glass Bowl, May Day, The Camel's Back, The Diamond as Big as the Ritz, The Rich Boy, Absolution, Crazy Sunday, Two Wrongs, Babylon Revisited.

The Stories of F. Scott Fitzgerald (Stories). Selected by Malcolm Cowley. New York: Charles Scribner's, 1951. The Diamond as Big as the Ritz, Bernice Bobs Her Hair, The Ice Palace, May Day, Winter Dreams, "The Sensible Thing," Absolution, The Rich Boy, The Baby Party, Magnetism, The Last of the Belles, The Rough Crossing, The Bridal Party, Two Wrongs, The Scandal Detectives, The Freshest Boy, The Captured Shadow, A Woman with a Past, Babylon Revisited, Crazy Sunday, Family in the Wind, An Alcoholic Case, The Long Way Out, Financing Finnegan, A Patriotic Short, Two Old-Timers, Three Hours between Planes, The Lost Decade.

Afternoon of an Author (AA). Princeton, N.J.: Princeton University Library, 1957; New York: Charles Scribner's, 1958. A Night at the Fair, Forging Ahead, Basil and Cleopatra, Outside the Cabinet-Maker's, One Trip Abroad, "I Didn't Get Over," Design in Plaster, "Boil Some Water—Lots of It," Teamed with Genius, No Harm Trying, News of Paris — Fifteen Years Ago.

The Bodley Head Scott Fitzgerald, Volume 1 (BH1). London: Bodley Head, 1958. May Day, The Diamond as Big as the Ritz, Crazy Sunday.

The Bodley Head Scott Fitzgerald, Volume 2 (BH2). London: Bodley Head, 1959. The Last of the Belles, Pat Hobby Himself, An Alcoholic Case, Financing Finnegan.

Babylon Revisited and Other Stories (Babylon). New York: Charles Scribner's, 1960 (Scribner Library #SL 22). The Ice Palace, May Day, The Diamond as Big as the Ritz, Winter Dreams, Absolution, The Rich Boy, The Freshest Boy, Babylon Revisited, Crazy Sunday, The Long Way Out.

The Bodley Head Scott Fitzgerald, Volume 3 (BH3). London: Bodley Head, 1960. The Cut-Glass Bowl, The Curious Case of Benjamin Button, The Lees of Happiness, The Rich Boy, The Adjuster, Gretchen's Forty Winks.

Six Tales of the Jazz Age and Other Stories (6TJA). New York: Charles Scribner's, 1960. The Jelly-Bean, The Camel's Back, The Curious Case of Benjamin Button, Tarquin of Cheapside, "O Russet Witch!," The Lees of Happiness, The Adjuster, Hot and Cold Blood, Gretchen's Forty Winks.

The Bodley Head Scott Fitzgerald, Volume 4 (BH4). London: Bodley Head, 1961. The Rough Crossing, Babylon Revisited.

The Stories of F. Scott Fitzgerald, Volume 1: The Diamond as Big as the Ritz and Other Stories (Penguin1). Harmondsworth, Middlesex: Penguin, 1962. The Cut-Glass Bowl, May Day, The Diamond as Big as the Ritz, The Rich Boy, Crazy Sunday, An Alcoholic Case, The Lees of Happiness.

The Pat Hobby Stories (PH). New York: Charles Scribner's, 1962. Pat Hobby's Christmas Wish, A Man in the Way, "Boil Some Water—Lots of It," Teamed with Genius, Pat Hobby and Orson Welles, Pat Hobby's Secret, Pat Hobby, Putative Father, The Homes of the Stars, Pat Hobby Does His Bit, Pat Hobby's Preview, No Harm Trying, A Patriotic Short, On the Trail of Pat Hobby, Fun in an Artist's Studio, Two Old-Timers, Mightier than the Sword, Pat Hobby's College Days.

The Bodley Head Scott Fitzgerald, Volume 5 (BH5). London: Bodley Head, 1963. The Diamond as Big as the Ritz, Bernice Bobs Her Hair, The Ice Palace, May Day, The Jelly-Bean, Winter Dreams, "The Sensible Thing,"

Absolution, The Rich Boy, The Baby Party, A Short Trip Home, The Bowl, Magnetism, Outside the Cabinet-Maker's, The Rough Crossing, Majesty, The Last of the Belles.

The Bodley Head Scott Fitzgerald, Volume 6 (BH6). London: Bodley Head, 1963. The Scandal Detectives, A Night at the Fair, The Freshest Boy, He Thinks He's Wonderful, The Captured Shadow, First Blood, A Woman with a Past, Babylon Revisited, Two Wrongs, The Bridal Party, One Trip Abroad, Family in the Wind, Crazy Sunday, An Alcoholic Case, The Long Way Out, Financing Finnegan, Design in Plaster, Boil Some Water—Lots of It, Teamed with Genius, A Patriotic Short, Two Old Timers, Three Hours between Planes, The Lost Decade.

The Fitzgerald Reader (Reader). Edited by Arthur Mizener. New York: Charles Scribner's, 1963. May Day, Winter Dreams, Absolution, "The Sensible Thing," The Rich Boy, Basil and Cleopatra, Outside the Cabinet-Maker's, Babylon Revisited, Crazy Sunday, Family in the Wind, The Long Way Out, Financing Finnegan, The Lost Decade.

The Apprentice Fiction of F. Scott Fitzgerald: 1909-1917 (AF). Edited by John Kuehl. New Brunswick, N.J.: Rutgers University Press, 1965. The Mystery of the Raymond Mortgage, Reade, Substitute Right Half, A Debt of Honor, The Room with the Green Blinds, A Luckless Santa Claus, The Trail of the Duke, Pain and the Scientist, The Ordeal, The Spire and the Gargoyle, Tarquin of Cheepside, Babes in the Woods, Sentiment—and the Use of Rouge, The Pierian Springs and the Last Straw.

The Stories of F. Scott Fitzgerald, Volume 2: The Crack-Up with Other Pieces and Stories (Penguin2). Harmondsworth, Middlesex: Penguin, 1965. Gretchen's Forty Winks, The Last of the Belles, Babylon Revisited, Pat Hobby Himself, Financing Finnegan.

The Stories of F. Scott Fitzgerald, Volume 3: The Pat Hobby Stories (Penguin3). Harmondsworth, Middlesex: Penguin, 1967. Pat Hobby's Christmas Wish, A Man in the Way, "Boil Some Water—Lots of It," Teamed with Genius, Pat Hobby and Orson Welles, Pat Hobby's Secret, Pat Hobby, Putative Father, The Homes of the Stars, Pat Hobby Does His Bit, Pat Hobby's Preview, No Harm Trying, A Patriotic Short, On the Trail of Pat Hobby, Fun in an Artist's Studio, Two Old-Timers, Mightier than the Sword, Pat Hobby's College Days.

The Stories of F. Scott Fitzgerald, Volume 4: Bernice Bobs Her Hair and Other Stories (Penguin4). Harmondsworth, Middlesex: Penguin, 1968. Bernice Bobs Her Hair, Winter Dreams, "The Sensible Thing," Absolution, The Baby Party, A Short Trip Home, Magnetism, The Rough Crossing.

The Stories of F. Scott Fitzgerald, Volume 5: The Lost Decade and Other Stories (Penguin5). Harmondsworth, Middlesex: Penguin, 1968. The Freshest Boy, A Woman with a Past, Two Wrongs, The Bridal Party, Crazy Sunday, Three Hours between Planes, The Lost Decade.

Francis Scott Fitzgerald: Selected Stories (Selected). Edited by Biancamaria Tedeschini Lalli. Milan: U. Mursia, 1970. The Diamond as Big as the Ritz, The Baby Party, The Scandal Detectives, The Freshest Boy, The Captured

Shadow, Babylon Revisited, The Long Way Out, Two Old-Timers, The Lost Decade.

Absolution May Day Babylon Revisited (Ab). Edited by A. Le Vot. Paris: Aubier-Flammarion, 1972. Absolution, May Day, Babylon Revisited.

The Basil and Josephine Stories (B&J). Edited by Jackson R. Bryer and John Kuehl. New York: Charles Scribner's, 1973. That Kind of Party, The Scandal Detectives, A Night at the Fair, The Freshest Boy, He Thinks He's Wonderful, The Captured Shadow, The Perfect Life, Forging Ahead, Basil and Cleopatra, First Blood, A Nice Quiet Place, A Woman with a Past, A Snobbish Story, Emotional Bankruptcy.

Bits of Paradise: 21 Uncollected Stories by F. Scott and Zelda Fitzgerald (Bits). Selected by Matthew J. Bruccoli with the assistance of Scottie Fitzgerald Smith. London: Bodley Head, 1973; New York: Charles Scribner's, 1973. The Popular Girl, Love in the Night, Our Own Movie Queen, A Penny Spent, The Dance, Jacob's Ladder, The Swimmers, The Hotel Child, A New Leaf, What a Handsome Pair!, Last Kiss, Dearly Beloved.

F. S. Fitzgerald e E. Hemingway: Selected Short Stories (FeH). Edited by P. Costa and D. Caldi. Turin: Petrini, 1973. Babylon Revisited, The Bridal Party, Financing Finnegan, Pat Hobby Himself, "The Sensible Thing," The Baby Party.

Bits of Paradise: 21 Uncollected Stories by F. Scott and Zelda Fitzgerald (BitsP). Selected by Matthew J. Bruccoli with the assistance of Scottie Fitzgerald Smith. New York: Pocket Books, 1976. The Popular Girl, Love in the Night, Our Own Movie Queen, A Penny Spent, The Dance, Jacob's Ladder, The Swimmers, The Hotel Child, A New Leaf, What a Handsome Pair!, Last Kiss, Dearly Beloved, Dice, Brass Knuckles, and Guitar.

The Price Was High: The Last Uncollected Stories of F. Scott Fitzgerald (Price). Edited by Matthew J. Bruccoli. New York: Harcourt Brace Jovanovich/ Bruccoli Clark, 1979. The Smilers, Myra Meets His Family, Two for a Cent, Dice, Brassknuckles & Guitar, Diamond Dick and the First Law of Woman, The Third Casket, The Pusher-in-the-Face, One of My Oldest Friends, The Unspeakable Egg, John Jackson's Arcady, Not in the Guidebook, Presumption, The Adolescent Marriage, Your Way and Mine, The Love Boat, The Bowl, At Your Age, Indecision, Flight and Pursuit, On Your Own, Between Three and Four, A Change of Class, Six of One—, A Freeze-Out, Diagnosis, The Rubber Check, On Schedule, More than Just a House, I Got Shoes, The Family Bus, In the Darkest Hour, No Flowers, New Types, Her Last Case, Lo, the Poor Peacock!, The Intimate Strangers, Zone of Accident, Fate in Her Hands, Image on the Heart, Too Cute for Words, Inside the House, Three Acts of Music, "Trouble," An Author's Mother, The End of Hate, In the Holidays, The Guest in Room Nineteen, Discard [Director's Special], On an Ocean Wave, The Woman from Twenty-One.

II. Books on Fitzgerald's Work Containing Discussion of the Short Stories

Discussions of individual stories included in the books listed in this section are detailed separately under the titles of the stories in Section VII. Essays and reviews reprinted in collections of material about Fitzgerald are listed here only if they are not included in Sections IV, V, or VI.

Allen, Joan M. *Candles and Carnival Lights: The Catholic Sensibility of F. Scott Fitzgerald.* New York: New York University Press, 1978.

Bruccoli, Matthew J. *The Composition of "Tender Is the Night."* Pittsburgh: University of Pittsburgh Press, 1963. [Referred to below as "Bruccoli (*Composition*")]

Bruccoli, Matthew J. *Some Sort of Epic Grandeur: The Life of F. Scott Fitzgerald.* New York: Harcourt Brace Jovanovich, 1981. [Referred to below as "Bruccoli (*Epic Grandeur*")]

Bruccoli, Matthew J., ed. *The Price Was High: The Last Uncollected Stories of F. Scott Fitzgerald.* New York: Harcourt Brace Jovanovich/Bruccoli Clark, 1979. [Referred to below as "Bruccoli (*Price*")]

Bruccoli, Matthew J., and Jackson R. Bryer, eds. *F. Scott Fitzgerald in His Own Time: A Miscellany.* Kent, Ohio: Kent State University Press, 1971.

Pp. 301–4: "Apprentice Work Done at Princeton," reprinted from *Daily Princetonian*, June 9, 1915; *Daily Princetonian*, February 24, 1917; *Daily Princetonian*, April 24, 1917; *Williams Literary Magazine*, November 1917.

Bryer, Jackson R., ed. *F. Scott Fitzgerald: The Critical Reception.* New York: Burt Franklin, 1978.

Pp. 53–54: Review of F&P by The Ringmaster, unidentified clipping in Fitzgerald's Scrapbook #1.

Pp. 54–55: " 'Flappers and Philosophers' " by A. L. S. W[ood?], unidentified clipping in Fitzgerald's Scrapbook #1.

Pp. 55–56: Review of F&P, reprinted from Duluth *Tribune* (?), unidentified clipping in Fitzgerald's Scrapbook #1.

P. 57: Review of F&P, reprinted from new London *Day* (?), unidentified clipping in Fitzgerald's Scrapbook #1.

Pp. 57–58: "Fitzgerald—One of the Most Promising American Writers of Fiction of the Present Day," review of F&P, unidentified clipping in Fitzgerald's Scrapbook #1.

Pp. 163–64: "Clever Stories of the Jazz Age by Fitzgerald" by H. B. D., review of TJA, reprinted from Philadelphia *Public Ledger* (?), unidentified clipping in Fitzgerald's Scrapbook #3.

Pp. 164–66: "The Jazz Age in Story" by A. A. White, review of TJA, reprinted from Long Island *Press* (?), unidentified clipping in Fitzgerald's Scrapbook #3.

Pp. 276–77: "Books and Their Authors" by Brooks Cottle, review of ASYM, unidentified clipping in Fitzgerald's Scrapbook #3.

Pp. 277–78: Review of ASYM by Clyde B. Davis, unidentified clipping in Fitzgerald's Scrapbook #3.

Pp. 278–79: " 'All the Sad Young Men' " by M. H. K., unidentified clipping in Fitzgerald's Scrapbook #3.

Pp. 279–80: "Jeunesse Doree," review of ASYM, unidentified clipping in Fitzgerald's Scrapbook #3.

Cross, K. G. W. *F. Scott Fitzgerald*. Edinburgh: Oliver and Boyd, 1964; New York: Grove Press, 1964.

Eble, Kenneth. *F. Scott Fitzgerald*. Revised Edition. Twayne's United States Authors Series, No. 36. Boston: Twayne, 1977. [Referred to below as "Eble (*Fitzgerald*)"]

Eble, Kenneth E., ed. *F. Scott Fitzgerald: A Collection of Criticism*. New York: McGraw-Hill, 1973. [Referred to below as "Eble (*Collection*)"]

Gallo, Rose Adrienne. *F. Scott Fitzgerald*. New York: Frederick Ungar, 1978.

Goldhurst, William. *F. Scott Fitzgerald and His Contemporaries*. Cleveland: World, 1963.

Higgins, John A. *F. Scott Fitzgerald: A Study of the Stories*. Jamaica, N.Y.: St John's University Press, 1971.

Hindus, Milton. *F. Scott Fitzgerald: An Introduction and Interpretation*. New York: Holt, Rinehart and Winston, 1968.

Hoffman, Frederick J., ed. *"The Great Gatsby": A Study*. New York: Charles Scribner's, 1962.

Pp. 115–17: *"The Great Gatsby* and Its World" by Frederick J. Hoffman.

Pp. 321–24: "The Untrimmed Christmas Tree: The Religious Background of *The Great Gatsby*" by Henry Dan Piper.

Kazin, Alfred, ed. *F. Scott Fitzgerald: The Man and His Work*. Cleveland: World, 1951.

Kuehl, John, ed. *The Apprentice Fiction of F. Scott Fitzgerald: 1909–1917*. New Brunswick, N.J.: Rutgers University Press, 1965.

Latham, Aaron. *Crazy Sundays: F. Scott Fitzgerald in Hollywood*. New York: Viking Press, 1971.

Lehan, Richard D. *F. Scott Fitzgerald and the Craft of Fiction*. Carbondale: Southern Illinois University Press, 1966.

Long, Robert Emmet. *The Achieving of "The Great Gatsby": F. Scott Fitzgerald, 1920–1925*. Lewisburg, Pa.: Bucknell University Press, 1979.

Miller, James E., Jr. *F. Scott Fitzgerald: His Art and His Technique*. New York: New York University Press, 1964.

Mizener, Arthur. *The Far Side of Paradise: A Biography of F. Scott Fitzgerald*. Revised Edition. Boston: Houghton Mifflin, 1965. [Referred to below as "Mizener (*Far Side*)"]

Mizener, Arthur, ed. *F. Scott Fitzgerald: A Collection of Critical Essays*. Englewood Cliffs, N.J.: Prentice-Hall, 1963. [Referred to below as "Mizener (*Collection*)"]

Perosa, Sergio. *The Art of F. Scott Fitzgerald.* Translated by Charles Metz and Sergio Perosa. Ann Arbor: University of Michigan Press, 1965.

Piper, Henry Dan. *F. Scott Fitzgerald: A Critical Portrait.* New York: Holt, Rinehart and Winston, 1965.

Shain, Charles E. *F. Scott Fitzgerald.* University of Minnesota Pamphlets on American Writers, No. 15. Minneapolis: University of Minnesota Press, 1961. [Reprinted in *Seven Modern American Novelists—An Introducton,* ed. William Van O'Connor. Minneapolis: University of Minnesota Press, 1964, pp. 81–117; and in *American Writers: A Collection of Literary Biographies,* ed. Leonard Unger. New York: Charles Scribner's, 1974, Vol. 2, pp. 77–100.]

Sklar, Robert. *F. Scott Fitzgerald: The Last Laocoön.* New York: Oxford University Press, 1967.

Stanley, Linda C. *The Foreign Critical Reputation of F. Scott Fitzgerald: An Analysis and Annotated Bibliography.* Westport, Conn.: Greenwood Press, 1980.

Way, Brian. *F. Scott Fitzgerald and the Art of Social Fiction.* London: Edward Arnold, 1980; New York: St. Martin's, 1980.

West, James L. W., III. *The Making of F. Scott Fitzgerald's "This Side of Paradise."* Columbia, S.C.: J. Faust, 1977.

Wilson, Edmund, ed. *The Crack-Up.* New York: New Directions, 1945.

III. Dissertations Containing Discussion of Fitzgerald's Short Stories

All abstracts are from *Dissertation Abstracts (DA)* or *Dissertation Abstracts International (DAI)*, unless otherwise indicated.

Allen, Joan Marie. "Residual Catholicism in Selected Works of F. Scott Fitzgerald," Ph.D., University of Massachusetts, 1973. [Abstract in *DAI*, 34 (July 1973), 302A]

Anderson, William Richard, Jr. "The Fitzgerald Revival, 1940–1974: A Study in Literary Reputation," Ph.D., University of South Carolina, 1974. [Abstract in *DAI*, 36 (August 1975), 883A–884A]

Atkinson, Jennifer Elizabeth. "Author and Agent: Appendices to As Ever, Scott Fitz—," Ph.D., University of South Carolina, 1971. [Abstract in *DAI*, 32 (November 1971), 2671A–2672A]

Bloom, Thomas Kenneth. "The Style of F. Scott Fitzgerald," Ph.D., Ohio University, 1972. [Abstract in *DAI*, 33 (August 1972), 746A]

Box, Patricia Ann Slater. "The Image of the Artist in the Works of F. Scott Fitzgerald," Ph.D., Texas Tech University, 1978. [Abstract in *DAI*, 39 (March 1979), 5509A]

Bronson, Dan E. "Vision and Revision: A Genetic Study of Scott Fitzgerald's Short Fiction with Some Excursions into His Novels," Ph.D., Princeton University, 1972. [Abstract in *DAI*, 33 (November 1972), 2362A]

Bruccoli, Matthew Joseph. "The Composition of F. Scott Fitzgerald's *Tender Is the Night*: A Study Based on the Manuscripts," Ph.D., University of Virginia, 1961. [Abstract in *DA*, 22 (November 1961), 1622–23]

Coleman, Thomas C., III. "The Social and Moral Criticism of F. Scott Fitzgerald," Ph.D., University of Southern California, 1959. [Abstract in *DA*, 20 (February 1960), 3289]

Doyle, Phyllis Louise. "The Search For Selfhood in the Fiction of F. Scott Fitzgerald," Ph.D., University of Rhode Island, 1980 [Abstract in *DAI*, 41 (February 1981), 3578A–3579A]

Durrell, John Blaine. "The Other Side of Paradise," Ph.D., University of South Carolina, 1971. [Abstract in *DAI*, 32 (April 1972), 5784A–5785A]

Elliot, James. "The Literary Reputation of F. Scott Fitzgerald," Ph.D., University of New Mexico, 1965. [Abstract in *DA*, 26 (April 1966), 6037–38]

Elmore, Albert Earl. "An Interpretation of *The Great Gatsby*," Ph.D., Vanderbilt University, 1968. [Abstract in *DAI*, 29 (February 1969), 2706A]

Farley, Pamella. "Form and Function: The Image of Woman in Selected Works of Hemingway and Fitzgerald," Ph.D., Pennsylvania State University, 1973. [Abstract in *DAI*, 35 (December 1974), 3735A]

Frederick, Kenneth Chester. "The Short Stories of F. Scott Fitzgerald," Ph.D., University of Michigan, 1963. [Abstract in *DA*, 24 (June 1964), 5406–7]

311

Goldhurst, William. "Scott Fitzgerald and His Contemporaries," Ph.D., Tulane University, 1962. [Abstract in *DA*, 23 (January 1963), 2525–26]

Hallam, Virginia Ann. "The Critical and Popular Reception of F. Scott Fitzgerald," Ph.D., University of Pennsylvania, 1966. [Abstract in *DA*, 27 (April 1967), 3456A]

Harris, Marie Philipsen. "A Critical Study of the Novels of F. Scott Fitzgerald," Ph.D., University of Maryland, 1952. [Abstract in *Abstracts of Dissertations* (University of Maryland), 5 (22 March 1953), 42–43]

Heseltine, Harry Payne. "The Development of the Fitzgerald Hero," Ph.D., Louisiana State University, 1956. [Abstract in *DA*, 17 (March 1957), 630]

Hewitt, Rosalie. "Aristocracy and the Modern American Novel of Manners: Edith Wharton, F. Scott Fitzgerald, Ellen Glasgow and James Gould Cozzens," Ph.D., Purdue University, 1970. [Abstract in *DAI*, 31 (February 1971), 4163A–4164A]

Higgins, John A. "F. Scott Fitzgerald as a Writer of the Short Story: A Critical Study of His Basic Motifs and Techniques," Ph.D., St. John's University, 1968. [Abstract in *DAI*, 30 (September 1969), 1169A–1170A]

Horodowich, Peggy Maki. "The Prose of F. Scott Fitzgerald," Ph.D., University of Delaware, 1978. [Abstract in *DAI*, 39 (September 1978), 1568A]

Kenyon, Nina Naomi. "Self-Hatred as a Basis for Criticism of American Society," Ph.D., St. Louis University 1968. [Abstract in *DA*, 29 (February 1969), 2713A]

Klug, Jack B. "Satire in the Early Works of F. Scott Fitzgerald," Ph.D., Texas A. & M. University, 1976. [Abstract in *DAI*, 37 (June 1977), 7752A]

Kuehl, John Richard. "Scott Fitzgerald: Romantic and Realist," Ph.D., Columbia University, 1958. [Abstract in *DA*, 19 (March 1959), 2345]

Kuhnle, John Harold. "Conscious Artistry in the Major Novels of F. Scott Fitzgerald," Ph.D., Vanderbilt University, 1971. [Abstract in *DAI*, 32 (May 1972), 6431A]

Latham, John Aaron. "The Motion Pictures of F. Scott Fitzgerald," Ph.D., Princeton University, 1970. [Abstract in *DAI*, 31 (June 1971), 6617A–6618A]

Lhamon, William Taylor, Jr. "The Horatio Alger Pattern in the Twentieth Century American Novel: Focus on Fitzgerald," Ph.D., Indiana University, 1972. [Abstract in *DAI*, 33 (May 1973), 6363A–6364A]

Long, Robert Emmet. "The Hero and Society in the Earlier Novels of F. Scott Fitzgerald: A Study in Literary Milieu," Ph.D., Columbia University, 1968. [Abstract in *DA*, 29 (February 1969), 2715A–2716A]

McCall, Raymond George. "Attitudes toward Wealth in the Fiction of Theodore Dreiser, Edith Wharton, and F. Scott Fitzgerald," Ph.D., University of Wisconsin, 1957. [Abstract in *DA*, 17 (October 1957), 2269]

Maimon, Elaine Plaskow. "The Biographical Myth of F. Scott Fitzgerald (1940–1970)," Ph.D., University of Pennsylvania, 1970. [Abstract in *DAI*, 32 (July 1971), 442A–443A]

Mangum, Anthony Bryant. "The Short Stories of F. Scott Fitzgerald: A Study in Literary Economics," Ph.D., University of South Carolina, 1974. [Abstract in *DAI*, 37 (October 1976), 2184A]

Margolies, Alan. "The Impact of Theatre and Film on F. Scott Fitzgerald," Ph.D., New York University, 1969. [Abstract in *DAI*, 30 (February 1970), 3467A]

Messenger, Christian Karl. "Sport in American Literature (1830–1930)," Ph.D., Northwestern University, 1974. [Abstract in *DAI*, 35 (April 1975), 6724A]

Miller, James E., Jr. "A Study of the Fictional Technique of F. Scott Fitzgerald," Ph.D., University of Chicago, 1950.

Moyer, Kermit Wonders, II. "The Historical Perspective of F. Scott Fitzgerald," Ph.D., Northwestern University, 1972. [Abstract in *DAI*, 33 (April 1973), 5738A–5739A]

Murthy, Sikha Satyanarayana. "Frank Norris and Scott Fitzgerald: Some Parallels in Their Thought and Art," Ph.D., University of Utah, 1976. [Abstract in *DAI*, 37 (December 1976), 3628A]

Piper, Henry Dan. "F. Scott Fitzgerald and the Origins of the Jazz Age," Ph.D., University of Pennsylvania, 1950.

Podeschi, John Battista. "The Writer in Hollywood," Ph.D., University of Illinois at Urbana–Champaign, 1971. [Abstract in *DAI*, 32 (February 1972), 4629A]

Potts, Stephen Wayne. "F. Scott Fitzgerald: His Career in Magazines," Ph.D., University of California, Berkeley, 1980. [Abstract in *DAI*, 41 (January 1981), 3110A]

Prigozy, Ruth Markoe. "The Stories and Essays of F. Scott Fitzgerald," Ph.D., City University of New York, 1969. [Abstract in *DAI*, 30 (December 1969), 2544A–2545A]

Reiter, Joan Govan. "F. Scott Fitzgerald: Hollywood as Literary Material," Ph.D., Northwestern University, 1972. [Abstract in *DAI*, 33 (April 1973), 5744A–5745A]

Schaeffer, Lynne Gail. "F. Scott Fitzgerald and the South," Ph.D., University of Detroit, 1977. [Abstract in *DAI*, 39 (March 1979), 5515A–5516A]

Schoonover, David Eugene. "The Long Way Home: American Literary Expatriates in Paris, 1919–1929," Ph.D., Princeton University, 1975. [Abstract in *DAI*, 37 (September 1976), 1556A]

Service, Eleanor Harnett. "Sense of Place in F. Scott Fitzgerald," Ph.D., Case Western Reserve University, 1976. [Abstract in *DAI*, 37 (June 1977), 7754A–7755A]

Seshachari, Neila C. "Myth in the Novels of F. Scott Fitzgerald," Ph.D., University of Utah, 1975. [Abstract in *DAI*, 36 (October 1975), 2203A–2204A]

Sklar, Robert A. "The Last Laocoön: A Study of F. Scott Fitzgerald," Ph.D., Harvard University, 1965.

Stanley, Linda Claire. "The Foreign Critical Reputation of F. Scott Fitzgerald: An Analysis and Annotated Bibliography," Ph.D., New York University, 1976. [Abstract in *DAI*, 38 (August 1977), 777A]

Steinberg, Michael Jay. "Dream and Disillusion: The Major Theme in F. Scott Fitzgerald's Fiction," Ph.D., Michigan State University, 1974. [Abstract in *DAI*, 35 (March 1975), 6162A–6163A]

West, James Lemuel Wills, III. "Materials for an Established Text of F. Scott Fitzgerald's *This Side of Paradise*," Ph.D., University of South Carolina, 1971. [Abstract in *DAI*, 32 (April 1972), 5754A–5755A]

Wexelblatt, Robert Bernard. "Disintegration in Works of F. Scott Fitzgerald and Nathanael West," Ph.D., Brandeis University, 1973. [Abstract in *DAI*, 34 (January 1974), 4296A]

Williams, Jere Lee. "The Cast of Glamour: A Study of Selected Short Stories of F. Scott Fitzgerald," Ph.D., Rice University, 1970. [Abstract in *DAI*, 31 (December 1970), 2945A]

Woodward, Jeffrey Harris. "F. Scott Fitzgerald and the Artist as Public Figure, 1920–1940," Ph.D., University of Pennsylvania, 1972. [Abstract in *DAI*, 33 (June 1973), 6937A–6938A]

IV. General Books Containing Discussion of Several Fitzgerald Short Stories

Material in this section which previously appeared in periodicals is also listed in Sections V and VI. Notations of reprintings refer to collections listed in Section II.

Aiken, Conrad. "Fitzgerald, F. Scott," in *A Reviewer's abc*. New York: Meridian, 1958, pp. 207–10. [Reprinted review of ASYM from *New Criterion*, 4 (October 1926), 773–76; reprinted in Bryer, ed., pp. 275–76]

Allen, Walter. *The Short Story in English*. New York: Oxford University Press, 1980, pp. 141–46.

Anderson, Charles R. "Scott Fitzgerald: 1896–1940," in *American Literary Masters*, ed. Charles R. Anderson. New York: Holt, Rinehart and Winston, 1965, Vol. 2, pp. 953–70.

Bewley, Marius. "Scott Fitzgerald: The Apprentice Fiction," in *Masks and Mirrors—Essays in Criticism*. New York: Atheneum, 1970, pp. 154–59. [Reprinted review of AF from *New York Review of Books*, September 16, 1965, pp. 22–24]

Bigsby, C. W. E. "The Two Identities of F. Scott Fitzgerald," in *The American Novel and the Nineteen Twenties*. London: Edward Arnold, 1971, pp. 129–49.

Blake, Nelson M. "The Pleasure Domes of West Egg and Tarmes," in *Novelist's America: Fiction as History, 1910–1940*. Syracuse, N.Y.: Syracuse University Press, 1969, pp. 45–74.

Blankenship, Russell. "F. Scott Fitzgerald (1896–1940)," in *American Literature as an Expression of the National Mind*. New York: Holt, Rinehart and Winston, 1958, pp. 742–45.

Bruccoli, Matthew J. See Smith, Scottie Fitzgerald.

Bryer, Jackson R., and John Kuehl. "Introduction," in *The Basil and Josephine Stories*, New York: Charles Scribner's, 1973, pp. vii–xxvi.

Cowley, Malcolm. "Introduction," in *The Stories of F. Scott Fitzgerald*. New York: Charles Scribner's, 1951, pp. vii–xxv.

Dardis, Tom. "F. Scott Fitzgerald: What Do You Do When There's Nothing to Do?," in *Some Time in the Sun*. New York: Charles Scribner's, 1976, pp. 18–77.

Fiedler, Leslie. "Some Notes on F. Scott Fitzgerald," in *An End to Innocence*. Boston: Beacon Press, 1955, pp. 174–82. [Reprinted from *New Leader*, 34 (April 9, 1951), 20–21; 34 (April 16, 1951), 23–24; reprinted in Mizener (*Collection*), pp. 70–76]

Geismar, Maxwell. "F. Scott Fitzgerald: Orestes at the Ritz," in *The Last of the Provincials*. Boston: Houghton Mifflin, 1943, pp. 287–352.

Gingrich, Arnold. "Introduction," in *The Pat Hobby Stories*. New York: Charles Scribner's, 1962, pp. ix–xxiii.

Hughes, Riley. "F. Scott Fitzgerald: The Touch of Disaster," in *Fifty Years of the American Novel*, ed. Harold C. Gardiner, S.C. New York: Charles Scribner's, 1951, pp. 135–49.

Kazin, Alfred. "Fitzgerald: An American Confession," in *The Inmost Leaf*. New York: Harcourt, Brace, 1955, pp. 116–26. [Reprinted from *Quarterly Review of Literature*, 2 (No. 4, 1945), 341–46]

Kazin, Alfred. *On Native Grounds*. New York: Reynal and Hitchcock, 1942, pp. 315–23.

Kuehl, John. See Bryer, Jackson R.

Lanahan, Frances Fitzgerald. "Introduction," in *Six Tales of the Jazz Age and Other Stories*. New York: Charles Scribner's, 1960, pp. 5–11.

Littlejohn, David. "Three," in *Interruptions*. New York: Grossman, 1970, pp. 102–5. [Reprinted review of AF from *Commonweal*, 82 (June 4, 1965), 358–60]

Mencken, H. L. "Two Years Too Late," in *H. L. Mencken's "Smart Set" Criticism*, ed. William H. Nolte. Ithaca, N.Y.: Cornell University Press, 1968, p. 286. [Reprinted review of F&P from *Smart Set*, 63 (December 1920), 140; reprinted in Bryer, ed., p. 48]

Mizener, Arthur. "Introduction," in *Afternoon of an Author*. New York: Charles Scribner's, 1958, pp. 3–12.

Mizener, Arthur. "Introduction," in *The Fitzgerald Reader*. New York: Charles Scribner's, 1963, pp. xv–xxvii.

Mizener, Arthur. "Introductory Essay," in *Flappers and Philosophers*. New York: Charles Scribner's, 1959, pp. 11–16.

O'Hara, John. "Introduction," in *The Portable F. Scott Fitzgerald*. Selected by Dorothy Parker. New York: Viking Press, 1945, pp. vii–xix.

Rosenfeld, Paul. "F. Scott Fitzgerald," in *Men Seen*. New York: Dial Press, 1925, pp. 215–24. [Reprinted in Kazin, ed., pp. 71–76; Wilson, ed., pp. 317–22]

Ross, Alan. "Preface," in *Borrowed Time*. London: Grey Walls Press, 1951, pp. 7–10.

Smith, Scottie Fitzgerald. "Foreword"; and Bruccoli, Matthew J. "Preface" in *Bits of Paradise: 21 Uncollected Stories By F. Scott and Zelda Fitzgerald*. New York: Charles Scribner's, 1973, pp. 1–7; and 8–13.

Tanner, Louise. "Babylon Revisited: F. Scott Fitzgerald," in *Here Today.* . . . New York: Thomas Y. Crowell, 1959, pp. 13–34.

Trilling, Lionel. "F. Scott Fitzgerald," in *The Liberal Imagination*. New York: Viking Press, 1950, pp. 243–54. [Reprinted in Hoffman, ed., pp. 232–43; Kazin, ed., pp. 194–204; Mizener (*Collection*), pp. 11–19]

Untermeyer, Louis. "F. Scott Fitzgerald," in *Makers of the Modern World*. New York: Simon and Schuster, 1955, pp. 691–701.

Untermeyer, Louis. "Introduction," in *The Diamond as Big as the Ritz and Other Stories*. New York: Editions for the Armed Services, 1945, pp. 7–8.

Voss, Arthur. *The American Short Story: A Critical Survey*. Norman: University of Oklahoma Press, 1973, pp. 208–14.

Wells, Walter. "The Hero and the Hack," in *Tycoons and Locusts: A Regional Look at Hollywood Fiction of the 1930s.* Carbondale: Southern Illinois University Press, 1973, pp. 103–21.

West, Ray B., Jr. *The Short Story in America, 1900–1950.* Chicago: Henry Regnery, 1952, pp. 64–68.

Wright, Austin McGiffert. *The American Short Story in the Twenties.* Chicago: University of Chicago Press, 1961, pp. 2, 5, 11, 14, 26–28, 30–31, 37, 39, 41, 46, 49, 52, 54, 57–60, 63–65, 69, 71–72, 77–82, 85–90, 98, 106, 113, 121, 123–24, 126, 128–29, 132–34, 138, 140, 143–44, 146, 151–52, 170, 181, 192, 199, 203, 212–15, 218, 253–54, 265, 276, 282, 284, 286–87, 293, 308, 319, 333, 336, 345, 350, 360, 374, 380–83, 385–91, 408.

v. General Articles Containing Discussion of Several Fitzgerald Short Stories

Notations of reprintings refer to collections listed in Section II and to books in Section IV.

Anderson, William R. "Fitzgerald after *Tender Is the Night*," *Fitzgerald/Hemingway Annual*, 11 (1979), 39–63.

Arnold, Edwin T. "The Motion Picture as Metaphor in the Works of F. Scott Fitzgerald," *Fitzgerald/Hemingway Annual*, 9 (1977), 43–60.

Atkinson, Jennifer McCabe. "Lost and Unpublished Stories by F. Scott Fitzgerald," *Fitzgerald/Hemingway Annual*, 3 (1971), 32–63.

Bennett, Warren. "Prefiguration of Gatsby, Eckleburg, Owl Eyes, and Klipspringer," *Fitzgerald/Hemingway Annual*, 11 (1979), 207–23.

Benson, Sally. "Fitzgerald's Heroine," New York *Times*, September 18, 1955, Sec. 2, pp. 1, 3. [Josephine Perry]

Berryman, John. "F. Scott Fitzgerald," *Kenyon Review*, 8 (Winter 1946), 103–12.

Bodeen, DeWitt. "F. Scott Fitzgerald and Films," *Films in Review*, 28 (May 1977), 285–94.

Boyd, Thomas Alexander. "Scott Fitzgerald Here on Vacation; 'Rests' By Outlining New Novels," St. Paul [Minn.] *Daily News*, August 28, 1921, "City Life-Books-Juvenile-Schools" Section, p. 6.

[Bruccoli, Matthew J.] "Two Issues of TAR," *Fitzgerald Newsletter*, No. 27 (Fall 1964), 1.

Cardwell, Guy A. "The Lyric World of Scott Fitzgerald," *Virginia Quarterly Review*, 38 (Spring 1962), 299–323.

Casty, Alan. " 'I and It' in the Stories of F. Scott Fitzgerald," *Studies in Short Fiction*, 9 (Winter 1972), 47–58.

Cowley, Malcolm. "F. Scott Fitzgerald: The Romance of Money," *Western Review*, 17 (Summer 1953), 245–55. [Reprinted in *Three Novels of F. Scott Fitzgerald: The Great Gatsby, Tender Is the Night, The Last Tycoon*. New York: Charles Scribner's, 1953, pp. ix–xx]

Cowley, Malcolm. "Third Act and Epilogue," *New Yorker*, 21 (June 30, 1945), 53–58. [Reprinted in Kazin, ed., pp. 146–53; Mizener (*Collection*), pp. 64–69]

Curry, Ralph, and Janet Lewis. "Stephen Leacock: An Early Influence on F. Scott Fitzgerald," *Canadian Review of American Studies*, 7 (Spring 1976), 5–14.

Daniels, Thomas E. "English Periodical Publications of Fitzgerald's Short Stories: A Correction of the Record," *Fitzgerald/Hemingway Annual*, 8 (1976), 124–29.

Daniels, Thomas E. "Pat Hobby: Anti-Hero," *Fitzgerald/Hemingway Annual*, 5 (1973), 131–39.

Daniels, Thomas E. "Toward a Definitive Edition of F. Scott Fitzgerald's Short Stories," *Publications of the Bibliographical Society of America*, 71 (July–September 1977), 295–310.

Donaldson, Scott. "Scott Fitzgerald's Romance with the South," *Southern Literary Journal*, 5 (Spring 1973), 3–17.

Drake, Constance. "Josephine and Emotional Bankruptcy," *Fitzgerald/Hemingway Annual*, 1 (1969), 5–13.

Elkin, P. K. "The Popularity of F. Scott Fitzgerald," *Australian Quarterly*, 29 (June 1957), 93–101.

Elstein, Rochelle S. "Fitzgerald's Josephine Stories: The End of the Romantic Illusion," *American Literature*, 51 (March 1979), 69–83.

Embler, Weller. "F. Scott Fitzgerald and the Future," *Chimera*, 4 (Autumn 1945), 48–55. [Reprinted in Kazin, ed., pp. 212–19]

Fiedler, Leslie A. "Notes on F. Scott Fitzgerald," *New Leader*, 34 (April 9, 1951), 20–21; 34 (April 16, 1951), 23–24. [Reprinted in *An End to Innocence*. Boston: Beacon Press, 1955, pp. 174–82; Mizener (*Collection*), pp. 70–76]

Forrey, Robert. "Negroes in the Fiction of F. Scott Fitzgerald," *Phylon*, 28 (Fall 1967), 293–98.

Foster, Richard. "Fitzgerald's Imagination: A Parable for Criticism," *Minnesota Review*, 7 (Nos. 1 & 2, 1967), 144–56.

Fussell, Edwin. "Fitzgerald's Brave New World," *ELH*, 19 (December 1952), 291–306. [Reprinted in Hoffman, ed., pp. 244–62; Mizener (*Collection*), pp. 43–56]

"The Future of Fitzgerald," Minneapolis *Journal*, December 31, 1922, Editorial Section, p. 6. [Reprinted in Bruccoli and Bryer, pp. 413–14]

G[ingrich], A[rnold]. "Scott Fitzgerald's Forgotten Comedy," *Esquire*, 58 (July 1962), 2. [Reprinted in expanded form as "Introduction," in *The Pat Hobby Stories*. New York: Charles Scribner's, 1962, pp. ix–xxiii]

"The Gossip Shop," *Bookman* (New York), 63 (May 1926), 374–75. [ASYM]

Greene, Ward. "Is the 'Jelly Bean' from Georgia?" Atlanta *Journal*, November 19, 1922, Magazine, p. 9.

Häusermann, H. W. "Fitzgerald's Religious Sense: Note and Query," *Modern Fiction Studies*, 2 (May 1956), 81–82.

Holmes, Charles S. "Fitzgerald: The American Theme," *Pacific Spectator*, 6 (Spring 1952), 243–52.

Houston, Penelope. "Visits to Babylon," *Sight and Sound*, 21 (April–June 1952), 153–56.

Hunt, Jan, and John M. Saurez. "The Evasion of Adult Love in Fitzgerald's Fiction," *Centennial Review*, 17 (Spring 1973), 152–69.

Kane, Patricia. "F. Scott Fitzgerald's St. Paul: A Writer's Use of Material," *Minnesota History*, 45 (Winter 1976), 141–48.

Kazin, Alfred. "Fitzgerald: An American Confession," *Quarterly Review of Literature*, 2 (No. 4, 1945), 341–46. [Reprinted in *The Inmost Leaf*. New York: Harcourt, Brace, 1955, pp. 116–26; Kazin, ed., pp. 172–81]

Koenigsberg, Richard A. "F. Scott Fitzgerald: Literature and the Work of Mourning," *American Imago*, 24 (No. 3, 1967), 248–70.

Kolbenschlag, Madonna C. "Madness and Sexual Mythology in Scott Fitzgerald," *International Journal of Women's Studies*, 1 (May/June 1978), 263–71.

Kreuter, Kent, and Gretchen Kreuter. "The Moralism of the Later Fitzgerald," *Modern Fiction Studies*, 7 (Spring 1961), 71–81.

Larsen, Erling. "The Geography of Fitzgerald's Saint Paul," *Carleton Miscellany*, 13 (Spring-Summer 1973), 3–30.

LeGates, Charlotte. "Dual-Perceptive Irony and the Fitzgerald Short Story," *Iowa English Yearbook*, 26 (1977), 18–20.

Lehan, Richard. "F. Scott Fitzgerald and Romantic Destiny," *Twentieth Century Literature*, 26 (Summer 1980), 137–56.

Lewis, Janet. "Fitzgerald's 'Philippe, Count of Darkness,'" *Fitzgerald/Hemingway Annual*, 7 (1975), 7–32.

Lewis, Janet. See Curry, Ralph.

Lubell, Albert J. "The Fitzgerald Revival," *South Atlantic Quarterly*, 54 (January 1955), 95–106.

Margolies, Alan. "A Note on Fitzgerald's Lost and Unpublished Stories," *Fitzgerald/Hemingway Annual*, 4 (1972), 335–36.

Marshall, Margaret. "Notes By the Way," *Nation*, 152 (February 8, 1941), 159–60. [Reprinted in Kazin, ed., pp. 159–60]

Mizener, Arthur. "The Maturity of Scott Fitzgerald," *Sewanee Review*, 67 (Autumn 1959), 658–75. [Reprinted in *The Sense of Life in the American Novel*. Boston: Houghton Mifflin, 1963, pp. 183–204; *Modern American Fiction: Essays in Criticism*, ed. A. Walton Litz. New York: Oxford University Press, 1963, pp. 113–26; Mizener (*Collection*), pp. 157–68]

Mizener, Arthur. "The Voice of Scott Fitzgerald's Prose," *Essays and Studies* (English Association), 16 (1963), 56–67.

Moyer, Kermit W. "Fitzgerald's Two Unfinished Novels: The Count and the Tycoon in Spenglerian Perspective," *Contemporary Literature*, 15 (Spring 1974), 238–56.

Oleksy, Walter, and Cynthia Scheer. "F. Scott Fitzgerald's America," *Discovery*, 14 (Autumn 1974), 9–13.

Piper, Henry Dan. "Scott Fitzgerald's Prep-School Writings," *Princeton University Library Chronicle*, 17 (Autumn 1955), 1–10.

Powers, J. F. "Cross Country: St. Paul, Home of the Saints," *Partisan Review*, 16 (July 1949), 714–21.

Powers, J. F. "Dealer in Diamonds and Rhinestones," *Commonweal*, 42 (August 10, 1945), 408–10. [Reprinted in Kazin, ed., pp. 182–86]

Prigozy, Ruth. "Gatsby's Guest List and Fitzgerald's Technique of Naming," *Fitzgerald/Hemingway Annual*, 4 (1972), 99–112.

Prigozy, Ruth. " 'Poor Butterfly': F. Scott Fitzgerald and Popular Music," *Prospects*, 2 (1976), 41–67.

Prigozy, Ruth. "The Unpublished Stories: Fitzgerald in His Final Stage," *Twentieth Century Literature*, 20 (April 1974), 69–90.

Rees, John O. "Fitzgerald's Pat Hobby Stories," *Colorado Quarterly*, 23 (Spring 1975), 553–62.

Robillard, Douglas. "The Paradises of Scott Fitzgerald," *Essays in Arts and Sciences*, 4 (May 1975), 64–73.

Savage, D. S. "The Significance of F. Scott Fitzgerald," *Envoy*, 5 (June 1951), 8–21; *Arizona Quarterly*, 8 (Autumn 1952), 197–210. [Reprinted in Mizener (*Collection*), pp. 146–56]

Scheer, Cynthia. See Oleksy, Walter.

Schoenwald, Richard L. "F. Scott Fitzgerald as John Keats," *Boston University Studies in English*, 3 (Spring 1957), 12–21; *M.I.T. Publications in the Humanities*, No. 28 (1958), 12–21.

Spencer, Benjamin T. "Fitzgerald and the American Ambivalence," *South Atlantic Quarterly*, 66 (Summer 1967), 367–81.

Suarez, John M. See Hunt, Jan.

Tanner, Stephen L. "Fitzgerald: 'What to Make of a Diminished Thing,' " *Arizona Quarterly*, 34 (Summer 1978), 153–61.

Trilling, Lionel. "F. Scott Fitzgerald," *Nation*, 161 (August 25, 1945), 182–84. [Reprinted in expanded form in *The Liberal Imagination*. New York: Viking Press, 1950, pp. 243–54; Hoffman, ed., pp. 232–43; Kazin, ed., pp. 194–204; Mizener (*Collection*), pp. 11–19]

Troy, William. "Scott Fitzgerald: The Authority of Failure," *Accent*, 6 (Autumn 1945), 56–60. [Reprinted in *Forms of Modern Fiction*, ed. William Van O'Connor. Minneapolis: University of Minnesota Press, 1948, pp. 80–86; *Modern American Fiction: Essays in Criticism*, ed. A. Walton Litz. New York: Oxford University Press, 1963, pp. 132–37; Hoffman, ed., pp. 224–31; Kazin, ed., pp. 187–93; Mizener (*Collection*), pp. 20–24]

Way, Brian. "Scott Fitzgerald," *New Left Review*, No. 21 (October 1963), 36–51.

Weir, Charles, Jr. " 'An Invite with Gilded Edges,' " *Virginia Quarterly Review*, 20 (Winter 1944), 100–13. [Reprinted in Kazin, ed., pp. 100–13]

Wescott, Glenway. "The Moral of Scott Fitzgerald," *New Republic*, 104 (February 17, 1941), 213–17. [Reprinted in *Novelists on Novelists: An Anthology*, ed. Louis Kronenberger. Garden City, N.Y.: Doubleday Anchor, 1962, pp. 374–87; Hoffman, ed., pp. 201–23; Kazin, ed., pp. 116–29; Wilson, ed., pp. 323–37]

White, Ray Lewis. "*The Pat Hobby Stories*: A File of Reviews," *Fitzgerald/ Hemingway Annual*, 11 (1979), 177–80.

Williams, Blanche Colton. "Magazine Short Stories," *Literary Review of the New York Evening Post*, June 5, 1920, p. 6.

Williams, Blanche Colton. "Short Stories in the May Magazines," *Literary Review of the New York Evening Post*, May 8, 1920, pp. 6, 9.

Wycherley, H. Alan. "Fitzgerald Revisited," *Texas Studies in Literature and Language*, 8 (Summer 1966), 277–83.

Yates, Donald A. "The Road to 'Paradise': Fitzgerald's Literary Apprenticeship," *Modern Fiction Studies*, 7 (Spring 1961), 19–31. [Reprinted in Eble (*Collection*), pp. 19–33]

vi. Reviews of Fitzgerald Story Collections

Material in this section is listed chronologically by date of first publication. For books by Fitzgerald which include short stories as well as other material, only reviews which comment on the stories are included. Abbreviations used are those introduced in Section I, with the addition of C-U for *The Crack-Up* (1945). Because of the dearth of material in print on Fitzgerald's short stories, very little selectivity has been exercised in listing the reviews which follow; much of the most worthwhile comment on the short stories is to be found in reviews. Notations of reprintings refer to collections listed in Section II and to books in Section IV.

Vane, Sibyl. Review of F&P, *Publishers Weekly*, 98 (September 18, 1920), 661–62. [Reprinted in Bryer, ed., p. 35]

"Sic Transit," review of F&P, *Nation*, 111 (September 18, 1920), 329–30. [Reprinted in Bryer, ed., pp. 35–36]

Hooper, Osman Castle. "Good Short Stories," review of F&P, Columbus [Ohio] *Dispatch*, September 19, 1920, "Passing Show" Section, p. 4.

Osborn, E. W. "Stories by Fitzgerald," review of F&P, New York *World*, September 19, 1920, p. 4 E.

Huse, William. "Stories by F. Scott Fitzgerald," review of F&P, Chicago *Evening Post*, September 24, 1920, p. 10. [Reprinted in Bryer, ed., pp. 36–37]

Review of F&P, *Literary Review of the New York Evening Post*, September 25, 1920, p. 9. [Reprinted in Bryer, ed., pp. 37–38]

Butcher, Fanny. Review of F&P, Chicago *Sunday Tribune*, September 26, 1920, Part 1, p. 9. [Reprinted in Bryer, ed., pp. 38–39]

"Latest Works of Fiction—Flappers," review of F&P, *New York Times Book Review and Magazine*, September 26, 1920, p. 24. [Reprinted in Bryer, ed., pp. 39–40]

Review of F&P, *Booklist*, 17 (October 1920), 31.

Dawson, N. P. Review of F&P, New York *Globe and Commercial Advertiser*, October 2, 1920, p. 8.

Review of F&P, *Outlook*, 126 (October 6, 1920), 238.

Ballard, Adele M. "Fitzgerald Has Punch in Light Short Stories," review of F&P, Seattle *Post-Intelligencer*, October 10, 1920, Part 7, p. 7.

"Stories by Fitzgerald," review of F&P, Springfield [Mass.] *Republican*, October 10, 1920, p. 9A. [Reprinted in Bryer, ed., p. 40]

"Fitzgerald Again," review of F&P, Minneapolis *Journal*, October 21, 1920, p. 3. [Reprinted in Bryer, ed., p. 41]

B., C. "Fitzgerald's New Book Is Disappointing," review of F&P, Baltimore *Evening Sun*, October 23, 1920, p. 8. [Reprinted in Bryer, ed., p. 42]

"A Young Man's Fancy," review of F&P, New York *Sun*, October 23, 1920, p. 9. [Reprinted in Bryer, ed., p. 42]

Coyle, David. "Short Stories by Scott Fitzgerald," review of F&P, New York *Herald*, October 24, 1920, Section 4, p. 11. [Reprinted in Bryer, ed., pp. 43–44]

Review of F&P, Galveston [Tex.] *Daily News*, October 31, 1920, p. 26. [Reprinted in Bryer, ed., p. 44].

R[iggs], S[trafford] P. Review of F&P, *Hamilton Literary Magazine* [Clinton, N.Y.], 55 (November 1920), 53.

Review of F&P, *Catholic World*, 112 (November 1920), 268. [Reprinted in Bryer, ed., pp. 44–45]

Broun, Heywood. "Books," review of F&P, New York *Tribune*, November 1, 1920, p. 10. [Reprinted in Bryer, ed., pp. 45–46]

L., I. W. "Flappers and Others," review of F&P, Boston *Evening Transcript*, November 6, 1920, Part 4, p. 4. [Reprinted in Bryer, ed., pp. 46–47]

Shinn, Charles H. "Fitzgerald Does It Again," review of F&P, Fresno [Calif.] *Republican*, November 28, 1920, p. 9A. [Reprinted in Bryer, ed., p. 47]

Mencken, H. L. "Chiefly Americans," review of F&P, *Smart Set*, 63 (December 1920), 140. [Reprinted in William H. Nolte, ed. *H. L. Mencken's "Smart Set" Criticism*. Ithaca, N.Y.: Cornell University Press, 1968, p. 286; Bryer, ed., p. 48]

Boyd, Alexander. "Mostly Flappers," review of F&P, St. Paul [Minn.] *Daily News*, December 26, 1920, Section 4, p. 6. [Reprinted in Bryer, ed., pp. 48–49]

Review of F&P, Los Angeles *Sunday Times*, January 9, 1921, Part 3, pp. 38, 39. [Reprinted in Bruccoli and Bryer, eds., pp. 315–17; Bryer, ed., pp. 49–51]

"Youth Insurgent," review of F&P, San Francisco *Chronicle*, January 23, 1921, p. 2E. [Reprinted in Bryer, ed., pp. 51–52] *

Gore, Russell. "F. Scott Fitzgerald—Flapper-Philosopher," review of F&P, Detroit *News*, February 20, 1921, Part 7, p. 3. [Reprinted in Bryer, ed., pp. 52–53]

Wegg, Silas. Review of F&P, Glasgow *Citizen*, March 23, 1922, p. 3.

"Youth and Age," review of F&P, Westminster [England] *Gazette*, March 29, 1922, p. 12.

"Clever Short Stories," review of F&P, Aberdeen [Scotland] *Daily Journal*, March 30, 1922, p. 2.

Review of F&P, London *Observer*, April 2, 1922, p. 4.

"Short Stories," review of F&P, Glasgow *Evening News*, April 6, 1922, p. 2.

Review of F&P, *Queen*, 151 (April 8, 1922), 428.

Review of F&P, *Punch*, 162 (April 19, 1922), 319.

C., I. A. "Eight Stories," review of F&P, London *Daily Herald*, April 26, 1922, p. 7.

C., A. E. Review of F&P, Manchester [England] *Guardian*, April 28, 1922, p. 7.

Review of F&P, *Country Life*, 51 (May 6, 1922), lxv.

McQuilland, Louis J. Review of F&P, *Passing Show*, 15 (May 13, 1922), 134.

Garland, Robert. " 'Tales of the Jazz Age' Both Silly and Profound," review of TJA, Baltimore *News*, September 30, 1922, p. 9. [Reprinted in Bryer, ed., pp. 139–40]

[Nelson, Frederic C.] "Fitzgerald on Flapperiana," review of TJA, Hartford [Conn.] *Daily Times*, September 30, 1922, p. 5.

Rascoe, Burton. "We Recommend—," review of TJA, New York *Tribune*, October 1, 1922, Section 5, p. 8.

R[obinson], T[ed]. "Some Artistic Short Stories Interpret Jazz Age," review of TJA, Cleveland *Plain Dealer*, October 7, 1922, p. 7. [Reprinted in Bryer, ed., pp. 140–41]

Farrar, John. Review of TJA, New York *Herald*, October 8, 1922, Section 7, pp. 12, 13. [Reprinted in Bryer, ed., pp. 141–42]

Maurice, Arthur Bartlett. Review of TJA, New York *Herald*, October 8, 1922, Section 7, p. 2.

Wallace, John T. "Short Stories by Fitzgerald," review of TJA, Detroit *Free Press*, October 8, 1922, Magazine, p. 6. [Reprinted in Bryer, ed., pp. 142–44]

"The Jazz Age," review of TJA, Columbus [Ohio] *Dispatch*, October 8, 1922, Section [4], p. 2. [Reprinted in Bryer, ed., p. 144]

"Jazz Tales Boil Fitzgerald Pot," review of TJA, San Francisco *Chronicle*, October 8, 1922, p. D5.

" 'Tales of the Jazz Age,' " review of TJA, New York *World*, October 8, 1922, p. E7.

Review of TJA, Portland [Me.] *Evening Express*, October 10, 1922, p. 19. [Reprinted in Bryer, ed., p. 145]

Minot, John Clair. "The Jazz Age," review of TJA, Boston *Herald*, October 11, 1922, p. 15. [Reprinted in Bryer, ed., pp. 145–46]

"Mr. Fitzgerald's Latest Book," review of TJA, *Princeton Alumni Weekly*, 23 (October 11, 1922), 40–41. [Reprinted in Bryer, ed., pp. 146–47]

Banning, Margaret Culkin. "Uneven Work of a Genius," review of TJA, Duluth [Minn.] *Herald*, October 13, 1922, Section 1, p. 21. [Reprinted in Bryer, ed., pp. 147–48]

Review of TJA, Buffalo [N.Y.] *Express*, October 15, 1922, Section 7, p. 4.

"Fitzgerald's Short Stories," review of TJA, New York *Sun*, October 21, 1922, p. 9. [Reprinted in Bryer, ed., p. 148]

Review of TJA, Denver *Post*, October 21, 1922, p. 5. [Reprinted in Bryer, ed., p. 149]

"Scott Fitzgerald Scores One More," review of TJA, Washington [D.C.] *Herald*, October 21, 1922, p. 7. [Reprinted in Bryer, ed., pp. 148–49]

Hazelton, Anna. "Freak Books," review of TJA, Milwaukee *Sentinel*, October 22, 1922, Fiction Section, p. 7.

Perkerson, Medora Field. " 'Tales of the Jazz Age,' " review of TJA, Atlanta *Journal*, October 22, 1922, Magazine, p. 8.

W[illiams], S[idney]. "Mr. Fitzgerald and Some Extra-Jazzy Fiction," review of TJA, Philadelphia *North American*, October 28, 1922, p. 4.

Review of TJA, Baltimore *Evening Sun*, October 28, 1922, p. 8.

Hawthorne, Hildegarde. Review of TJA, *New York Times Book Review*, October 29, 1922, p. 12. [Reprinted in Bryer, ed., pp. 149–51]

" 'Tales of the Jazz Age,' " review of TJA, Springfield [Mass.] *Sunday Republican*, October 29, 1922, p. 7A. [Reprinted in Bryer, ed., pp. 151–52]

Wilson, Edmund, Jr. "The Jazz King Again," review of TJA, *Vanity Fair*, 19 (November 1922), 24–25. [Reprinted in Bryer, ed., pp. 152–53]

M[unson], G[orham] B. Review of TJA, *New Republic*, 32 (November 1, 1922), 257. [Reprinted in Bryer, ed., p. 153]

S[wan], M[ary] B[elle]. *"Tales of the Jazz Age* Caviar for Jaded Taste," review of TJA, Buffalo [N.Y.] *Sunday Courier*, November 5, 1922, Magazine, p. 14. [Reprinted in Bryer, ed., pp. 153–54]

Gunther, John. "Fitzgerald 'Collects,' " review of TJA, Chicago *Daily News*, November 8, 1922, p. 13. [Reprinted in Bryer, ed., pp. 154–55]

Benét, Stephen Vincent. "Plotting an Author's Curve," review of TJA, *Literary Review of the New York Evening Post*, November 18, 1922, p. 219. [Reprinted in Bryer, ed., pp. 155–56]

Lambright, E. D. Review of TJA, Tampa [Fla.] *Tribune*, November 19, 1922, p. 9.

"F. Scott Fitzgerald Puffs as Jazz Age Outpaces Him," review of TJA, Philadelphia *Evening Public Ledger*, November 28, 1922, p. 30. [Reprinted in Bryer, ed., p. 157]

Review of TJA, *Commerce and Finance*, 11 (December 6, 1922), 1845. [Reprinted in Bryer, ed., pp. 157–58]

D[awson], N. P. " 'Tales of the Jazz Age,' " review of TJA, New York *Globe and Commercial Advertiser*, December 7, 1922, p. 19.

Boyd, Woodward. "The Fitzgerald Legend," review of TJA, St. Paul [Minn.] *Daily News*, December 10, 1922, "City Life-Books-Juvenile-Schools" Section, p. 6. [Reprinted in Bruccoli and Bryer, eds., pp. 338–41; Bryer, ed., pp. 158–61]

" 'Tales of the Jazz Age,' " review of TJA, Rochester [N.Y.] *Democrat and Chronicle*, December 10, 1922, Section 3, p. 6. [Reprinted in Bryer, ed., pp. 161–62]

"Too Much Fire Water," review of TJA, Minneapolis *Journal*, December 10, 1922, Women's Section, p. 12. [Reprinted in Bryer, ed., pp. 162–63]

Curtis, William. Review of TJA, *Town & Country*, 79 (December 15, 1922), 60.

Butcher, Fanny. "As If They Were Extraordinary," review of TJA, Chicago *Sunday Tribune*, December 31, 1922, Part 6, p. 11.

L., I. E. Review of TJA, *Churchman* [New York], 127 (January 13, 1923), 5. [Reprinted in Bryer, ed., p. 163]

Gore, Russell. "New Tales of the Jazz Age," review of TJA, Detroit *News*, January 21, 1923, Metropolitan Section, p. 11.

Review of TJA, *Dial* [London], 74 (March 1923), 311.

K., K. "The Jazz Age," review of TJA, London *Evening Standard*, March 29, 1923, p. 12.

Harwood, H. C. Review of TJA, *Outlook* [London], 51 (March 31, 1923), 270.

Review of TJA, *Weekly Dispatch* [London], April 1, 1923, p. 2.

Review of TJA, London *Daily Herald*, April 4, 1923, p. 7.

"A Brilliant American," review of TJA, Glasgow *Evening News*, April 5, 1923, p. 2.

Gould, Gerald. Review of TJA, *Saturday Review* [London], 135 (April 7, 1923), 469.

Review of TJA, *Observer* [London], April 8, 1923, p. 5.

"American Short Stories," review of TJA, *Times Literary Supplement* [London], April 19, 1923, p. 264.

"Tales," review of TJA, *Nation & the Athenaeum*, 33 (April 28, 1923), 125–26.

Review of TJA, *Queen*, 153 (May 3, 1923), 598.

Review of TJA, London *Daily Telegraph*, June 1, 1923, p. 6.

McQuilland, Louis J. Review of TJA, *Passing Show*, 17 (June 2, 1923), 4.

Review of TJA, *Spectator*, 130 (June 2, 1923), 931.

D. " 'More of the Beautiful and Damned,' " review of TJA, Glasgow *Bulletin*, June 13, 1923, p. 14.

Review of TJA, Southport [England] *Guardian*, June 13, 1923, p. 7.

Mencken, H. L. Review of TJA, *Smart Set*, 71 (July 1923), 141. [Reprinted in Bryer, ed., p. 163]

Pringle, Henry F. "F. Scott Fitzgerald Grows Older and Serene in His Book of Stories," review of ASYM, New York *World*, February 28, 1926, p. 6M. [Reprinted in Bryer, ed., pp. 253–54]

Gray, James. "The World of Art, Books, and Drama," review of ASYM, St. Paul [Minn.] *Dispatch*, March 2, 1926, p. 15. [Reprinted in Bryer, ed., pp. 254–55]

Hansen, Harry. "The Boy Grows Older," review of ASYM, Chicago *Daily News*, March 3, 1926, p. 16. [Reprinted in Bruccoli and Bryer, eds., pp. 365–66; Bryer, ed., pp. 255–56]

Currie, George. "Passed in Review," review of ASYM, Brooklyn *Eagle*, March 6, 1926, p. 5. [Reprinted in Bryer, ed., pp. 256–57]

Boyd, Thomas. "Genius and Pains," review of ASYM, Minneapolis *Journal*, March 7, 1926, Editorial Section, p. 11.

"Scott Fitzgerald Turns a Corner," review of ASYM, *New York Times Book Review*, March 7, 1926, p. 9. [Reprinted in Bryer, ed., pp. 257–58]

"Stories About 'All the Sad Young Men,' " review of ASYM, Milwaukee *Journal*, March 12, 1926, p. 12. [Reprinted in Bryer, ed., pp. 258–59]

Beckwith, E. C. "Volume of F. Scott Fitzgerald Stories in Which 'Absolution' Reigns Supreme," review of ASYM, *Literary Review of the New York Evening Post*, March 13, 1926, p. 4. [Reprinted in Bryer, ed., pp. 260–61]

McCardell, Lee. "Short Stories From the Maturing Pen of Scott Fitzgerald," review of ASYM, Baltimore *Evening Sun*, March 13, 1926, p. 6.

"Touchstone," Review of ASYM, *New Yorker*, 2 (March 13, 1926), 51.

"List of Collections of Short Stories Augmented by Four Notable Volumes," review of ASYM, Newark [N.J.] *Evening News*, March 13, 1926, p. 4–X.

"Short Stories by Fitzgerald," review of ASYM, Cleveland *Plain Dealer*, March 14, 1926, All-Feature Section, p. 3. [Reprinted in Bryer, ed., p. 261]

Rochford, Daniel. "The Devious Ways of Sad Young Men," review of ASYM, Boston *Evening Transcript*, March 20, 1926, Part 6, p. 4.

" 'All the Sad Young Men' Is Scott Fitzgerald's Latest," review of ASYM, Philadelphia *Record*, March 20, 1926, p. 10. [Reprinted in Bryer, ed., pp. 261–62]

Review of ASYM, *Independent*, 116 (March 20, 1926), 335. [Reprinted in Bryer, ed., pp. 262–63]

B., R. A. "Another Collection of Fitzgerald Stories for the Blasé Younger Set," review of ASYM, Minneapolis *Sunday Tribune*, March 21, 1926, Section [5], p. 4.

[Hooper, Osman C.] Review of ASYM, Columbus [Ohio] *Sunday Dispatch*, March 21, 1926, "Passing Show" Section, p. 2. [Reprinted in Bryer, ed., p. 263]

"Mr. Fitzgerald's Young Men," review of ASYM, Springfield [Mass.] *Sunday Union and Republican*, March 21, 1926, p. 5A.

Larsson, R. Ellsworth. "The Young, Sad Years," review of ASYM, New York *Sun*, March 27, 1926, p. 6. [Reprinted in Bryer, ed., pp. 263–65]

"Pierrot Penseroso," review of ASYM, *Time*, 7 (March 29, 1926), 39. [Reprinted in Bryer, ed., p. 265]

Field, Louise Maunsell. "Three Exhibits of Drifting Americans," review of ASYM, *Literary Digest International Book Review*, 4 (April 1926), 315–16. [Reprinted in Bryer, ed., pp. 266–67]

Leonard, Baird. Review of ASYM, *Life*, 87 (April 1, 1926), 25. [Reprinted in Bryer, ed., p. 267]

Benét, William Rose. "Art's Bread and Butter," review of ASYM, *Saturday Review of Literature*, 2 (April 3, 1926), 682. [Reprinted in Bruccoli and Bryer, eds., 366–68; Bryer, ed., pp. 267–68]

McClure, John. "Literature and Less—*All the Sad Young Men*," review of ASYM, New Orleans *Times-Picayune*, April 11, 1926, Sunday Magazine, p. 4. [Reprinted in Bryer, ed., p. 269]

Review of ASYM, Hartford [Conn.] *Daily Courant*, April 11, 1926, Part 6, p. 5.

" 'All the Sad Young Men,' " review of ASYM, Indianapolis *News*, April 14, 1926, p. 24.

"From the House of the Interpreter," review of ASYM, Louisville [Ky.] *Courier-Journal*, April 18, 1926, Section 3, p. 8.

"Scott Fitzgerald Shines in 'All the Sad Young Men,' " review of ASYM, Kansas City *Star*, April 24, 1926, p. 6.

Newman, Frances, "One of the Wistful Young Men," review of ASYM, *New York Herald Tribune Book Review*, April 25, 1926, p. 4. [Reprinted in Bruccoli and Bryer, eds., pp. 368–70; Bryer, ed., pp. 270–71]

Cowley, Malcolm. Review of ASYM, *Charm*, 5 (May 1926), 80–81. [Reprinted in Bryer, ed., pp. 271–72]

Paterson, Isabel. "Other Books Worth Reading," review of ASYM, *McNaught's Monthly*, 5 (May 1926), 155.

"The Best of His Time," review of ASYM, *Bookman* [New York], 63 (May 1926), 348–49. [Reprinted in Bryer, ed., p. 272]

Review of ASYM, *Century*, 112 (May 1926), 128. [Reprinted in Bryer, ed., p. 273]

Partridge, Bellamy. "Some Good Short Stories," review of ASYM, *Brentano's Book Chat*, 5 (May-June 1926), 49. [Reprinted in Bryer, ed., p. 273]

Review of ASYM, *Outlook*, 143 (May 5, 1926), 33. [Reprinted in Bryer, ed., pp. 273–74]

Gaines, Clarence. Review of ASYM, *North American Review*, 223 (June 1926), 368–69. [Reprinted in Bryer, ed., p. 274]

Review of ASYM, *Dial*, 80 (June 1926), 521. [Reprinted in Bryer, ed., p. 274–75]

Whipple, Leon. Review of ASYM, *Survey*, 56 (June 1, 1926), 331. [Reprinted in Bryer, ed., p. 275]

Review of ASYM, *Booklist*, 22 (July 1926), 421.

Review of ASYM, *Cleveland Open Shelf*, Nos. 7–8 (July–August 1926), 96.

Carpenter, Helene Collins. "Fitzgerald Strikes His Pace as Writer," review of ASYM, Oklahoma City *Oklahoman*, August 8, 1926, Section C, p. 10.

Aiken, Conrad. Review of ASYM, *New Criterion*, 4 (October 1926), 773–76. [Reprinted in *A Reviewer's abc*. New York: Meridian, 1958, pp. 207–10; Bryer, ed., pp. 275–76]

Gray, James. "Scott Fitzgerald Brilliance Bared in Short Stories," review of TAR, St. Paul [Minn.] *Dispatch*, March 20, 1935, Section 1, p. 8. [Reprinted in Bryer, ed., pp. 337–38]

B., G. "Short Stories by Scott Fitzgerald," review of TAR, Montgomery [Ala.] *Advertiser*, March 24, 1935, p. 16.

Coleman, Arthur. "Stories by F. Scott Fitzgerald Are Merely Entertaining," review of TAR, Dallas *Morning News*, March 24, 1935, Section 3, p. 8. [Reprinted in Bryer, ed., pp. 338–39]

H., P. "Three New Books from Fictioneers of Varied Merit," review of TAR, Providence [R.I.] *Sunday Journal*, March 24, 1935, Section 6, p. 4. [Reprinted in Bryer, ed., pp. 339–40]

Anderson, Katherine McClure. Review of TAR, Macon [Ga.] *Telegraph*, March 27, 1935, p. 4.

Chamberlain, John. "Books of The Times," review of TAR, New York *Times*, March 27, 1935, p. 19. [Reprinted in Bryer, ed., pp. 340–42]

Review of TAR, *New Yorker*, 11 (March 30, 1935), 89.

Hart, Elizabeth. "F. Scott Fitzgerald, Looking Backward," review of TAR, *New York Herald Tribune Book Review*, March 31, 1935, p. 4. [Reprinted in Bruccoli and Bryer, eds., pp. 393–95; Bryer, ed., pp. 342–43]

Walton, Edith H. "Scott Fitzgerald's Tales," review of TAR, *New York Times Book Review*, March 31, 1935, p. 7. [Reprinted in Broccoli and Bryer, eds., pp. 395–96; Bryer, ed., pp. 344–45]

"Mr. Fitzgerald Grows Up," review of TAR, Milwaukee *Journal*, March 31, 1935, Section 5, p. 3. [Reprinted in Bryer, ed., pp. 345–46]

H., N. "Short Stories," review of TAR, New York *Sun*, April 5, 1935, p. 30. [Reprinted in Bryer, ed., pp. 346–47]

P., M. E. Review of TAR, Boston *Evening Transcript*, April 6, 1935, Book Section, p. 2.

Matthews, T. S. Review of TAR, *New Republic*, 82 (April 10, 1935), 262. [Reprinted in Bryer, ed., p. 347; Kazin, ed., p. 108]

Seldes, Gilbert. "True to Type," review of TAR, New York *Evening Journal*, April 11, 1935, p. 21.

Train, Lilla. "*Taps at Reveille*: Stories by F. Scott Fitzgerald," review of TAR, Savannah [Ga.] *Morning News*, April 14, 1935, Section 3, p. 2.

" 'Taps at Reveille,' " review of TAR, Atlanta *Journal*, April 14, 1935, Magazine, p. 12.

"Fitzgerald Figments," review of TAR, *Time*, 25 (April 15, 1935), 80.

Troy, William. "The Perfect Life," review of TAR, *Nation*, 140 (April 17, 1935), 454–56. [Reprinted in Bruccoli and Bryer, eds., pp. 397–99; Bryer, ed., pp. 347–49]

Tyler, A. Ranger. "Youth Scanned by Fitzgerald," review of TAR, Albany [N.Y.] *Knickerbocker Press*, April 21, 1935, Section 4, p. 7.

Beck, Clyde. Review of TAR, Detroit *News*, April 28, 1935, Women's Section, p. 17.

Nourse, Joan. "Better Short Stories by Fitzgerald," review of TAR, San Francisco *Chronicle*, May 5, 1935, p. 4D. [Reprinted in Bryer, ed., pp. 350–51]

Perry, Anne. Review of TAR, Brooklyn *Citizen*, May 10, 1935, p. 5. [Reprinted in Bryer, ed., pp. 351–52]

" 'Taps at Reveille,' " review of TAR, Springfield [Mass.] *Sunday Union and Republican*, May 12, 1935, p. 7E.

M., P. D. "Fitzgerald Tales Are Ably Told," review of TAR, Richmond [Va.] *Times-Dispatch*, May 26, 1935, Section 5, p. 11.

Review of TAR, *Booklist*, 31 (June 1935), 345.

Baker, Howard. Review of TAR, *Southern Review*, 1 (July 1935), 190. [Reprinted in Bryer, ed., p. 352]

Jackson, Charles. "F. Scott Fitzgerald—from the Heart," review of C-U, *Saturday Review of Literature*, 28 (July 14, 1945), 9–10.

Poore, Charles. "Books of The Times," review of *Portable*, New York *Times*, September 27, 1945, p. 19.

M[izener], A[rthur]. Review of *Portable*, *Kenyon Review*, 8 (Spring 1946), 342–43.

Review of *Stories*, *Kirkus*, 19 (February 1, 1951), 72–73.

Toklas, Alice B. "Between Classics," review of *Stories*, *New York Times Book Review*, March 4, 1951, p. 4.

Prescott, Orville. "Books of The Times," review of *Stories*, New York *Times*, March 7, 1951, p. 31.

Alpert, Hollis. "The Lost Generation Revisited," review of *Stories*, *Saturday Review of Literature*, 34 (March 10, 1951), 13–14.

Seligman, Daniel. Review of *Stories*, *Commonweal*, 53 (March 23, 1951), 595.

Maloney, John J. "Fitzgerald Stories, a Long Time Later," review of *Stories*, *New York Herald Tribune Book Review*, March 25, 1951, p. 5.

Clark, John Abbot. "Fitzgerald's Best Short Stories Here," review of *Stories*, *Chicago Sunday Tribune Magazine of Books*, April 8, 1951, p. 4.

S., M. "Stories by Fitzgerald," review of *Stories*, San Francisco *Chronicle*, April 15, 1951, "This World" Section, p. 19.

Review of *Stories*, *Booklist*, 47 (May 1, 1951), 310.

Johnson, Pamela Hansford. "Books and Writers," review of BT, *Spectator*, 186 (May 18, 1951), 657.

Beach, Joseph Warren. Review of *Stories*, *Yale Review*, 40 (June 1951), 750–51.

Piper, Henry Dan. "Fitzgerald Once More," review of *Stories*, *New Republic*, 125 (July 2, 1951), 20.

Miller, Perry. "Departure and Return," review of *Stories*, *Nation*, 173 (October 27, 1951), 356–57.

"The Boy Grew Older," review of AA, *Newsweek*, 50 (December 23, 1957), 78–79.

Butcher, Fanny. "He Transmuted Experience into Literature," review of AA, *Chicago Sunday Tribune Magazine of Books*, December 29, 1957, p. 3.

"The Story Behind the Story," review of AA, *Times Literary Supplement* [London], January 24, 1958, p. 41.

[Bruccoli, Matthew J.] Review of AA, *Fitzgerald Newsletter*, No. 1 (Spring 1958), 1–2.

B., C. "Mizener Strikes Paydirt," review of AA, *Florida Times-Union* [Jacksonville], April 20, 1958, p. 72.

Kirsch, Robert R. "The Book Report," review of AA, Los Angeles *Times*, April 22, 1958, Part 3, p. 5.

Hutchens, John K. " 'Afternoon of an Author,' " review of AA, New York *Herald Tribune*, April 25, 1958, p. 19.

Roberts, Edwin A., Jr. "A Lamp in the Forest," review of AA, *Wall Street Journal*, April 25, 1958, p. 8.

Geismar, Maxwell. "Fitzgerald: Bard of the Jazz Age," review of AA, *Saturday Review*, 41 (April 26, 1958), 17–18.

O'Leary, Theodore M. "Fitzgerald Stories and Essays," review of AA, Kansas City *Star*, April 26,1958, p. 16.

Cowley, Malcolm. "Twenty by Scott Fitzgerald," review of AA, *New York Herald Tribune Book Review*, April 27, 1958, p. 5.

Lanahan, Frances Scott. "Fitzgerald as He Really Was," review of AA, Washington [D.C.] *Post and Times-Herald*, April 27, 1958, p. E7.

L[aycock], E[dward] A. "Fabulous Fitzgerald," review of AA, Boston *Sunday Globe*, April 27, 1958, p. A-27.

Little, Elizabeth T. "The Special Sort of Light Created by Writer of 20s," review of AA, *Virginian-Pilot* and the Portsmouth *Star* [Norfolk-Portsmouth, Va.], April 27, 1958, p. 4-G.

McGrory, Mary. "Stories Show Limitations of Fitzgerald's Talent," review of AA, Washington [D.C.] *Star*, April 27, 1958, p. E-7.

May, William. "New Collection Has Fitzgerald's Magic," review of AA, Newark [N.J.] *Sunday News*, April 27, 1958, Section 4, p. S 12.

Mooney, Harry, Jr. "Legend from Ruins," review of AA, Pittsburgh *Press*, April 27, 1958, Section 5, p. 8.

S[izer], A[lvin] V. "Stories in New Collection Tell Much about Fitzgerald," review of AA, New Haven [Conn.] *Register*, April 27, 1958, Section 7, p. 8.

Weideman, Hugh. "Footnotes to His Career," review of AA, Worcester [Mass.] *Telegram*, April 27, 1958, p. D 9.

Wilkinson, Burke. "The Magic Is Authentic," review of AA, *New York Times Book Review*, April 27, 1958, p. 5.

"Fitzgerald Gains More Recognition," review of AA, Philadelphia *Sunday Bulletin*, April 27, 1958, Section 4, p. 9.

Hanscom, Leslie. "F. Scott Fitzgerald in His Own Words," review of AA, New York *World-Telegram and Sun*, April 28, 1958, p. 17.

H[artmann], F[rederick]. Review of AA, Wilmington [Del.] *Morning News*, April 28, 1958, p. 11.

Doyle, Paul A. Review of AA, *Best Sellers*, 18 (May 1, 1958), 61.

Walbridge, Earle F. Review of AA, *Library Journal*, 83 (May 1, 1958), 1438.

Review of AA, Easton [Pa.] *Express*, May 2, 1958, p. 18.

McCormick, Jay. "Active Leisure—Then, Now," review of AA, Detroit *Times*, May 4, 1958, Section C, p. 6.

Murphy, Robert E. " 'Afternoon' Sheds Light on Fitzgerald," review of AA, Minneapolis *Sunday Tribune*, May 4, 1958, p. E-6.

Hogan, William. "Sweet Princeliness of F. Scott Fitzgerald," review of AA, San Francisco *Chronicle*, May 5, 1958, p. 33.

Bruccoli, Matthew J. "Scott Fitzgerald Writings Revived," review of AA, Richmond [Va.] *News Leader*, May 10, 1958, p. 8.

Simmons, Edgar, Jr. Review of AA, Natchez [Miss.] *Times*, May 11, 1958, Section B, p. 4.

Maddocks, Melvin. "Counting His Falling Stars," review of AA, *Christian Science Monitor*, May 12, 1958, p. 7.

Bruni, Thomas G. Review of AA, *Valley Vanguard* [Allentown, Pa.], May 14, 1958, p. 16.

Fecher, Charles A. "Fitzgerald Fragments," review of AA, Baltimore *Evening Sun*, May 15, 1958, p. 20.

Hanrahan, Virginia. "The Literary Grapevine," review of AA, Napa [Calif.] *Register*, May 17, 1958, p. 11A.

Hindus, Milton. "The Great Fitzgerald," review of AA, *New Leader*, 41 (May 19, 1958), 23–24.

Andrews, William G. "Fitgerald Stories Now Collected," review of AA, Ithaca [N.Y.] *Journal*, May 21, 1958, p. 9.

W[eissblatt], H[arry] A. "Fitzgerald," review of AA, Trenton [N.J.] *Times-Advertiser*, June 1, 1958, Part 4, p. 12.

Schoenwald, Richard L. "Random Pieces from an Eminent Career," review of AA, *Commonweal*, 68 (June 6, 1958), 259–60.

Friedrich, Otto. "The Hole in Fitzgerald's Pocket," review of AA, *Reporter*, 18 (June 12, 1958), 37.

A., P. "Fitzgerald Book," review of AA, Columbia *Missourian*, June 17, 1958, p. 4.

M., T. "Fitzgerald Writings Revived," review of AA, Houston *Chronicle*, June 22, 1958, p. 29.

Adams, Phoebe. Review of AA, *Atlantic Monthly*, 202 (July 1958), 84.

Schoch, Russ. "They Stand Test of Time," review of AA, Des Moines [Iowa] *Register*, August 24, 1958, p. 15-G.

Baumwell, Dorothy. Review of AA, *Books Abroad*, 32 (Autumn 1958), 450.

Griscom, Isobel. "Another Look at Fitzgerald," review of AA, Chattanooga [Tenn.] *Times*, September 14, 1958, p. 18.

"A Beautiful Talent," review of AA, London *Times*, October 9, 1958, p. 13.

"The Beautiful Rich," review of AA, *Times Literary Supplement* [London], October 17, 1958, p. 592.

Harding, D.W. "Cost of Living," review of AA, *Spectator*, 201 (October 31, 1958), 591.

Hightower, Rosalind. "Fitzgerald Fans Will 'Flip' with This One," review of AA, Shreveport [La.] *Times*, November 16, 1958, p. 4F.

Review of AA, *Listener*, 60 (November 27, 1958), 891.

Review of AA, *British Book News*, 220 (December 1958), 826–27.

[Bruccoli, Matthew J.] "F&P," review of 1959 F&P, *Fitzgerald Newsletter*, No. 6 (Summer 1959), 1.

Carter, Lane. "Fitzgerald Short Stories Reissued," review of 1959 F&P, Birmingham [Ala.] *News*, July 26, 1959, Section E, p. 7.

H[all], B[arbara] H[odge]. "Fitzgerald Collection Is Reissued," review of 1959 F&P, Anniston [Ala.] *Star*, July 26, 1959, p. 6B.

Arndt, Carol. "Fitzgerald Revisited," review of 1959 F&P, *Army Times* [Washington, D.C.], August 8, 1959, p. 24.

Brady, Charles A. "The Beautiful Talent of Fitzgerald Reviewed," review of 1959 F&P, Buffalo [N.Y.] *Evening News*, August 15, 1959, p. B-6.

Beatty, Richmond C. "Fitzgerald Stories Reissued Along with a New Rebel Diary," review of 1959 F&P, Nashville *Tennessean*, August 16, 1959, p. 11-C.

Brown, Alexander C. "A Short Story Collection by a Master of the Trade," review of 1959 F&P, Newport News [Va.] *Daily Press*, August 16, 1959, Section D, p. 4.

Lubeck, Robert E. "Strictly For Fitzgerald's Fans," review of 1959 F&P, Detroit *News*, August 16, 1959, "Passing Show" Section, p. 18.

Norris, Hoke. "Fitzgerald: A Light Glittering Yet Remote," review of 1959 F&P, Chicago *Sun-Times*, August 16, 1959, Section 3, p. 4.

P[eck], D[avid] T. "Early Stories of Fitzgerald," review of 1959 F&P, New Haven [Conn.] *Register*, August 16, 1959, Section 7, p. 8.

Snyder, Mary Rennels. "Of Books & Authors," review of 1959 F&P, Gary [Ind.] *Post-Tribune*, August 16, 1959, p. D-4.

Schulberg, Budd. "These for the Love of Zelda," review of 1959 F&P, *Saturday Review*, 42 (August 22, 1959), 14.

E., J. "New Reader May Wonder," review of 1959 F&P, Des Moines [Iowa] *Sunday Register*, August 23, 1959, p. 15-G.

Fielding, Wanda. "Eight Stories by Fitzgerald," review of 1959 F&P, Fresno [Calif.] *Bee*, August 23, 1959, p. 39-D.

O'Mara, Roger. "Fitzgerald Shorts Aren't Up to Par of Today's Styles," review of 1959 F&P, *Arizona Daily Star* [Tucson], August 23, 1959, Section D, p. 9.

Shaw, Fred. "Bibliophile Mans the Barricades," review of 1959 F&P, Miami [Fla.] *News*, August 23, 1959, p. 6B.

Viele, Charles. "Fitzgerald Reprint Is Well Received," review of 1959 F&P, Charleston [S.C.] *News and Courier*, August 23, 1959, p. 13-C.

W[eissblatt], H[arry] A. "More of Fitzgerald," review of 1959 F&P, Trenton [N.J.] *Sunday Times-Advertiser*, August 23, 1959, Part 4, p. 12.

Hibbets, Laura. "Publication of Early Stories Is Disservice to Fitzgerald," review of 1959 F&P, Ft. Wayne [Ind.] *News-Sentinel*, August 29, 1959, p. 4.

Beck, Warren. "Intriguing Ghost of F. Scott Fitzgerald," review of 1959 F&P, *Chicago Sunday Tribune Magazine of Books*, August 30, 1959, p. 2.

M., T. "Early Fitzgerald Stories Show Budding Genius," review of 1959 F&P, Houston *Chronicle*, August 30, 1959, p. 31.

H[artmann], F[rederick]. Review of 1959 F&P, Wilmington [Del.] *Morning News*, August 31, 1959, p. 9.

Bruccoli, M[atthew] J. "The Flapper Age: Scott Fitzgerald's Stories Reveal Genius, Talent," review of 1959 F&P, Richmond [Va.] *News Leader*, September 2, 1959, p. 15.

"Ride Him While He's Still Hot," review of 1959 F&P, Charlotte [N.C.] *News*, September 12, 1959, Section B, p. 8.

Whalen, Gerald F. "Roaring Twenties Revisited," review of 1959 F&P, Peoria [Ill.] *Journal Star*, September 12, 1959, p. B-6.

Shore, Sherman. "A Revival of Fitzgerald," review of 1959 F&P, Winston-Salem [N.C.] *Journal & Sentinel*, September 13, 1959, p. C7.

O'Reilly, Virginia. "Fitzgerald Collection Has Charm," review of 1959 F&P, Anchorage [Alaska] *Daily News*, September 26, 1959, p. 5.

B[uckley], R[obert] M. "Fitzgerald's 'Slick' Tales Have Depth," review of 1959 F&P, Buffalo [N.Y.] *Courier-Express*, October 25, 1959, p. 30D.

Heppenstall, Rayner. "Jazz Age Echoes," review of BH2, *Observer* [London], November 15, 1959, p. 21.

Hughes, Riley. Review of 1959 F&P, *Critic*, 18 (December 1959–January 1960), 78.

Kirsch, Robert R. "An End-of-the-Year Miscellany," review of 1959 F&P, Los Angeles *Times*, December 18, 1959, Part 3, p. 5.

Matthews, Mrs. K. B. "Reviews of Late Books," review of 1959 F&P, Ludington [Mich.] *News*, January 9, 1960, p. 2.

Walbridge, Earle F. Review of 6TJA, *Library Journal*, 85 (January 15, 1960), 275–76.

[Bruccoli, Matthew J.] Review of 6TJA, *Fitzgerald Newsletter*, No. 9 (Spring 1960), 2.

Kinnaird, Clark. "Fitzgerald—Sing His Praises," review of 6TJA, Harrisburg [Pa.] *Sunday Patriot-News*, March 6, 1960, "TV Magazine" Section, p. 6.

Hicks, Granville. "For the Slicks, He Was Slick," review of 6TJA, *Saturday Review*, 43 (March 12, 1960), 18.

B[rock], C[harles]. "More Fitzgerald—and Welcome," review of 6TJA, *Florida Times-Union* [Jacksonville], March 13, 1960, p. 76.

Carter, Lane. "Flappers Are Few in This Collection by Fitzgerald," review of 6TJA, Birmingham [Ala.] *News*, March 13, 1960, Section E, p. 7.

Crosby, Ralph W. "Short Stories by F. Scott F.," review of 6TJA, Washington [D.C.] *Post*, March 13, 1960, p. E7.

K., E. Review of 6TJA, Boston *Sunday Globe*, March 20, 1960, p. A-51.

W[eissblatt], H[arry] A. "Fitzgerald's Stories," review of 6TJA, Trenton [N.J.] *Sunday Times-Advertiser*, March 20, 1960, Part 4, p. 12.

Norris, Hoke. "Seekers for Eternity in the Jazz Age," review of 6TJA, Chicago *Sun-Times*, March 27, 1960, Section 3, p. 6.

Poore, Charles. "Books of The Times," review of 6TJA, New York *Times*, March 29, 1960, p. 35.

Schoch, Russ. "A Volume for F.S.F. Fans," review of 6TJA, Des Moines [Iowa] *Sunday Register*, April 3, 1960, p. 15-G.

Hilgenstuhler, Ted. " 'Six Tales of the Jazz Age,' " review of 6TJA, Los Angeles *Herald-Express*, April 4, 1960, Section B, p. 3.

May, William. "Have You Read . . . ?," review of 6TJA, Newark [N.J.] *Evening News*, April 5, 1960, p. 26.

Engelberg, Morton A. "Jazz Age and Bathtub Gin—Fitzgerald Stories Re-create an Era," review of 6TJA, Columbia *Missourian*, April 10, 1960, Section B, p. 9.

McCaslin, Walt. Review of 6TJA, Dayton [Ohio] *Daily News*, April 10, 1960, Section 3, p. 22.

P[eck], D[avid] T. "Stories of the Jazz Age Tame by 1960 Standards," review of 6TJA, New Haven [Conn.] *Register*, April 10, 1960, Section 7, p. 8.

H[artmann], F[rederick]. Review of 6TJA, Wilmington [Del.] *Morning News*, April 11, 1960, p. 19.

Review of 6TJA, Charlotte [N.C.] *News*, April 23, 1960, Section A, p. 6.

Meriwether, James B. "The Odds and Ends of Scott Fitzgerald," review of 6TJA, Houston *Post*, May 1, 1960, "Houston Now" Section, p. 22.

"Symbol of Jazz Age," review of 6TJA, Savannah [Ga.] *Morning News*, May 8, 1960, Magazine, p. 12.

Goodspeed, John. "Fitzgerald Stories," review of 6TJA, Baltimore *Sunday Sun*, May 22, 1960, Section A, p. 5.

[Bruccoli, Matthew J.] "*Taps at Reveille*," review of 1960 TAR, *Fitzgerald Newsletter*, No. 10 (Summer 1960), 1–2.

Rodgers, Glen M. "Fitzgerald's Short Fiction," review of 6TJA, *Southwest Review*, 45 (Summer 1960), 283–84.

Didion, J[oan]. Review of 6TJA, *National Review*, 8 (June 18, 1960), 403.

Daniel, Frank. "Fitzgerald Revisited—Life without Price Tags," review of 1960 TAR, Atlanta *Journal and Constitution*, July 24, 1960, p. 2-E.

Minot, George E. "Fitzgerald's Light Bright Despite Years," review of 1960 TAR, Boston *Sunday Herald*, July 24, 1960, Section 3, p. 2.

Shogan, Robert. "Fitzgerald for a New Generation," review of 1960 TAR, Miami [Fla.] *News*, July 24, 1960, p. 6B.

Markson, Robert J. "Echoes of Our Past in Jazz Idiom," review of 6TJA, Sacramento [Calif.] *Bee*, July 31, 1960, "Valley Leisure" Section, p. 27.

Hogan, William. Review of 1960 TAR, San Francisco *Chronicle*, August 1, 1960, p. 29.

Laut, Stephen J., S.J. Review of 1960 TAR, *Best Sellers*, 20 (August 1, 1960), 156.

D[uran], M[arlys]. Review of 1960 TAR, Albuquerque [N. Mex.] *Tribune*, August 6, 1960, Section A, p. 4.

McSherry, Sara. "Collection Is Best of Fitzgerald," review of 1960 TAR, Indianapolis *News*, August 6, 1960, p. 2.

Lubeck, Robert E. "Skill Undimmed by Time," review of 1960 TAR, Detroit *News*, August 7, 1960, p. 13-E.

Brown, David. Review of 1960 TAR, Greenville [Miss.] *Delta Democrat-Times*, August 14, 1960, p. 16.

S[izer], A[lvin] V. "Fitzgerald—Teenage Antics of Jazz Age Seem Dated Now," review of 1960 TAR, New Haven [Conn.] *Register*, August 14, 1960, Section 7, p. 8.

Roll, Florence. Review of 1960 TAR, San Francisco *Call-Bulletin*, August 20, 1960, p. 6.

May, William. "Fitzgerald's Stories," review of 1960 TAR, Newark [N.J.] *Sunday News*, August 21, 1960, Section 3, p. E7.

"Basil Duke Lee Pops Up Again," review of 1960 TAR, Long Beach [Calif.] *Sunday Independent-Press-Telegram*, August 21, 1960, "Southland" Section, p. 28.

"Fitzgerald Stories," review of 1960 TAR, Baltimore *Sun*, August 21, 1960, Section A, p. 5.

Bruccoli, M[atthew] J. "*Taps at Reveille*: Eighteen Short Stories Tell Much of F. Scott Fitzgerald's Life," review of 1960 TAR, Richmond [Va.] *News Leader*, August 24, 1960, p. 11.

De Filippo, Frank. "Drink, Drink, Drink!," review of 1960 TAR, *Catholic Review* [Baltimore], August 26, 1960, p. 9.

B., A. G. Review of 1960 TAR, Charleston [S.C.] *News and Courier*, September 4, 1960, p. 7-C.

Covert, Harry, Jr. "A Collection of Stories by F. Scott Fitzgerald," review of 1960 TAR, Newport News [Va.] *Daily Press*, September 4, 1960, Section D, p. 4.

Thomas, Alma S. "Delineator of the 20's," review of 1960 TAR, Savannah [Ga.] *Morning News*, September 4, 1960, Magazine, p. 10.

Calvin, Tommie. "Tales of Flapper Era from Fitzgerald Pen," review of 1960 TAR, Tulsa [Okla.] *Daily World*, September 11, 1960, "Your World" Section, p. 25.

C[urtis], F[rancis] M. "Fitzgerald Admirers: Attention," review of 1960 TAR, New Bedford [Mass.] *Standard-Times*, September 11, 1960, p. 33.

Duncan, Jacqueline. "Fitzgerald Classic Items Are Reprinted," review of 1960 TAR, Sacramento [Calif.] *Bee*, September 11, 1960, "Valley Leisure" Section, p. 26.

Review of 1960 TAR, *New York Herald Tribune Book Review*, September 25, 1960, p. 15.

Bowers, John. "Fitzgerald Stories Make Book Debut," review of PH, Washington [D.C.] *Post*, July 15, 1962, p. G7.

Bunke, Joan. "Pat Was Good Provider," review of PH, Des Moines [Iowa] *Sunday Register*, July 15, 1962, p. 15-G.

"Collections," review of PH, Boston *Sunday Globe*, July 15, 1962, p. 72-A.

Goodspeed, John. "F. Scott Fitzgerald's Pat Hobby Tales," review of PH, Baltimore *Sun*, July 15, 1962, Section A, p. 5.

Hatfield, Don. "Fitzgerald Farewell—Last Work Not Major," review of PH, Huntington [W. Va.] *Herald-Advertiser*, July 15, 1962, p. 29.

Pine, George J. "Delectably Readable—Scott Fitzgerald's Last Short Tales," review of PH, Boston *Sunday Herald*, July 15, 1962, Section 4, p. 7.

Hogan, William. "Fitzgerald's 'Pat' Stories Collected," review of PH, San Francisco *Chronicle*, July 16, 1962, p. 45.

Mooney, Harry, Jr. "Fitzgerald on Hollywood," review of PH, Pittsburgh *Press*, July 16, 1962, p. 22.

Kupferberg, Herbert. " 'The Pat Hobby Stories,' " review of PH, New York *Herald Tribune*, July 17, 1962, p. 19.

Mariano, Louis. " 'The Pat Hobby Stories'—Fitzgerald's Hollywood," review of PH, Chicago *Daily News*, July 18, 1962, p. 38.

Poore, Charles. "Books of The Times," review of PH, New York *Times*, July 19, 1962, p. 25.

Butcher, Fanny. "Pat Hobby Stories Add Little to Fitzgerald Fame," review of PH, *Chiago Sunday Tribune Magazine of Books*, July 22, 1962, p. 2.

Freshwater, Phillip C. "An Unhappy Journey from NY to Hollywood with Fitzgerald," review of PH, Sacramento [Calif.] *Bee*, July 22, 1962, "Valley Leisure" Section, p. 18.

Hood John. "Swan Songs of Scott Fitzgerald," review of PH, Houston *Chronicle*, July 22, 1962, "TV-Radio Pullout" Section, p. 10.

Jackson, Katherine Gauss. Review of 1960 TAR, *Harper's*, 221 (October 1960), 112.

Nagelschmidt, Joe. Review of 1960 TAR, Chapel Hill [N.C.] *Weekly*, October 6, 1960, p. 8.

Review of 1960 TAR, Louisville [Ky.] *Courier-Journal*, October 16, 1960, Section 4, p. 7.

G[arvick], J[ohn] D. Review of 1960 TAR, *Dateline Delaware*, 1 (November–December 1960), 47.

L., R. Review of 6TJA, *Story*, 33 (November–December 1960), 94.

Olyphant, Winifred R. Review of 1960 TAR, *Nevada State Journal* [Reno], December 25, 1960, p. 5.

Review of 1960 TAR, *English Journal*, 50 (March 1961), 200.

Review of 6TJA, *English Journal*, 50 (March 1961), 220.

Bruccoli, M[atthew] J. "Jazz Age: Selection of Fitzgerald's Stories Inadequate," review of 6TJA, Richmond [Va.] *News Leader*, September 6, 1961, p. 13.

[Bruccoli, Matthew J.] "Review," review of PH, *Fitzgerald Newsletter*, No. 18 (Summer 1962), 1–2.

Pollock, Wilson. "Pat Hobby Rides Again," review of PH, *Partisan Review*, 29 (Summer 1962), 464–65.

Griffin, Lloyd W. Review of PH, *Library Journal*, 87 (July 1962), 2567.

Beau-Seigneur, Jay. "Mr. Hyde," review of PH, Palo Alto [Calif.] *Times*, July 14, 1962, "Peninsula Living" Section, p. 19.

B[rady], C[harles] A. "Fitzgerald Book Details His Final Disillusion," review of PH, Buffalo [N.Y.] *Evening News*, July 14, 1962, p. B-6.

Richards, Keith. "Fitzgerald's 'Pat Hobby' Stories Add Up to Portrait," review of PH, St. Louis *Globe-Democrat*, July 14-15, 1962, p. 4F.

Hoyt, Elizabeth N. "Fitzgerald's Last," review of PH, Cedar Rapids [Iowa] *Gazette*, July 22, 1962, Section C, p. 2.

O'Leary, Theodore M. "Two Burnt Out in Hollywood," review of PH, Kansas City *Star*, July 22, 1962, p. 8E.

"Pat Hobby Stories," review of PH, Philadelphia *Inquirer*, July 22, 1962, Section D, p. 8.

S[izer], A[lvin] V. "Fitzgerald's 'Pot Boilers' Finally Appear in Book Form," review of PH, New Haven [Conn.] *Register*, July 22, 1962, Section 4, p. 6.

Turnbull, Andrew. "The Last Buffoon," review of PH, *New York Times Book Review*, July 22, 1962, p. 6.

Powers, Dennis. "Pat Hobby Stories Were Author's Last," review of PH, Oakland [Calif.] *Tribune*, July 25, 1962, p. 20.

Pearre, Howell. "Important Figure of Contemporary Humor," review of PH, Nashville [Tenn.] *Banner*, July 27, 1962, p. 21.

Boger, Mary Snead. Review of PH, Charlotte [N.C.] *Observer*, July 29, 1962, p. 5-E.

Brown, Leonard. "F. Scott Fitzgerald's Pat Hobby Tales Reprinted," review of PH, Pasadena [Calif.] *Independent Star-News*, July 29, 1962, "Scene" Section, p. 9.

Conant, Mike. "Fitzgerald's Fall," review of PH, Olympia [Wash.] *Sunday Olympian*, July 29, 1962, p. 12.

P[rather], G[ibson]. "Fitzgerald's Last Effort," review of PH, Fayetteville [N.C.] *Observer*, July 29, 1962, Section D, p. 3.

Review of PH, *Critic*, 21 (August–September 1962), 64–65.

Walsh, William J., S.J. Review of PH, *Best Sellers*, 22 (August 1, 1962), 186.

"Wire the Money," review of PH, *Time*, 80 (August 3, 1962), 61.

Staley, Thomas F. Review of PH, Tulsa [Okla.] *World*, August 5, 1962, p. 14.

Powers, Dennis. "Scott Fitzgerald's 'Pat Hobby' Stories,' " review of PH, Oakland [Calif.] *Tribune*, August 10, 1962, p. 24.

Norris, Hoke. "Fitzgerald Canon Completed," review of PH, Chicago *Sun-Times*, August 12, 1962, Section 3, p. 2.

Moore, Harry T. "Behind the Screens Report," review of PH, *Saturday Review*, 45 (August 18, 1962), 32.

"Pat Stories Fill Fitzgerald Gap," review of PH, Syracuse [N.Y.] *Herald*, August 19, 1962, "Stars" Section, p. 4.

Valenti, Michael. "Scott Fitzgerald's Last Stories Are Stripped of Unessentials," review of PH, Louisville [Ky.] *Courier-Journal*, August 19, 1962, Section 4, p. 5.

Davis, Paxton. "No One Is Safe if Successful," review of PH, Roanoke *Times*, August 26, 1962, p. B-8.

L., F. "Fitzgerald Reborn in Pat Hobby," review of PH, Buffalo *Courier-Express*, August 26, 1962, Section D, p. 26.

Conn, Peter J. "Scott Fitzgerald's Last Testimony," review of PH, Providence [R.I.] *Visitor*, August 31, 1962, p. 16.

Review of PH, *Booklist*, 59 (September 1, 1962), 29.

Blizzard, William C. "Fitzgerald's Hollywood Hell," review of PH, Charleston [W.Va.] *Sunday Gazette-Mail*, September 2, 1962, p. 10C.

Dickson, Frank A. "World of Books," review of PH, Anderson [S.C.] *Independent*, September 2, 1962, p. 5.

Gould, Ray. " 'The Pat Hobby Stories,' " review of PH, Montgomery [Ala.] *Advertiser*, September 2, 1962, p. 4E.

Stern, Catherine G. "Scott Fitzgerald's Hollywood Hack," review of PH, Greensboro [N.C.] *Daily News*, September 2, 1962, p. D3.

Review of PH, New Orleans *Times-Picayune*, September 9, 1962, Section 2, p. 19.

Howe, Marjorie. Review of PH, Burlington [Vt.] *Free Press*, September 12, 1962, p. 13.

Wade, Gerald. "Fitzgerald's Last Efforts Not His Best," review of PH, Beaumont [Tex.] *Journal*, September 14, 1962, Section A, p. 21.

Carter, Lane. "Fitzgerald At His Peak in 'Pat Hobby Stories,' " review of PH, Birmingham [Ala.] *News,* September 16, 1962, p. E-6.

M'Clary, Ben. "Huge Talent, Scenario Hack," review of PH, Chattanooga [Tenn.] *Times*, September 30, 1962, p. 18.

Adams, Phoebe. Review of PH, *Atlantic*, 210 (October 1962), 149.

Heath, Gary E. "Readers and Writers," review of PH, St. Albans [Vt.] *Messenger*, October 5, 1962, p. 8.

Price, Ann. "Penetrating, Endearing—Collection of Scott Fitzgerald Funny, Semi-Tragic, Poignant," review of PH, Baton Rouge [La.] *Advocate*, October 14, 1962, p. 2-E.

Wall, Mary R. Review of PH, *Woods County Enterprise* [Waynoka, Okla.], October 25, 1962, p. 9.

Shroyer, Frederick. "Spotlighting the Movie World," review of PH, Los Angeles *Herald Examiner*, November 11, 1962, p. E-7.

Moers, Ellen. "F. Scott Fitzgerald: Reveille at Taps," review of PH, *Commentary*, 34 (December 1962), 526–30.

Review of PH, *Modern Fiction Studies*, 8 (Winter 1962–63), 421.

O'Leary, Theodore M. "But He Has Never Read 'Gone With the Wind,'" review of PH, Kansas City *Star*, December 2, 1962, Section G, p. 1.

Sewell, John B. "Pat Hobby Stories Are Not Great Literature, but They Are Fun," review of PH, Jamestown [N.Y.] *Post-Journal*, December 22, 1962, p. 13M.

Review of PH, *Films in Review*, 14 (May 1963), 298.

White, Terence de Vere. "Whom the Gods Love," review of BH5 & BH6, *Irish Times* [Dublin], October 26, 1963, p. 8.

Rosselli, John. "Collector's Items," review of BH5 & BH6, Manchester *Guardian*, November 1, 1963, p. 17.

"Two into Six," review of BH5 & BH6, *Times Literary Supplement* [London], November 1, 1963, p. 885.

Rees, David. "Trust the Tale," review of PH and BH5 & BH6, *Spectator*, No. 7064 (November 15, 1963), 631–32.

"Scott Fitzgerald," review of BH5 & BH6, *Eastern Daily Press* [Norwich, England], November 21, 1963, Christmas Book Supplement, p. v.

Ellmann, Richard. "A Talent as Big as the Ritz," review of BH5 & BH6, *New Statesman*, n.s. 66 (November 22, 1963), 746.

Nye, Robert. "Only the Hands Were Old," review of BH5 & BH6, *Scotsman* [Edinburgh], November 30, 1963, Week-end Magazine, p. 2.

Richards, Anne. "Short Stories," review of BH5 & BH6, Birmingham [England] *Post*, December 3, 1963, Christmas Books Supplement, p. 4.

Muggeridge, Malcolm. "The Man Who Captured the American Dream," review of BH5 & BH6, London *Evening Standard*, December 17, 1963, p. 14.

"Short and Bitter," review of BH5 & BH6, London *Times*, December 19, 1963, p. 13.

Laws, Frederick. "Books: A Few Well-Chosen Words," review of BH5 & BH6, London *Daily Herald*, January 2, 1964, p. 4.

Clive, Jeremy. "Scott Fitzgerald," review of BH5 & BH6, London *Sunday Times*, January 5, 1964, p. 29.

Barrell, John. "American SF," review of BH5 & BH6, *Granta*, January 25, 1964.

[Bruccoli, Matthew J.] Review of AF, *Fitzgerald Newsletter*, No. 28 (Winter 1965), 1–2.

Review of AF, *Kirkus*, 33 (March 15, 1965), 73.

Dillon, John J. "Fitzgerald's Earliest," review of AF, Baltimore *Sun*, March 21, 1965, Section D, p. 7.

Kirsch, Robert R. "The Book Report," review of AF, Los Angeles *Times*, March 26, 1965, Part 5, p. 4.

Brown Doris E. "Roots of Literary Genius," review of AF, New Brunswick [N.J.] *Sunday Home News*, April 4, 1965, p. 33.

Miller, James E., Jr. "Early Fitzgerald," review of AF, *Chicago Tribune Books Today*, April 4, 1965, p. 10.

La Houd, John. "Evolution of a Talent—Even as a Lad, F. Scott Fitzgerald Flashed Signs of Writing Skill Ahead," review of AF, *National Observer*, April 5, 1965, p. 18.

Thompson, Francis J. "Words About Words and the Men Who Use Words," review of AF, Roanoke [Va.] *Times*, April 18, 1965, p. B-8.

Review of AF, *Booklist*, 61 (May 1, 1965), 584.

Turnbull, Andrew. "Young Man with a Style," review of AF, *New York Times Book Review*, May 2, 1965, pp. 38–39.

Hamlin, William C. "Between Book Ends: Scott Fitzgerald as a Young Man Writing," review of AF, St. Louis *Post-Dispatch*, May 6, 1965, p. 2B.

Carberry, Edward. "Turning New Leaves—Young Man's Fancy," review of AF, Cincinnati *Post & Times Star*, May 8, 1965, "All Week" Magazine, p. 2.

Hicks, Granville. Review of AF, *Saturday Review*, 48 (May 22, 1965), 57.

Littlejohn, David. "A Collection of Fitzgerald's Early Stories," review of AF, *Commonweal*, 82 (June 4, 1965), 358–60. [Reprinted in *Interruptions*. New York: Grossman, 1970, pp. 102–5]

Review of AF, *Modern Fiction Studies*, 11 (Summer 1965), 200.

Review of AF, *Choice*, 2 (July–August 1965), 296.

Pinkerton, Wm. Stewart, Jr. "The Bookshelf: Early Fitzgerald Bears Stamp of Gifted Writer," review of AF, *Wall Street Journal*, July 13, 1965, p. 14.

N., J. R. "More Cheers for F. Scott," review of AF, *Literary Times* [Chicago], September–October 1965.

Bewley, Marius. "Great Scott," review of AF, *New York Review of Books*, September 16, 1965, pp. 22–24. [Reprinted in *Masks and Mirrors: Essays in Criticism*. New York: Atheneum, 1970, pp. 154–59]

Eble, Kenneth E. Review of AF, *College English*, 27 (December 1965), 258.

Eble, Kenneth E. Review of AF, *Western Humanities Review*, 20 (Winter 1966), 89–90.

Bryer, Jackson R. Review of AF, *Studies in Short Fiction*, 3 (Summer 1966), 469–71.

Hedges, Elaine. Review of AF, *Wisconsin Studies in Contemporary Literature*, 7 (Summer 1966), 217–18.

Harris, Robert R. Review of B&J, *Library Journal*, 98 (July 1973), 2071.

Review of B&J, *Kirkus*, 41 (July 1, 1973), 702.

Bannon, Barbara A. Review of B&J, *Publishers Weekly*, 204 (July 16, 1973), 110.

Review of B&J, *Choice*, 10 (September 1973), 974.

Morton, Kathryn. "About Books: Fitzgerald—Our Perpetual Boy Wonder," review of B&J, Norfolk *Virginian-Pilot*, September 23, 1973, p. C6.

Latham, Aaron. "Stories in the Juvenile Tradition," review of B&J, Washington [D.C.] *Post*, September 24, 1973, p. B 4.

Brady, Charles A. "Fitzgerald Memories of Buffalo Boyhood," review of B&J, Buffalo [N.Y.] *Evening News*, September 29, 1973, p. C-12.

Balakian, Nona. "Books of The Times: Beautiful and Undamned," review of B&J, New York *Times*, October 2, 1973, p. 41.

Williams, Erma. "A Fitzgerald Collection: Stories Reproduce His Years as Youth," review of B&J, Buffalo [N.Y.] *Courier-Express*, October 7, 1973, "Focus" Section, p. 16.

"Fitzgerald Frenzy Is Merited," review of B&J, St. Paul [Minn.] *Sunday Pioneer Press*, October 7, 1973, "Focus" Section, p. 8.

Norris, Hoke. "Out of a Dead Past, Fitzgerald's Glittering Boy-Girl Stories," review of B&J, Chicago *Daily News*, October 13–14, 1973, "Panorama" Section, p. 9.

Long, Fern. "Taking a 'Pentimento' Journey," review of B&J, Cleveland *Press*, October 19, 1973, "Showtime" Section, p. 18.

Review of B&J, *New Times*, 1 (October 19, 1973), 32.

Finocchiarro, Ray. "For Fitzgerald Addicts," review of B&J, Wilmington [Del.] *Morning News*, October 25, 1973, p. 59.

Baker, Jackson, "And Yet Another Round of Scott Fitzgerald," review of B&J, Memphis *Commercial Appeal*, October 28, 1973, Section 6, p. 6.

Denison, Paul. "Fitzgerald Prose Still Glows White," review of B&J, Monterey [Calif.] *Sunday Peninsula Herald*, October 28, 1973, p. 8C.

Hartley, Lodwick. "Scott Fitzgerald's 'Basil and Josephine' Tales," review of B&J, Raleigh [N.C.] *News and Observer*, October 28, 1973, p. 6-IV.

"Fitzgerald Remembered," review of B&J, Big Spring [Tex.] *Herald*, November 4, 1973, p. 3-D.

"F. Scott Fitzgerald Stories Lead November List," review of B&J, *Rocky Mountain News* [Denver], November 4, 1973, "Startime" Section, p. 18.

Glotzer, David. "A Fitzgerald Delight," review of B&J, *Valley Advocate* [Amherst, Mass.], November 14, 1973, p. 16.

Sudler, Barbara. " 'Basil and Josephine' Series Put Together," review of B&J, Denver *Sunday Post*, November 25, 1973, "Roundup" Magazine, p. 6.

Nye, Robert. "Money and Scott Fitzgerald," review of *Bits*, *Scotsman* [Edinburgh], December 1, 1973, "The Weekend Scotsman," p. 2.

Toynbee, Philip. "Fitzgerald Industry," review of *Bits*, *Observer* [London], December 2, 1973, p. 36.

Snow, C. P. "Scott and Mrs. Scott," review of *Bits*, *Financial Times* [London], December 6, 1973, p. 18.

Masters, Anthony. "The Myth of Scott and Zelda," review of *Bits*, Birmingham [England] *Post*, December 8, 1973, Saturday Magazine, p. 2.

Dick, Kay. "Monday Books: Gabbling On About Scott," review of *Bits*, London *Times*, December 10, 1973, p. 14.

Kermode, Frank. "Scottie on the Make," review of *Bits*, Manchester [England] *Guardian*, December 22, 1973, p. 25.

Eble, Kenneth. Review of B&J, *Fitzgerald/Hemingway Annual*, 6 (1974), 261–63.

Eble, Kenneth. Review of *Bits*, *Fitzgerald/Hemingway Annual*, 6 (1974), 263–64.

"This Side of Pardise," review of *Bits*, *Times Literary Supplement* [London], January 4, 1974, p. 13.

Cady, Richard. " 'Basil, Josephine Stories' Light Tales by Fitzgerald," review of B&J, Indianapolis *Star*, January 6, 1974, Section 8, p. 5.

Review of B&J, Portland *Sunday Oregonian*, January 6, 1974, "Oregonian SunDAY" Section, p. 19.

Moynihan, John. "Scott on the Rocks," review of *Bits*, London *Sunday Telegraph*, January 13, 1974, p. 14.

Brown, Michael. "Fitzgerald Revival," review of B&J, San Francisco *Chronicle*, January 27, 1974, "This World" Section, p. 25.

Corrin, Stephen. "Agent of Despair," review of *Bits*, London *Daily Telegraph*, January 31, 1974, p. 12.

M[oody], M[innie] H[ite]. "Recent & Readable," review of B&J, Columbus [Ohio] *Sunday Dispatch*, February 3, 1974, p. 7D.

Blumberg, Leslie. "Two Who Never Met," review of B&J, *New Leader*, 57 (February 4, 1974), 25–26.

Seward, William W., Jr. "Fitzgerald's Short Stories," review of B&J, Richmond [Va.] *Times-Dispatch*, February 10, 1974, p. F-3.

Keister, Don A. "Some Lesser Fitzgerald," review of B&J, Cleveland *Plain Dealer*, March 3, 1974, p. 8-F.

Scott, L. Wayne. "Fitzgerald Nostalgia Booms Big," review of B&J, San Antonio [Tex.] *Sunday Express and News*, March 3, 1974, p. 72.

Flora, Joseph M. Review of B&J, *Studies in Short Fiction*, 11 (Spring 1974), 210–12.

[Keegan, Timothy]. Review of B&J, *Jeffersonian Review*, 2 (Spring 1974), 65–66.

Thomas, Phil. "The Short Stories of Scott Fitzgerald," review of B&J, Cincinnati *Enquirer*, April 11, 1974, p. 38.

Jones, Cal. "Devilish Duo's Exploits Relived," review of B&J, Oklahoma City *Sunday Oklahoman*, April 21, 1974, "Showcase" Section, p. 8.

Bell, Michael Davitt. "Fitzgerald's Josephine," review of B&J, *Princeton Alumni Weekly*, 74 (May 28, 1974), unpaged.

Salzman, Jack. "Waiting for Gatsby," review of B&J, *Nation*, 218 (June 1, 1974), 700.

Casper, Leonard. Review of B&J, *Thought*, 49 (September 1974), 330–31.

H[all], R[ichard] R[andall]. "The Fitzgeralds As Collaborators," review of *Bits*, Anniston [Ala.] *Star*, September 29, 1974, Section D, p. 2.

H[obbs], J[ohn]. "Scott's, Zelda's Stories Form 'Bits of Paradise,' " review of *Bits*, Galesburg [Ill.] *Register-Mail*, October 7, 1974, p. 9.

Review of *Bits*, Burlington [Vt.] *Free Press*, October 8, 1974, p. 30.

Corriveau, Verna Cutter. "By Their Life Together," review of *Bits*, Worcester [Mass.] *Sunday Telegram*, October 13, 1974, p. 6E.

Shackelford, Arn. "Some Choice 'Warmed-Over Fare,' " review of *Bits*, Grand Rapids [Mich.] *Press*, October 13, 1974, p. 2-H.

Tolson, Michael. "Book Revives Fitzgerald Works," review of *Bits*, *Daily Texan* [University of Texas, Austin], October 17, 1974, p. 19.

Hagemann, E. R. "Zelda in Writing Glory, and Scott in Her Shadow," review of *Bits*, Louisville [Ky.] *Courier-Journal & Times*, October 20, 1974, p. E 5.

Smith, James M. " 'Bits' Probably the Last of Fitzgerald Canon," review of *Bits*, Nashville *Tennessean*, October, 20, 1974, p. 10-F.

Hogan, William. "World of Books: Fitzgeralds Are Still with Us," review of *Bits*, San Francisco *Chronicle*, October 23, 1974, p. 47.

M[oody], M[innie] H[ite]. Review of *Bits*, Columbus [Ohio] *Sunday Dispatch*, October 27, 1974, p. I-7.

"Two Meteors: Scott and Zelda," review of *Bits*, Savannah [Ga.] *News Press*, October 27, 1974, Magazine, p. 5F.

Meacham, Harry M. "Uncollected Writings: Book Marks End of Fitzgerald Canon," review of *Bits*, Richmond [Va.] *News Leader*, October 30, 1974, p. 13.

Review of B&J, *Journal of Modern Literature*, 4 (November 1974), 322.

Fink, Ira. "Theater—Paradise in Bits and Pieces," review of *Bits*, *Harvard Crimson*, November 12, 1974, p. 2.

Friend, Beverly. "Bits of Paradise—and Bits of Hell," review of *Bits*, Chicago *Daily News*, November 16–17, 1974, "Panorama" Section, p. 7.

Oberbeck, S. K. " 'Writer at Work,' " review of *Bits*, Washington [D.C.] *Post*, November 21, 1974, p. C12.

Scott, Ellen. "Books in Review—You Can Make Book on It: People Love Printed Word," review of *Bits*, Albany [N.Y.] *Times-Union*, December 8, 1974, p. G-8.

Gregg, Louise. "The Flapper Years," review of *Bits*, Wichita Falls [Tex.] *Times*, December 15, 1974, Magazine, p. 4.

Kouidis, Virginia. Review of *Bits*, *Southern Humanities Review*, 11 (Summer 1977), 70–71.

Mangum, Bryant. Review of *Price*, *Fitzgerald/Hemingway Annual*, 10 (1978), 389–95.

Review of *Price*, *Kirkus*, 46 (November 15, 1978), 1263.

Bannon, Barbara A. Review of *Price*, *Publishers Weekly*, 214 (November 20, 1978), 51.

Just, Ward. "Leftovers from the Files of Scott Fitzgerald," review of *Price*, Chicago *Tribune*, December 24, 1978, "Book World" Section, p. 2.

L[atour], M[artine]. Review of *Price*, *Mademoiselle*, 85 (January 1979), 44.

Tavernier-Courbin, Jacqueline. Review of *Price*, *Library Journal*, 104 (January 15, 1979), 210.

Olsen, Carol. Review of *Price*, *Arizona Republic* [Phoenix], January 21, 1979, p. N-8.

Rollings, Alane. "Fitzgerald Wrote Them for Money," review of *Price*, Chicago *Sunday Sun-Times*, January 21, 1979, "Show" Section, p. 8.

Hunter, William B., Jr. "Fitzgerald: A Career's Interesting Leftovers," review of *Price*, Houston *Chronicle*, January 28, 1979, "Zest" Section, p. 15.

Seib, Philip. "Fitzgerald: Fine Even at His Worst," review of *Price*, Dallas *Times Herald*, January 28, 1979, "Perspective" Section, p. 4-G.

Sermon, Charles. "Last of Fitzgerald Is Notable but Not Best," review of *Price*, *State* [Columbia, S.C.], January 28, 1979, Section E, p. 4-E.

Manning, Margaret. "No Rest for Fitzgerald," review of *Price*, Boston *Globe*, February 1, 1979, p. 20.

B[arkham], J[ohn]. "No Masterpieces in Fitzgerald's 49 Magazine Stories," review of *Price*, Youngstown [Ohio] *Vindicator*, February 4, 1979, p. B-4.

Dretzka, Gary. "The Last Word(s) on Fitzgerald," review of *Price*, Los Angeles *Herald-Examiner*, February 4, 1979, p. F-12.

Harris, Roger. "The Book Shelf: Scholar Spins a Fascinating Mystery Web," review of *Price*, Newark [N.J.] *Sunday Star-Ledger*, February 4, 1979, Section 4, p. 24.

Yardley, Jonathan. " 'New' Fitzgerald: Shining Moments at a High Cost," review of *Price*, Washington [D.C.] *Sunday Star*, February 4, 1979, pp. E-1, E-8.

Cook, Malcolm. "No Dumb Dolls," review of *Price*, *Village Voice* [New York], 24 (February 5, 1979), 73, 82.

Fox, Thomas, "Written to Pay the Bills," review of *Price*, Memphis *Commercial Appeal*, February 11, 1979, Section G, p. 6.

Latham, Aaron. "Slick Fiction from F. Scott Fitzgerald," review of *Price*, Washington [D.C.] *Post*, February 11, 1979, "Book World" Section, pp. 1, 4.

Wilson, Leon. "Wildly Uneven Fitzgerald Tales," review of *Price*, San Francisco *Sunday Examiner & Chronicle*, February 11, 1979, "This World" Section, p. 53.

Mysak, Joe. "American Writers of 20's and 30's: Yet Another Fitzgerald Book," review of *Price*, *Columbia Spectator* [Columbia University, New York], February 13, 1979, p. 5.

B[utscher], E[dward]. Review of *Price*, *Booklist*, 75 (February 15, 1979), 913–14.

Boardman, Kathryn. "49 Fitzgerald Short Stories in Collection," review of *Price*, Macon [Ga.] *Telegraph & News*, February 18, 1979, Section F, p. 3.

Brown, Dennis. "Fitzgerald by the Yard," review of *Price*, St. Louis *Post-Dispatch*, February 18, 1979, p. 4C.

Buchanan, Bill. "Last Scott Fitzgerald Collection Is a Bust," review of *Price*, Nashville *Tennessean*, February 18, 1979, p. 10-F.

Gervais, Ronald J. "Fitzgerald's Lesser Works Re-Examined," review of *Price*, San Diego *Union*, February 18, 1979, "Currents in Books" Section, pp. 1, 4.

Noland, Thomas. "Fitzgerald's Short Stories—Writer Paid the Price," review of *Price*, Anniston [Ala.] *Star*, February 18, 1979, Section L, p. 2.

Pintarich, Paul. "Writing Good for Study—Stories by Fitzgerald Prove Disappointing," review of *Price*, Portland *Sunday Oregonian*, February 18, 1979, p. D4.

Williams, Paul. " 'The Price Was High'—Will Appeal to Scholars and Fitzgerald Lovers," review of *Price*, Quincy [Mass.] *Patriot Ledger*, February 23, 1979, "Limelight" Section, p. 19.

Anderson, David. "Short Stories with a Touch of Class—Fitzgerald's Prose Is Still Fresh," review of *Price*, San Jose [Calif.] *Mercury News*, February 25, 1979, p. 8B.

Hibbert, Dorothy. "A Desperate Search for Pleasure—Memorable Fitzgerald Stories Mirror the '20s and '30s," review of *Price*, Atlanta *Journal and Constitution*, February 25, 1979, p. 5E.

Milazzo, Lee. "F. Scott Fitzgerald: He Truly Wrote to Live," review of *Price*, Dallas *Morning News*, February 25, 1979, p. 4G.

Stiles, Lehman. "Fitzgerald Stories a Curious Mix," review of *Price*, *Gamecock* [University of South Carolina, Columbia], March 2, 1979, p. 14.

Cowley, Malcolm. "A Book of Last Things," review of *Price*, *New York Times Book Review*, March 4, 1979, p. 7.

Fuller, Richard. ". . . and Checks and Balances of Scott," review of *Price*, Philadelphia *Inquirer*, March 4, 1979, p. 12-H.

Jaynes, Roger. "More Good Fitzgerald," review of *Price*, Milwaukee *Journal*, March 4, 1979, Lively Arts Section, p. 5.

Fanzone, Joseph, Jr. "Fitzgerald and Adolescence Mingle in the Memory," review of *Price*, Baltimore *Sunday Sun*, March 11, 1979, p. D5.

Vogel, Jim. "Bad Collection of Fitzgerald Not Too Bad," review of *Price*, Memphis *Press-Scimitar*, March 17, 1979, p. 8.

Kirsch, Robert. "Fitzgerald's Short Stories: A Master at Work for the Masses," review of *Price*, Los Angeles *Times*, March 18, 1979, Book Review Section, pp. 1, 8.

Kloer, Phil. " 'Price Was High' Has Beauty, Tragedy," review of *Price*, Jacksonville [Fla.] *Times-Union and Journal*, March 18, 1979, p. G-7.

Lavine, Harold. "Fitzgerald Payed [*sic*] High Price For Fortunes," review of *Price*, *Arizona Republic* [Phoenix], March 18, 1979, p. ET-8.

Mintz, Phil. "Fitzgerald's Potboilers," review of *Price*, *Newsday* [Garden City, N.Y.], March 18, 1979, "Ideas" Section, p. 18.

Dugas, Joseph H. Review of *Price*, Grand Rapids [Mich.] *Press*, March 25, 1979, p. 7-G.

Thomas, Phil. "F. Scott Fitzgerald Wrote for Money," review of *Price*, Omaha *Sunday World-Herald*, March 25, 1979, Magazine Section, p. 38.

Wukas, Mark. "Scott's Shorts—Leftovers Need Salt, Pepper," review of *Price*, *The Daily Illini* [University of Illinois, Champaign-Urbana], March 31, 1979, Spectrum Section, p. 9.

Bonham, Roger. "Bruccoli-Edited Works Add to Writers' Canon," review of *Price*, Columbus [Ohio] *Dispatch*, April 1, 1979, p. K-8.

Hagemann, E. R. "Fitzgerald Potboilers Unearthed," review of *Price*, Louisville [Ky.] *Courier-Journal*, April 15, 1979, p. D 5.

Feeney, Joseph J., S.J. Review of *Price*, *Best Sellers*, 39 (May 1979), 42.

Peabody, Richard. Review of *Price*, *Washington Book Review*, 1 (May 1979), 16.

Staley, Thomas F. Review of *Price*, Tulsa [Okla.] *Home & Garden*, 3 (May 1979), 72–73.

Marder, Dan. Review of *Price*, Tulsa [Okla.] *World*, May 13, 1979, Section F, p. 3.

Benson, Joseph. "Fitzgerald's Fine Forty-Nine," review of *Price*, Greensboro [N.C.] *Daily News*, May 27, 1979, p. G5.

Powell, Larry. "Scott Fitzgerald: The Other Stories," review of *Price*, Savannah [Ga.] *News-Press*, June 3, 1979, p. 5G.

Hart, Jeffrey. "Swell Letters—Tough Professional," review of *Price*, *National Review*, 31 (June 8, 1979), 750–51.

Middleton, Harry. "The Last of All Scott Fitzgerald Had to Say," review of *Price*, *Figaro* [New Orleans], June 25, 1979, p. 35.

Pye, Michael. "Short Stories—Autopsy on Fitzgerald," review of *Price*, *Now!*, 2 (September 21, 1979), 105.

Review of *Price*, *Harpers and Queen*, October 1979, p. 276.

Reynolds, Stanley. "Cracked Up, Still Tops," review of *Price*, *New Society*, 50 (October 4, 1979), 32.

McNeil, Helen. "Dream Factory," review of *Price*, *New Statesman*, n.s. 98 (October 5, 1979), 520.

Keates, Jonathan. "Fitzgerald's Leftovers," review of *Price*, *Literary Review*, No. 3 (November 2–15, 1979), 8–9.

Blythe, Ronald. "Fitzgerald's Dream-Men," review of *Price*, *Listener*, 102 (November 15, 1979), 685–86.

Reynolds, Stanley. "Good Times, Bad Times," review of *Price*, Manchester [England] *Guardian*, November 21, 1979, p. 16.

Burgess, Anthony. "Dollars and Dolours," review of *Price*, *Observer* [London], December 2, 1979, p. 36.

Review of *Price*, *Queen's Quarterly*, 86 (Winter 1979/80), 739.

Milicia, Joe. Review of *Price*, *Studies in Short Fiction*, 17 (Winter 1980), 87–88.

Lothian, Andrew. Review of *Price*, *Blackwood's Magazine*, 327 (May 1980), 399–400.

Hill, Barry. "Domestic Chronicles and Crass Regurgitations," review of *Price*, *National Times* [Sydney, Australia], July 13, 1980, p. 47.

VII. Criticism, Explication, and Commentary on Individual Stories, Listed by Story— Including Specific Articles, Segments from Books on Fitzgerald's Work, and Segments from General Books

Each title below is followed by parentheses containing the following information: (date of composition/date of first publication/place of first publication/ abbreviations of Fitzgerald story collections in which the story has been reprinted). Items below which consist of last names followed by page numbers refer to books solely devoted to Fitzgerald's works; complete publication information for these books is given in Section II of this checklist. Again because comment on Fitzgerald's stories is so rare, relatively little selectivity has been exercised in determining what to include; all but the most descriptive or brief mentions have been listed. For information on the unpublished stories, see Jennifer McCabe Atkinson's "Lost and Unpublished Stories by F. Scott Fitzgerald," *Fitzgerald/Hemingway Annual*, 3 (1971), 32–63.

1. **Absolution**

(June 1923/June 1924/*American Mercury*/ASYM, LT, *Portable*, BT, *Stories*, *Babylon*, BH5, *Reader*, Penguin4, Ab)

Allen, pp. 93–101.

Bruccoli (*Composition*), p. 28.

Bruccoli (*Epic Grandeur*), pp. 191–92.

Cross, pp. 73–74.

Cushman, Keith. "Scott Fitzgerald's Scrupulous Meanness: 'Absolution' and 'The Sisters,' " *Fitzgerald/Hemingway Annual*, 11 (1979), 115–21.

Eble (*Fitzgerald*), pp. 32–33, 106.

Gallo, pp. 92–94.

Hagemann, E. R. " 'Small *Latine*' in the Three Printings of F. Scott Fitzgerald's 'Absolution,' " *Notes on Modern American Literature*, 4 (Spring 1980), Item 7.

Higgins, pp. 65–67.

Kuehl, John. "A la Joyce: The Sisters Fitzgerald's Absolution," *James Joyce Quarterly*, 2 (Fall 1964), 2–6.

LaHurd, Ryan. " 'Absolution': *Gatsby*'s Forgotten Front Door," *College Literature*, 3 (Spring 1976), 113–23.

Lehan, p. 105.

Long, pp. 71–77.

Martin, Robert A. "The Hot Madness of Four O'Clock in Fitzgerald's 'Absolution' and *Gatsby*," *Studies in American Fiction*, 2 (Autumn 1974), 230–38.

Miller, pp. 103–5.

Mizener (*Far Side*), p. 214.

Morrison, Gail Moore. "Faulkner's Priests and Fitzgerald's 'Absolution,' " *Mississippi Quarterly*, 32 (Summer 1979), 461–65.

Morse, J. I. "Fitzgerald's *Sagitta Volante in Dei:* An Emendation and a Possible Source," *Fitzgerald/Hemingway Annual*, 4 (1972), 321–22.

Perosa, pp. 59–60.

Piper, pp. 103–7.

Rideout, Walter B., and James K. Robinson, eds. *A College Book of Modern Fiction*. Evanston, Ill.: Row, Peterson, 1961, p. 642.

Sklar, pp. 159–60.

Stavola, Thomas J. *Scott Fitzgerald: Crisis in an American Identity*. New York: Barnes & Noble, 1979, pp. 125–29.

Stewart, Lawrence D. " 'Absolution' and *The Great Gatsby*," *Fitzgerald/ Hemingway Annual*, 5 (1973), 181–87.

Way, pp. 80–82.

West, p. 33.

2. **The Adjuster**

(December 1924/September 1925/*Red Book*/ASYM, *Diamond*, 6TJA, BH3)

Bruccoli (*Epic Grandeur*), p. 212.

Cross, p. 75.

Eble (*Fitzgerald*), pp. 104–5.

Goldhurst, pp. 197–200.

Higgins, pp. 90–91.

Hindus, pp. 32–33.

Mizener (*Far Side*), p. 214.

Sklar, p. 203.

3. **The Adolescent Marriage**

(December 1925/March 6, 1926/*Saturday Evening Post*/Price)

Bruccoli (*Price*), p. 203.

Higgins, p. 95.

Sklar, p. 216.

4. **An Alcoholic Case**

(December 1936/February 1937/*Esquire*/*Stories*, BH2, Penguin1, BH6)

Higgins, p. 166.

Perosa, p. 143.

5. **An Author's Mother**

(1936/September 1936/*Esquire*/Price)

Bruccoli (*Composition*), p. 22.

Bruccoli (*Epic Grandeur*), p. 409.

Bruccoli (*Price*), p. 736.

Higgins, p. 164.

6. **At Your Age**

(June 1929/August 17, 1929/*Saturday Evening Post*/Price)

Bruccoli (*Composition*), p. 84.

Bruccoli (*Epic Grandeur*), pp. 281–82.
Bruccoli (*Price*), p. 278.
Higgins, pp. 112–13.
Linn, James Weber, and Houghton Wells Taylor. *A Foreword to Fiction.*
New York: D. Appleton-Century, 1935, pp. 73–75.
Sklar, p. 236.

7. **Babes in the Woods**
(January 1917/May 1917/*Nassau Literary Magazine*/AF)
Bruccoli (*Epic Grandeur*), p. 71.
Higgins, pp. 8–9.
Kuehl, pp. 13–14, 124–31.
Piper, pp. 32–35.
West, pp. 41–42.

8. **Babylon Revisited**
(December 1930/February 21, 1931/*Saturday Evening Post*/ TAR,
Portable, Diamond, BT, *Stories, Babylon*, BH4, BH6, *Reader*, Penguin2,
Selected, Ab, FeH)
Allen, pp. 119–21.
Bruccoli (*Composition*), pp. 72–73.
Bruccoli (*Epic Grandeur*), p. 309.
[Bruccoli, Matthew J.] "Misinformation," *Fitzgerald Newsletter*, No. 24
(Winter 1964), 6.
Cross, pp. 93–94.
Eble (*Fitzgerald*), pp. 130–31.
Gallo, pp. 101–5.
Gervais, Ronald J. "The Snow of Twenty-Nine: 'Babylon Revisited' as *ubi
sunt* Lament," *College Literature*, 7 (Winter 1980), 47–52.
Gessner, Robert. *The Moving Image: A Guide to Cinematic Literacy.*
New York: E.P. Dutton, 1968, pp. 240–48.
Griffith, Richard R. "A Note on Fitzgerald's 'Babylon Revisited,' " *American Literature*, 35 (May 1963), 236–39.
Gross, Seymour L. "Fitzgerald's 'Babylon Revisited,' " *College English*,
25 (November 1963), 128–35.
Hagopian, John V. "A Prince in Babylon," *Fitzgerald Newsletter*, No. 19
(Fall 1962), 1–3.
Harrison, James M. "Fitzgerald's 'Babylon Revisited,' " *Explicator*, 16
(January 1958), Item 20.
Higgins, pp. 121–24.
Hoffman, Frederick J. *The Twenties.* New York: Viking Press, 1955, pp.
371–72.
Johnson, Ira. "Roundheads and Royalty in 'Babylon,' " *English Record*,
14 (October 1963), 32–35.
Kennedy, James G., ed. *Stories East and West.* Glenview, Ill.: Scott,
Foresman, 1971, pp. 255–57.
Lehan, pp. 144–46.

Lindfors, Bernth. "Paris Revisited," *Fitzgerald Newsletter*, No. 16 (Winter 1962), 4.

Ludwig, Jack Barry, and W. Richard Poirier. *Instructor's Manual to Accompany "Stories: British and American."* Boston: Houghton Mifflin, 1953, pp. 17–18.

McCollum, Kenneth. " 'Babylon Revisited' Revisited," *Fitzgerald/Hemingway Annual*, 3 (1971), 314–16.

Male, Roy R. " 'Babylon Revisited': A Story of the Exile's Return," *Studies in Short Fiction*, 2 (Spring 1965), 270–77.

Maugham, W. Somerset, ed. *Great Modern Reading*. Garden City, N.Y.: Nelson Doubleday, 1943, p. 157.

Mizener (*Far Side*), p. 284.

Morgan, Wanda. "Fitzgerald's Babylon," in *Increase in Learning: Essays in Honor of James G. Van Buren*, eds. Robert J. Owens, Jr., and Barbara E. Hamm. Manhattan, Kan.: Manhattan Christian College, [c. 1979], pp. 37–42.

North, Paul H., Jr. "Another Note on the ASE," *American Book Collector*, 15 (November 1964), 25.

Osborne, William R. "The Wounds of Charlie Wales in Fitzgerald's 'Babylon Revisited,' " *Studies in Short Fiction*, 2 (Fall 1964), 86–87.

Perosa, pp. 95–98.

Piper, pp. 165–66.

Schrader, Richard J. "F and Charles G. Norris," *Fitzgerald Newsletter*, No. 26 (Summer 1964), 3–4.

[Schramm, Wilbur L.] *"Babylon Revisited,"* in *50 Best American Short Stories: 1915–1939*, ed. Edward J. O'Brien. Boston: Houghton Mifflin, 1939, pp. 899–900.

Shain, p. 39.

Sklar, pp. 243–45.

Slattery, Sister Margaret Patrice. "The Function of Time in GG and 'Babylon,' " *Fitzgerald Newsletter*, No. 39 (Fall 1967), 1–4.

Staley, Thomas F. "Time and Structure in Fitzgerald's 'Babylon Revisited,' " *Modern Fiction Studies*, 10 (Winter 1964–65), 386–88.

Toor, David. "Guilt and Retribution in 'Babylon Revisited,' " *Fitzgerald/Hemingway Annual*, 5 (1973), 155–64.

Twitchell, James B. " 'Babylon Revisited': Chronology and Characters," *Fitzgerald/Hemingway Annual*, 10 (1978), 155–60.

Way, pp. 90–92.

White, William. "Mr. North, Mr. Bruccoli and Mr. Fitzgerald," *American Book Collector*, 15 (November 1964), 25–26.

White, William. "The Text of 'Babylon Revisited,' " *Fitzgerald Newsletter*, No. 28 (Winter 1965), 4–7.

White, William. "Two Versions of F. Scott Fitzgerald's 'Babylon Revisited': A Textual and Bibliographical Study," *Papers of the Bibliographical Society of America*, 60 (Fourth Quarter 1966), 439–52.

9. **The Baby Party**
   (February 1924/February 1925/*Hearst's International*/ASYM, *Portable, Stories,* BH5, Penguin4, *Selected,* FeH)
   Cross, p. 75.
   Current-Garcia, Eugene, and Walton R. Patrick, eds. *American Short Stories: 1820 to the Present.* Chicago: Scott, Foresman, 1952, pp. 289–90.
   Dashiell, Alfred. *Editor's Choice.* New York: G.P. Putnam's, 1934, p. 190.
   Early, James, et al., eds. *Adventures in American Literature.* New York: Harcourt, Brace & World, 1968, p. 558.
   Eble (*Fitzgerald*), pp. 104–5.
   Higgins, pp. 72–73.
   Kennedy, X. J. *Instructor's Manual to Accompany "An Introduction to Fiction."* Boston: Little, Brown, 1976, p. 13.
   Kennedy, X. J., ed. *An Introduction to Fiction.* Boston: Little, Brown, 1976, pp. 90, 103–4.
   Rehder, Jessie, ed. *The Story at Work: An Anthology.* New York: Odyssey Press, 1963, p. 40.

10. **Basil and Cleopatra**
    (February 1929/April 27, 1929/*Saturday Evening Post*/AA, *Reader,* B&J)
    Cross, p. 93.
    Eble (*Fitzgerald*), pp. 30–32.
    Higgins, p. 108.
    Perosa, pp. 90–91.

11. **Benediction** (revised from "The Ordeal")
    (October 1919/February 1920/*Smart Set*/F&P)
    Allen pp. 43–45.
    Eble (*Fitzgerald*), p. 58.
    Higgins, pp. 17–18.
    Perosa, pp. 30–31.
    Sklar, pp. 13, 65–66.

12. **Bernice Bobs Her Hair**
    (January 1920/May 1, 1920/*Saturday Evening Post*/F&P, *Stories,* BH5, Penguin4)
    Bruccoli (*Epic Grandeur*), p. 112.
    Bruccoli, Matthew J. "On F. Scott Fitzgerald and 'Bernice Bobs Her Hair,' " in *The American Short Story,* ed. Calvin Skaggs. New York: Dell, 1977, pp. 219–22.
    Eble (*Fitzgerald*), pp. 58–59, 64–65.
    Higgins, pp. 23–24.
    Perosa, p. 31.
    Piper, p. 67.
    Shain, p. 26.
    Sklar, p. 68.
    Way, pp. 56–57.

13. **Between Three and Four**
    (June 1931/September 5, 1931/*Saturday Evening Post/Price*)
    Bruccoli (*Price*), p. 339.
    Higgins, p. 150.
    Sklar, pp. 245–46.
14. **"Boil Some Water—Lots of It"**
    (September 1939/March 1940/*Esquire*/AA, PH, BH6, Penguin3)
    Higgins, pp. 173–74.
    Perosa, p. 150.
15. **The Bowl**
    (November 1927/January 21, 1928/*Saturday Evening Post*/BH5, *Price*)
    Bruccoli (*Price*), p. 256.
    Higgins, pp. 100–1.
    Sklar, p. 230.
    Way, pp. 74–75.
16. **The Bridal Party**
    (May 1930/August 9, 1930/*Saturday Evening Post/Stories*, BH6, Penguin5, FeH)
    Bruccoli (*Epic Grandeur*), p. 293.
    Eble (*Fitzgerald*), pp. 123–24.
    Higgins, pp. 119–20.
    Hindus, pp. 104–5.
    Perosa, p. 87.
    Sklar, p. 242.
17. **The Camel's Back**
    (January 1920/April 24, 1920/*Saturday Evening Post*/TJA, BT, 6TJA)
    Bruccoli (*Epic Grandeur*), p. 113.
    Cross, p. 42.
    Higgins, p. 24.
    Hindus, p. 106.
    Margolies, Alan. " 'The Camel's Back' and *Conductor 1492*," *Fitzgerald/Hemingway Annual*, 6 (1974), 87–88.
    Perosa, p. 31.
    Piper, p. 67.
    Sklar, pp. 67–68.
    Williams, Blanche Colton. *O. Henry Memorial Award Prize Stories—1920*. Garden City, N.Y.: Doubleday, Page, 1921, p. xiii.
18. **The Captured Shadow**
    (September 1928/December 29, 1928/*Saturday Evening Post*/TAR, *Stories*, BH6, *Selected*, B&J)
    Eble (*Fitzgerald*), p. 28.
    Perosa, p. 90.
19. **A Change of Class**
    (July 1931/September 26, 1931/*Saturday Evening Post/Price*)
    Bruccoli (*Price*), p. 352.
    Higgins, pp. 150–51.
    Sklar, p. 246.

20. **The Count of Darkness**
    (October 1934/June 1935/*Redbook*)
    Goldhurst, pp. 172–73.
    Perosa, pp. 134–35.
21. **The Couple** (Unpublished)
    (?/ . . . / . . .)
22. **Crazy Sunday**
    (January 1932/October 1932/*American Mercury*/TAR, LT, *Portable*,
    Diamond, BT, *Stories*, BH1, *Babylon*, Penguin1, BH6, *Reader*,
    Penguin5)
    Bruccoli, (*Composition*), p. 84.
    Bruccoli (*Epic Grandeur*), pp. 323–24.
    Cross, p. 95.
    Eble (*Fitzgerald*), pp. 125–26.
    Gallo, pp. 97–99.
    Higgins, pp. 127–28, 152–54.
    Johnston, Kenneth. "Fitzgerald's 'Crazy Sunday': Cinderella in Holly-
    wood," *Literature/Film Quarterly*, 6 (Summer 1978), 214–21.
    Latham, pp. 70–75.
    Lehan, p. 163.
    Perosa, pp. 99–100.
    Piper, p. 167.
    Taylor, Dwight. "Scott Fitzgerald in Hollywood," *Harper's*, 218 (March
    1959), 67–71. [Reprinted in *Joy Ride*. New York: G.P. Putnam's, 1959,
    pp. 234–50]
    Way, pp. 93–95.
23. **The Curious Case of Benjamin Button**
    (February 1922/May 27, 1922/*Collier's*/TJA, BH3, 6TJA)
    Bruccoli (*Epic Grandeur*), pp. 138, 169.
    Crosland, Andrew. "Sources for Fitzgerald's 'The Curious Case of Benja-
    min Button,' " *Fitzgerald/Hemingway Annual*, 11 (1979), 135–39.
    Cross, p. 42.
    Eble (*Fitzgerald*), p. 79.
    Gery, John. "The Curious Grace of Benjiman [*sic*] Button," *Studies in
    Short Fiction*, 17 (Fall 1980), 495–97.
    Harris, Mark, Josephine Harris, and Hester Harris, eds. *The Design of
    Fiction*. New York: Thomas Y. Crowell, 1976, pp. 479–80.
    Higgins, pp. 58–59.
    Hindus, pp. 106–7.
    Lehan, p. 103.
    Perosa, p. 55.
24. **The Cut-Glass Bowl**
    (October 1919/June 1920/*Scribner's Magazine*/F&P, *Portable*, BT, BH3,
    Penguin1)
    Cross, p. 33.
    Eble (*Fitzgerald*), pp. 57–58.

Gallo, pp. 85–87.
Higgins, pp. 18–19.
Mizener (*Far Side*), p. 160.
Perosa, p. 35.
Shain, p. 27.
Sklar, p. 67.

25. **Cyclone in Silent Land** (Unpublished)
    (1936/ . . . / . . .)
26. **Daddy Was Perfect** (Unpublished)
    (1934/ . . . / . . .)
27. **Dalyrimple Goes Wrong**
    (September 1919/February 1920/*Smart Set*/F&P)
    Cross, pp. 33–34.
    Eble (*Fitzgerald*), p. 66.
    Higgins, pp. 16–17.
    Mizener (*Far Side*), p. 160.
    Perosa, p. 34.
    Shain, p. 27.
    Sklar, pp. 64–65.
28. **The Dance**
    (January 1926/June 1926/*Red Book*/*Bits, BitsP*)
    Bruccoli (*Epic Grandeur*), p. 246.
    Higgins, pp. 95–96.
    Sklar, p. 216.
29. **Dearly Beloved**
    (January–February 1940/1969/*Fitzgerald/Hemingway Annual/Bits, BitsP*)
    Bruccoli (*Epic Grandeur*), p. 473.
    Mangum, Bryant. "The Reception of *Dearly Beloved*," *Fitzgerald/ Hemingway Annual*, 2 (1970), 241–44.
    West, James L. W., III. "F. Scott Fitzgerald to Arnold Gingrich: A Composition Date for 'Dearly Beloved,' " *Publications of the Bibliographical Society of America*, 67 (Fourth Quarter 1973), 452–54.
30. **A Debt of Honor**
    (1909–1910/March 1910/*St. Paul Academy Now and Then*/AF)
    Higgins, pp. 3–4.
    Kuehl, pp. 34–35.
31. **Design in Plaster**
    (July 1939/November 1939/*Esquire*/AA, BH6)
    Bruccoli (*Epic Grandeur*), p. 471.
    Higgins, pp. 168–69.
    Perosa, p. 144.
    Sklar, p. 326.
32. **Diagnosis**
    (October 1931/February 20, 1932/*Saturday Evening Post*/Price)
    Bruccoli (*Price*), p. 402.

Eble (*Fitzgerald*), p. 122.

Higgins, pp. 151–52.

33. **The Diamond as Big as the Ritz**
    (October 1921/June 1922/*Smart Set*/TJA, LT, *Diamond*, BT, *Stories*, BH1, *Babylon*, Penguin1, BH5, *Selected*)
    Allen, pp. 85–88.

    Bewley, Marius. "Scott Fitzgerald and the Collapse of the American Dream," in *The Eccentric Design*. New York: Columbia University Press, 1959, pp. 259–87.

    Bloom, Nancy. "Coincidence: *21 Balloons* & 'Diamond,' " *Fitzgerald Newsletter*, No. 28 (Winter 1965), 3.

    Bruccoli (*Epic Grandeur*), pp. 160–61.

    Cross, pp. 45–50.

    Eble (*Fitzgerald*), pp. 79–81.

    Gallo, pp. 82–85.

    Higgins, pp. 55–57.

    Holmes, Charles S. "Fitzgerald: The American Theme," *Pacific Spectator*, 6 (Spring 1952), 243–52.

    Kelley, David J. F. "The Polishing of 'Diamond,' " *Fitzgerald Newsletter*, No. 40 (Winter 1968), 1–2.

    Latham, p. 38.

    Lehan, pp. 103–4.

    Long, pp. 60–67.

    Miller, pp. 56–59.

    Mordden, Ethan. *That Jazz!* New York: G.P. Putnam's, 1978, pp. 163–64.

    Perosa, pp. 55–57.

    Piper, pp. 77–78.

    Shain, p. 28.

    Sklar, pp. 140–47.

    Spatz, Jonas. "Fitzgerald, Hollywood, and the Myth of Success," in *The Thirties: Fiction, Poetry, Drama*, ed. Warren French. Deland, Fla.: Everett/Edwards, 1967, pp. 31–37.

    Way, pp. 67–71.

34. **Diamond Dick and the First Law of Woman**
    (December 1923/April 1924/*Hearst's International*/*Price*)
    Bruccoli (*Price*), p. 69.

    Higgins, pp. 68–70.

    Jones, Daryl E. "Fitzgerald and Pulp Fiction: From Diamond Dick to Gatsby," *Fitzgerald/Hemingway Annual*, 10 (1978), 137–39.

35. **Dice, Brass Knuckles & Guitar**
    (January 1923/May 1923/*Hearst's International*/*BitsP*, *Price*)
    Bruccoli (*Epic Grandeur*), p. 180–81.

    Bruccoli (*Price*), p. 47.

    Eble (*Fitzgerald*), p. 77.

Higgins, pp. 62–64.

Perosa, p. 55.

36. **Discard** ("Director's Special")

    (July 1939/January 1948/*Harper's Bazaar*/*Price*, as "Discard [Director's Special]")

    Bruccoli (*Price*), p. 764.

    Higgins, pp. 179–80.

    Sklar, p. 326.

37. **Emotional Bankruptcy**

    (June 1931/August 15, 1931/*Saturday Evening Post*/B&J)

    Bruccoli (*Composition*), p. 72.

    Eble (*Fitzgerald*), pp. 118–19.

    Higgins, p. 117.

    Lehan, pp. 57–58.

    Perosa, pp. 92–93.

    Sklar, p. 241.

38. **The End of Hate**

    (August 1936, June 1939/June 22, 1940/*Collier's*/*Price*)

    Bruccoli (*Price*), p. 740.

    Higgins, p. 179.

39. **The Family Bus**

    (September 1933/November 4, 1933/*Saturday Evening Post*/*Price*)

    Bruccoli (*Price*), p. 488.

    Higgins, p. 157.

40. **Family in the Wind**

    (April 1932/June 4, 1932/*Saturday Evening Post*/TAR, *Stories*, BH6, *Reader*)

    Bruccoli (*Epic Grandeur*), p. 331.

    Cross, pp. 94–95.

    Eble (*Fitzgerald*), pp. 122, 127.

    Gallo, pp. 99–101.

    Higgins, pp. 126–27.

    Mizener (*Far Side*), pp. 284–85.

    Perosa, pp. 98–99.

    Piper, p. 168.

41. **Fate in Her Hands**

    (June–July 1935/April 1936/*American Magazine*/*Price*)

    Bruccoli (*Price*), p. 646.

    Higgins, p. 178.

42. **The Fiend**

    (September 1934/January 1935/*Esquire*/TAR)

    Higgins, pp. 160–61.

    Perosa, pp. 136–37.

43. **Financing Finnegan**

    (June 1937/January 1938/*Esquire*/*Stories*, BH2, BH6, *Reader*, *Penguin2*,

FeH)
Bruccoli (*Epic Grandeur*), p. 417.
Higgins, pp. 167–68.
Lehan, p. 57.
Perosa, pp. 143–44.
Way, p. 97.
44. **First Blood**
   (January 1930/April 5, 1930/*Saturday Evening Post*/TAR, BH6, B&J)
   Bruccoli (*Composition*), p. 69.
   Eble (*Fitzgerald*), p. 116.
   Higgins, pp. 115–16.
   Perosa, pp. 91–92.
45. **Flight and Pursuit**
   (April 1931/May 14, 1932/*Saturday Evening Post*/Price)
   Bruccoli (*Price*), p. 308.
   Higgins, pp. 149–50.
46. **Forging Ahead**
   (January 1929/March 30, 1929/*Saturday Evening Post*/AA, B&J)
   Eble (*Fitzgerald*), pp. 29–30.
   Higgins, p. 108.
   Perosa, p. 90.
   Scharnhorst, Gary. "Scribbling Upward: Fitzgerald's Debt of Honor to
   Horatio Alger, Jr.," *Fitzgerald/Hemingway Annual*, 10 (1978), 161–69.
47. **The Four Fists**
   (May 1919/June 1920/*Scribner's Magazine*/F&P)
   Bruccoli (*Epic Grandeur*), p. 129.
   Eble (*Fitzgerald*), pp. 59–60.
   Higgins, p. 15.
   Perosa, pp. 31–32.
   Piper, p. 71.
   Sklar, p. 67.
48. **A Freeze-Out**
   (September 1931/December 19, 1931/*Saturday Evening Post*/Price)
   Bruccoli (*Price*), p. 382
   Higgins, p. 126.
49. **The Freshest Boy**
   (April 1928/July 28, 1928/*Saturday Evening Post*/TAR, *Portable, Stories,
   Babylon*, BH6, Penguin5, *Selected*, B&J)
   Cross, pp. 92–93.
   Eble (*Fitzgerald*), pp. 26–27.
   Higgins, p. 107.
   Lesser, M. X., and John N. Morris, eds. *Modern Short Stories: The
   Fiction of Experience*. New York: McGraw-Hill, 1962, p. 250.
   Perosa, pp. 89–90.
   Tressin, Deanna. "Toward Understanding," *English Journal*, 55 (December
   1966), 1170–74.

50. **Fun in an Artist's Studio**
    (1940/February 1941/*Esquire*/PH, Penguin3)
    Higgins, p. 176.
51. **Gods of Darkness**
    (December 1934/November 1941/*Redbook*)
    Perosa, p. 135.
52. **Gretchen's Forty Winks**
    (January 1924/March 15, 1924/*Saturday Evening Post*/ASYM, Diamond, BH3, 6T, JA, Penguin2)
    Eble (*Fitzgerald*), p. 104.
    Higgins, pp. 71–72.
53. **The Guest in Room Nineteen**
    (March 1937/October 1937/*Esquire*/Price)
    Higgins, pp. 166–67.
54. **Head and Shoulders**
    (November 1919/February 21, 1920/*Saturday Evening Post*/F&P)
    Bruccoli (*Epic Grandeur*), p. 107.
    Eble (*Fitzgerald*), pp. 63–64.
    Higgins, p. 19.
    Perosa, p. 34.
    Piper, p. 66.
    Sklar, p. 67.
55. **Her Last Case**
    (August 1934/November 3, 1934/*Saturday Evening Post*/Price)
    Bruccoli (*Price*), p. 571.
    Eble (*Fitzgerald*), p. 122.
    Higgins, pp. 158–59.
56. **He Thinks He's Wonderful**
    (July 1928/September 29, 1928/*Saturday Evening Post*/TAR, BH6, B&J)
    Cross, pp. 92–93.
    Eble (*Fitzgerald*), pp. 27–28.
    Higgins, p. 107.
    Perosa, p. 89.
    His Russet Witch (see "O Russet Witch!")
57. **The Homes of the Stars**
    (1940/August 1940/*Esquire*/PH, Penguin3)
    Higgins, pp. 176–77.
    Perosa, p. 150.
58. **The Honor of the Goon**
    (April 1937/June 1937/*Esquire*)
    Higgins, p. 195, fn. 78.
59. **Hot & Cold Blood**
    (April 1923/August 1923/*Hearst's International*/ASYM, Diamond, 6TJA)
    Bruccoli (*Epic Grandeur*), p. 181.
    Higgins, p. 64.

60. **The Hotel Child**
    (November 1930/January 31, 1931/*Saturday Evening Post*/*Bits, BitsP*)
    Bruccoli (*Composition*), p. 72.
    Higgins, pp. 120–21.
    Sklar, p. 243.
61. **The I.O.U.** (Unpublished)
    (1920/ . . . / . . .)
62. **The Ice Palace**
    (December 1919/May 22, 1920/*Saturday Evening Post*/F&P, *Stories, Babylon*, BH5)
    Bruccoli (*Epic Grandeur*), p. 110.
    Butwin, David. "In the Days of the Ice Palace," *Saturday Review*, 55 (January 29, 1972), 55–56.
    Cross, p. 33.
    Eble (*Fitzgerald*), pp. 56–57, 65.
    Fulkerson, Tahita N. "Ibsen in 'The Ice Palace,' " *Fitzgerald/Hemingway Annual*, 11 (1979), 169–71.
    Galloway, David, and John Whitley, eds. *Ten Modern American Short Stories*. London: Methuen, 1968, pp. 45–48.
    Gervais, Ronald J. "A Miracle of Rare Device: Fitzgerald's 'The Ice Palace,' " *Notes on Modern American Literature*, 5 (Summer 1981), Item 21.
    Higgins, pp. 20–23.
    Mills, Nicolaus, ed. *Comparisons: A Short Story Anthology*. New York: McGraw-Hill, 1972, p. 64.
    Mizener (*Far Side*), p. 160.
    Moses, Edwin. "F. Scott Fitzgerald and the Quest to the Ice Palace," *CEA Critic*, 36 (January 1974), 11–14.
    Perosa, pp. 34–35.
    Piper, p. 66.
    Shain, p. 26.
    Sklar, pp. 66–67.
    Way, pp. 55–56.
63. **I'd Die for You** (Unpublished; "The Legend of Lake Lure")
    (1935–1936/ . . . / . . .)
64. **"I Didn't Get Over"**
    (August 1936/October 1936/*Esquire*/AA, *Reader*)
    Eble (*Fitzgerald*), p. 142.
    Higgins, p. 165.
65. **I Got Shoes**
    (July 1933/September 23, 1933/*Saturday Evening Post*/*Price*)
    Bruccoli (*Price*), p. 476.
    Higgins, p. 157.
66. **Image on the Heart**
    (September 1935/April 1936/*McCall's*/*Price*)

Bruccoli (*Price*), p. 661.
Higgins, p. 178.
Sklar, p. 309.

67. **Indecision**
(January–February 1931/May 16, 1931/*Saturday Evening Post*/*Price*)
Bruccoli (*Composition*), pp. 72, 84.
Bruccoli (*Price*), p. 292.
Higgins, pp. 124–25.
Sklar, p. 245.

68. **Inside the House**
(April 1936/June 13, 1936/*Saturday Evening Post*/*Price*)
Eble (*Fitzgerald*), p. 131.
Higgins, p. 178.

69. **In the Darkest Hour**
(April 1934/October 1934/*Redbook*/*Price*)
Bruccoli (*Price*), pp. 512–13.
Perosa, p. 134.

70. **In the Holidays**
(February 1937/December 1937/*Esquire*/*Price*)
Higgins, p. 166.

71. **The Intimate Strangers**
(February–March 1935/June 1935/*McCall's*/*Price*)
Bruccoli (*Epic Grandeur*), p. 396.
Bruccoli (*Price*), p. 608.
Higgins, p. 177.

72. **Jacob's Ladder**
(June 1927/August 20, 1927/*Saturday Evening Post*/*Bits, BitsP*)
Bruccoli (*Composition*), pp. 50, 66, 84, 97, 127.
Bruccoli (*Epic Grandeur*), p. 262.
Higgins, pp. 96–98.
Sklar, pp. 228–30.

73. **The Jelly-Bean**
(May 1920/October 1920/*Metropolitan Magazine*/TJA, 6TJA, BH5)
Blair, Thomas M. H., ed. *Fifty Modern Stories*. New York: Harper & Row, 1960, p. 131.
Cross, pp. 42–43.
Eble (*Fitzgerald*), pp. 76–77.
Higgins, pp. 29–33.
Lehan, p. 103.
Mizener (*Far Side*), pp. 160–61.
Perosa, p. 31.
Piper, pp. 68–69.
Shain, p. 26.
Shaw, Harry, and Douglas Bement, eds. *Reading the Short Story*. New York: Harper, 1941, p. 353.

Sklar, pp. 87–88.

Way, p. 60.

74. **Jemina A Story of the Blue Ridge Mountains by John Phlox, Jr.**

("Jemina, the Mountain Girl [One of Those Family Feud Stories of the Blue Ridge Mountains with Apologies to Stephen Leacock]")

(October 1916/December 1916/Nassau Literary Magazine/TJA, as "Jemina")

75. **John Jackson's Arcady**

(April 1924/July 26, 1924/Saturday Evening Post/Price)

[Bruccoli, Matthew J.] "John Jackson's Arcady," Fitzgerald Newsletter, No. 19 (Fall 1962), 6.

Bruccoli (Price), p. 143.

Eble, Kenneth. " 'John Jackson's Arcady' and GG," Fitzgerald Newsletter, No. 21 (Spring 1963), 1–2.

Higgins, pp. 74–76.

[Meriwether, James]. "J J's Arcady Again," Fitzgerald Newsletter, No. 20 (Winter 1963), 7.

Sklar, pp. 161–62.

76. **The Kingdom in the Dark**

(November 1934/August 1935/Redbook)

Perosa, p. 135.

77. **Last Kiss**

(1939–1940/April 16, 1949/Collier's/Bits, BitsP)

Bruccoli (Epic Grandeur), p. 473.

Higgins, pp. 180–81.

Mizener (Far Side), pp. 325–26.

78. **The Last of the Belles**

(November 1928/March 2, 1929/Saturday Evening Post/TAR, Stories, BH2, BH5, Penguin2)

Bruccoli (Epic Grandeur), p. 270–71.

Eble (Fitzgerald), pp. 126–27.

Higgins, pp. 104–5.

Lehan, pp. 140–41.

Lynskey, Winifred. Reading Modern Fiction. 2d Edition. New York: Charles Scribner's, 1957, pp. 200–202.

Mizener (Far Side), pp. 283–84.

Perosa, pp. 85–86.

Sklar, p. 234.

Way, pp. 82–84.

79. **The Lees of Happiness**

(July 1920/December 12, 1920/Chicago Tribune/TJA, BH3, 6TJA, Penguin1)

Bruccoli (Epic Grandeur), p. 145.

Cross, p. 43.

Eble *(Fitzgerald)*, pp. 78–79.

Higgins, pp. 33–35.

Mizener *(Far Side)*, p. 160.

Perosa, pp. 35–36.

Sklar, pp. 88–89.

80. **The Long Way Out**

(May 1937/September 1937/*Esquire*/*Stories*, *Babylon*, BH6, *Reader*, *Selected*)

[Bruccoli, Matthew J.] "A Source for 'The Long Way Out,' " *Fitzgerald Newsletter*, No. 34 (Summer 1966), 1.

Higgins, p. 167.

Mizener *(Far Side)*, p. 322.

Perosa, p. 143.

81. **The Lost Decade**

(July 1939/December 1939/*Esquire*/*Stories*, BH6, *Reader*, Penguin5, *Selected*)

Bruccoli *(Epic Grandeur)*, p. 472.

Cross, p. 99.

Higgins, pp. 169–70.

Mizener *(Far Side)*, p. 322.

Perosa, p. 145.

Sklar, p. 326.

82. **Lo, the Poor Peacock!**

(1935/September 1971/*Esquire* [abridged]/*Price* [unabridged])

Bruccoli *(Epic Grandeur)*, pp. 396–97.

Bruccoli *(Price)*, p. 591.

83. **The Love Boat**

(August 1927/October 8, 1927/*Saturday Evening Post*/*Price*)

Bruccoli *(Composition)*, p. 84.

Bruccoli *(Price)*, p. 237.

Higgins, pp. 98–99.

Sklar, pp. 229–30.

84. **Love in the Night**

(November 1924/March 14, 1925/*Saturday Evening Post*/*Bits*, *BitsP*)

Bruccoli *(Composition)*, p. 18.

Bruccoli *(Epic Grandeur)*, p. 212.

Higgins, pp. 88–89.

Sklar, p. 203.

85. **A Luckless Santa Claus**

(1912/Christmas 1912/*Newman News*/AF)

Bruccoli *(Epic Grandeur)*, p. 35.

Higgins, p. 4.

Kuehl, pp. 12–13, 44–47.

86. **Magnetism**

(December 1927/March 3, 1928/*Saturday Evening Post*/*Stories*, BH5,

Penguin4)

[Bruccoli, Matthew J.] "F Parodies F," *Fitzgerald Newsletter*, No. 25 (Spring 1964), 8.

Eble (*Fitzgerald*), p. 125.

Higgins, pp. 101–2.

Perosa, pp. 94–95.

Sklar, pp. 230–31.

87. **Majesty**

(May 1929/July 13, 1929/*Saturday Evening Post*/TAR, BH5)

Bruccoli (*Composition*), p. 84.

Bruccoli (*Epic Grandeur*), p. 281.

Higgins, p. 111–12.

Sklar, p. 236.

Way, pp. 45–46.

88. **A Man in the Way**

(1939/February 1940/*Esquire*/PH, Penguin3)

Higgins, p. 173.

Lehan, p. 164.

Perosa, p. 150.

89. **May Day**

(March 1920/July 1920/*Smart Set*/TJA, LT, *Portable, Diamond*, BT, *Stories*, BH1, *Babylon*, Penguin1, BH5, *Reader*, Ab)

Bruccoli (*Epic Grandeur*), pp. 141–42.

Cass, Colin S. "Fitzgerald's Second Thoughts About 'May Day': A Collation and Study," *Fitzgerald/Hemingway Annual*, 2 (1970), 69–95.

Cross, pp. 43–45, 50.

Eble (*Fitzgerald*), pp. 77–78.

Gallo, pp. 87–90.

Gruber, Michael P. "Fitzgerald's 'May Day': A Prelude to Triumph," *Essays in Literature* [University of Denver], 2 (No. 1, 1973), 20–35.

Higgins, pp. 26–29.

Hindus, p. 33.

Lehan, pp. 84–85.

Long, pp. 30–38.

Martin, Robert K. "Sexual and Group Relationships in 'May Day': Fear and Longing," *Studies in Short Fiction*, 15 (Winter 1978), 99–101.

Mazzella, Anthony J. "The Tension of Opposites in Fitzgerald's 'May Day,' " *Studies in Short Fiction*, 14 (Fall 1977), 379–85.

Miller, pp. 53–56.

Mizener (*Far Side*), pp. 88–89.

Perlis, Alan. "The Narrative Is All: A Study of F. Scott Fitzgerald's *May Day*," *Western Humanities Review*, 33 (Winter 1979), 65–72.

Perosa, pp. 32–33.

Piper, Henry Dan. "Frank Norris and Scott Fitzgerald," *Huntington Library Quarterly*, 19 (August 1956), 393–400.

Piper, pp. 69–71.
Shain, pp. 27–28.
Sklar, pp. 71–78.
Way, pp. 77–79.

90. **Mightier than the Sword**
    (1939/April 1941/*Esquire*/PH, Penguin3)
    Higgins, p. 175.
    Perosa, p. 151.

91. **More than Just a House**
    (April 1933/June 24, 1933/*Saturday Evening Post*/*Price*)
    Bruccoli (*Epic Grandeur*), pp. 356–57.
    Bruccoli (*Price*), p. 455.
    Higgins, pp. 155–56.

92. **Myra Meets His Family**
    (April, December 1919/March 20, 1920/*Saturday Evening Post*/*Price*)
    Bruccoli (*Price*), p. 11.
    Eble (*Fitzgerald*), p. 55.
    Higgins, pp. 19–20.
    Piper, p. 67.

93. **The Mystery of the Raymond Mortgage**
    (June 1909/October 1909/*St. Paul Academy Now and Then*/AF)
    Bruccoli (*Epic Grandeur*), pp. 27–28.
    [Bruccoli, Matthew J.] " 'Raymond Mortgage' Activity," *Fitzgerald Newsletter*, No. 12 (Winter 1961), 4.
    Gray, James. "Scott Fitzgerald at 13 Wrote Detective Story for School," St. Paul *Dispatch*, May 17, 1932, Section 1, p. 10.
    Higgins, p. 3.
    Kuehl, pp. 17–19.

94. **A New Leaf**
    (April 1931/July 4, 1931/*Saturday Evening Post*/*Bits, BitsP*)
    Bruccoli (*Composition*), p. 84.
    Eble (*Fitzgerald*), p. 121.
    Higgins, pp. 125–26.
    Sklar, p. 245.

95. **News of Paris—Fifteen Years Ago**
    (1940?/Winter 1947/*Furioso*/AA)
    Higgins, pp. 171–72.
    Mizener (*Far Side*), p. 322.
    Mizener, Arthur. "A Note on 'News of Paris,' " *Furioso*, 3 (Winter 1947), 11–12.
    Perosa, pp. 145–47.
    Sklar, pp. 326–27.

96. **New Types**
    (July 1934/September 22, 1934/*Saturday Evening Post*/*Price*)
    Bruccoli (*Price*), p. 548.

Higgins, p. 158.

Sklar, pp. 300–301.

97. **A Nice Quiet Place**

 (March 1930/May 31, 1930/*Saturday Evening Post*/TAR, B&J)

 Bruccoli (*Composition*), p. 69.

 Eble (*Fitzgerald*), pp. 116–17.

 Higgins, p. 116.

 Perosa, p. 92.

98. **A Night at the Fair**

 (May 1928/July 21, 1928/*Saturday Evening Post*/AA, BH6, B&J)

 Allen, pp. 23–25.

 Bruccoli (*Composition*), p. 84.

 Eble (*Fitzgerald*), pp. 25–26.

 Higgins, p. 107.

 Perosa, p. 89.

99. **The Night before Chancellorsville** ("The Night at Chancellorsville")

 (November 1934/February 1935/*Esquire*/TAR, as "The Night at Chancellorsville")

 Higgins, p. 161.

 Perosa, p. 137.

100. **Nightmare** (Unpublished; "Fantasy in Black")

 (1932/ . . . / . . .)

101. **No Flowers**

 (May 1934/July 21, 1934/*Saturday Evening Post*/Price)

 Bruccoli (*Price*), p. 530.

 Higgins, pp. 157–58.

 Sklar, p. 300.

102. **No Harm Trying**

 (1939/November 1940/*Esquire*/AA, PH, Penguin3)

 Higgins, p. 174.

 Perosa, p. 150.

103. **Not in the Guidebook**

 (February 1925/November 1925/*Woman's Home Companion*/Price)

 Bruccoli (*Price*), p. 162.

 Higgins, pp. 89–90.

 Sklar, pp. 203–4.

104. **The Offshore Pirate**

 (February 1920/May 29, 1920/*Saturday Evening Post*/F&P, *Portable*)

 Atkinson, Jennifer McCabe. "The Discarded Ending of 'The Offshore Pirate,' " *Fitzgerald/Hemingway Annual*, 6 (1974), 47–49.

 Bruccoli (*Epic Grandeur*), p. 112.

 Eble (*Fitzgerald*), p. 65.

 Goldhurst, pp. 121–24.

 Higgins, pp. 24–26.

 Hindus, p. 106.

 Latham, pp. 36–37.

Perosa, p. 31.
Piper, p. 68.
Shain, pp. 26–27.
Sklar, pp. 68–71.
105. **Offside Play** (Unpublished; "Athletic Interview," "Athletic Interval")
(1937/ . . . / . . .)
106. **On an Ocean Wave** (by Paul Elgin)
(September? 1940/February 1941/*Esquire*/*Price*)
Bruccoli (*Price*), p. 778.
Higgins, pp. 170–71.
107. **One Interne**
(August 1932/November 5, 1932/*Saturday Evening Post*/TAR)
Higgins, p. 155.
Perosa, pp. 86–87.
108. **One of My Oldest Friends**
(March 1924/September 1924/*Woman's Home Companion*/*Price*)
Bruccoli (*Price*), p. 112.
Higgins, p. 73.
109. **One Trip Abroad**
(August 1930/October 11, 1930/*Saturday Evening Post*/AA, BH6)
Bruccoli (*Composition*), pp. 66, 69, 71, 72, 84.
Bruccoli (*Epic Grandeur*), pp. 308–9.
Eble (*Fitzgerald*), pp. 124–25.
Higgins, p. 120.
Lehan, p. 143.
Miller, pp. 131–32.
Mizener (*Far Side*), pp. 237–39.
Perosa, pp. 100–101.
Piper, p. 165.
Shain, pp. 38–39.
Sklar, pp. 242–43.
Way, pp. 89–90.
110. **On Schedule**
(December 1932/March 18, 1933/*Saturday Evening Post*/*Price*)
Bruccoli (*Price*), p. 437.
Eble (*Fitzgerald*), pp. 121–22.
Higgins, p. 155.
111. **On the Trail of Pat Hobby**
(1940/January 1941/*Esquire*/PH, Penguin3)
Higgins, p. 176.
112. **On Your Own** ("Home to Maryland")
(Spring 1931/1979/*Price*)
Bruccoli, Matthew J. "Epilogue: A Woman, a Gift, and a Still Unanswered
Question," *Esquire*, 91 (January 30, 1979), 67.
Bruccoli (*Price*), p. 323.

[Introduction to "On Your Own"], *Esquire*, 91 (January 30, 1979), 56–57.

Maddocks, Melvin. "Fitzgerald's Green Light—A Half Century Later," *Christian Science Monitor*, January 29, 1979, p. 30.

113. **The Ordeal** (revised into "Benediction")
    (1915/June 1915/*Nassau Literary Magazine*/AF)
    Allen, pp. 42–45.
    Bruccoli (*Epic Grandeur*), p. 58.
    Eble (*Fitzgerald*), p. 58.
    Higgins, pp. 5–6.
    Kuehl, pp. 7–9, 78–80.
    Sklar, pp. 12–13.
    Van Winkle, Cortlandt. "Prose Surpasses Verse in June Number of Lit," *Daily Princetonian*, June 9, 1915, pp. 1, 4. [Reprinted in Bruccoli and Bryer, eds., p. 301]

114. **"O Russet Witch!"** (His Russet Witch)
    (November 1920/February 1921/*Metropolitan Magazine*, as "His Russet Witch"/TJA, 6TJA)
    Eble (*Fitzgerald*), p. 79.
    Higgins, pp. 35–37.
    Lehan, p. 103.
    Perosa, p. 35.
    Sklar, p. 90.

115. **Our Own Movie Queen** (by F. Scott and Zelda Fitzgerald)
    (November 1923/June 7, 1925/Chicago *Sunday Tribune*/Bits, BitsP)
    Perosa, p. 55.

116. **Outside the Cabinet-Maker's**
    (1927/December 1928/*Century Magazine*/AA, BH5, *Reader*)
    Higgins, pp. 102–4.
    Perosa, p. 95.

117. **Pain and the Scientist**
    (1912–1913/1913/*Newman News*/AF)
    Bruccoli (*Epic Grandeur*), p. 35.
    Higgins, p. 5.
    Kuehl, pp. 44–47.

118. **The Passionate Eskimo**
    (February 1935/June 8, 1935/*Liberty*)
    Bruccoli (*Epic Grandeur*), p. 400.
    Piper, p. 232.

119. **Pat Hobby and Orson Welles**
    (1940/May 1940/*Esquire*/PH, Penguin3)
    Higgins, p. 176.
    Perosa, p. 150.

120. **Pat Hobby Does His Bit**
    (1940/September 1940/*Esquire*/PH, Penguin3)
    Higgins, p. 176.

Pat Hobby Himself (combination of "A Patriotic Short" and "Two Old-Timers")

(1939, 1940/ . . . / . . . /BH2, Penguin2, FeH)

121. **Pat Hobby, Putative Father**

(1939/July 1940/*Esquire*/PH, Penguin3)

Higgins, p. 175.

122. **Pat Hobby's Christmas Wish**

(1939/January 1940/*Esquire*/PH, Penguin3)

Higgins, p. 174.

Lehan, p. 164.

Perosa, p. 150.

123. **Pat Hobby's College Days**

(1939/May 1941/*Esquire*/PH, Penguin3)

Higgins, p. 175.

Perosa, p. 151.

124. **Pat Hobby's Preview**

(1939/October 1940/*Esquire*/PH, Penguin3)

Higgins, p. 174.

Perosa, p. 150.

125. **Pat Hobby's Secret**

(1940/June 1940/*Esquire*/PH, Penguin3)

Higgins, p. 176.

Perosa, p. 150.

126. **A Patriotic Short** (See also "Pat Hobby Himself")

(1940/December 1940/*Esquire*/*Stories*, BH2, as part of "Pat Hobby Himself," PH, BH6, Penguin2, as part of "Pat Hobby Himself," Penguin3, FeH, as part of "Pat Hobby Himself")

Higgins, pp. 175–76.

Lehan, p. 165.

Perosa, pp. 150–51.

127. **The Pearl and the Fur** (Unpublished)

(1936/ . . . / . . .)

128. **A Penny Spent**

(July 1925/October 10, 1925/*Saturday Evening Post*/*Bits*, BitsP)

Bruccoli (*Composition*), p. 84.

Higgins, p. 90.

129. **The Perfect Life**

(October 1928/January 5, 1929/*Saturday Evening Post*/TAR, B&J)

Allen, pp. 31–32.

Eble (*Fitzgerald*), pp. 28–29.

Higgins, pp. 107–8.

Perosa, p. 90.

130. **The Pierian Springs and the Last Straw**

(Spring? 1917/October 1917/*Nassau Literary Magazine*/AF)

Bakeless, John. "In Other Colleges: *Nassau Literary Monthly*," *Williams*

Literary Monthly [Williams College], 33 (November 1917), 525–27. [Reprinted in Bruccoli and Bryer, eds., pp. 303–4]
Bruccoli (*Epic Grandeur*), pp. 78–79.
Higgins, pp. 10–11.
Kuehl, John. "A Note on the Begetting of *Gatsby*," *University* [Princeton University], No. 21 (Summer 1964), 26–31.
Kuehl, pp. 15–16, 160–62.
Lehan, pp. 96, 101.
"Recent Lit Shows Effect of War on the University," *Daily Princetonian*, November 26, 1917, pp. 1, 2.
Sklar, pp. 21–23.

131. **The Popular Girl**
(November 1921/February 11 & 18, 1922/*Saturday Evening Post*/*Bits*, *BitsP*)
Higgins, pp. 57–58.

132. **Presumption**
(November 1925/January 9, 1926/*Saturday Evening Post*/*Price*)
Bruccoli (*Price*), p. 177.
Higgins, pp. 94–95.
Sklar, pp. 215–16.

133. **The Pusher-in-the-Face**
(March 1924/February 1925/*Woman's Home Companion*/*Price*)
Bruccoli (*Price*), p. 98.
Eble (*Fitzgerald*), p. 56.
Higgins, pp. 73–74.

134. **Rags Martin-Jones and the Pr-nce of W-les**
(December 1923/July 1924/*McCall's*/ASYM)
Eble (*Fitzgerald*), p. 104.
Higgins, pp. 70–71.
Latham, pp. 47–48.
Miller, pp. 96–97.
Mizener, (*Far Side*), pp. 127–28.

135. **Reade, Substitute Right Half**
(1909–1910/February 1910/*St. Paul Academy Now and Then*/AF)
Bruccoli (*Epic Grandeur*), p. 28.
Higgins, p. 3.
Kuehl, pp. 28–30.

136. **Recklessness** (Unpublished)
(1922/ . . . / . . .)

137. **The Rich Boy**
(April–August 1925/January & February 1926/*Red Book*/ASYM, LT, *Portable*, *Diamond*, BT, *Stories*, *Babylon*, BH3, Penguin1, BH5, *Reader*)
Arnold, Aerol. "Why Structure in Fiction: A Note to Social Scientists," *American Quarterly*, 10 (Fall 1958), 325–37.

Beebe, Lucius. "Who Said It?" San Francisco *Chronicle*, November 10, 1963, "This World" Section, p. 31.

Brooks, Cleanth, John Thibaut Purser, and Robert Penn Warren. *An Approach to Literature.* 3d Edition. New York: Appleton-Century-Crofts, 1952, pp. 240–41.

Bruccoli (*Epic Grandeur*), pp. 231–34.

Cross, pp. 71–72, 75.

Eble (*Fitzgerald*), pp. 66, 106–7.

Gallo, pp. 94–97.

Goldhurst, pp. 141, 163–64.

Higgins, pp. 91–94.

Hindus, pp. 96–102.

Katz, Joseph. "The Narrator and 'The Rich Boy,' " *Fitzgerald Newsletter*, No. 32 (Winter 1966), 2–3.

Lehan, pp. 141–42.

Mizener (*Far Side*), pp. 213–14.

Perosa, pp. 84–85.

Piper, pp. 156–58.

Rees, Robert A., and Barry Menikoff. *Manual to Accompany "The Short Story—An Introductory Anthology."* Boston: Little, Brown, 1969, pp. 8–9.

Shain, pp. 37–38.

Sklar, pp. 210–12.

Stein, William Bysshe. "Two Notes on 'The Rich Boy,' " *Fitzgerald Newsletter*, No. 14 (Summer 1961), 1–3.

Way, pp. 84–87.

Weimer, David R., ed. *Modern American Classics: An Anthology of Short Fiction.* New York: Random House, 1969, p. 83.

Wells, Elizabeth. "A Comparative Statistical Analysis of the Prose Styles of F. Scott Fitzgerald and Ernest Hemingway," *Fitzgerald/Hemingway Annual*, 1 (1969), 47–67.

West, James L. W., III, and J. Barclay Inge. "F. Scott Fitzgerald's Revision of 'The Rich Boy,' " *Proof*, 5 (1975), 127–46.

138. **The Room with the Green Blinds**
     (1909–1911/June 1911/*St. Paul Academy Now and Then*/AF)
     Higgins, p. 4.

     Kuehl, pp. 34–35.

139. **The Rough Crossing**
     (March 1929/June 8, 1929/*Saturday Evening Post*/*Stories*, BH4, BH5, Penguin4)
     Bruccoli (*Composition*), pp. 59, 66, 84.

     Bruccoli (*Epic Grandeur*), p. 279.

     Eble (*Fitzgerald*), p. 124.

     Higgins, pp. 110–11.

     Lehan, pp. 57, 143–44.

     Miller, p. 131.

Perosa, pp. 100–101.

Sklar, pp. 234–36.

Way, pp. 87–88.

140. **The Rubber Check**
(May 1932/August 6, 1932/*Saturday Evening Post*/*Price*)
Bruccoli (*Price*), p. 417.
Eble (*Fitzgerald*), p. 122.
Higgins, pp. 154–55.
Sklar, p. 248.

141. **The Scandal Detectives**
(March 1928/April 28, 1928/*Saturday Evening Post*/TAR, *Stories*, BH6, *Selected*, B&J)
Cross, pp. 92–93.
Eble (*Fitzgerald*), p. 25.
Higgins, p. 106.
Perosa, p. 89.

142. **"Send Me In, Coach"**
(October 1936/November 1936/*Esquire*)
Eble (*Fitzgerald*), pp. 142–43.
Higgins, pp. 165–66.

143. **"The Sensible Thing"**
(November 1923/July 5, 1924/*Liberty*/ASYM, *Diamond*, *Stories*, BH5, *Reader*, Penguin4, FeH)
Bruccoli (*Epic Grandeur*), p. 191.
Cross, pp. 74–75.
Eble (*Fitzgerald*), pp. 103–4.
Higgins, pp. 67–68.
Hindus, p. 103.
Lehan, pp. 104–5.
Long, pp. 70–71.
Miller, pp. 102–3.
Mizener (*Far Side*), p. 214.
Perosa, pp. 57–59.
Piper, pp. 101–2.

144. **Sentiment—and the Use of Rouge**
(1917/June 1917/*Nassau Literary Magazine*/AF)
Allen, pp. 54–55.
Bruccoli (*Epic Grandeur*), p. 71.
Higgins, pp. 9–10.
Kuehl, pp. 141–43.
Sklar, pp. 23–24.

145. **Shaggy's Morning**
(March 1935/May 1935/*Esquire*)
Bruccoli (*Epic Grandeur*), p. 400.
Higgins, pp. 192–93, fn. 51.

146. **A Short Trip Home**
(October 1927/December 17, 1927/*Saturday Evening Post*/TAR, BH5, Penguin4)
Bruccoli (*Composition*), pp. 70, 241.
Bruccoli (*Epic Grandeur*), p. 263.
Eble (*Fitzgerald*), pp. 127–29.
Higgins, pp. 99–100.
Perosa, p. 86.
Sklar, p. 230.

147. **Six of One—**
(July 1931/February 1932/*Redbook*/Price)
Bruccoli (*Epic Grandeur*), p. 314.
Bruccoli (*Price*), p. 369.
Higgins, p. 151.
Sklar, pp. 246–47, 257–58.

148. **The Smilers**
(September 1919/June 1920/*Smart Set*/Price)
Bruccoli (*Price*), p. 3.
Eble (*Fitzgerald*), pp. 55–56.
Higgins, pp. 15–16.

149. **A Snobbish Story**
(September 1930/November 29, 1930/*Saturday Evening Post*/B&J)
Bruccoli (*Composition*), p. 69.
Eble (*Fitzgerald*), p. 118.
Higgins, p. 117.
Perosa, p. 92.
Sklar, p. 241.

150. **The Spire and the Gargoyle**
(1916/February 1917/*Nassau Literary Magazine*/AF)
[Benét, William Rose]. "February Nassau Lit Is Reviewed by Benét," *Daily Princetonian*, February 24, 1917, pp. 3–4. [Reprinted in Bruccoli and Bryer, eds., p. 302]
Bruccoli (*Epic Grandeur*), p. 71.
Higgins, pp. 7–8.
Kuehl, pp. 8, 102–4.
West, p. 37.

151. **Strange Sanctuary** ("Make Yourself at Home")
(1935/December 9, 1939/*Liberty*)
Bruccoli (*Epic Grandeur*), p. 402.
Higgins, p. 179.

152. **The Swimmers**
(July-August 1929/October 19, 1929/*Saturday Evening Post*/Bits, BitsP)
Bruccoli (*Composition*), p. 84.
Bruccoli (*Epic Grandeur*), pp. 279–81.
Eble (*Fitzgerald*), pp. 120–21.

Higgins, pp. 113–14.

Sklar, pp. 236–39, 256.

153. **Tarquin of Cheepside** ("Tarquin of Cheapside")
   (February 1917/April 1917/*Nassau Literary Magazine*/TJA, as "Tarquin of Cheapside," 6TJA, as "Tarquin of Cheapside," AF, as "Tarquin of Cheepside")
   Cross, p. 42.
   Eble (*Fitzgerald*), p. 79.
   [Gerould, Katherine Fullerton]. "April Lit Successful Because of Grim Note," *Daily Princetonian*, April 24, 1917, pp. 1, 3. [Reprinted in Bruccoli and Bryer, eds., p. 303]
   Higgins, p. 8.
   Kuehl, pp. 115–17.
   Sklar, p. 24.
   Swinnerton, A. C. "In Other Colleges: *Nassau Literary Magazine*," *Williams Literary Monthly* [Williams College], 33 (May 1917), 411–12.
   Way, pp. 16–17.

154. **Teamed with Genius**
   (1939/April 1940/*Esquire*/AA, PH, BH6, Penguin3)
   Higgins, p. 174.
   Perosa, p. 150.

155. **Temperature** (Unpublished; "The Women in the House")
   (1939/ . . . / . . .)
   Bruccoli (*Epic Grandeur*), p. 457.

156. **Thank You for the Light** (Unpublished)
   (1936/ . . . / . . .)

157. **That Kind of Party**
   (1928/Summer 1951/*Princeton University Library Chronicle*/B&J)
   Allen, pp. 9–12.
   Bruccoli (*Composition*), p. 55.
   Bruccoli (*Epic Grandeur*), p. 418.
   Eble (*Fitzgerald*), pp. 23–24.
   Higgins, p. 106.

158. **They Never Grow Older** (Unpublished)
   (1937/ . . . / . . .)
   Bruccoli (*Epic Grandeur*), p. 418.

159. **The Third Casket**
   (March 1924/May 31, 1924/*Saturday Evening Post*/Price)
   Bruccoli (*Price*), p. 86.
   Higgins, p. 74.

160. **Three Acts of Music**
   (February 1936/May 1936/*Esquire*/Price)
   Bruccoli (*Price*), p. 711.
   Higgins, pp. 161–62.

161. **Three Hours between Planes**
   (1939/July 1941/*Esquire*/Stories, BH6, Penguin5)

Eble *(Fitzgerald)*, p. 145.
Higgins, p. 170.
Perosa, p. 145.
Sklar, p. 326.
Way, p. 84.
162. **Too Cute for Words**
(December 1935/April 18, 1936/*Saturday Evening Post*/*Price*)
Bruccoli *(Price)*, p. 679.
Eble *(Fitzgerald)*, p. 131.
Higgins, p. 178.
163. **The Trail of the Duke**
(1912–1913/June 1913/*Newman News*/AF)
Bruccoli *(Epic Grandeur)*, p. 35.
Higgins, pp. 4–5.
Kuehl, pp. 13, 44–47.
164. **Travel Together** (Unpublished)
(1935/ . . . / . . .)
165. **"Trouble"**
(June 1936/March 6, 1937/*Saturday Evening Post*/*Price*)
Bruccoli *(Price)*, p. 717.
Higgins, p. 179.
166. **Two for a Cent**
(September 1921/April 1922/*Metropolitan Magazine*/*Price*)
Bruccoli *(Price)*, p. 33.
Higgins, pp. 54–55.
167. **Two Old-Timers** (See also "Pat Hobby Himself")
(1939/March 1941/*Esquire*/*Stories*, BH2, as part of "Pat Hobby Himself," PH, BH6, Penguin2, as part of "Pat Hobby Himself," Penguin3, *Selected*, FeH, as part of "Pat Hobby Himself")
Higgins, p. 175.
Perosa, p. 151.
168. **Two Wrongs**
(October-November 1929/January 18, 1930/*Saturday Evening Post*/ TAR, BT, *Stories*, BH6, Penguin5)
Bruccoli *(Epic Grandeur)*, p. 279.
Eble *(Fitzgerald)*, pp. 122–23.
Higgins, pp. 114–15.
Lehan, pp. 142–43.
Perosa, pp. 95–96.
Sklar, pp. 239–40, 256.
169. **The Unspeakable Egg**
(April 1924/July 12, 1924/*Saturday Evening Post*/*Price*)
Bruccoli *(Price)*, p. 126.
Higgins, pp. 74–75.
170. **The Vanished Girl** (Unpublished)
(1937/ . . . / . . .)

171. **What a Handsome Pair!**
    (April 1932/August 27, 1932/*Saturday Evening Post*/*Bits, BitsP*)
    Bruccoli (*Epic Grandeur*), pp. 330–31.
    Eble (*Fitzgerald*), p. 121.
    Higgins, p. 154.
172. **What to Do About It** (Unpublished)
    (1933/ . . . / . . .)
173. **Winter Dreams**
    (September 1922/December 1922/*Smart Set*/TJA, *Diamond, Stories, Babylon*, BH5, *Reader*, Penguin4)
    Boggan, J. R. "A Note on 'Winter Dreams,' " *Fitzgerald Newsletter*, No. 13 (Spring 1961), 1–2.
    Brown, Clarence A., and John T. Flanagan, eds. *American Literature: A College Survey*. New York: McGraw-Hill, 1961, pp. 716–17.
    Bruccoli (*Epic Grandeur*), pp. 173–74.
    Burhans, Clinton S., Jr. " 'Magnificently Attune to Life': The Value of 'Winter Dreams,' " *Studies in Short Fiction*, 6 (Summer 1969), 401–12.
    Cross, pp. 72–73.
    Daniels, Thomas E. "The Texts of 'Winter Dreams,' " *Fitzgerald/Hemingway Annual*, 9 (1977), 77–100.
    Eble (*Fitzgerald*), pp. 33–34, 105–6.
    Gallo, pp. 90–92.
    Goldhurst, pp. 136–38.
    Higgins, pp. 59–62.
    Hindus, pp. 102–3.
    Ishikawa, Akiko. "From 'Winter Dreams' to *The Great Gatsby*," *Persica* (*Journal of the English Society of Okayama*), No. 5 (January 1978), 79–92.
    Lid, R. W., ed. *The Short Story: Classic & Contemporary*. Philadelphia: J. B. Lippincott, 1966, pp. 5–6, 29–30.
    Long, pp. 67–70.
    Magalaner, Marvin, and Edmond L. Volpe. *Teacher's Manual to Accompany "Twelve Short Stories."* New York: Macmillan, 1961, pp. 5–7.
    Miller, pp. 98–102.
    Mizener (*Far Side*), pp. 51, 211–13.
    Perosa, pp. 57–59.
    Piper, p. 101.
    Sklar, pp. 158–59.
174. **The Woman from Twenty-One**
    (?/June 1941/*Esquire*/Price)
175. **A Woman with a Past**
    (June 1930/September 6, 1930/*Saturday Evening Post*/TAR, *Stories*, BH6, Penguin5, B&J)
    Bruccoli (*Composition*), p. 69.
    Eble (*Fitzgerald*), pp. 117–18.
    Higgins, pp. 116–17.

Lehan, pp. 91–93.

Perosa, p. 92.

Sklar, p. 241.

Wachner, Clarence W., Frank E. Ross, and Eva Marie Van Houten, eds. *Contemporary American Prose*. New York: Macmillan, 1963, pp. 125–26.

176. **The World's Fair**
(?/Autumn 1948/*Kenyon Review*)
Eble (*Fitzgerald*), pp. 135–36.
Mizener, Arthur. "A Note on 'The World's Fair,'" *Kenyon Review*, 10 (Autumn 1948), 701–4.

177. **Your Way and Mine**
(February 1926/May 1927/*Woman's Home Companion*/Price)
Bruccoli (*Price*), p. 219.
Higgins, p. 96.
Sklar, pp. 216–17.

178. **Zone of Accident**
(Fall 1932, May 1935/July 13, 1935/*Saturday Evening Post*/Price)
Bruccoli (*Price*), p. 628.
Higgins, pp. 177–78.
[Thomas, Ed G.] "F. Scott Fitzgerald Staying at Hotel Here," Asheville [N.C.] *Citizen-Times*, July 21, 1935, pp. 1, 2. [Reprinted in Bruccoli and Bryer, eds., pp. 289–92]

CONTRIBUTORS

CARLOS BAKER, Woodrow Wilson Professor of Literature, Emeritus, Princeton University, has written and edited many books, including *Hemingway: The Writer as Artist; Ernest Hemingway: A Life Story;* and *Ernest Hemingway: Selected Letters 1907–1961.*

JACKSON R. BRYER is Professor of English at the University of Maryland, College Park. He is the author of *The Critical Reputation of F. Scott Fitzgerald* and has edited or co-edited *F. Scott Fitzgerald in His Own Time: A Miscellany; Dear Scott/Dear Max: The Fitzgerald-Perkins Correspondence; The Basil and Josephine Stories;* and *F. Scott Fitzgerald: The Critical Reception.* Between 1971 and 1978 he contributed the Fitzgerald and Hemingway chapter to *American Literary Scholarship: An Annual.*

LAWRENCE BUELL is Professor of English at Oberlin College. He is the author of *Literary Transcendentalism: Style and Vision in the American Renaissance.* His essays have appeared in *American Quarterly, American Literature, ELH, Texas Studies in Literature and Language,* and other journals. He has held research fellowships from the Howard Foundation and the National Endowment for the Humanities.

SCOTT DONALDSON, Professor of English at the College of William and Mary, has written *By Force of Will: The Life and Art of Ernest Hemingway; Poet in America: Winfield Townley Scott;* and *The Sub-*

urban Myth. He is the editor of the Viking Critical Edition of Jack Kerouac's *On the Road* and has contributed essays to *American Literature, New England Quarterly, Modern Fiction Studies, Southern Literary Journal, Studies in American Fiction,* and other journals. He currently contributes the Fitzgerald and Hemingway chapter to *American Literary Scholarship: An Annual.*

Victor Doyno is Associate Professor of English at the State University of New York at Buffalo. His essays on Fitzgerald and on other writers have appeared in *Modern Fiction Studies, Fitzgerald Newsletter, Hartford Studies, Studies in Contemporary Satire,* and *Essays in Criticism.* He is currently completing a genetic study of *The Adventures of Huckleberry Finn.*

Kenneth E. Eble is Professor of English at the University of Utah and served as chairman from 1964 to 1969. He is the author of *F. Scott Fitzgerald; The Profane Comedy: American Higher Education in the Sixties; A Perfect Education;* and *The Craft of Teaching.* He is the editor of *F. Scott Fitzgerald: A Collection of Criticism* and of *Howells: A Century of Criticism,* and has contributed essays to *College English, Western Humanities Review, American Scholar, American Literature,* and *College Literature.*

Melvin J. Friedman is Professor of Comparative Literature and English at the University of Wisconsin–Milwaukee. He is the author or editor of books on Samuel Beckett, William Styron, Flannery O'Connor, Eugene Ionesco, and the twentieth-century Catholic novel, and has contributed essays and reviews to *The Nation, New Republic, Massachusetts Review, Contemporary Literature, American Literature, Southern Literary Journal, Studies in American Fiction,* and other journals. He has held fellowships from the Fulbright Commission and the American Council of Learned Societies.

Sheldon Grebstein is President of the State University of New York, College at Purchase. He was formerly Dean of Arts & Sciences and Harpur College at the State University of New York at Binghamton, where he was also Professor of English from 1963 until 1981. He is the author of *Sinclair Lewis; John O'Hara;* and *Hemingway's Craft.* He has edited *Monkey Trial; Perspectives in Contemporary Criticism;* and *Studies in "For Whom the Bell Tolls,"* and has contributed essays to *New England Quarterly, American Scholar, Philological Quarterly, University of Kansas City Review,* and other journals.

C. HUGH HOLMAN was Kenan Professor of English at the University of North Carolina at Chapel Hill until his death on October 13, 1981. He also served as Special Assistant to the Chancellor, and was the author of *The Immoderate Past: The Southern Writer and History; The Roots of Southern Writing: Essays on the Literature of the American South; Three Modes of Modern Southern Fiction: Ellen Glasgow, William Faulkner, Thomas Wolfe; John P. Marquand; Thomas Wolfe;* and *Windows on the World: Essays on American Social Fiction.* He was the editor or co-editor of *The Short Novels of Thomas Wolfe; The World of Thomas Wolfe; The Thomas Wolfe Reader; The Letters of Thomas Wolfe to His Mother;* and *Southern Writing 1585–1920.*

NEIL D. ISAACS is Professor of English and American Studies at the University of Maryland, College Park. He is the author or co-author of *Structural Principles in Old English Poetry; Eudora Welty; Fiction into Film: "A Walk in the Spring Rain"; All the Moves: A History of College Basketball; Checking Back: The Story of NHL Hockey; Jock Culture, U.S.A.; Covering the Spread: How to Bet Pro Football;* and *Sports Illustrated Basketball.* He has edited or co-edited *Approaches to the Short Story; Tolkien and the Critics; The Sporting Spirit: Athletes in Literature and Life;* and *Tolkien: New Critical Perspectives.*

CHRISTIANE JOHNSON teaches American Literature at the University of Paris VII. Her essays have appeared in *Études Anglaises* and the *Fitzgerald/Hemingway Annual,* and she is a co-editor of *Les Américanistes: New French Criticism on Modern American Fiction.*

JOHN KUEHL, Professor of English at New York University, is the author of *The Apprentice Fiction of F. Scott Fitzgerald, 1909–1917* and *John Hawkes and the Craft of Conflict.* He is the editor or co-editor of *Write & Rewrite: A Study of the Creative Process; Thoughtbook of Francis Scott Key Fitzgerald; Dear Scott/Dear Max: The Fitzgerald-Perkins Correspondence;* and *The Basil and Josephine Stories.* His essays and reviews on Fitzgerald have appeared in *Texas Studies in Literature and Language, Princeton University Library Chronicle, Modern Fiction Studies, Fitzgerald Newsletter, Georgia Review, Yale Review, Modern Language Journal,* and the *Fitzgerald/Hemingway Annual.*

RICHARD LEHAN, Professor of English at the University of California, Los Angeles, is the author of *F. Scott Fitzgerald and the Craft of Fiction; Theodore Dreiser: His World and His Novels;* and *A Dangerous Crossing: French Literary Existentialism and the Modern Ameri-*

can Novel. He is presently at work on a study of the city in history and literature.

IRVING MALIN, Professor of English at City College of New York, is the author of *William Faulkner: An Interpretation; Isaac Bashevis Singer; New American Gothic; Saul Bellow's Fiction; Jews and Americans;* and *Nathanael West's Novels.* He has edited or co-edited *The Achievement of William Styron; Critical Views of Isaac Bashevis Singer; Saul Bellow and the Critics; Truman Capote's "In Cold Blood": A Critical Handbook; William Styron's "The Confessions of Nat Turner": A Critical Handbook; Breakthrough: A Treasury of Contemporary American-Jewish Literature; Contemporary American-Jewish Literature: Critical Essays;* and *Psychoanalysis and American Fiction.*

JOSEPH MANCINI, JR., is Assistant Professor of English at the University of Maryland, College Park. He has contributed articles with psychological orientations to *Notes on Modern American Literature, Psychocultural Review, Modern Language Studies,* and the *Journal of Evolutionary Psychology.* He recently completed a book-length study of John Berryman which assimilates the insights of Gestalt psychology.

ALAN MARGOLIES is Professor of English at John Jay College of Criminal Justice, C.U.N.Y. He is the editor of *F. Scott Fitzgerald's St. Paul Plays: 1911–1914* and co-compiler of *American Literary Manuscripts* (2nd edition). His essays and reviews have appeared in *Princeton University Library Chronicle, Resources for American Literary Study,* the *Fitzgerald/Hemingway Annual,* and *Journal of Modern Literature.*

ROBERT A. MARTIN is Professor of English in the Department of Humanities at the University of Michigan. He is the editor of *The Theater Essays of Arthur Miller; Arthur Miller: New Perspectives;* and *The Writer's Craft.* His work has appeared in *Modern Drama, CEA Critic, Studies in American Fiction, Michigan Quarterly Review, Theatre Journal,* and *American Notes and Queries.*

JAMES J. MARTINE is Professor of English at St. Bonaventure University. He is the author of *Fred Lewis Pattee and American Literature* and the editor of *Critical Essays on Arthur Miller.* He is the editor of three volumes of the *Dictionary of Literary Biography.*

GEORGE MONTEIRO is Professor of English at Brown University. He has written *Henry James and John Hay: The Record of a Friendship* and has edited or co-edited *Poems By Emily Dickinson; The Complete Poetical Works of Henry Wadsworth Longfellow; John Hay-Howells Letters;* and *The Man Who Never Was: Essays on Fernando Pessoa.*

RUTH PRIGOZY is Professor of English and former chairman of the department at Hofstra University. She has co-edited *Short Stories: A Critical Anthology,* and her essays have appeared in the *Fitzgerald/ Hemingway Annual, Commonweal, Twentieth Century Literature,* and *Prospects.*

JAMES W. TUTTLETON, Professor of English and chairman of the department at New York University, is the author of *The Novel of Manners in America* and *Thomas Wentworth Higginson.* His essays have appeared in *Modern Fiction Studies, English Language Notes, American Imago, The Personalist, American Literature, Yale Review,* and *Sewanee Review.*

JAMES L. W. WEST III is Associate Professor of English at Virginia Polytechnic Institute and State University. He is the author of *William Styron: A Descriptive Bibliography* and textual editor of the recent Pennsylvania Edition of Dreiser's *Sister Carrie.* His essays on Fitzgerald have appeared in *Proof, Resources for American Literary Study, Publications of the Bibliographical Society of America,* and *Studies in Bibliography.*

PETER WOLFE, Professor of English at the University of Missouri at St. Louis, has published books on Iris Murdoch, Mary Renault, Rebecca West, Graham Greene, John Fowles, Ross Macdonald, Dashiell Hammett, and Jean Rhys.

INDEX

Aiken, Conrad, 151
Andersen, Hans Christian: "The Ice Maiden," 176, 177
Anderson, Sherwood, 165, 188; "Why I Am a Socialist," 188
Apparel Arts, 150

Baker, Hobey, 202
Baker, Josephine, 270
Baltimore, Maryland, 28, 169–70, 189
Barthelme, Donald, 37
Baudelaire, Charles, 251
Benét, Stephen Vincent, 151
Berger, Yves, 251, 252, 253, 255, 260; *Le Sud (The Garden)*, 252, 256, 260
Berlin, Irving, 159, 160–61
Bishop, John Peale, xiii
Booth, John Wilkes, 26
Bourjaily, Vance, 157
Bow, Clara, 70
Braddock, Edward, 31*n*
Bridges, Robert, 66
Butler, Jack, 169
Butler, Samuel, 34
Byron: "The Prisoner of Chillon," 269, 273

Cabell, James Branch: *Jurgen*, 33, 34
Caldwell, Erskine, 151
Call, The, 187
Callaghan, Morley, 151
Century Magazine, 165
Civil War, 15, 169, 170
Clay, Henry, 257
Coleridge, Samuel Taylor: "Kubla Khan," 176
Collier's, 147
Columbia Pictures, 274
Conrad, Joseph, 35, 185
Coover, Robert, 207
Cosmopolitan, 146
Cowan, Lester, 274
Crane, Stephen, 191
cummings, e. e., 151

Dana, Viola, 67
Dartmouth College, 161
Debs, Eugene V., 187
Debussy, Claude, 251
DeLillo, Don, 202
Depression (1929), 15, 16, 111–26, 147, 151, 164, 169
Doctorow, E. L.: *Ragtime*, 203
Dos Passos, John, 151, 154–55
Dreiser, Theodore, 151, 182
Dwan, Allen, 70

Eastman, Max, 293
Eglov, Margaret, 90
Elgin, Paul, 157
Eliot, T. S.: *The Waste Land*, 16
Esquire, xvi, 20, 113, 124, 149–58, 161, 164–66, 291
Exley, Frederick, 202–3

Famous-Lasky-Paramount, 134, 137
Film Daily, 67, 68, 70
Film Guild, 70, 71
Fitzgerald, Edward, 48, 49, 50, 170, 179
Fitzgerald, Frances Scott, 130, 148, 179, 189, 236, 274–76
Fitzgerald, Francis Scott, individual works:
—"Absolution," xii, xvi, 12, 27, 76, 175, 204, 209–16, 224, 227, 239, 240, 289
—"Adjuster, The," xvii, 9, 26, 28, 35, 49, 70, 71, 72, 85, 224, 227–40
—"Adolescent Marriage, The," 80, 81
—"Advice to a Young Writer," 158*n*
—*Afternoon of an Author*, 113
—"Afternoon of an Author," 47, 125, 126, 155
—"Alcoholic Case, An," 45, 47
—*All the Sad Young Men*, 70, 71, 127, 199, 204, 223, 224, 225, 227
—"Ants at Princeton, The," 155
—"At Your Age," 118
—"Auction—Model 1934," 152
—"Author's House," 126, 155

385

JACKET DESIGNED BY MIKE JAYNES
TEXT DESIGNED BY IRA NEWMAN
COMPOSED BY LANDMANN ASSOCIATES, INC., MADISON, WISCONSIN
MANUFACTURED BY INTER-COLLEGIATE PRESS, INC.
SHAWNEE MISSION, KANSAS
TEXT AND DISPLAY LINES ARE SET IN CALEDONIA

Library of Congress Cataloging in Publication Data
Main entry under title:
The Short stories of F. Scott Fitzgerald.
Bibliography: pp. 303–77.
Includes index.
1. Fitzgerald, F. Scott (Francis Scott), 1896–1940—
Criticism and interpretation—Addresses, essays, lectures.
I. Bryer, Jackson R.
PS3511.I9Z853 1982   813'.52   81-69815
ISBN 0-299-09080-9
ISBN 0-299-09084-1 (pbk.)